New Masters of Photoshop

Volume 2

TEODORU BADIU
ALICIA BUELOW
RYAN CLARK AND DON CLARK
CORNÉ VAN DOOREN
MAURO GATTI
PER GUSTAFSON
SEUNG HO HENRIK HOLMBERG
JIM HSIEH
KAREN INGRAM
JASON MORRISON
MARIN MUSA
OLIVER OTTNER
JORGE RESTREPO
COLIN SMITH

New Masters of Photoshop: Volume 2

ISBN (pbk): 1-59059-315-4

Printed and bound in China 9 8 7 6 5 4 3 2 1

Distributed to the book trade in the United States by Springer-Verlag New York, Inc., 175 Fifth Avenue, New York, NY 10010 and outside the United States by Springer-Verlag GmbH & Co. KG, Tiergartenstr. 17, 69112 Heidelberg, Germany.

In the United States: phone 1-800-SPRINGER, e-mail orders@springer-ny.com, or visit http://www.springer-ny.com. Outside the United States: fax +49 6221 345229, e-mail orders@springer.de, or visit http://www.springer.de.

For information on translations, please contact Apress directly at 2560 Ninth Street, Suite 219, Berkeley, CA 94710.
Phone 510-549-5930, fax 510-549-5939, e-mail info@apress.com, or visit http://www.apress.com.

Commissioning Editor:
Gavin Wray

Technical Editors:
Luke Harvey and Gavin Wray

Editorial Board:
Steve Anglin, Dan Appleman, Ewan Buckingham, Gary Cornell, Tony Davis, John Franklin, Jason Gilmore, Chris Mills, Steve Rycroft, Dominic Shakeshaft, Jim Sumser, Karen Watterson, Gavin Wray, John Zukowski

Project Manager:
Beckie Stones

Copy Edit Manager:
Nicole LeClerc

Copy Editor:
Rebecca Rider

Production Manager:
Kari Brooks

Graphic Designer and Compositor:
Katy Freer

CD Design:
Pete Aylward

Copyright Research:
Beckie Stones

Proofreader:
Katie Stence

Indexer:
Kevin Broccoli

Cover Design:
Oliver Ottner, Katy Freer and Kurt Krames

Manufacturing Manager:
Tom Debolski

WELCOME TO *NEW MASTERS OF PHOTOSHOP: VOLUME 2*

Photoshop is a culture in its own right. It receives adoration from its users worldwide and is at the heart of the creative professional's toolkit. However, it is much more than a piece of software; it represents one of the widest mechanisms and opportunities for individual artistic expression. With ideas, Photoshop, and a website, anyone can communicate their visions to the world. The door is wide open.

The digital art world has experienced tremendous shifts—new techniques, combinations of vectors and pixels, 3D elements, high-end complexity, and formal super-clean simplicity. There is also a growing imitation of handmade collages incorporating wide arrays of type, scratched biro sketches, or scanned scrapbooks of life's everyday packaging. A digital art culture has developed and diversified, has cross-pollinated with ideas, styles, and influences from around the globe, and has never been more widely accessible. The book you have in your hands is a showcase of 15 artists from different backgrounds, with different ideas, yet all speaking the same language of creativity and artistic endeavor: they all use Photoshop to bring their ideas to life.

They also have Photoshop firmly under control. Control is knowing when less is more, enabling an image to express its full potential, and possessing precise mastery of the tools to transfer a vision to print or screen.

How to use this book

These artists are not necessarily the planet's top experts in using every feature of the program. This book will not teach you How To Use Photoshop. However, through the combination of each author's creative essay on their artistic influences and tutorials that deconstruct their artwork, it will, we hope, open your eyes to the vast creative possibilities with the program, inspire you to develop your own work to greater heights, and give you an insight into the digital artist's creative process.

We love how great ideas evolve. Cross-pollinate. Sketch. Believe in what you see. Pour your heart and soul into your work. Be brave and share your visions. You can inspire others.

friends of ED
23 April 2004

Special thanks for ideas and inspiration: Jens Karlsson, Richard May, Ryan Shelton, and Colin Smith.

P.S. Different artists use different platforms. To avoid boring repetition throughout the text, we only supply the key combinations for the platform being used in context. The conversions are:

(PC) Right-click = (Mac) Ctrl-click
(PC) Ctrl-click = (Mac) Command-click

Ideas, comments, and feedback: newmasters@friendsofed.com

ABOUT THE AUTHORS

TEODORU BADIU

www.theodoru.com

www.apocryph.net

Teodoru Badiu was born and grew up in the beautiful town of Sibiu, Romania. In the 1989 revolution, at the age of 23, Teodoru was wounded and brought to a hospital in Vienna where he had to stay for four months until he was able to walk again and go back home. After a short time, he came back to Vienna where he has lived ever since with his eight-year-old son and his wife. Teodoru had some hard times as a foreigner, and it was not easy to learn a new language and start building a new life from scratch, but he did manage it at last. He was also able to follow his dreams and study art and design in addition to his day job, working in an iron foundry. Even when it wasn't easy, Teodoru learned that nothing is impossible. Today, he is studying for his Creative Media Diploma at SAE, in Vienna, and seeing his artistic aspirations fulfilled.

ALICIA BUELOW

www.aliciabuelow.com

Alicia Buelow is a San Francisco–based illustrator and designer who specializes in Photoshop collage-based illustration. Her clients include publications and agencies such as *National Geographic*, *PlayStation Magazine*, *US News & World Report*, Saatchi & Saatchi, Lucas Books, and Adobe Systems. Alicia received a Bachelor's degree in Graphic Design from San Jose State University and attended the MA Art Design program. As a student, she worked at various design agencies until 1987, when she was hired by Adobe Systems to help test and demonstrate a new version of Adobe Illustrator. Alicia was part of the in-house communications department, where she designed support materials and software packaging for Adobe Illustrator, PageMaker, Photoshop, and other products. She also teaches Photoshop at the University of California, Berkeley.

RYAN CLARK AND DON CLARK

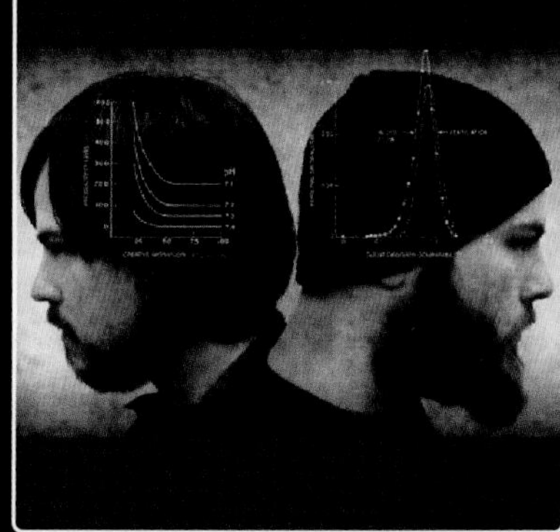

www.asterikstudio.com

Asterik Studio was founded in 2000 by Don Clark, Demetre Arges, and Ryan Clark, who joined forces to create a company where quality, creativity, and fun came first. Originally from Sacramento, CA, the trio relocated to the Northwest. Asterik is a full-time, fully functional design firm specializing in CD packaging, poster art, web design, merchandise design, and everything in between. Asterik's client list includes numerous record labels such as Atlantic, Capitol, DreamWorks, Elektra, EMI, Warner Brothers, Geffen, Island, and Ferret. Artists Asterik has worked with include The Strokes, Liz Phair, Good Charlotte, Jimmy Eat World, The White Stripes, and Puddle of Mudd. Asterik Studio has appeared in numerous publications such as *Communication Arts*, *Print*, *HOW*, and *Computer Arts*. Their work has appeared in more than six books, and the studio has been nominated for four Dove awards. Asterik Studio continues to keep it simple: they just do what they love and love what they do.

CORNÉ VAN DOOREN

www.cornevandooren.com

Corné was born in autumn 1979 in Hooge Mierde, a village in the south of the Netherlands. He grew up being an avid cartoonist, until he discovered the infinite world of multimedia at the age of 17. He has since become a time-served Interactive Multimedia Developer. His journey of discovery hasn't stopped since. Corné spends most of his time working with the Adobe and Macromedia packages for both online and offline use. In addition to these, he uses many other visualization packages and follows his mantra, "The only limit to multimedia is the imagination." Over the past four years, Corné has found success after success. He has worked for many international clients, has been featured in multimedia magazines, and has edited a number of books on Photoshop and digital video. His portfolio can be seen at www.cornevandooren.com.

MAURO GATTI

www.thebrainbox.com

www.gluebalize.com

Mauro is Creative Director at theBrainbox, a collective of four Italian designers with a wide range of skills in print, motion graphics, interactivity, application development, and video production. In addition to his personal projects, Mauro has worked as Art Director for fashion house Idea Italia (www.1ideaitalia.it/eng) and as Creative Director on the Blogwork project (http://blogwork.gluebalize.com). As a freelance concept artist and graphic designer, Mauro's clients include Peugeot, Tim, MTV, and Biennale di Venezia.

PER GUSTAFSON

www.MODERNSTYLE.NU

www.geidemarkgustafson.nu

Per is a graphic designer and digital artist from Sweden, the land of the northern lights and the midnight sun. In addition to being the founder of the digital art site and freelance brand MODERNSTYLE.NU, he is also the founder of the Swedish-based Internet media company geidemark gustafson, where he holds the position of Creative Director. Per's digital art has been used by clients such as Ericsson, Graphicscene, Digital Vision, Adidas, UEFA, and several record labels. Currently, Per is also the Creative Director of Sonic Nerve Clothing, a brand he cofounded.

SEUNG HO HENRIK HOLMBERG

http://henrik.cgcommunity.com

Seung Ho Henrik was born in 1980 in Seoul, South Korea, and was adopted by Swedish parents when he was 13 months old. He grew up in Mönsterås, a very small and quiet town in southern Sweden. Because the town is small and close to nature, living near beautiful landscapes has always been a great source of inspiration for him. Drawing has been an important part of his life for as long as he can remember. Today Seung Ho Henrik works as a conceptual designer and digital painter for games, TV, and feature films. He has worked as Matte Painter, Concept Designer, Storyboarder, and Character Animator for companies such as PDI/DreamWorks, The Mill, The Moving Picture Company, Outlaw Studios, and Amuze Electronic Media.

JIM HSIEH

www.jimbotron.com
www.FistsOfCurry.com

Jim Hsieh is a graphic designer, illustrator, and animator based in Alhambra, California. He launched www.jimbotron.com in 2001 to showcase his commercial portfolio. Based on a combination of groovy sounds and Flash animation, jimbotron.com helped Jim establish his signature DJ and turntable graphic style. While working and gaining experience in various top media companies, Jim contributed to a large number of projects, including the movie sites of *Tomb Raider: The Cradle of Life*, *Tupac: Resurrection*, and Richard Donner's *Timeline*. On Jim's personal site, www.FistsOfCurry.com, he mixes his interests in art, hip-hop music, and far eastern culture into a dynamic whole, exploring new aesthetic ground. Jim looks forward to the many more projects to come in his life.

KAREN INGRAM

www.kareningram.com
www.krening.com

As a painting graduate of the University of North Carolina at Greensboro, Karen started her design career as a pattern designer for a textile company in the southern United States. Leaving the world of ditsies, neats, jaquards, and foulards behind, she became involved in creating motion illustrations for the Web. Her experiments and collaborations are displayed at www.krening.com. Karen has been profiled, featured, and reviewed in a number of online and printed publications such as *This is a Magazine*, *Neomu*, and *Half Empty*'s first printed edition. Clients include Absolut Vodka, friends of ED, Spike TV, Monkeyclan, and Virgin Atlantic for *Carlos Magazine*. Karen has participated in many festivals and shows including FlashintheCan, in Toronto, Canada; BD4D, in London and New York; South By Southwest (SXSW) in Austin, Texas; and Curvy, Design is Kinky, and *Yen* magazine's ladies designer showcase, in Sydney, Australia. Karen is a crew member of the Australian-based site, designiskinky.net, and is a happy news contributor at K10k.net.

JASON MORRISON

www.dubtastic.com

Located in south Metro Atlanta, Jason works as Creative Director for a local web development and consulting firm. He is largely responsible for the "grunge" digital art trend, and supports this with his own large collection of free Photoshop brushes, textures, and tutorials via Dubtastic Design Labs.

"I have always been involved with art, as long as I can remember. I pursued anything artistic in high school, was nominated for Governor's Honors twice, and was voted as a senior superlative ('Most Artistic'). I continued my training in college, receiving an Associate degree in Art. However, then the fear of being a starving artist set in, so I pursued my Associate degree in General Business, and Bachelor's degree in Business with an emphasis on Marketing."

MARIN MUSA

www.tartartmagazine.com
www.pauskruske.com

Marin Musa is a digital artist and illustrator born in Mostar, Bosnia and Hercegovina. He studied at the Faculty of Graphic Arts in the University of Zagreb, Republic of Croatia, and graduated in 2002 as a Graduate Engineer of Printing Technology and Graphic Arts. Now living and working in Mostar, Marin's main creative outlet is running the noncommercial global design magazine *Tartart* (www.tartartmagazine.com), which has featured digital artwork, photography, and illustrations by designers from over 50 countries. Commercially, Marin works as a freelance graphic designer and also as a part-time graphic designer for a Mostar marketing agency. He was the Chief Designer for the political party that won the Bosnia and Hercegovina 2002 elections, designed all the graphic material for Pope John Paul II's visit to Bosnia and Hercegovina in July 2003, and was the Chief Designer for the International Investment Conference held in Bosnia and Hercegovina in February 2004.

OLIVER OTTNER

www.effectlab.com
www.naturemorphosis.com

Oliver Ottner was born in 1974 and lives in Vienna, Austria. In 1999, he founded the advertising agency iService, which works for clients such as Estée Lauder and the famous Vienna Zoo. His private works, such as his naturemorphosis and dualism series, as well as original Photoshop tutorials, can be found on his personal site www.effectlab.com. Oliver has been a National Association of Photoshop Professionals (NAPP) member since 2001, and his work has been recognized in various photography and digital art publications, including *Computer Arts*.

JORGE RESTREPO

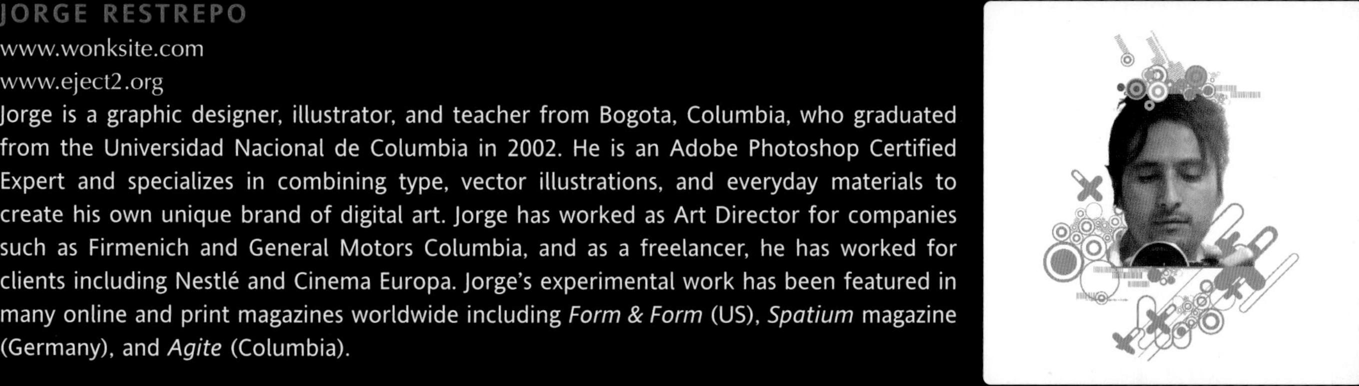

www.wonksite.com
www.eject2.org
Jorge is a graphic designer, illustrator, and teacher from Bogota, Columbia, who graduated from the Universidad Nacional de Columbia in 2002. He is an Adobe Photoshop Certified Expert and specializes in combining type, vector illustrations, and everyday materials to create his own unique brand of digital art. Jorge has worked as Art Director for companies such as Firmenich and General Motors Columbia, and as a freelancer, he has worked for clients including Nestlé and Cinema Europa. Jorge's experimental work has been featured in many online and print magazines worldwide including *Form & Form* (US), *Spatium* magazine (Germany), and *Agite* (Columbia).

COLIN SMITH

www.photoshopcafe.com
Colin Smith is an award-winning graphic designer who has caused a stir in the design community with his stunning photorealistic illustrations that he composes entirely in Photoshop. He is also founder of the popular PhotoshopCAFE web resource. He has won several design contests and awards including: 1st Place, Illustration, Photoshop World Guru Awards 2001, Los Angeles; Finalist, Macworld Design Contest 2002, New York; and 1st Place, Illustration, Photoshop World Guru Awards 2002, San Diego. Colin has coauthored six books for friends of ED including *From Photoshop to Dreamweaver*, *Photoshop Most Wanted 2*, and *Photoshop 7 Trade Secrets*. His latest book is *How to Do Everything with Photoshop CS* (McGraw-Hill Osborne, 2003). Colin writes weekly columns for Planet Photoshop and the NAPP member's site and is a contributing writer for the *Photoshop User* and *Mac Design* magazines.

ABOUT THE TECHNICAL EDITOR

LUKE HARVEY

Luke Harvey was born in Bristol and traveled a roundabout route to Birmingham, England, where he now lives. Along the way, he went scuba diving on the Great Barrier Reef, enjoyed Devon country life, walked the Inca Trail, and taught English in Eastern Europe. He first came across Photoshop in Lithuania while staying late at work to do his first image editing on a painfully slow machine. Then in Hungary, he ran into it again where the old Macs weren't much better and free time was taken up by studying for a teaching diploma. He finally got access to some decent computers during a brief stint as a Web Editor in London and could truly start to explore the vast Photoshop world. He came to Birmingham for a position at friends of ED as Technical Editor and has worked on almost all the Photoshop books they have published, either as Commissioning Editor, Content Architect, or Technical Reviewer.

To date, the world of digital art has been but a small scratch on the timescale of humankind's existence, especially when contrasted to the duration of the artistic media that have preceded it. But these are new times, with new media. I think what we are experiencing now is a reemergence of the artistic spirit. The boundaries of the art world have been starting to crumble ever since we realized that we have the power to change the landscape of artistic media with new and challenging ideas that have not yet been explored and with the programs that give us the flexibility to explore these landscapes.

When confronted with the task of examining the modern design culture of the 21st century, I typically find myself searching for verbal or artistic mechanisms that our generation can easily relate to—empty quantifications of what it means to be a part of the "new media" phenomenon, or how broadband affects the psyche of the artist who specializes in the "moving image." Very rarely, however, am I afforded the opportunity to stand aside and let the work flow through as pure art, as untouched and as raw as the revered classics of past cultures. Rarely have we seen a breakthrough in stylistic modality than the one we have experienced in the past five years.

It seems that those of us born after the time of the modernists who were breaking away from the medieval church in the early 1920s were born into some sort of pseudo-continuance of modern values in art, fashion, and literature. These have been distorted and confined to a narrow view of the world, one that is constantly changing and can never fit our worldview as it exists today. Out of this, arose a standstill in the realm of artistic novelty. It seems that with the birth of Photoshop, however, we have put the pedal to the floor in the artistic domain.

Art itself has been a global mode of expression as far back as we can remember because its influence is so far-reaching without being defined as an "ideology." It is something pure and clean that comes from the individual without being subject to the rules of a cultural institution. But more interesting to me is the increasing globalization of the digital art medium. The spread of technology has replaced the paintbrush with a whole new set of tools that open up new possibilities never conceived by traditional artists.

Terence McKenna states that we are becoming aware that "beneath the surface of societal convention is utter Terra Incognito, a no-man's land, the unexplored territory behind cultural assumptions, suddenly, starkly, totally incontrovertibly, illuminated to the inspection of the individual." I think only now are we starting to explore what it is that lies beneath the surface.

In the past two years, we have seen an explosion of Photoshop artists exploring pieces built around shards of abstract light and structures, stretching into an infinite level of spatial dimensions. Some artists have been integrating 3D renderings into their compositions to create ever more seductive and inspiring pieces, which I think represent the peak of bleeding-edge artistic momentum to date. In the professional realm, this has caused a shift in the mindset of corporations and small businesses. It seems that more and more, companies are embracing a certain openness to the interpretations of their values and processes by digital artists.

CONDUIT

What this has led to is a very interesting divergence from the drab, corporate aesthetic that plagued much of the last decade into a new stylistic breakthrough that has reshaped traditional branding and marketing. The chasm that existed between corporate advertising and what was defined as “art” preceding this breakthrough has been greatly narrowed by the increasing understanding that humans respond to artistic expression with passion. Only now is there a convergence of artistic expression and business marketing that allows designers the freedom to take risks and break the mold. This is good news for freelancers and students looking to break into the arena of professional design, because anyone with artistic inclination, talent, and Photoshop now has the opportunity to use that ability to shape even the largest of corporate brands or marketing campaigns.

There is a strong idea I cling to that centers around an interesting concept: the level of novelty exerted by humans over the course of time increases exponentially, as if pulled by an “attractor” at the end of time. That is to say that our innovation becomes sharper and more complex than the generations preceding the last, because we are being drawn toward something that compels us to create and express, as if trying to paint a picture of the attractor itself. I think this provides a very interesting platform for modern design of the 21st century and beyond, as the concept illustrates that we have nowhere to go but up. I believe that new generations of artists will build and grow on the foundations of modern digital art, and that they will reach even further into the depths of their imaginations in an attempt to steer our civilization toward this attractor. And this will lead straight to the essence of who we are and what our dreams are telling us lies ahead.

Eric Jordan

President/Chief Creative Officer
2Advanced Studios
www.2advanced.com

01

01 RECONSTRUCTING WEMBLEY

“CHANGES AND CHALLENGES KEEP YOU EXPERIMENTING. EXPERIMENTATION BRINGS CREATIVITY.”
CORNÉ VAN DOOREN
WWW.CORNEVANDOOREN.COM

I can remember those rainy autumn days when I used to sit at the big table at my parents' house. I was always drawing and sketching. (I love the work of Albert Uderzo; his work made me want to become a comic book artist. He is best known for his Asterix comics, but his other comics are also very impressive.)

At that age—I was probably around 8 or 9 years old—I really thought I had already figured out what I wanted to do with my life. I wanted to become a comic book artist and there was nothing that would get in my way . . . .

The title of this book tells you that it didn't all turn out as I thought it would at that young age. In the summer of 2000, I graduated as an interaction designer from a Dutch graphics school. An interaction designer both designs and develops user-friendly interfaces for CD-ROMs, websites, and DVDs. The four years I spent there also taught me much about computers. Before I began my education at this school, I had barely touched a computer.

The school also offered me a broader view of art. Before I began my studies, I was mostly influenced by comics, but during my time there I started looking more closely at music videos, magazines, television shows, and much more. People like Tim Burton (film director and artist), Anton Corbijn (photographer and video artist), Ridley Scott (film director), and Guy Ritchie (film director) really inspired me. But I wasn't just inspired by people working in the entertainment industry. Multimedia artists like Brian Taylor (www.rustboy.com) and companies like Neostream (www.neostream.com) also greatly influenced me. It didn't take long before their influences became a challenge.

www.neostream.com

© Brian Taylor 2003

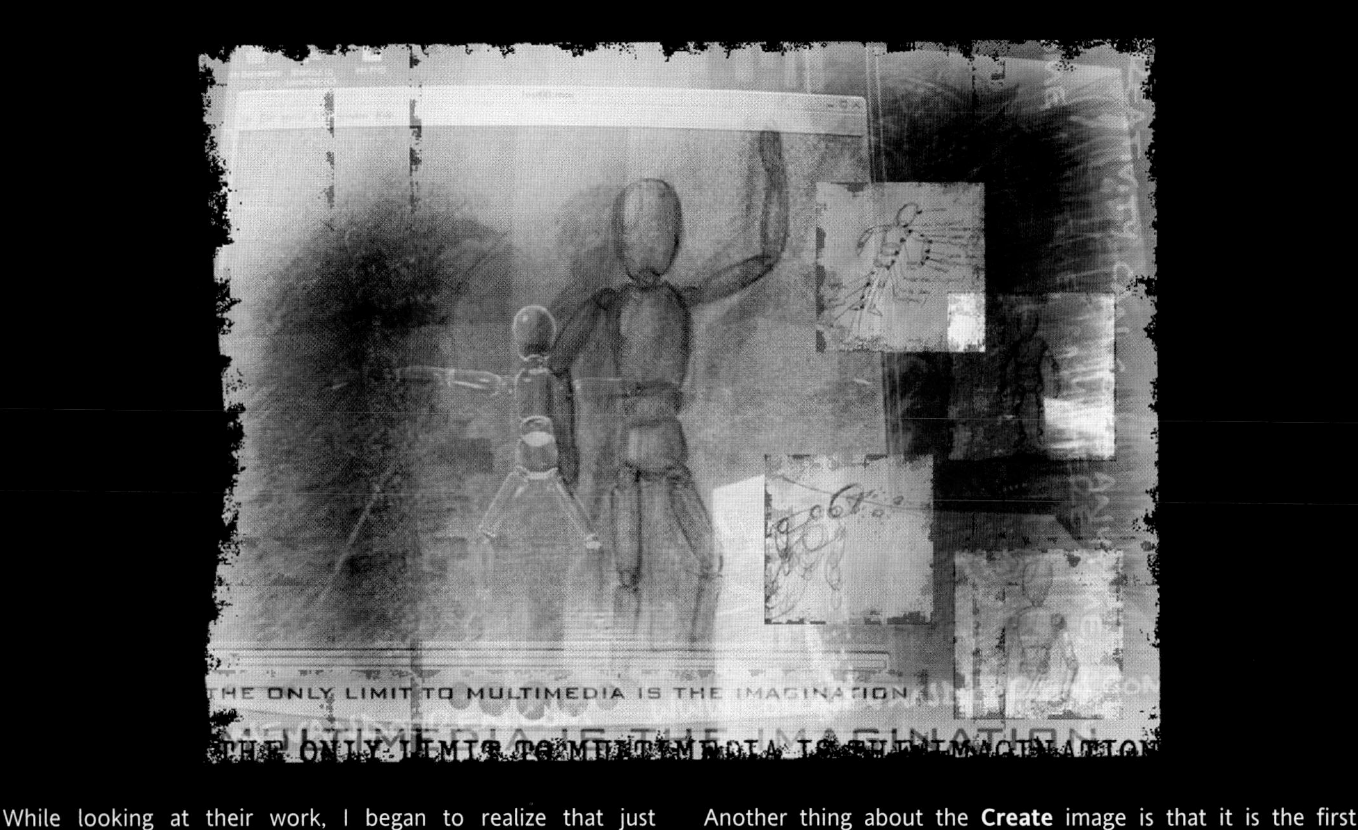

While looking at their work, I began to realize that just designing menus and making them work was a bit boring—I like change and challenges—so I started to experiment using all kinds of tools such as 3D software, video software, and, of course, Adobe Photoshop. These experiments inspired me to go on and combine the skills I had acquired. That's why I think the image **Create** represents me best. This image is all about experimenting; the collage shows several steps of an experiment. Originally, I was trying to produce a short 3D movie about a guy made out of glass who was being attacked by all kinds of elements that he had to dodge in order to stay in one piece. The image combines some of my storyboard sketches on the right with a sketch of the main character in the center. Just behind the main character sketch, you can see the same character rendered in 3D. The background represents the multimedia that I do, and you might be able to spot the

Another thing about the **Create** image is that it is the first image where I used the *dirt factor*. As you can see, the edges look a bit dirty and I also added some paint effects that give the image the feeling that something went wrong—it's not a clean or crystal clear image.

Sometimes I like to see a bit of dirt in an image. For me, an image doesn't always have to look perfectly polished. The inspiration for the dirt factor approach probably came from the entertainment industry. The CD covers for The Prodigy's *Fat of the Land*, Linkin Park's *Meteora*, or Fatboy Slim's *You've Come a Long Way, Baby* have really impressed me in that way. Besides great music, for me, they represent the fact that something doesn't have to look perfectly clean to make sense.

Another aspect of those types of CD and DVD covers that really impressed me was that the designers weren't reluctant to use various types of fonts and font sizes in the design. Engaged by the way these fonts were used, I started experimenting on my own. The image **Every Door** is one of those tests where I tried to use fonts in a subtle way and also to treat them as a design element. I used various fonts in the text lines and think it worked well. The text supports the image, rather than distracting the eye, and fits in nicely with the theme of exploration and experimentation as a whole.

I really enjoy making those unpolished images. Normally I don't get to make this type of image for my clients, because up until now, I have mainly worked for business-to-business clients. This type of client often expects something clean and polished, which is logical, to be honest, because the images I create for them are designed to represent their companies in the most professional way possible. However, it also means that the work I do for clients is quite different from my personal experiments. I think that's a good thing, because changes in the type of work you do can be very motivating. Even though I have to admit that sometimes the clean world of the business-to-business marketing industry tends to demotivate me slightly, this can be a good thing—it's at these moments that I get extremely motivated to express my feelings through my images.

EVERY DOOR
IS ANOTHER ONE 2 EXPLORE

One of my most appreciated images was made at a time when I was a bit down because of the type of work I had been doing that month. I honestly admit that I was a bit frustrated with it. But then I realized that frustration is one of the best motivators for being imaginative and creative. It felt really good to produce a piece of work that released the feelings inside. By making the image **Creativity**, I got those feelings out of my system in a creative way without damaging anyone or, most importantly, without harming the work I had to do for the clients or negatively affecting the clients themselves.

The idea behind **Creativity** is that at that point I felt creatively boxed, so I made this boxing ring in a 3D software package (Cinema 4D). I chose this kind of boxing ring because it is pretty open, and this enhanced the feeling that I felt boxed by some metal bars rather than by a big solid wall, for example. After rendering the image, I added the lighting effects in Photoshop. The lighting effects represent me and my creativity escaping from the boxing ring. As you can see, I made absolutely no reference to anyone or any client. The image just represents me trying to get frustration out of my system without hurting or damaging anyone, but it made me understand that such frustration can lead to great inspiration.

CREATIVITY IS LIKE L

IT CANNOT

I am very thankful that others appreciate this type of personal image. Actually, this process I went through is pretty strange. Normally, I'm not eager to talk about feelings, but most of my images do contain a personal feeling or message. Although I have changed in that sense over the past years, every now and then I do go back to my roots—the interaction designer. Nowadays, I do make the most out of Photoshop's features for those types of projects.

Take **Interface** for instance. I designed this image to be used on a CD-ROM resume about myself (run `start.exe` in the presentation folder on this book's CD to view an adjusted working version). Actually, this image is just one part of an animation. I wanted the CD-ROM to be really impressive, which is why I included a lot of animation. About 90 percent of the project was made in Photoshop, and 10 percent through programming.

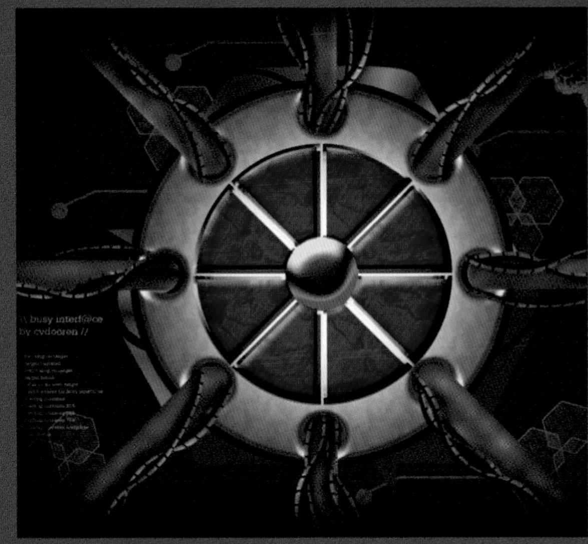

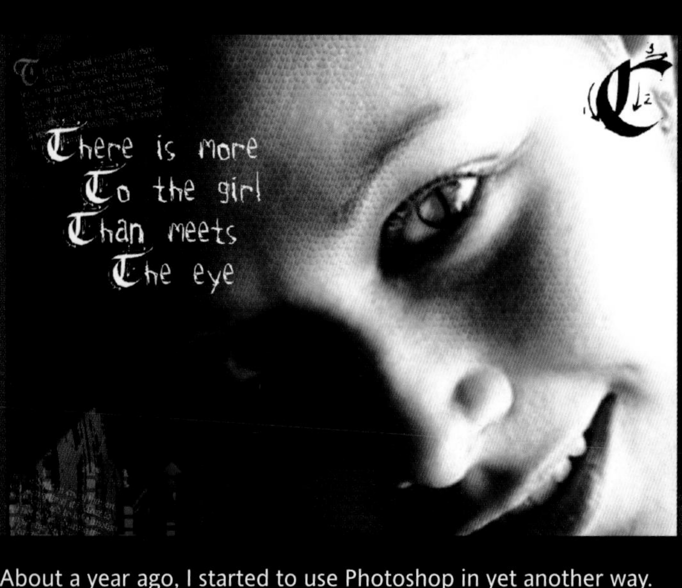

About a year ago, I started to use Photoshop in yet another way. I began this new approach when I got to know some fashion models. Before these encounters, I never thought models had a tough career. I mean models like Naomi Campbell and Laetitia Casta certainly don't have a problem finding work, but the models that aren't so well known have a difficult task, and an impressive portfolio is the most important thing in building their career. These people are selected based on their portfolio, and there are literally thousands of models out there, so what makes one individual attract attention? Probably something

The image **Eye** is an example of such a digital enhancement, although perhaps it is not such a good portfolio image. Because this image has been enhanced too obviously, it's difficult to see what might have been changed from the original image, so it's difficult to see the real model, which isn't good for a portfolio. However, it does show that this model is gracious enough to let me experiment with her photos to create this type of image. The **Eye** image shows a confident girl, and I wanted the text to state that there's more to a person than just her appearance. I think I made the **Eye** image for two reasons: the main reason

The images **Toxicitizans** and **Industrial** are examples where I used the dirt factor on images of a different fashion model. In fact, this second model was enlisted into a model contest after the judges saw these digitally enhanced images. **Industrial** shows another element of my experiments. You know the way it's sometimes hard to take a photo yourself? I wanted the **Industrial** image to include an old rusty factory, but where I live there aren't really any old abandoned factories. So, every now and then I use photos from stock libraries on the Internet. I have several CD-ROMs from PhotoDisc (www.photodisc.com) that I use as a resource when it's difficult to make an image completely out of my own material. I'd rather make every element of an image myself, but sometimes using stock photos can offer an easier or better solution.

Toxicitizans, above

Industrial, below

Dark Face

I also started using stock photos when I was working with the models. Because I had never worked with models in my images before, I decided to do some tests using stock photos. I could also have taken some photos from the family album but, because they were just experiments, why not use stock photos? Those CDs had to come in useful sometime, right? So, before I started working on the photos for the models, I wanted to make sure I knew what was involved. The image **Dark Face** was one of these experiments.

Bolder

However, it was probably the **Bolder** image that turned out to be the best of these experiments. What I tried to do in these images was combine various skills, such as merging 3D elements with real photos. Not only did I use fully rendered 3D elements, I also decided to use wireframes. I believe these elements provide something extra for the images, giving them more depth. Subconsciously, I was probably influenced by images from Derek Lea (www.dereklea.com), whose work just looks amazing. After seeing his work, I think I also started to try to play a bit with the human body in the sense of taking skin off and adding other elements.

With the **Bolder** image, I also did some testing on the colors. I wanted to see whether the green-yellow color scheme was actually the best. Green is normally a positive color for me. For instance, a green traffic light means "go!" but I wasn't sure whether green would look bold. I guess just looking at designs for *The Matrix* trilogy would have already told me that green can be pretty impressive . . . still, these color tests gave me more certainty that I had chosen the correct color setup.

What you have seen and read up until now is basically my development and the development of my designs over the past years. For the tutorial in this chapter, I have tried to combine all these elements.

Reconstructing Wembley

Because this tutorial features quite a lot of steps in the process of making the final image, I've divided it into several sections. First, we'll look at the idea behind the project because the idea is where everything starts. Next, we'll dive into making the background visual; this combines the use of photos, Photoshop effects, and some 3D elements. We won't use Photoshop to make the 3D elements, but I will show you how a combination of software packages can work together.

Once the background visual is in place, we'll take a photo of a model and place it in the background setting. At the end of this process, we'll add some text and some small design elements to complete it.

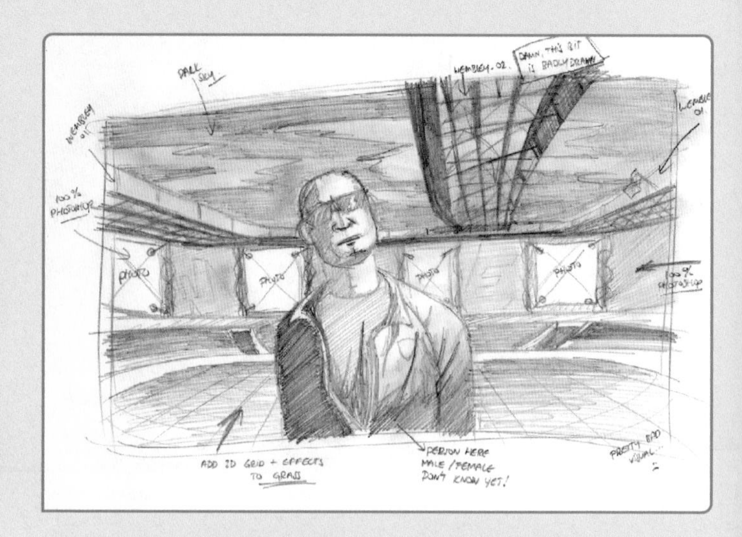

Idea

The most important part of any visual, design, or whatever terminology you use, is the *idea*. Because I'm used to working for clients in advertising, I am also used to making a sketch or visual of the idea first. Clients often don't understand an idea if it's only described in words, and a good visual can say more than a thousand words.

The idea for this tutorial came to me when I was looking at the recently published photos of a new Wembley Stadium in London, England (the stadium where England won the 1966 World Cup Final). The stadium has a great and significant history for millions of people. When I visited Wembley back in 1995, I found it to be the most impressive stadium I had ever seen, something I still think to this day. It had character. I say "had" because it has since been demolished and is currently being rebuilt into a new modern stadium, scheduled to open in 2006.

Because I had taken photos when I was there almost ten years ago, I thought it would be a great scene for this visual. The fact that it isn't there anymore in this form adds a little more weight and atmosphere. Almost automatically, I decided to make it into a dark, slightly futuristic new arena, and this led me to a first sketch.

The sketch shows that I wanted to make some changes to the stadium itself and also add a person to the visual. When I was sketching, I drew a sports fan because people tend to think of sports fans as being male, as I initially did. But then I realized I could make something of a statement, so I changed my mind and used a female fan instead. In any case, now that the idea is outlined in a sketch, we can easily place a female model in an adjusted Wembley stadium.

Background

We'll start with the two photos I took of Wembley Stadium in 1995 (`photoWembley1.tif` and `photoWembley2.tif` on the CD), and use various techniques to turn it into a modern arena. As you can see in the panoramic photo, the first thing we have to do is retouch the photo of the stadium, as my finger was a bit too close to the lens (right side of the photo).

To retouch that entire photo would be quite some work, so instead we want to copy the left side of the photo, flip it horizontally and use a mask to make it fit, which is exactly how I started this project. I made a Photoshop document (landscape A3 size at 200dpi), which is the same size as the planned final visual. I didn't want the photo to span the whole visual, because I liked the panorama effect of it, so I copied the photo over to the new document—I always tend to call it "working" because I look at it as a work in progress. I also always start in the RGB mode. This is a screen mode and will not show how the printed visual looks, but when you work with the RGB mode, it allows you to use all the Photoshop filters, whereas CMYK mode doesn't. To make sure I know what the print will look like, I use View ➤ Proof Colors.

The light/dark image below shows the setup I used to get rid of the finger on the right. The bottom layer is the original photo copied into the document. The copy above it is a copy of the original photo in which I adjusted the brightness/contrast of the image. On top of that is a horizontally flipped layer with the same photo as the copy layer. The top layer contains the black bars, while the selected Layer 6 is only in there temporarily. It simply contains the red line I placed in there to indicate where the mask should go. The part that is masked out of the flipped layer is also darker for the same reason.

The light portion on the right side of this image is copied from the left side of the photo

As you can see, the mask has a couple of indents. The stand on the other end says "Wembley," and it should still say that when we flip the image horizontally. When we're comfortable with the adjusted part, we can merge the copy layer and the one above it into a single layer. Once that's done, it's time to add a part to the stadium. To do this, we'll want to use the second photo of Wembley. On the left side of this photo there's a section of the stadium's roof.

Combining the two photos was actually pretty easy. I just cut out the roof part of the image and copied it into the working document. To make it more believable, I then copied the added layer and flipped it vertically. I placed the flipped layer on the ground of the stadium using the **Darken** blending mode and an opacity of 60 percent.

This helped break up the light and shadows on the image. After all, I added a part to the roof, so there had to be a corresponding shadow on the ground.

I always start the business of real manipulating when the lighting and shadows have been set out. Of course, these can change during the process, but I find it easier to place other elements in the image when the lighting and shadows are already set. So, to finish this off in our Wembley image, we want to add a dark sky to it. In this case, I have already made such an image (`clouds.tif`) from about five photos of clouds. When you look at it, you might think that it doesn't look very nice. To be honest, I've never seen clouds like these before, but that's okay, because they only add to the strange atmosphere we want in this image once they are placed in the working document.

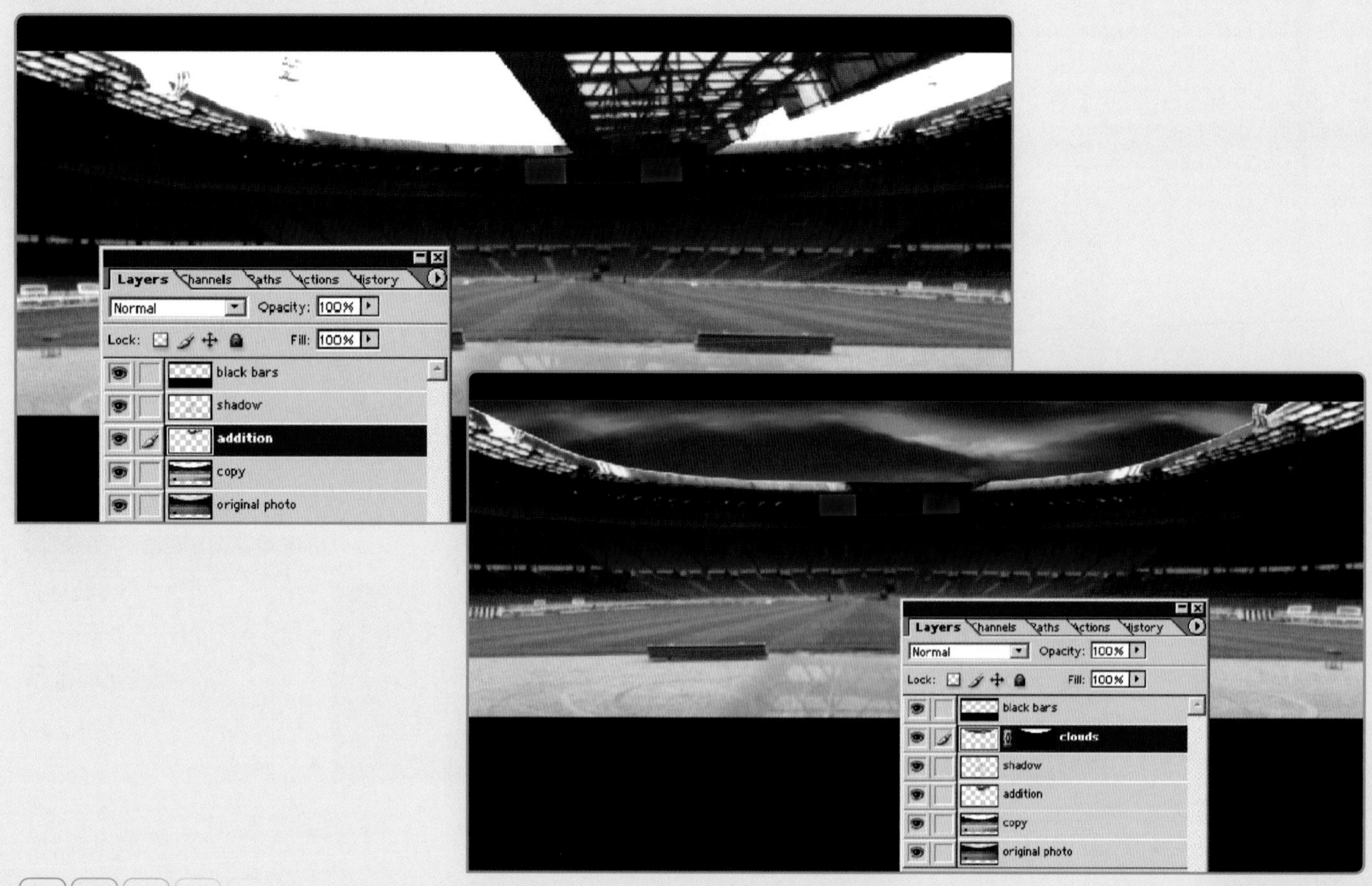

There's something terribly wrong here. I placed the sky above the roof addition. I had every intention of placing the clouds above the addition layer, because it would be very time-consuming to cut out the pieces of sky where the roof addition goes. Also, because the roof addition contains some transparent elements, it would take even more time. To save on this time you can play a bit with the layer **transparency**. After applying the layer mask and adding a light blur, the **Linear Burn** transparency seemed to work best in this image. It kept the roof addition intact, which was the main priority.

However, just as with the roof addition, adding clouds also generates the need for shadows. I could have used the **Clouds** filter for this, but I don't think that would have generated the realistic clouds I had in mind. So, I used the existing clouds layer to make the shadows. I made a grayscale image of the clouds (`shadow.tif`) and played a bit with the brightness/contrast.

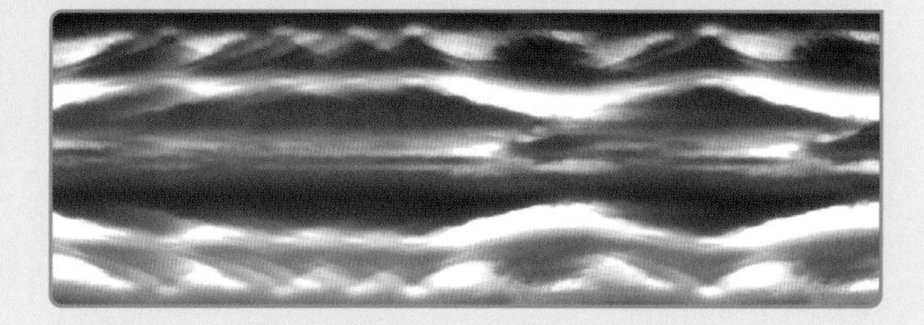

I then placed this image in the working document and flipped it vertically. Again, playing with the transparency of a layer proved very helpful. Adding the shadows for the clouds will make the image a bit darker and also a bit more believable (as you can see on the left side).

Now that the roof addition and sky have been placed and the shadows for these extra elements set, it's time to add the 3D effects. Sometimes these types of effects can be simple to implement, yet they add a whole new dimension to an image.

An example of an easy effect would be a wireframe render of the floor. I decided to focus on the grass field a bit more and to add a light wireframe effect to it (`wireframe.tif` on the CD).

Adding a wireframe render makes it seem as if the grass was made using a 3D package, although in reality, it's a photo. Again I am using the layer transparency capabilities to make it fit with the rest of the image without having to cut out all the black parts. This time, the **Linear Dodge** seemed to be the best answer. I set it at 20 percent, because I didn't want the wireframe to be too obvious in the image.

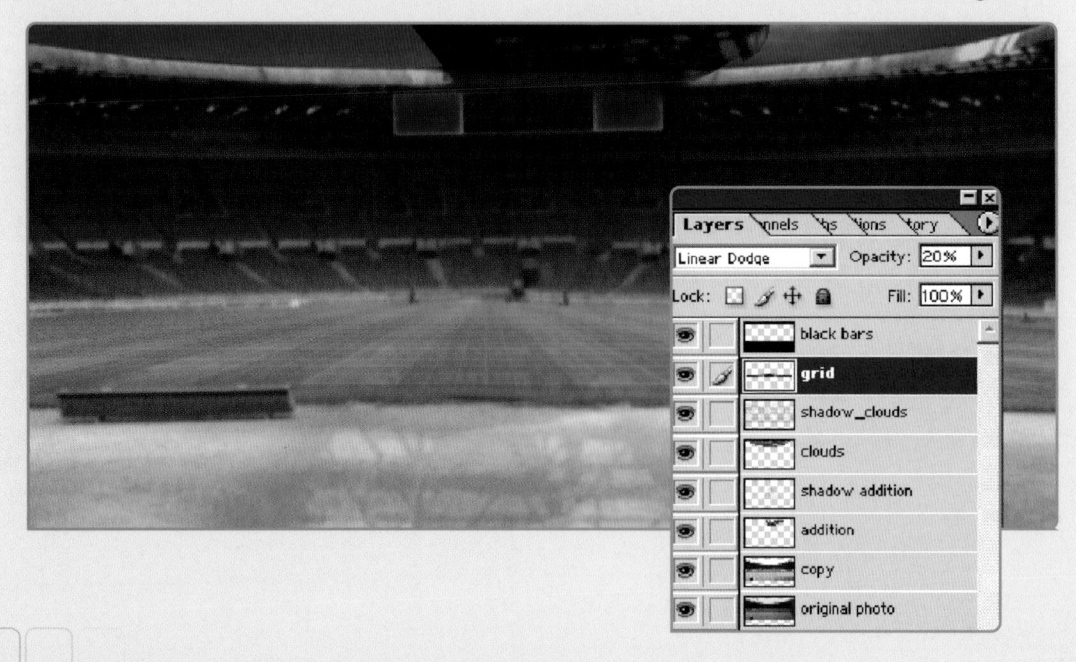

However, I wanted to add more than just a wireframe, so I decided to rebuild part of the stadium in 3D and add some new screens in the stand. Here's a useful trick to make sure whatever you build in 3D fits into the image. First, I saved a JPEG copy of the Photoshop document. In the 3D package (I used Maxon Cinema 4D), I placed a box with dimensions of the exact size of the image. Next, I placed the JPEG file on the box, which gave me an ideal view of where to add the elements. Before rendering, I removed the box, leaving just the added 3D elements to be rendered as a PSD file with mask. You'll find that most 3D packages support this kind of output.

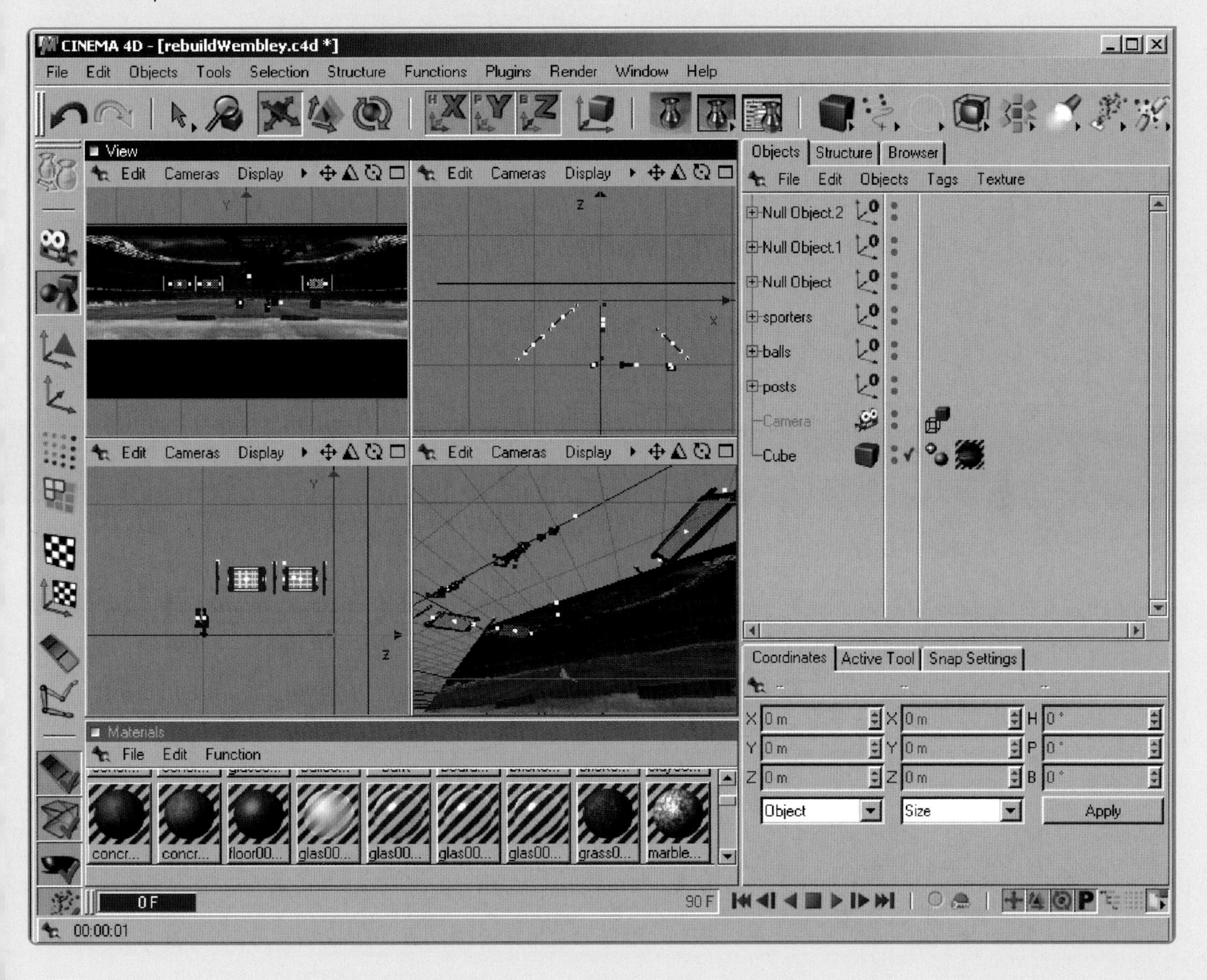

Building something in 3D can be very time-consuming depending on the quality you're looking for. Imagine a cylinder. For the top and bottom to be perfectly round you'd need 360 points or references—one point for every degree. Depending on your system's performance, it may take quite a while for your computer to render all 360 points. If the machine isn't able to render all the points, then you can always set the amount of points to a lower rate. For screen resolution, a circle will still look like a circle if the points are set to 24. I tend to work with 24 points when the 3D scene becomes overly complex or simply too heavy. In this case, I have worked at those minimum settings too.

I decided to add three jumbo TV screens and some light, transparent sports players to the image. The idea for these players came to me while I was working on the piece. It often happens that I just think of things to add as I go along—I find this refreshing. Sometimes, it's quite hard to plan everything from the start. In this case, I thought that the addition of transparent sports players could give the image a nice surreal feeling. My initial suspicion proved to be correct—the 3D elements look way too sharp in comparison to the photo behind them. But, because of the atmosphere I am looking for, this is okay.

At this stage in any project, I would check the entire photo in more detail to find any small errors. Are there any areas of the image I can improve? For this image, I copied the light masts to another layer and made them a bit darker, corrected the tilt in the scoreboard, and removed the remaining letters on the tribune. I also tried to make the stadium look a bit sharper using the Filter ➤ Sharpen ➤ Unsharp Mask option, and make the sky a bit darker and give it a little blur where it meets the stadium.

I still want to change something else. I want to add a score on the scoreboard or, if not a score, at least some kind of text, but I will add this in at a later stage. I always add text later because the colors are then set and I can see how the text fits into the image. At this point, you'll probably agree that this image still has room for improvement. Too many contrasting colors are present and it has no clear overall "feeling." So before I added the text on the scoreboard, I colored the image to a suitable color palette.

As mentioned earlier, I find green a great color to work with and, because the playing field is an important element in the image, I decided to choose a green color to use as the basis for the coloring process. Using the color at different layer transparencies ensures that the image gets its own identity. I always tend to work this way, first selecting a color and then changing the image section by section. This time I divided the image into four separate sections starting with the floor, then the grass, the stands, and the sky, coloring them one by one.

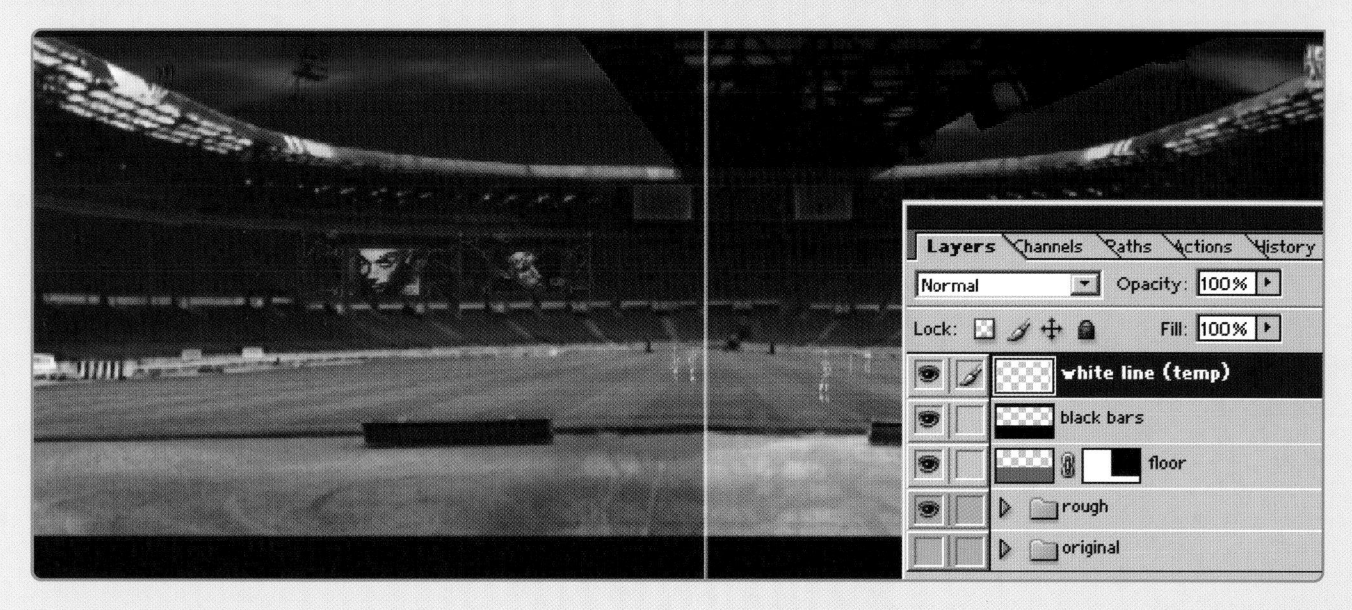

It doesn't matter if it doesn't look right from the start, because you'll always have room to tweak it a little after all the parts have been colored. You might notice in the previous screenshot that I've placed the original photo in a **layer set** called original and all the images in another set called rough. I have used these sets quite a lot since the introduction of layer sets in Photoshop 6.0. They are really useful, especially in an environment where more than one person works on your documents, because they make things much easier to find. Later in this project, all the colored layers will also be placed in a layer set.

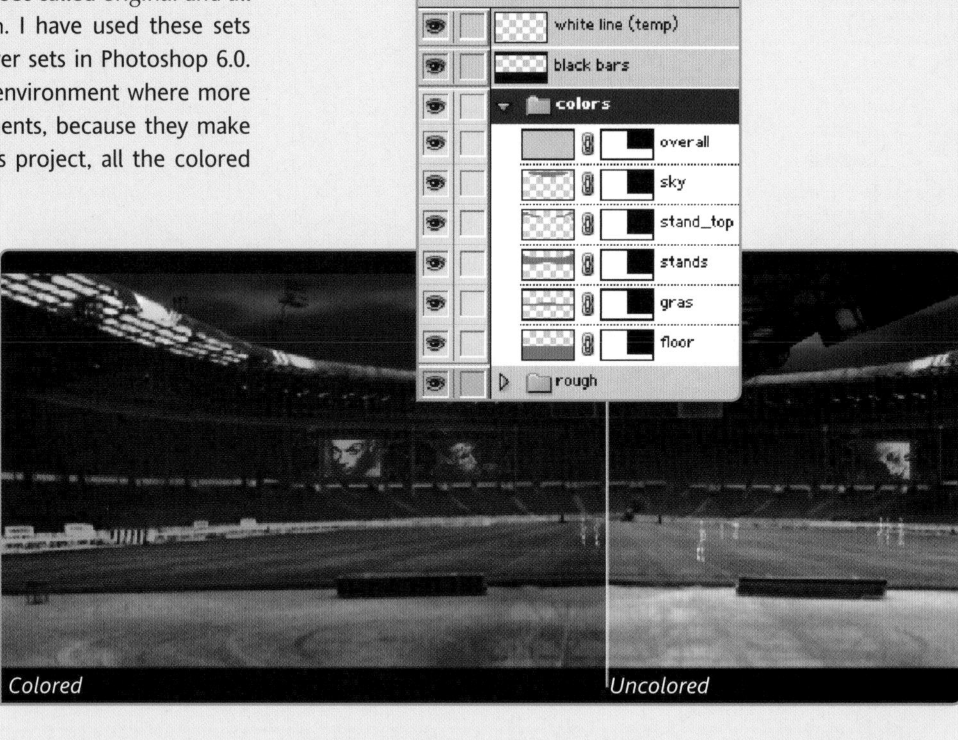

Colored *Uncolored*

When working on coloring, sometimes you might find that things don't always work out. That's exactly what happened in this image. I thought the color setup wouldn't work in its original setup, given the red and blue stands in the image, and so on. In fact, when I printed both a color version and a green version, I actually preferred the color version. So, I decided to reduce the green and emphasize the different colors in the image by copying the whole background, giving it a blur, and then playing with the transparency settings of that blurred layer.

When I was happy with the image and tested it by printing it, I merged the background layers together (this does not include the colors layers). At this point, I saved the document as `working2.psd`. Now we can go onto the next step: adding the model (the sports fan).

The model

How do you find a good model for an image? It's not quite as difficult as you might think. There are lots of online resources for photographers and models. Once you find these, it's basically just a matter of asking and offering. My post immediately led to quite a few replies. Knowing what I wanted to do with this visual made the search a lot easier, especially when I received a reply from Suzanne Engel.

Suzanne Engel photographed by Martijn Ronche

Suzanne is an excellent Dutch model who often works with the talented photographer Martijn Ronche (www.ronche.nl). Suzanne's surname actually translates to "angel" in English—pretty apt in this case. The combination of skills and art from these two people were combined in this photo, which I immediately loved and felt I could use for this piece. Actually, what I really like about Martijn's photos is the way he uses makeup. He isn't afraid to try new things, and neither am I, and that's probably why this photo immediately caught my eye. I really felt that this girl, and the way she was looking and was photographed, just fit in with the piece perfectly. I am very thankful I was allowed to use their creativity in this piece of my own.

Having said all that, though, I still had to make some changes to the photo. Because of the canvas, some parts of Suzanne have fallen off the image. So what I wanted to do with this photo was add some shoulders, remove the flowers from her dress, color the stones in the necklace green, and cut her out from the original background, since it will be replaced by the background I have already made.

The first step is to remove the background. I didn't really pay great attention to cutting out the hair. For this image, I thought it would work better if not every hair was nicely cut out. I was also thinking of adding a glow around the model in the final piece. What's more, I like the hair to be sharply cut out because this will add an "unnatural" feeling to the image.

After cutting her out of the background, I changed the clothing to a black dress and adjusted the color of the stones around her neck using the Image ➤ Adjustments ➤ Hue/Saturation tool.

At this point, I debated whether I should also change the color of her eyes to green, but decided not to do so. After all, with Photoshop, I can always do this later when I can see what she looks like in her new environment. I didn't want to change much on this picture, because I felt it could fit directly into the scene, but since the image already has a surreal feel to it, I wanted the model to match this kind of surreal quality too.

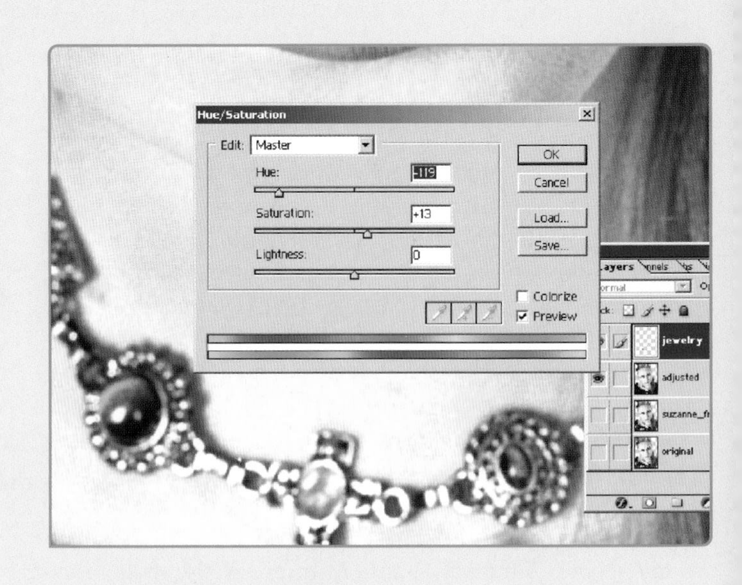

So, knowing I didn't want to change that much, I decided to go for the Chrome filter. I selected the left side of the model's face, copied it onto a new layer, and filtered it.

I found that this looked stupid at first and discovered that playing with layer transparencies once again helped out. Changing the layer transparency to Soft Light was the answer.

The chrome works well with the Soft Light settings. It makes the face a bit lighter on one side, whereas the little elements it adds next to the hairline, eye, and mouth make her look just a little surreal. At the same time, I also answered my own wish to not make too many changes to this already great photo.

Now it's time to place the model in her new background to see how much of her shoulder we'll have to draw.

Placing the model in the background

I opened the `working2` document and copied the model in there. I placed her on the left side of the image because we'll be adding some text and design elements to the right side of the image later. However, placing her in a nice position immediately shows that we'll have to add more to the shoulder than I expected. Also notice where I placed the photo in the Layers palette. It's beneath the overall color tone, which instantly gives the model photo the same feel as the background.

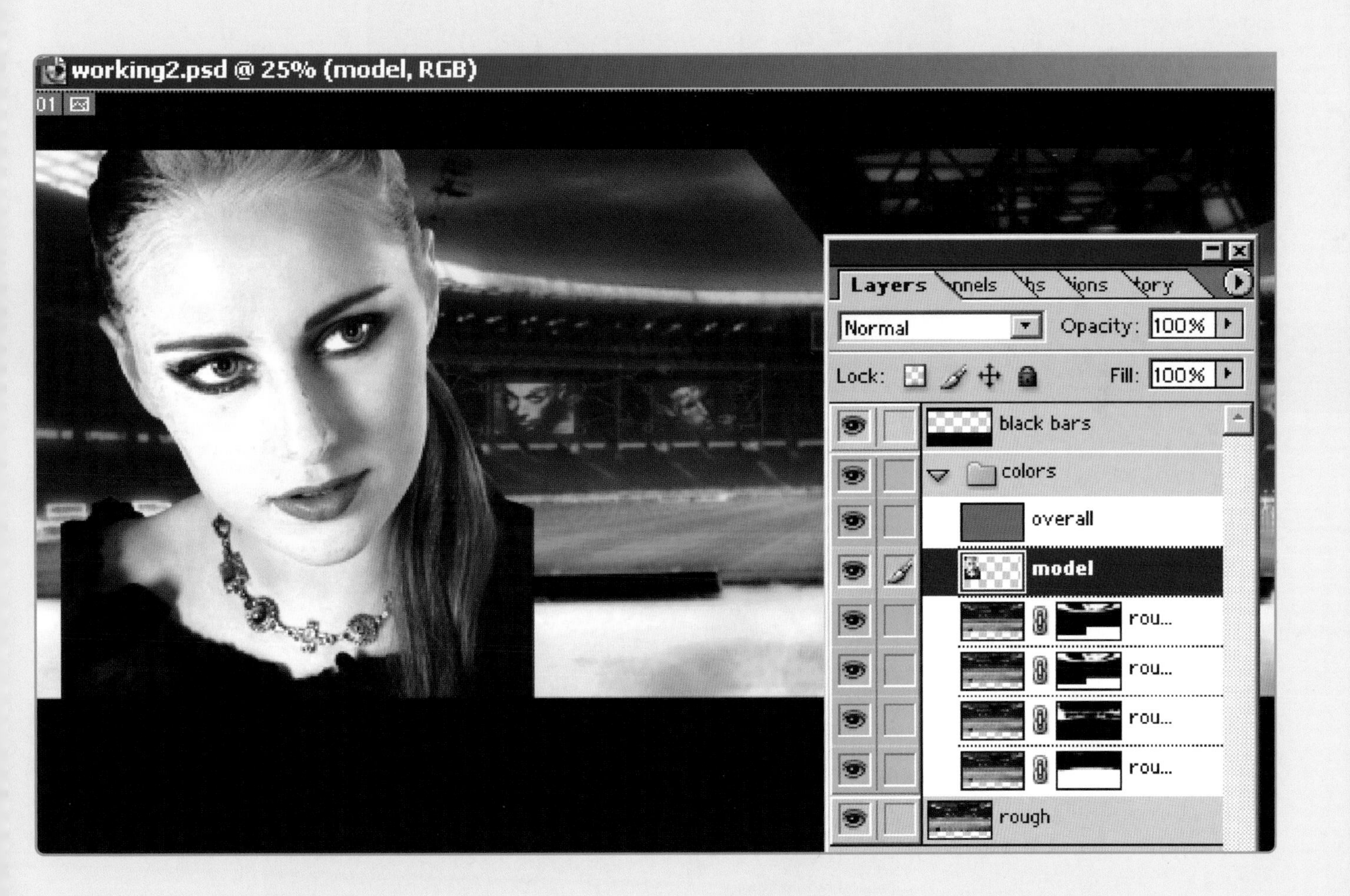

Once I was satisfied with the position of the model, I took a black brush and drew the shoulders and part of the arms—just what you would expect to see in this image. Now you'll also know why I wanted the model to be in a black dress—it makes the drawing part here that much easier. I also had a clothing catalog next to me, which I referenced while I was drawing to make sure that the shoulder was realistic.

The first thing to do here is look at the pose of the model. Models often tend to pose with one of their shoulders higher than the other, but that's not the case with this picture. The clothing material looks pretty thin, so if I imagine that there's no shoulder padding, it means I'll have to try and follow the curve quite closely to a real shoulder and arm. Knowing all this makes it's easier to find a reference in the catalog. This requires a bit of imagination, but it works really well. Look for an image of a girl with the same pose in a clothing catalog and draw the shoulder and arm by following the curve on that photo. You could, for instance, scan the photo in the catalog and trace over it in Photoshop to get the curve right.

Certainly it's not perfect—adding body parts isn't the easiest of tasks—but because I'll be using some blur effects on the model, it doesn't matter that much. At this point, I'm pleased I didn't change the color of her eyes because I feel it isn't necessary after placing her in the piece. It wouldn't add anything to the image so I'll use a blur effect instead.

Once I was satisfied with the blur effect and had the model placed in the background, I thought it was about time to add the text and design elements. Before adding these, I had to make some changes to the Layers palette, because the colors layer set didn't make sense with the addition of the new elements. So, I divided the image into several sections to make it easier to work with in the next stage.

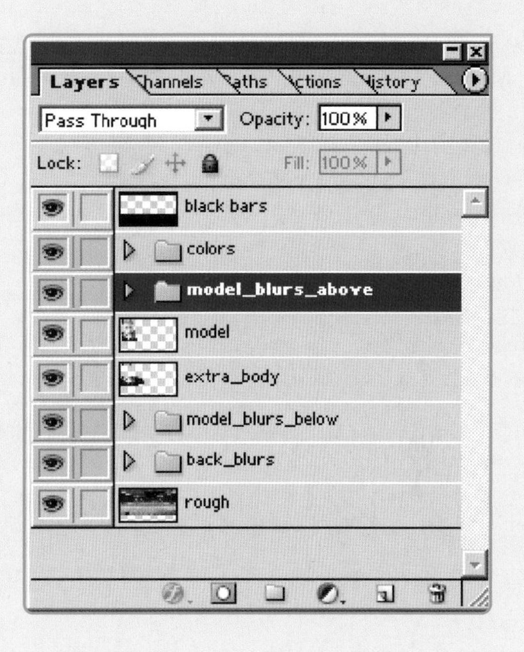

Adding text and other design elements

To finish this piece, I want to add some text and design elements, starting with the scoreboard. You might remember from earlier that I chose not to add text during the first stages of the image. This was simply because it's easier to add text (the score in this case) at this point in the process. If I place the text layer underneath the overall colors layer, the text automatically gets green edges, which makes it fit better into the scene. The only changes I made were to reduce the layer opacity a bit and give the text a small blur to make sure it fit perfectly.

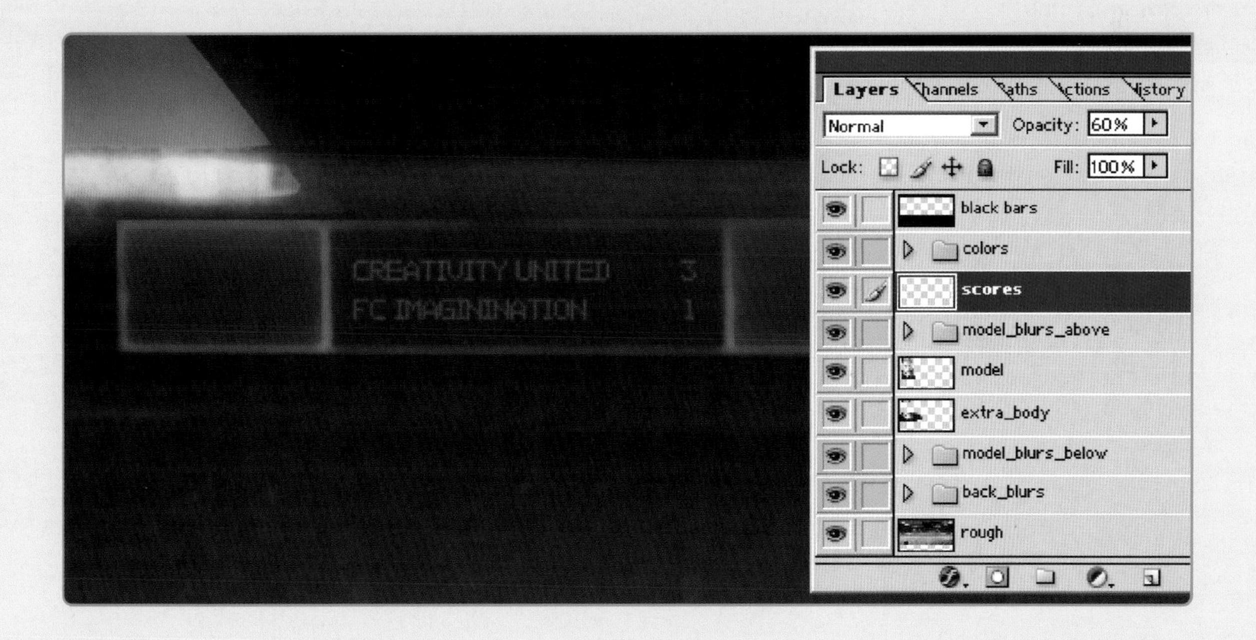

On the right side of the image I've added several layers of text. Some have been blurred a little to give the text layers a slight feeling of depth. When I was satisfied with the text layers, I merged them together and made a copy of the layer to give it a Twirl filter. When I use this filter, it looks as if the text is flowing a bit more, again creating extra depth. I also placed some text layers on the ground in the bottom of the image.

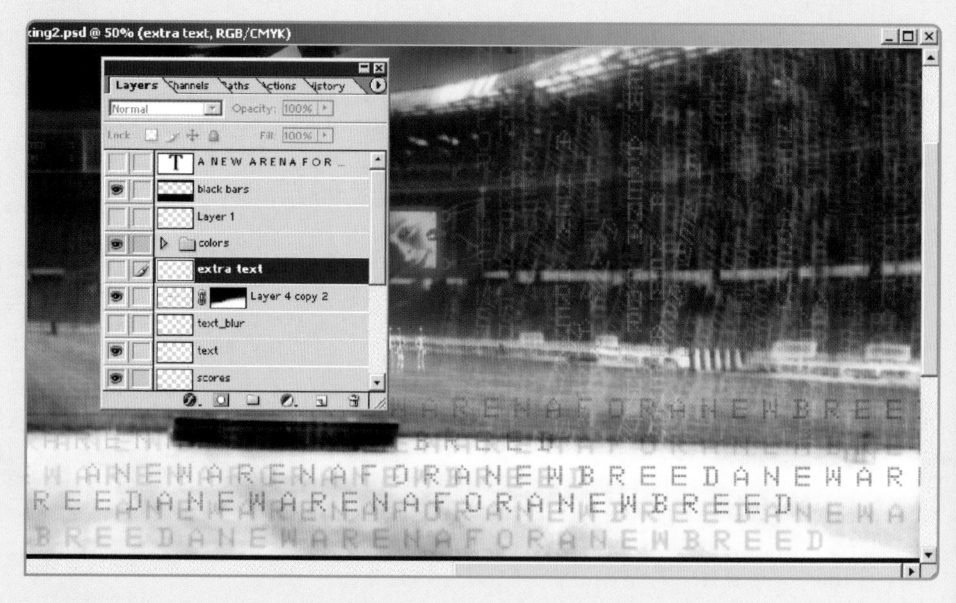

I always try to put readable text into my images. In this case, I decided to add a few extra words and some kind of title. So, on the right side of the image I added "A new era, a new arena." I chose to use the font I also used on the scoreboard. By using this font, I tried to ensure that it all fits together. This font is a digital typeface, which is appropriate because I've been working on this image digitally; I also think a digital font just fits with a modern stadium. The previous Wembley arena is no more and I have used images of the old arena to create a new one, a new environment.

Once I had placed the text, it was time to take a look at the image as a whole. When I looked at it, I noticed one thing that I did not like. So far, everything has been placed between the black bars, but by boxing an image you take away some of the depth. To get a feeling of more depth, I placed some elements outside the boxed image.

One of the first things I did was to take a closer look at the clouds image. I found that by placing a grass layer on top of the clouds and by playing with the transparency settings, I could create ideal dust. Placing the grass on top of the clouds looks strange at first, but setting the image mode to Grayscale made it into perfect dust. As you've probably noticed by now, I often use the layer blending modes and opacity to find new things and, although it doesn't always work out, these experiments can lead to amazing visual elements.

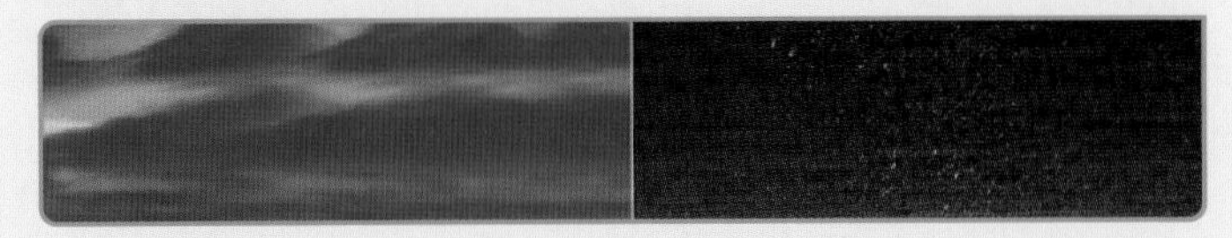

I then copied this new texture into the `working2.psd` document, placing the texture in there twice: above the bottom black bar and also at the right side of the image, rotated by 90 degrees. Placing it at the right accentuates the text effects already going on there. I think adding this texture reinforced the image somewhat. Even though I already liked it, I wanted to add just one or two more things.

I wanted to add a few more elements to the image and add text to give credit where it is due—I never have and never will use something not made by me without giving credit. So, somewhere in this image I want some names, made very light, and in a way that you would really have to search for them (but I do want them in there).

For these elements, I used the **Custom Shape tool**, which provides lots of vector shapes. I chose the Club Card, Heart Card, Spade Card, Diamond Card, and some layers with the Splatter shape. (All these shapes come preinstalled in Photoshop.)

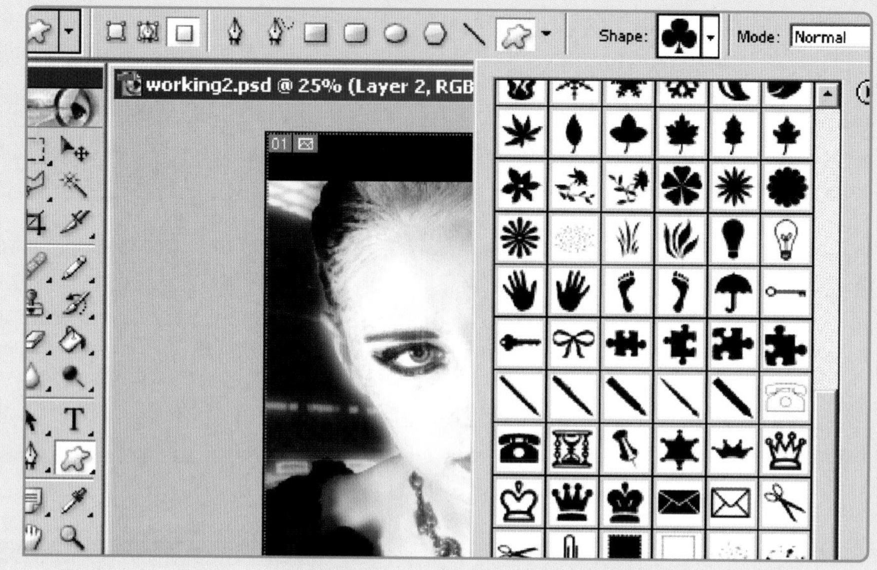

Once I was satisfied with these extra elements in the image and liked the overall view of the piece, I saved the file as `final.psd` (which you can find on the CD). I have indicated the different types of layers by coloring the layer sets:

- Blue layers and layer sets indicate an element, shape, or photo on the layer.
- Green layers or layer sets adjust the color of the overall image.

Another thing I check is the difference between print and screen quality. I often work in the RGB mode, because this is the screen mode and, as a multimedia designer, I often work on files to be used on screen. To make sure I know what it will look like when printed, I use View ➤ Proof Colors (CTRL+Y). When I am certain that the image works both on screen and in print, I once again save the document as `final.psd`.

Conclusion

I am pretty pleased with the end result. I think it could have been just a bit better if the original photo of Wembley had been sharper, but I can only blame myself, because it was the picture I took back in 1995. Apart from that, though, I think we turned the original photo of Wembley into a new and refreshing piece.

Given the fact that I am a multimedia designer and tend to work on 72dpi images, I think I did pretty well with this "ready-to-print" work. I would also be one of the first to admit that being able to use the existing photo of the model saved me a lot of time and effort. But it also proved another valuable point to me. Lots of people out there are willing to share and combine their skills with yours.

Whether you love or hate the piece I made in this chapter, the thing I really wanted to try and show you is how to experiment and not follow existing rules. In the long run, I think that existing rules don't sell. One of the reasons I'm never completely pleased with my work is that I am always focused on trying new things, on continuing to share my skills and expertise with others, and on experimenting.

Just let your imagination flow, be bold, experiment, try new things, and don't pay attention to what people say—do your own thing. Apart from that, I can only say open Photoshop and go, go, go!

A NEW ERA
A NEW ARENA
Let The Energy Out <
Express Yourself <
Let Photoshop Be Your Tool <
Your Tool For Expression <
ANEWARENAFORANEWBREED
> New Masters of Photoshop
> Corné van Dooren
> With many thanks to
> Gerry Black - feedback
> Suzanne Engel - model
> Martijn Ronche - photographer

02 IMAGINATION

"FANTASTIC WORLDS AND CREATURES LIVE IN MY IMAGINATION. ALL I WANT TO DO IS OPEN A DOOR TO THAT WORLD AND SET THEM FREE. PHOTOSHOP IS THE KEY TO THAT FANTASTIC REALM."
TEODORU BADIU
WWW.APOCRYPH.NET

Hello, and welcome to my chapter. My name is Teodoru Badiu and I was born 37 years ago in a small town called Sibiu in Romania. Today I live in the beautiful city of Vienna, Austria, with my family. I'm a freelance artist and multimedia designer and am currently studying for my Creative Media Director Diploma at the SAE Institute in Vienna. My creative seed was sown by my father, who I always looked up to as a child. He wasn't a famous artist, but he drew, sculpted, and did a lot of wonderful stuff that impressed me. Later, when I went to art school in Vienna, I learned all the basics about art from color theory to composition, from drawing to paint techniques. It was there that I developed my artistic background and started to explore my artistic side.

The Beginning

As I mentioned, my father was the first person I looked up to. By the time I reached school age, I had started drawing and doodling, but it was nothing serious. This doodling persisted for years—in fact, I've never stopped—but these doodles have no meaning. However, in 1995, I decided to learn about art to get an idea of how and what I wanted to create, so I started attending the People's Art School in Vienna. I learned a lot, and although it wasn't easy, it was a pleasure. It was a wonderful experience in which I learned a lot about art theory combined with practice; I studied color theory, color psychology, composition, drawing, nude drawing, animal drawing, aquarelle painting, oil techniques, and so on.

It was during this time that I started to analyze old master paintings: their color composition and how and why they used the color they did. Then I moved on to modern art such as dadaism, cubism, surrealism, and futurism. I was totally caught up in cubism at that time. Picasso and Braque impressed and influenced me a lot, as you can see in my oil paintings of that period. Of course, the themes and subjects I studied at art school aren't possible to describe here, nor are they the point of this chapter, but I wanted to express that going to art school was the best idea I had. Without it, I would not be able to do the things I can today.

In 1995, my son was born, and in 1997, I had to give up and leave the school. Some troublesome years followed in which I didn't create anything at all. But these bad times came to an end, and good times followed. This is when I started working with Photoshop, which marked the beginning of my real creative phase.

Everything really started for me in 1999, when a friend gave me Bryce and Photoshop. Like most beginners, I had no idea what Photoshop was or what you could do with it besides using the filters. So I went to a bookstore to take a look at the Photoshop books. This was the first time I realized what this software could do. I was simply overwhelmed by the artwork I saw, because at that moment, I couldn't imagine how it could be created using software. At that point, the use of layer techniques in a program was unknown territory for me. Then I saw a tutorial in one of these books and a light bulb switched on. I understood that it was just like working on an oil painting—you work in layers—and these layers are the key, the reason why Photoshop is what it is.

With that tutorial in mind, I returned home and searched the Internet for more Photoshop tutorials. I started following tutorials almost daily from sites such as DesignsByMark (www.designsbymark.com), phong (www.phong.com), Computer Arts (www.computerarts.co.uk), PS Workshop (http://psworkshop.net), Eyes on Design (www.eyesondesign.net), and many others. This phase lasted more than a year, but it was worth the work and time. After that, I was familiar with most of Photoshop's capabilities, but I was still only able to re-create those things I had learned: interfaces, fancy buttons, wires, textures, and all the other eye candy that Photoshop is able to do, mostly using layer styles with bevels, shadows, and filters.

The next big step in my learning process was when I joined some online forums. One of these had an important role in my creative growth—PyrosPixelmassaker (http://pyros.pixelmassaker.net/phpBB2), a forum set up by Christian Heinrich. A photo was posted each week on his "Playground," and everyone was suppose to work on it and try to do something new. It was a great place where I could experiment, try new techniques, and work, and I met a lot of wonderful people with similar interests to mine, people that I am proud to call friends and for whom I have a great respect, such as Dennis Sibeijn (www.damnengine.net), Sebastian Holmer (www.illuminated-alley.org), and Thomas Melldgaard (www.epoxy5.com), all of whom are superb artists with wonderful imaginations and great skills. During this time period, I also set up www.apocryph.net and started to display my first experimental work.

As my Photoshop childhood ended, I let the traditional photo manipulation drift away and found my own way of working and expressing myself artistically. I was finally able to work in a way that let my ideas, vision, and dreams become a reality using Photoshop as my new tool. This tool helped me quench my creative thirst and offered ways of working that I had never thought about before. It has developed from just being a digital tool for creating digital art to a tool where digital and traditional media can be fused, and it still continues to evolve.

This way of working gave me the ability to create artwork such as *Living in a Box*, an image from a series where I used handmade wire sculptures placed in a cardboard box. I digitally photographed and imported the wire figure in the box into Photoshop where I added the skin, body, and TV elements to the image using layers and blending techniques. I did this to create the illusion that the figure lives in its own world, has its own space in which to act, is able to communicate, and has a unique look. This image in particular deals with the idea of "Big Brother is watching you," that every step of our lives is followed and we are manipulated through media. At some point, we become slaves of propaganda, start to act like robots following programs, like puppets on strings. We believe we are free, but we are really living in a box.

Another image that involves this kind of fusion is *How to Create an Angel*, where I used oil-painted canvases to get the desired look and feel. I painted two small canvases, then took some photographs of my own body, one of a stuffed pigeon I bought at a flea market, and some general shots of the sky and the landscape where I live. This piece deals with the idea of creating from two points of view: as a part of the divine creation in the way the church deals with it, and creation from an artistic viewpoint, where the artist creates a piece of art that represents his/her ideas and meanings. I took these two ideas and merged them so that the artist is the one who creates a piece of art that starts living, and that as soon the artwork is ready, it will live its own life. I gave the artist divine powers, and it seems that the angel is just waking up from sleep.

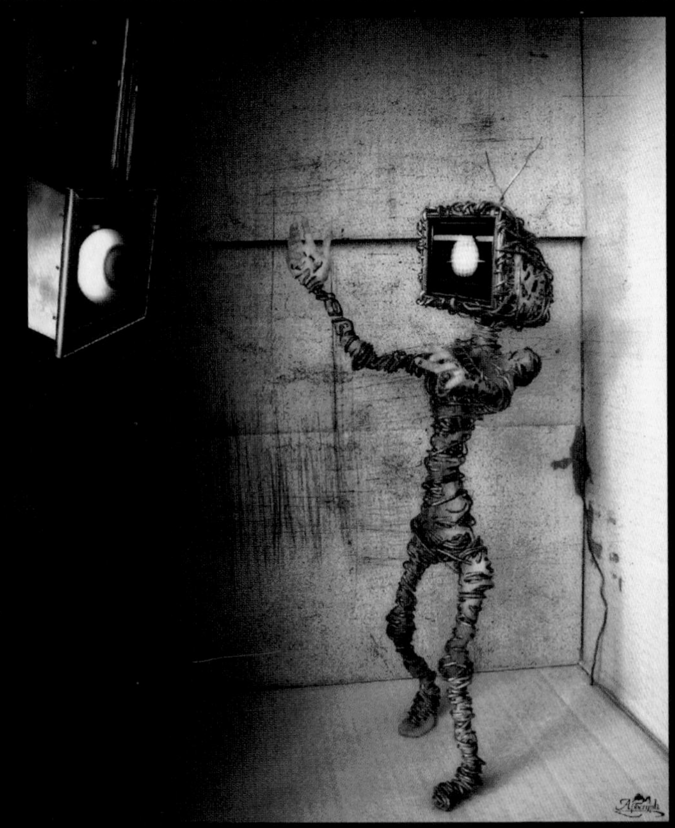

Living in a Box

How to Create an Angel

At the same time, I thought it would be interesting to shake things up a bit—to let the artist be from the "evil half of the creation" and, at the same time, not follow the cliché of the artist creating an evil creature. Instead, the artist is creating a good creature, a creature of light, an angel. I wanted to say that evil could give birth to good, that dark can turn to light, but at the same time, the creator must be afraid of the bridge he has created between good and evil. He can't give up, though; the creative process has to continue, as it's his aim to create and he has to follow his destiny. That angel on the easel has to be woken from sleep.

In *The Bird Hunter* and *The Sentinels*, I used a wire and ton (clay) sculpture for a series called Dreizehn; this series of 13 works is based on that same sculpture, but each piece tells its own story with its own feeling. To produce something like this series with another media would have taken months and months of work, but with Photoshop, I was able to finish that project in about two months. That's one of the reasons I work with Photoshop; it isn't as time-consuming.

These works are the result of my creative struggle; the satisfaction I got during this process is unlike anything else I've experienced. The ability to turn my ideas and visions into real artwork, and to share them with the rest of the world, makes me very happy. This is a road that never ends and a search that will never stop. There will always be a next step, a new idea, a new image to be realized.

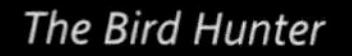

The Bird Hunter

The Sentinels

Another important moment for me was when I accepted Keith Kennedy and Luis C. Araujo's invitation to join the Raster Group at www.rasterized.org, a group of wonderful artists who release a selected monthly collection of artwork. It's great to be part of such a talented group, and I'm happy such groups are out there today. Just looking back at the history of art, you can see that there were always groups who introduced new ideas and new impulses in art (groups like Der Blaue Reiter, Die Brucke, Bauhaus, the surrealists), so why not today too? Although digital art is fast becoming accepted as being as good as a traditional art form, it will never surpass or substitute traditional art. However, I believe it's enough that they both run parallel to complement each other.

In the time since I joined Raster, I've create a large number of images that I possibly would never have made if it weren't for this group. It has played a dynamic role in my artistic development, giving me the energy to keep going and to create works like *Eve's Umbrella*, *Don Quixote*, and *Eve and the Apple*.

Eve's Umbrella

Don Quixote

Eve and the Apple

Paradise Lost

The End of the Holy Spirit

The Inspiration

Like most artists before me, and surely those who will follow, I get my inspiration from a very wide spectrum of sources, and this is mirrored in my artwork.

This *Paradise Lost* piece was triggered by John Milton's book of the same name, which is where my obsession with angels comes from. These ideas merged with my reading of the Apocryphal books, where a lot more stories about angels are written (ones not included in the Bible), stories that have caused me to think about religion from a different point of view. I was raised without much thought given to religion until I came to Austria, where religion plays an important role in everyday life. Those books awoke my curiosity about the history of Christianity. With the Bible, religion, church, faith, historical facts, and all the religious wonders and myths circling around in my head, I am still searching for the place that I can consider my own religious standpoint, and this is reflected in my work too.

Like many of us, I have to fight my fight and find my balance between the spiritual part of religion and the historical reality of it. My search for a way I can believe has given birth to works like *The End of the Holy Spirit* and *Adam's Experiment*. These reflect the way I have tried to find my path in this question of faith, and because I still have not found my balance, they are full of the questions and doubts resulting my search.

The End of the Holy Spirit deals with these questions and my search to find an answer. I took the problem that the church in general faces today: more and more people are leaving, those who are losing their faith. The person in my artwork has stopped believing in a divine power that takes care of her life and chooses to be her own protector instead, which is symbolized by the umbrella. But, because of this, a small part of the divine power that protects and cares dies, which opens a bleeding wound, and from the sad dark sky falls a heavy rain of blood.

I composed this artwork using the same techniques that we'll use in the Tutorial section—I use real-life elements such as trees, grass, a body, a heart, and an umbrella to create a surreal image. I wanted to cause a kind of confusion where the artwork has an initial realistic look at first glance, but that disappears the moment the artwork is seen as a whole. In that moment, everything is just an illusion, fantasy, and imagination.

Another frequent source of inspiration for me is Greek mythology, which has influenced works like the *Capture of Pegasus*, and *Heracles and Nessos*. These works show my interpretation of those myths; I use my skills to create new, fresh-looking versions of those subjects. Once again, I created these using combinations of handmade, traditional media, and digital media elements. The figures have their own environment, their own place to act, and hopefully, they give the viewer a starting point for his imagination from which he can continue and imagine how Pegasus would be captured, or how Nessos fights with Heracles.

I also get impulses from the daily events of the world that surrounds us. Our world has problems that we cannot ignore—such as the destruction of our natural environment, flora, and fauna—and I deal with these in my own way. Uses of genetic technology, like cloning and artificial madness, are reflected in works like *Freak of Nature* where nature strikes back or *Ripeness*, which deals with the genetic and artificial reproduction questions.

The idea behind *Freak of Nature* is that someday, all of the things we do to our environment, including destroying our forests, driving so many animal species to extinction, and polluting our atmosphere and water—all to make our lives easier—will result in the total opposite. It is we who will suffer. I want to show how nature could strike back. Because the evolutionary process is continuous, nature will find its way out of the problem. If the environment can find new ways to evolve, new terrains will be used for that, and the human body will be one of them. Wood will grow on our heads, animal parts will become new organs, and all kinds of mutations will result. That is the main idea behind this image, and I hope it will make people think for a few seconds about what is happening all around them before they act.

Of course, it is simply a work of my imagination and, as in all my artwork, the imagination plays the key role. Without it, I would not be able to realize all my art. You can be a master of all the techniques that Photoshop has to offer, but without imagination all those techniques are useless. If you dare to give your imagination enough freedom, you'll be able to create wonderful pieces of art using basic techniques like layer blends, masking, cloning, and adjustment layers.

Ripeness is another image in which I am working out my thoughts about events around us and, as you can see, I've used another method and technique to express them. I chose to use 3D figures imported from Poser, but the way normal Poser figures usually look was not what I wanted for my images. They are *too* realistic, and didn't match my thoughts, so I imported the final Poser renderings into Photoshop and edited their form using the Transform and Liquify tools to change proportions, stretch, and modify the figure. This gave me that surreal, disproportional look, but it only goes so far. The viewer is still able to link what she sees with reality, and so she grasps the main thought behind the image—this artwork deals with today's genetic manipulation madness, cloning, and artificial reproduction questions. I combined the 3D Poser figures with photos of a bunch of tomatoes and a few scanned textures. I combined the mother figure with the tomatoes to represent a possible new hybrid creature, half human, half plant.

Sources of inspiration are endless. A simple emotion can be the trigger, as can a song I hear, a movie I see, something I have just learned about, or books I have read by writers such as John Milton, Dante Aligieri, Goethe, and the expressionist Alfred Kubin, whose novel, *The Other Side*, is one of my favorites. Among these is one source who has not only inspired me but who has also had an impact on and influenced my work: Hieronymus Bosch, in particular works like *The Garden of Earthly Delights*.

His paintings look marvelous but are terrifying at the same time. They are filled with light and color, but they make you associate them more with the darker part of the creation. His imagination is one of horror dressed in humor and colors; it is full of strange creatures that remind me of the grotesque antique wall ornaments, creatures made from the fusion of people, animals, and plants. Some of my creatures are the result of this influence and also the way in which I make my images in full color, yet try to show a dark feeling emanating from them.

For example, in *The Other Side*, I created trees that can fly or walk, fish that are able to fly, and a living home that's half human, half plant, which acts as a portal between our side (the real world) and another fantasy world where the imagination is at home, everything is possible, and real-world rules have no value. I also use the idea of the third eye, and through that eye it's possible to see inside this fantastic realm.

Another influence on my work is the surrealist movement, especially André Breton's *Manifesto of Surrealism* (1924), which opened my eyes, allowed me to get rid of logic, and let my imagination and fantasy play the key roles in the creative process. This gave birth to *Slaves of Logic*, an image that deals with this influence. I wanted to show that not everyone is able to do this. Some people are totally enslaved by logic—they would just look at this image and think, "What the hell is this?" Others try to free themselves, to understand how to let their imagination roam, but they don't dare break the last chain of logic. Finally, there are those who can clearly see what it is all about, who also have dreams and visions and want to share them with the rest of us.

In this same style are artists like Picasso, Dali, Magritte, and Max Ernst. Together, they have helped me give in to the impulse that I have to deal with in my own way of working; search to find my own style, fingerprint, and expression; and be myself and say what I have to say using their surrealist techniques combined with new ones in Photoshop and other digital tools like Poser or Bryce. You can see this in *Moonlover* and *Angry Venus*. I made these using mainly Photoshop's Liquify and Transform tools to get the desired form. This technique allows me to create images full of emotion, to reach the viewer and communicate with him/her.

As you can see, the possibilities are huge. You can achieve different results using the same technique, as in *Moonlover*, where I use a 3D Poser figure combined with scanned textures. In *Angry Venus*, I used a digital photo of the main subject and some more scanned textures for the background. I'm sure there is much room for experimentation here, which is why Photoshop is my tool of choice. I do not find any restrictions as I search for new ways to express my thoughts. I can set my imagination free. The end of such a process, when I get results that I'm really happy with, is the real kicker that simply makes me feel high. Of course, this is one of the reasons why I can't stop working and searching for new ways to realize my ideas and imagination using Photoshop.

Last but not least, an important place is held by today's artists, like Tim Burton, Dave McKean, and Brian Warner, who through their films, artwork, and music, let us be part of the world that they are able to see. They share it with us, and help us understand the ideas, emotions, or thoughts they have to share. These guys are part of that group of successful artists who are able to stand out, even in a world where we're saturated with images. Only by achieving this kind of success will your work stand apart and rise above the masses.

All these influences have helped me find the person I am today, the way I work, and the look and feel that my artwork has. It was a long journey to reach this point, but it was full of joy, and you can see the results. But this is surely not the end. It is good to find your own style and to be recognized through your work, but beware the danger of falling into "the style trap," which can be lethal. Sometimes, when you try to dress an idea in a specific style, instead of giving birth to that idea, you pretty much kill it, just because you're so intent on trying to apply a style that doesn't fit the idea. My opinion is that being able to change, finding new techniques, and developing and changing your style is just as important, if not more important, than searching for your personal style. Just keeping a fingerprint of style is enough, and if you have new ideas that deserve a new way of working, change the way you work, don't hesitate. After doing this, you'll be pleased with what you've done, even when it looks completely different from what you have created before.

Moonlover

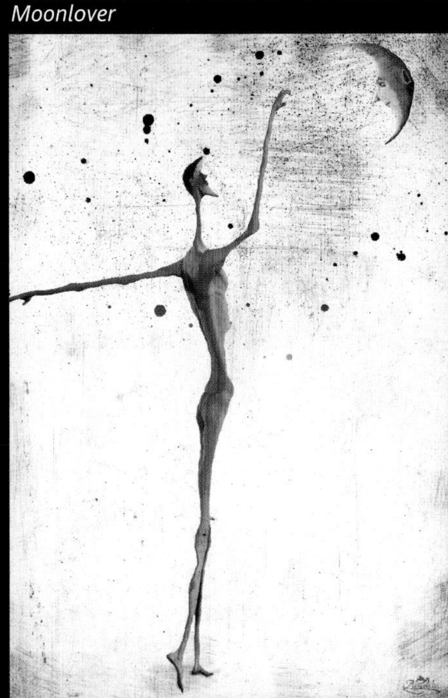

Angry Venus

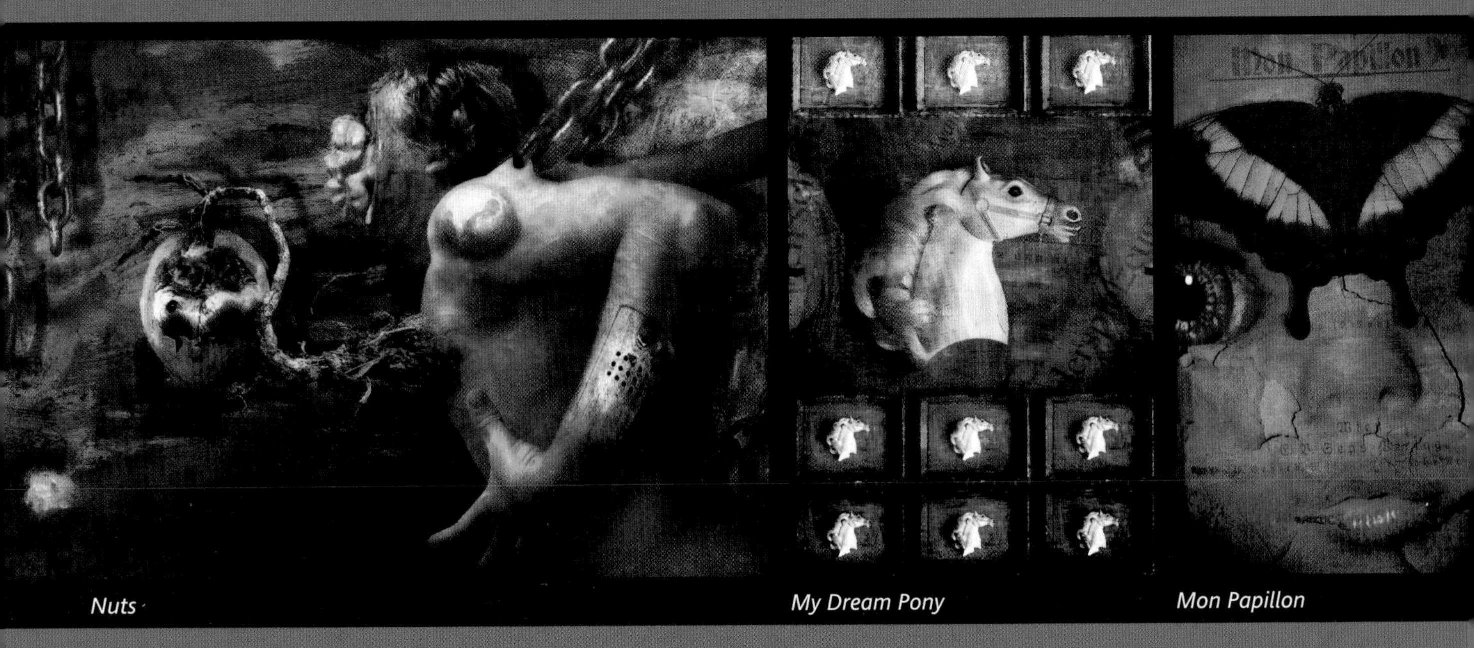

Nuts *My Dream Pony* *Mon Papillon*

The Message

Because I started working as I do today, any messages that I want to communicate are portrayed through my images. If I don't have something to say, I don't do anything, because all my work is useless if I don't have a message to send. Of course, I could tell a whole story with every image, every time, but it can be enough when I only want to share an emotion, like I have done in *Nuts* where the dominant feeling is madness and rage that has to be chained. The image lives from these emotions.

Images like *Mon Papillon* and *My Dream Pony* are part of a series that displays my childhood memories and events that have left a deep imprint and have formed me into the person I am today.

Most of the time I spend creating these images is taken up by making my thoughts, ideas, message, and emotions understandable to the viewer. I want to say something and I want to give you the chance to understand it, whether it is in my way or in your own way, because an image lives from this.

If different viewers understand an image in different ways, you have created something that has soul. Most of my ideas develop in my mind like a short story with a beginning and an end, and I want to share that story with other people. But unlike a storyteller who uses words to tell the story, I have to compress my story into an image that's a frozen moment in the middle of the story—just one frame of a film.

However, all of this is just until the point where my image reaches a viewer. That is the moment when my image starts to react, to unfold in the viewer's mind. It decompresses, sets emotions free, and the viewer's fantasy and imagination does the work. That single image becomes a story again, but now it's a personal one with its own beginning and end, personalized by each person who sees that image.

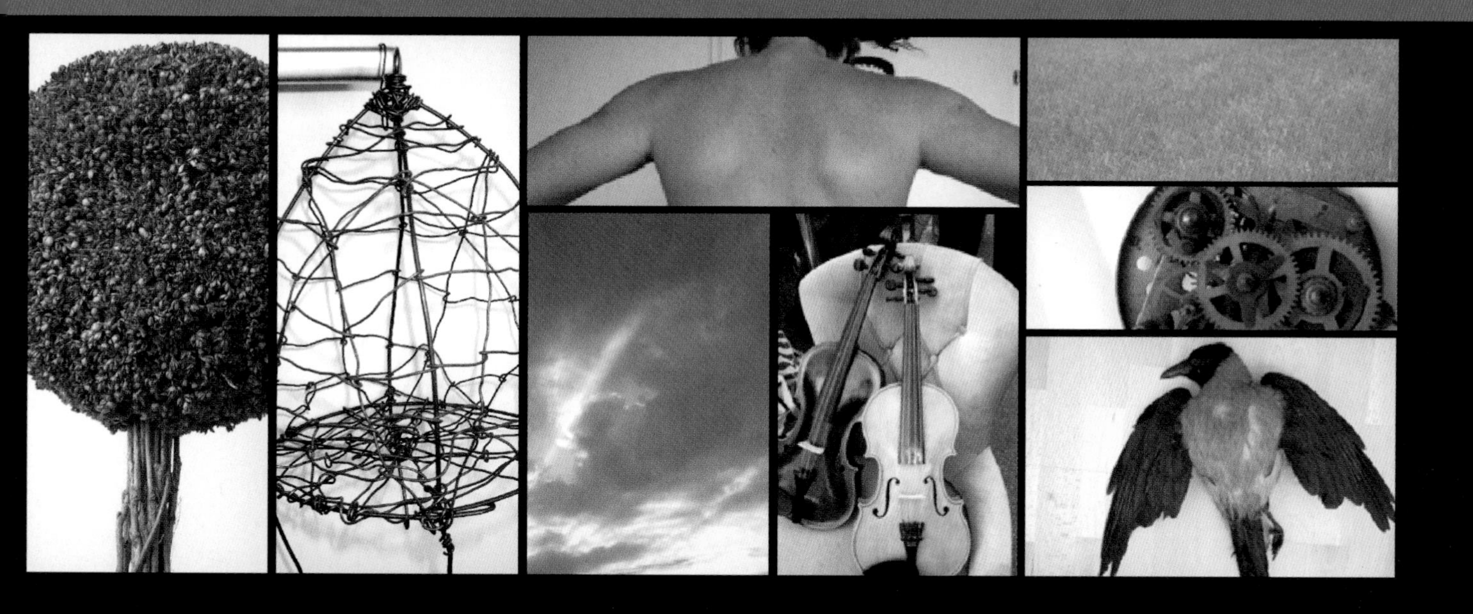

The Image

The basic idea of this tutorial image is a short story about a world without music, a world where the music is the prisoner of harpies that are part man, part bird, and part mechanical creatures. These harpies are called the Keepers of the Notes. They are the servants of a power that wants to make the world forget the delights of music and the happiness and emotions music can share. They want to substitute a deep silence for all of that. This silence is one you can feel; it overwhelms you and lets you fall into sadness. That is the message of this piece that I've named *Feel the Silence*.

Once the story had formed in my mind, I started searching for a way to make it understandable and to collect the images I needed to realize it.

As always, I use only source images and photography that I have made or shot myself. I decided to use a cage that I made from wire combined with photos of my body and of a dead crow that I found one day on a road.

Then I came across an old watch at a flea market that I just had to buy. In addition, there are also some shots of a small decorative tree, a photo of a grass field in front of my house, and a photo of the sky. To symbolize the music, I photographed a fiddle at the same flea market (always a treasure chest for my needs). These are all the photos we need to form the basis of the surreal image (all these are in the source files folder on the CD).

It is always a good idea to make a sketch of the basic idea for the piece. It's good to have a plan, rather than go any further without thinking first, but I don't need one here because I already have a concrete image in my mind of what I want. Also, because I have a small story in my mind too, I'm not in danger of forgetting it soon. Now, it's time to go further with the second part of this chapter, the tutorial.

The Tutorial

In this tutorial, we'll aim to create the image I have been talking about. We're going to create a fantasy creature that we build from different image sources. Even though it isn't a real creature, we'll try to make it look as natural as possible. Like the creature, the world that surrounds it will be made from different elements and image sources; we'll try to bring all these different parts together harmoniously and then make the composition look as realistic as possible by using different blending and adjustment settings to create a colorful, yet dark and depressing mood to fit the story behind the image.

The first step is to name the document and set its size and resolution. I've set the width to 1600 and the height to 2400 pixels. The resolution is 300ppi. It's up to you to choose what size you use for this tutorial (if the size I'm using is too large); you could halve my dimensions and use 1200x800 pixels, which will be good enough for this tutorial. This is a 1.5:1 image aspect ratio that I've had good experience with in the past, and it's also a good ratio to use when you print your work. To determine your image's aspect ratio, simply divide the largest dimension in your image by the smallest (in this example, 2400/1600 = 1.5). We'll work in RGB color mode for now (you can convert to CMYK before printing) because it's easier to work with in Photoshop.

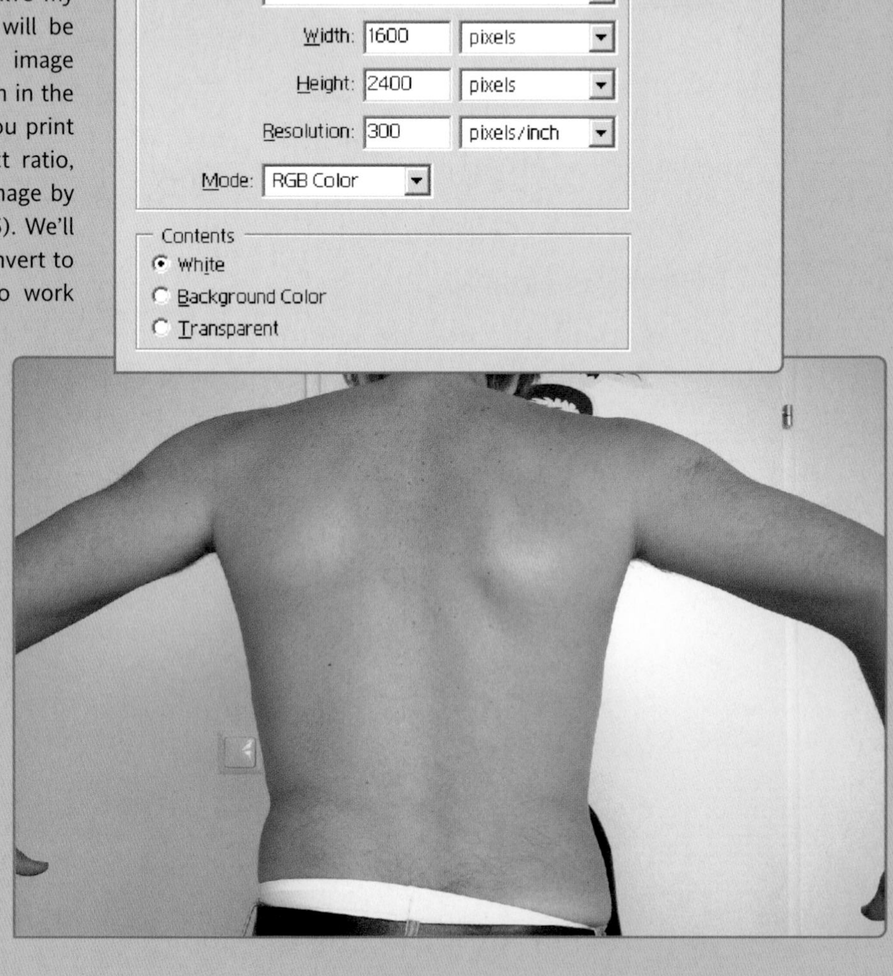

Now we need to prepare the images for the Harpy creature. Open `body.tif` from the CD and draw a close path with the Pen tool around the body, omitting the hair and the sections of the arms past the elbows.

Once you have completed the path, generate a selection and copy and paste it into your working document. Scale it to about 80 percent and name the layer "body." Before you close `body.tif`, it's a good idea to save your selection as an alpha channel (via the Channels palette), in case you need to use it again. This is also the reason why I didn't feather the selection—in order to keep all the possibilities open for the future.

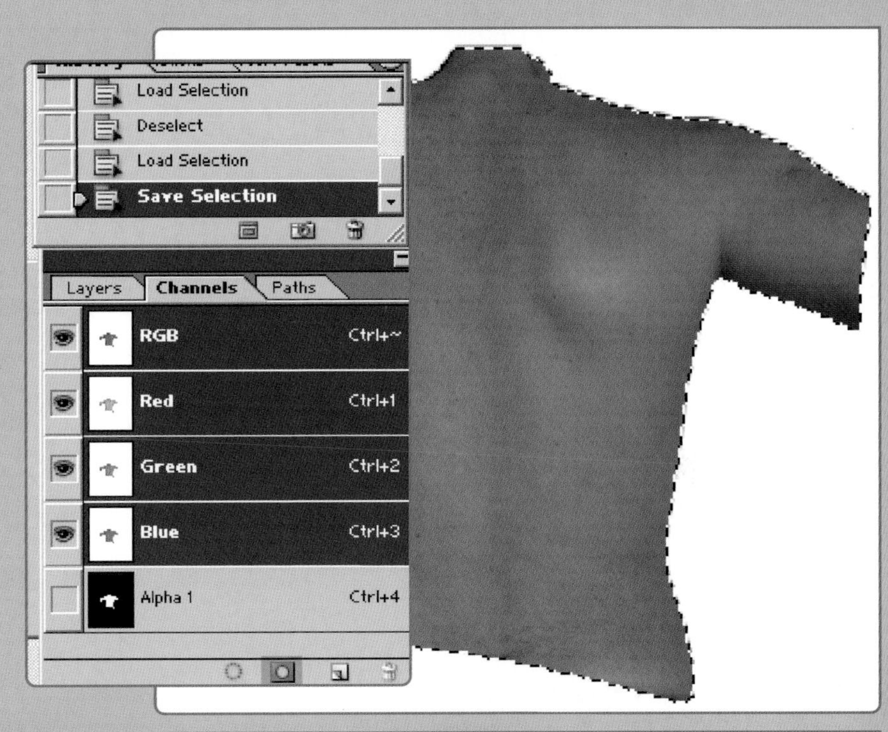

On the body layer, choose Select ➤ Load Selection and then choose Select ➤ Modify ➤ Contract to shrink the selection by 1 pixel. Next, use Select ➤ Modify ➤ Feather to feather the selection with a 1-pixel radius. Now invert the selection and press DELETE to get rid of the ugly background and smooth the edges a bit. Of course, the results will depend on how carefully you generated your selection. If you still have problems getting rid of the remaining background, repeat the previous steps and use the Eraser and Lasso tools to erase any extraneous background.

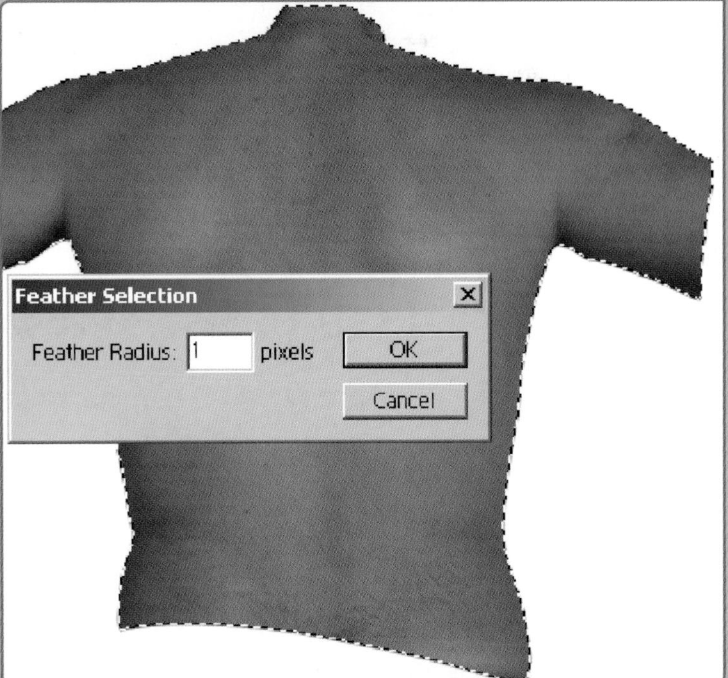

Open `cage.tif` from the CD. This step is going to involve a lot of work because I will use the Pen tool to knock out the cage, but this tool also gives the best results. There are other ways to knock out the cage, such as by using the Extract or the Magic Wand tools, but I'm not happy with their results. Because the cage is built of thin wire, I don't have too much of the image there, therefore the Pen tool is necessary because it is so precise.

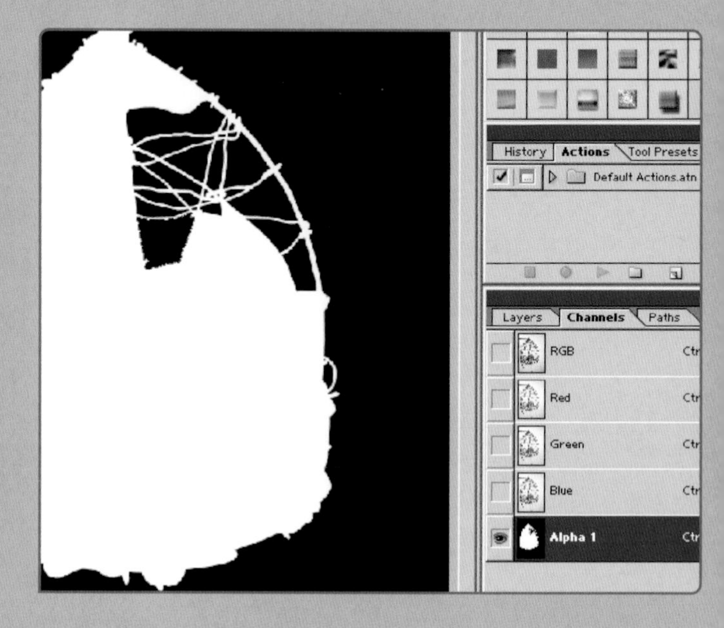

To get the best result, before you begin selecting, set the master opacity for the shape layer to 0 so that you have an unencumbered view. It is also important to start drawing the first path outside the cage and, immediately after that, move inside the cage. When you begin drawing with the Pen tool, a new path is created in the Paths palette named Work Path by default. When the path is inactive and you start to draw again, a new path is created that replaces the old path. In our case, we'll need a lot of paths to knock out the cage, so one way to save the paths is to name them by double-clicking the path icon. Or, you could always make a selection from the path you have just drawn and save it as an alpha channel, using the same alpha channel (in our case Alpha 1) each time until you have selected the whole cage (as you can see in the following image). Next, simply generate a selection from this channel, and copy and paste the cage into your working document. It will take a lot of time, but the effort is worth it because we will have a clean, good-looking cage that you can use again and again. (If you don't want to go through this, you can use the prebuilt image `cageknockout.psd` on the CD).

Open `crow.tif` and knock it out from the background. This time, I used the Magnetic Lasso tool because the image has a good contrast between the crow's body and the background and it gives a good quick result.

Now, just repeat what you did for the body: create an alpha channel from the selection, copy and paste the selection into the working document, and save the `crow.tif` file. Contract the selection by 1 pixel (Select ➤ Modify ➤ Contract), invert it, and press DELETE. We'll retouch the crow later, so for now, just resize the body, crow, and the cage so that they'll fit together. The cage and the body aren't finalized yet, but they are accurate enough to give us an idea of how the creature will look. Now is also a good time to make a Layer Set for the creature. Note that to retain the correct order when you add a layer to a set, you must drag the items into the Layer Set from the top to bottom. Layer Sets are great for grouping layers with individual masks, and they also makes it possible to alter blending modes for the entire set.

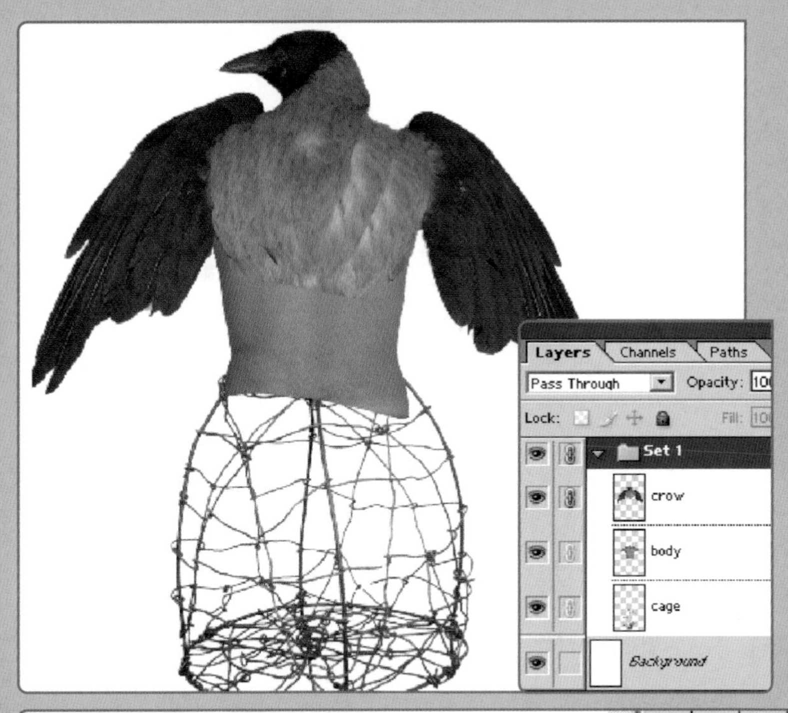

Hide the crow and cage layers, activate the body layer, and use the Rectangular Marquee tool to select the bottom part of the body. Duplicate the body layer, select Edit ➤ Transform ➤ Flip Vertical, and nudge the layer into position so that it perfectly mirrors the other body part. Merge the two body layers. We'll need the mirrored bottom part of the body to create the connection between the cage and the body.

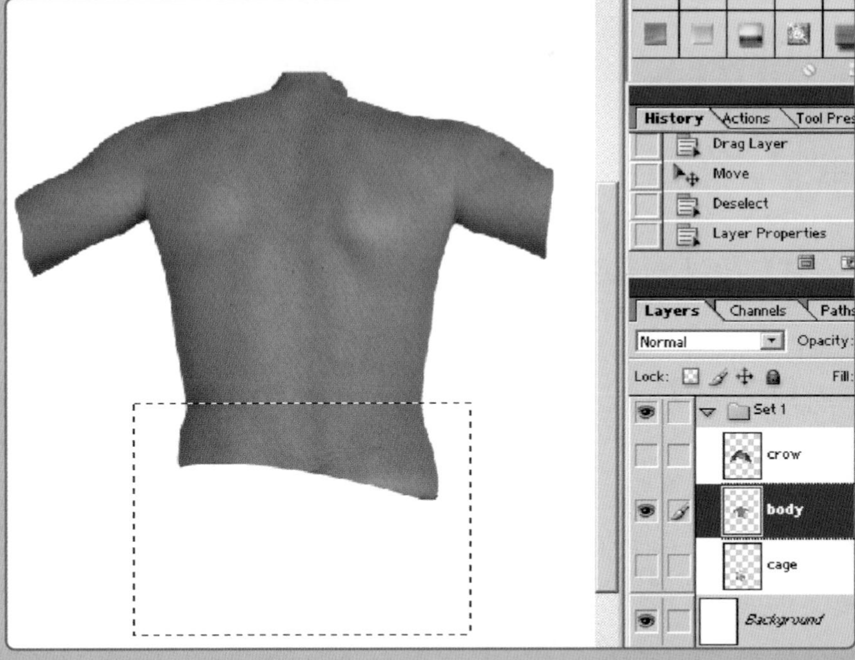

Open `clockwork.tif` and use the Magnetic Lasso tool again to knock it out from its background, then paste it into the working document on a new layer called "clockwork."

Hide the clockwork layer and make the crow layer visible again. Also, go to the History palette and create a new snapshot before continuing. With the crow layer active, go to Image ➤ Adjustments ➤ Hue/Saturation, check Colorize, and set the sliders as shown here to change the color of the crow. This adjustment is necessary so that the color of the crow matches the body in preparation for combining these two parts of the harpy-like creature together; this adjustment will also get rid of the patchy look that results from using two different image sources.

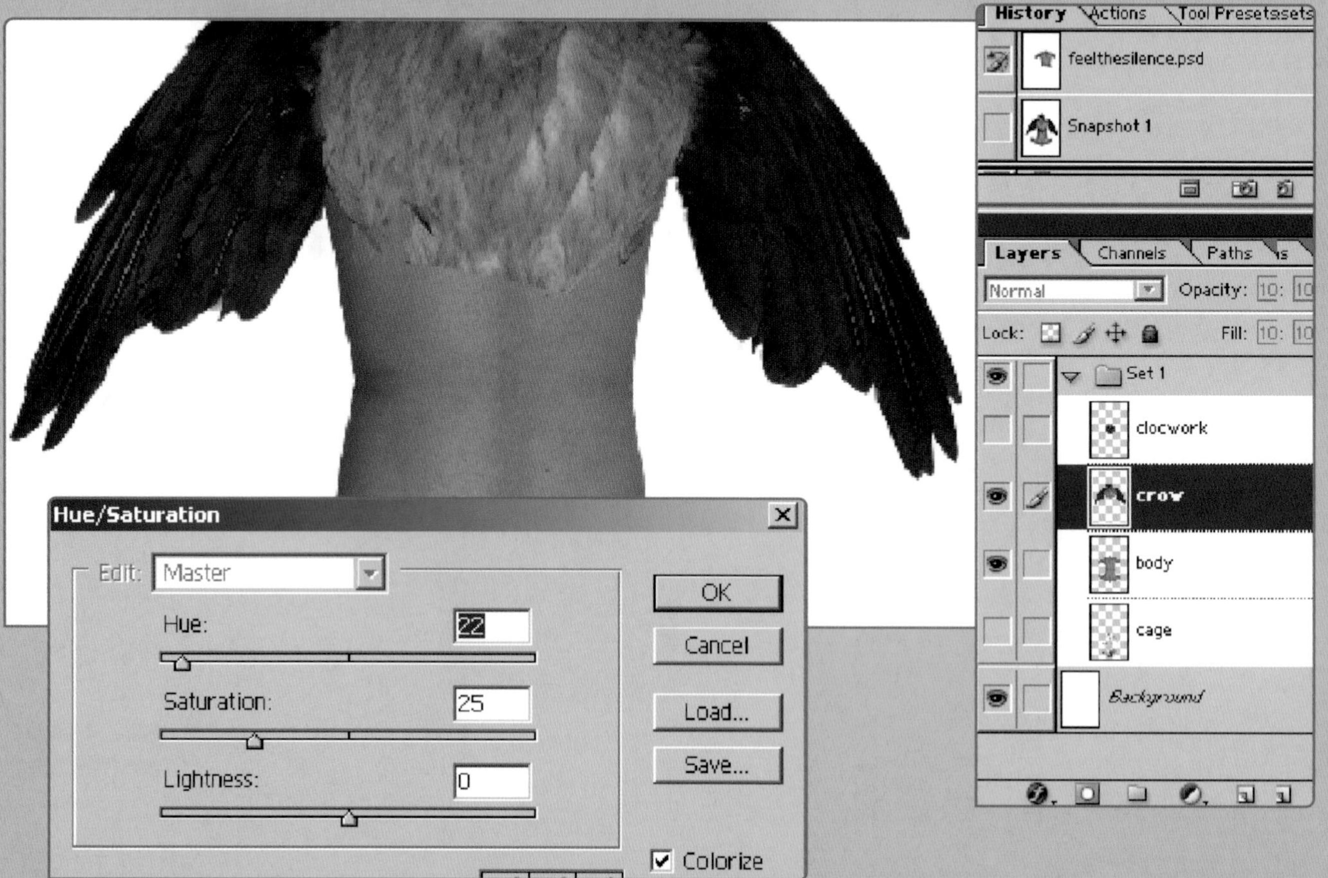

Now duplicate the body and the crow layers. Drag the clockwork layer under the crow copy layer, activate the crow copy layer, and, using a large brush, erase the bottom part of the crow so that the clockwork image is visible. We're now going to place the clockwork image inside the body. Drag the crow copy layer over the body copy layer and select Layer ➤ Merge Down again. Name this layer "bodycrow" and drag it over the clockwork layer. Now you have the clockwork image between the body and the bodycrow layers. Select the bodycrow layer and set its opacity to 70 percent so that you can see the clockwork between the layers. Next, select the Elliptical Marquee Tool and SHIFT+drag a circle that fits inside the clockwork, as shown here:

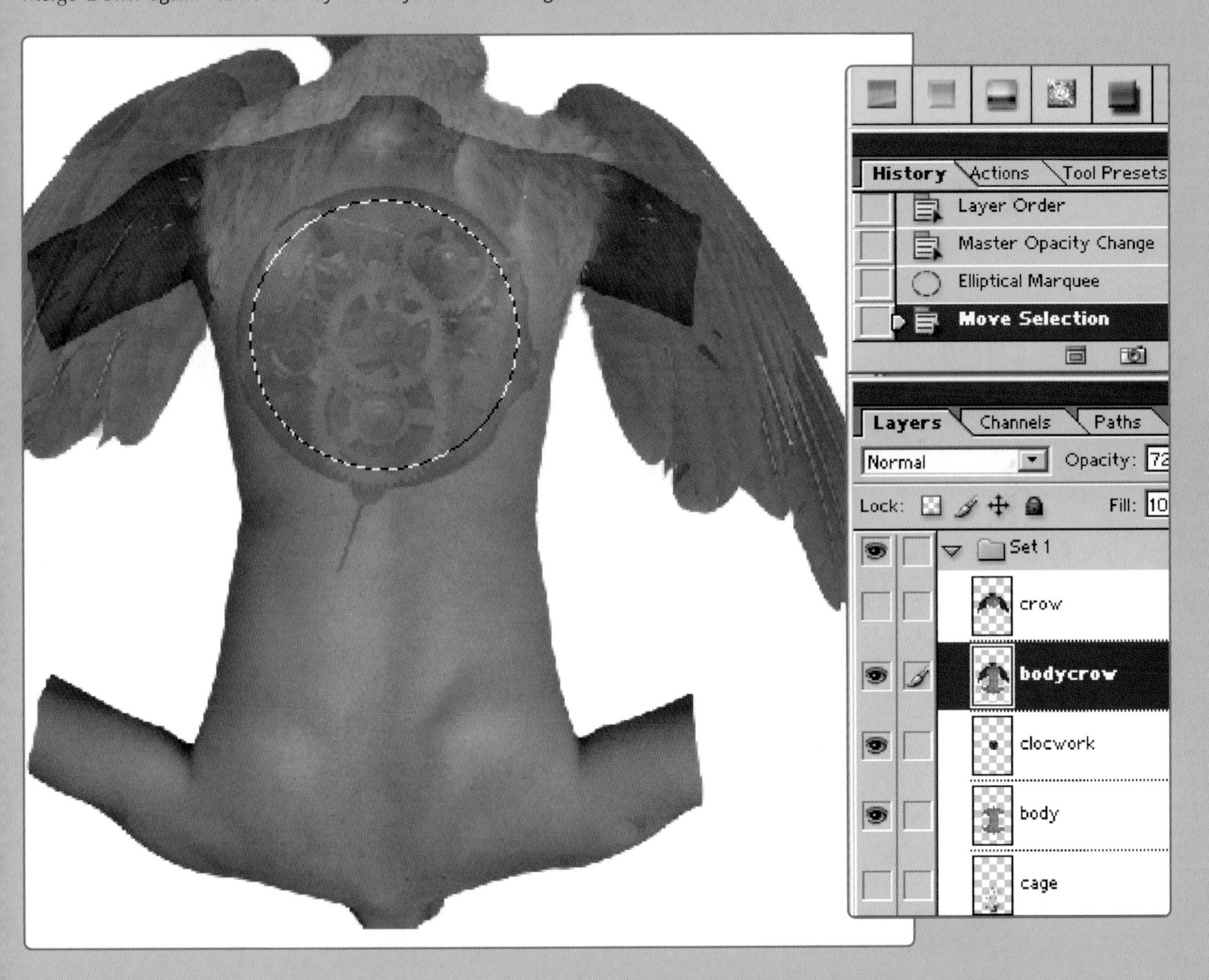

Set the opacity of the bodycrow layer back to 100 percent and, with this layer and the selection active, copy and paste to create a new layer from the copied selection, and name the new layer "bevel." While you're still in the bevel layer, load the selection and choose Select ➤ Modify ➤ Contract to shrink it by 10 pixels. Press DELETE, activate the bodycrow layer, and hit DELETE again.

You can see the clockwork now, but I don't like the way the edge looks too clean and flat. It would look more natural if the harpy had a healed scar around the edge of the hole in its body. Select the bevel layer and add a bevel (Layer ➤ Layer Style ➤ Bevel and Emboss) using the settings shown here:

What I want to do next is add a new light to the clock inside the body, a kind of red light that is a reflection of the flesh that surrounds the clock. Of course, I also want to add a shadow that is produced by the edges of the hole, once again trying to achieve the most natural look possible. I am hoping the effect will create a kind of confusion in the viewer; at fist glance, it will seem natural, but the mind will say that can't be real. This gives the creature a very special look and feel.

To accomplish this effect, follow these steps. With the bevel layer active, select the Magic Wand tool and click inside the bevel selection. Duplicate the body layer and name it "insidelight." Set its blending mode to Hard Light and its opacity to 70 percent. Make a copy of it and drag it under the clockwork layer. Now set the blending mode to Multiply and its opacity to 100 percent to give it a much darker shadow underneath the clock.

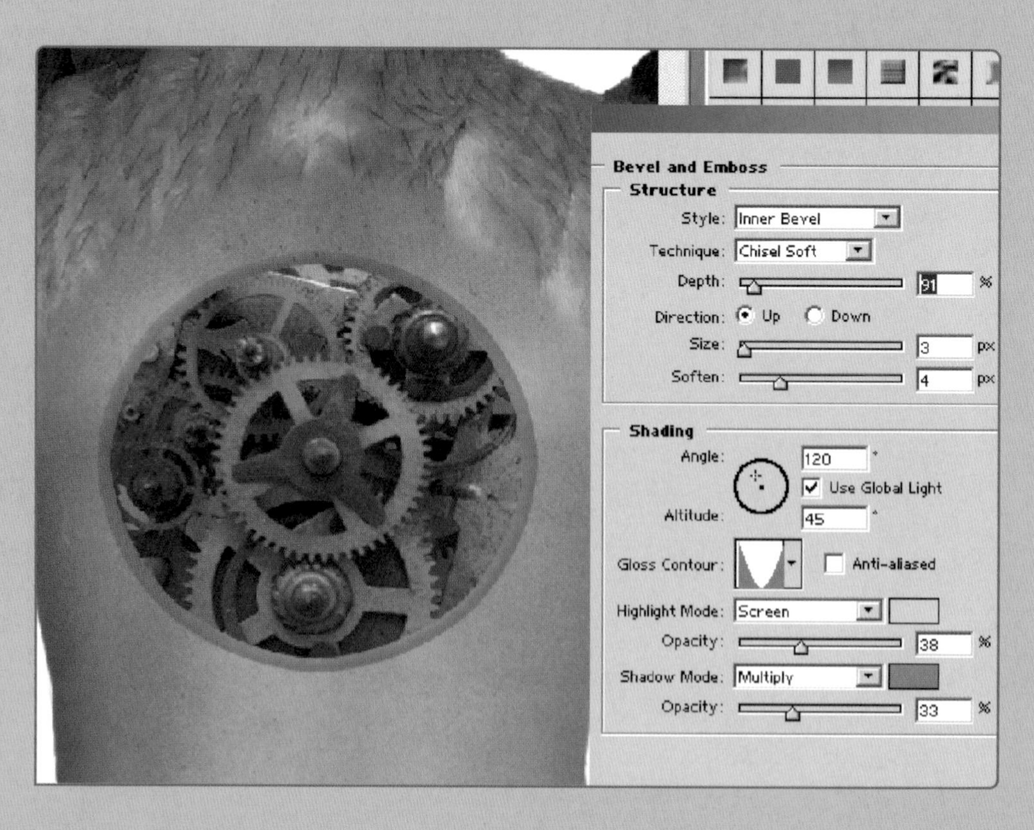

Once again, load the insidelight selection, create a new layer, and name it "insideshadow." Fill it with a dark brown color and drag it above the insidelight layer. This will be the edge shadow inside the body. Contract the selection by 20 pixels, then choose Select ➤ Modify ➤ Feather to feather it with a 10-pixel radius. Hit DELETE three times to get a smooth transition from light to shadow. Select the insidelight layer and change the levels (CTRL+L), dragging the left marker to darken the selection. Now the clockwork inside the body looks the way I want it to, as if it actually belongs inside the body.

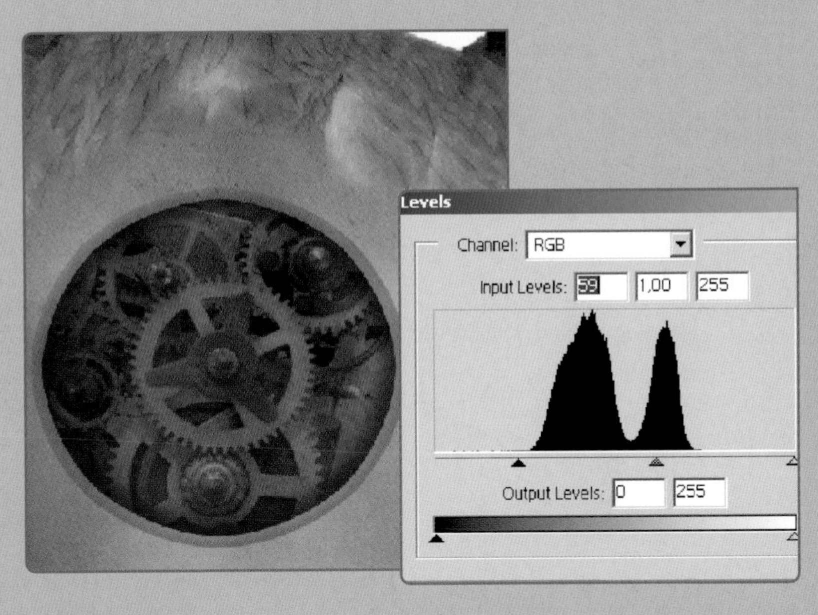

Now let's add the cage to the body. Drag the cage layer above the body layer, select the bodycrow layer, and hit 5 to reduce the opacity to 50 percent so that you can see through it. Nudge the cage so that it conforms to the body's edges.

Now, back on the bodycrow layer, we'll use the Elliptical Marquee tool and Eraser tool with a large brush to cut out the body parts we don't want, but not before we create a new snapshot in the History palette. Once you have erased the parts, select the Burn tool with a 25 percent Exposure and a Soft Round Brush; then softly burn the edges you just created. Now select the body layer and repeat these steps, only remember that the back part must be visible, as you can see here:

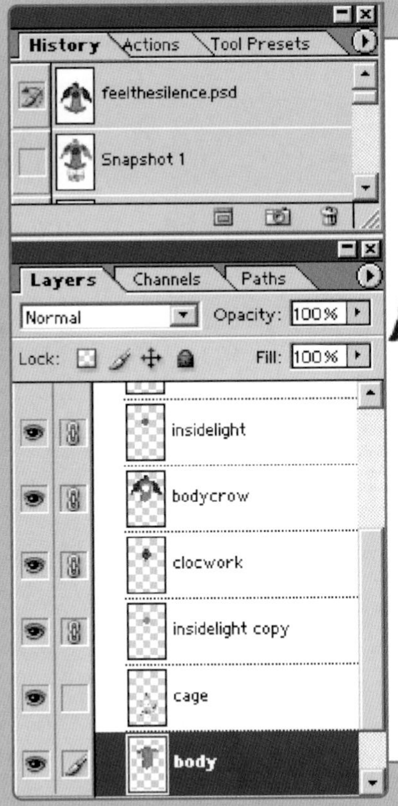

We'll darken the back part now to create the inner part of the body and, at the same time, put the cage inside the body. To do so, first duplicate the body layer and use the Rectangular Marquee tool to delete the upper part of the bodycopy because you only need the lower part. Set the blending mode to Multiply and the opacity to 80 percent to darken the inner part of the body. I used the Multiply mode because you can see it darken, but at the same time, it looks like soft light shimmering through. Also, with the opacity settings, you have total control over this effect and you can try different settings until you get your desired result.

Now zoom in and use the Burn tool with a small Soft Round brush to darken those parts of the cage that are inside the body. I used the Burn tool because it gives me total control over Ranges, Exposure, and brush size, and I can work in small steps as if painting. When used in combination with a sensitive pen, Burn is an even more powerful tool.

After this, duplicate the bodycopy layer that you just created and drag it above the cage layer. Then set the blending mode to Soft Light and the opacity to 60 percent to intensify the shimmering light appearance. Now use the Eraser tool and a small brush to erase above the parts of the body that currently cover the front side of the cage. Select the bodycrow layer and using the Eraser tool with a small brush and a 20-percent opacity, carefully erase those parts where the body meets the cage wire to create a soft transition from the cage to the body.

Now open `fiddle.tif` and use the Pen tool to cut out and paste the yellow fiddle into our document under the cage layer. Then duplicate it and drag the fiddle copy layer above the cage layer. Select the cage layer and then choose Select ➤ Load Selection. With the cage selected, select the fiddle copy layer, and use the Eraser tool with a small Round Brush to delete the parts of the fiddle that cover the front part of the cage wire. This part is a bit tricky and we have to work carefully, so zoom in to see what you're doing better. By using the Eraser tool to erase the parts of the cage and the fiddle copy, you can make the fiddle appear as if it's inside the cage.

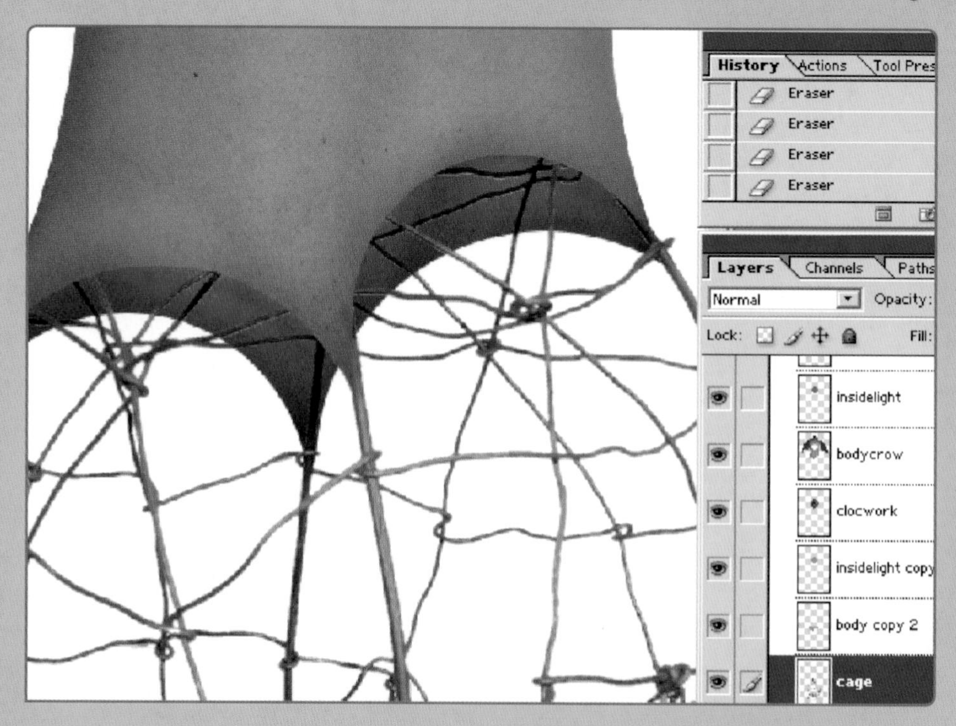

Select the Burn tool again with a small brush and set the Exposure to 40 percent to draw the shadows on the fiddle copy. Next, use a bigger brush to slightly darken the bottom area of the fiddle copy and the upper part that's inside the body to create the illusion of shadow. Also, using the Burn tool and a medium-sized brush, darken the body copy part behind the fiddle a bit to create a shadow dropped by the fiddle. Now that the fiddle is inside the cage, you can go into more detail and create lights and shadows on the fiddle using the Burn and Dodge tools. Let your creativity roam free. For example, you could add some light at the center-left side of the fiddle and more shadow at the bottom, This is a creative process and a guide only—it is not compulsory—so use your own judgment here to get the appearance you prefer.

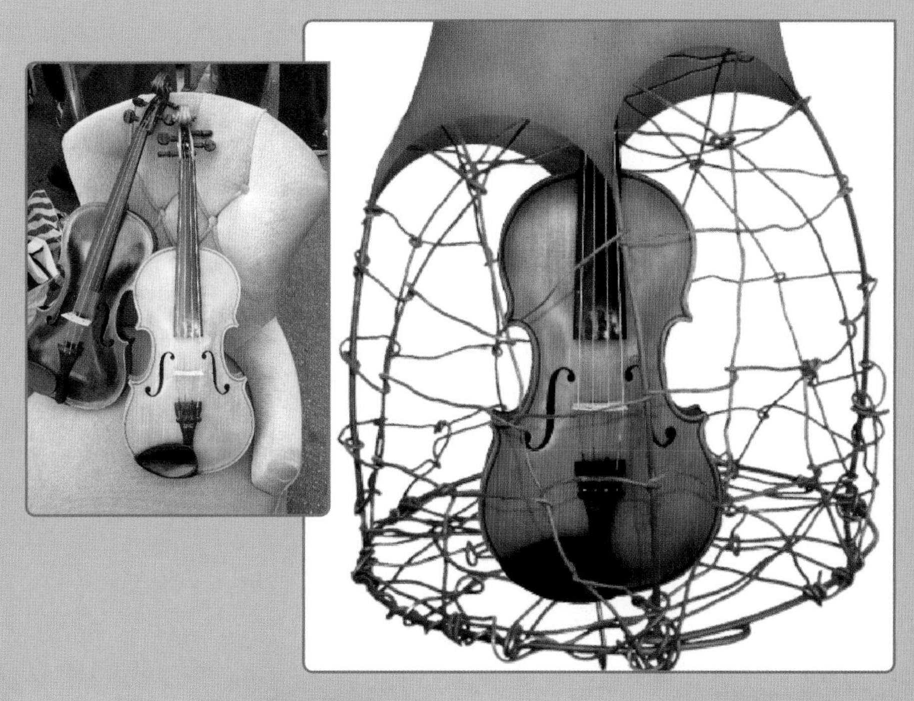

Activate the crow layer, nudge the crow to fit with the crow body below, and set the opacity to 85 percent. Now use the Eraser tool to get rid of the parts you don't need, such as those covering the clockwork. This next step is a bit time-consuming because you have to do the final retouching on the crow's wings and head. By using the Eraser combined with the Clone Stamp tool, you can make the crow's head and wings look more real to get rid of that clean-cut edge. At this point, a sensitive pen helps a lot. A good idea is to fill the Background layer with black so that you can better see the sections you've erased. Then fill it with white again when you start to work with the Clone Stamp tool. When everything is ready, your creature should look like this:

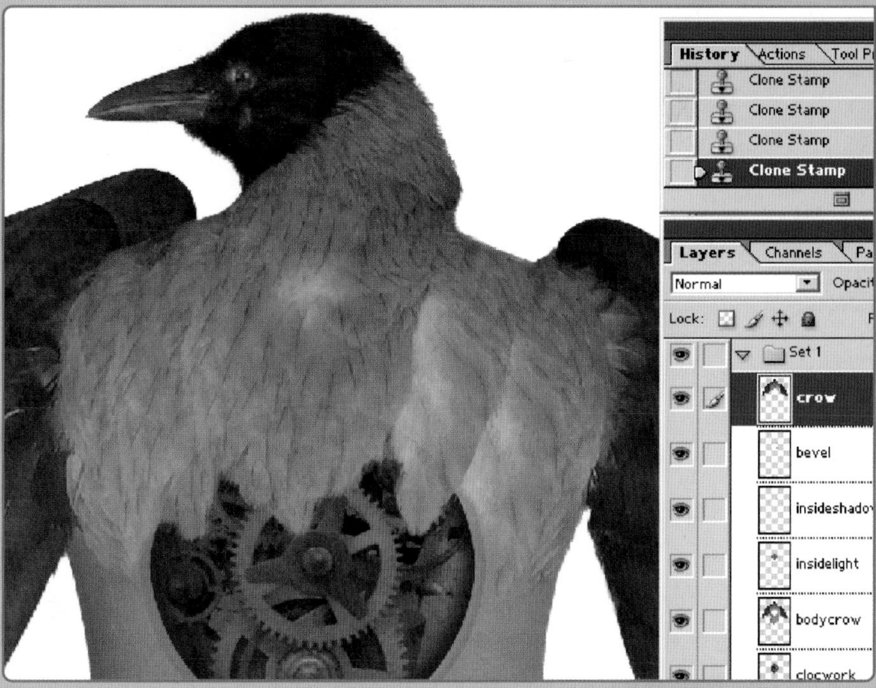

Now we'll move on and start creating the world around the creature. Open thesky.tif from the CD and drag it into your working document onto a new layer called "sky." Hide the Set 1. Go to Edit ➤ Transform ➤ Scale, hold SHIFT, and scale the image to fit in the document.

Now you must get rid of the digital artifacts and smooth the sky. So, with the sky layer selected, add a Gaussian Blur with a 3-pixel radius. Duplicate the sky layer and blur it again, but now use a radius of 5 pixels. Set the blending mode for the sky layer to Color, and in the Levels dialog box (CTRL+L), drag the left marker slightly to the right to darken the sky a little for a more dramatic effect.

At this point, you may be thinking that the light from the sky doesn't fit with the light that the creature seems to be exposed to. Once again, let me point out that it's not my goal to duplicate reality but to show what is possible in an imaginary world. So, it's possible that there could be two different light sources in that world, like two suns for example. This is why I deliberately use lights that will look strange or surreal.

Open thegreen.tif and drag it into your document, calling the new layer "green." Using the Eraser tool with a big Soft Round brush, erase the upper part of the green. Now duplicate the layer, name it "hill," drag it beneath the green layer, and scale it to about 60 percent. Duplicate this layer and use the Eraser tool again to give the two hills the desired form. Duplicate *both* hill layers and set the blending mode of the copies to Multiply. Change the opacity of the front hill to 50 percent and make the opacity 60 percent for the hill at the back. Finally, select the green layer and go to Edit ➤ Transform ➤ Distort to add perspective to the green.

Open tree.tif, and use the Magic Wand tool to knock out the tree and paste it into our document (call the new layer "tree").

Activate the tree layer and go to Select ➤ Modify ➤ Contract to shrink by about 1 pixel, then choose Select ➤ Modify ➤ Feather with 1-pixel radius, invert, and press DELETE. Scale the tree to 35 percent (constrain it with SHIFT while you do so) and drag the layer under the hill layer. Now duplicate it and scale this second tree to 90 percent. Duplicate the layer again and scale it to 80 percent. Duplicate it again and go to Edit ➤ Transform ➤ Again.

Now arrange the tree copy layers from first to last, placing the largest one in the sequence at the bottom all the way to the smallest one at the top. Now link the tree layers and go to Layer ➤ Merge Linked to create the surreal-looking tree. Use the Burn tool to darken the bottom parts and trunks of the top two trees and use a blur with a 1-pixel radius. Now, make sure the tree layers are under the hills layers, select the tree layer, Select ➤ Load Selection and select the hill copy layer. With the tree selected, erase those parts of the hill that cover the tree trunk, and repeat this for the other hill.

Open both `grass.tif` and `grasses.tif`, go to Edit ➤ Define Brush, and name the first one "Grass" and the second "Grasses." Select the Brush tool with the newly created Grasses brush, set the master diameter to 50 pixels and, in the Brush Presets palette, check Shape Dynamics, Scattering, Color Dynamics, and Other Dynamics. Select the Clone Stamp tool and activate the hill layer, zoom in, and by using the Clone tool and the Grass brush, add some more grass at the edges of the hills to make them nice and natural looking.

With the Grasses brush, start to create grass at the edge of the hill and to slightly cover the tree trunk. Use the same technique for the other hill and for the edge of the green in front of the hills. Don't forget to change the master diameter to vary the size of the grass, and also remember to switch between the two brushes you created to get a better result. After completing the new grass, blur the two hills with a 0.7-pixel radius.

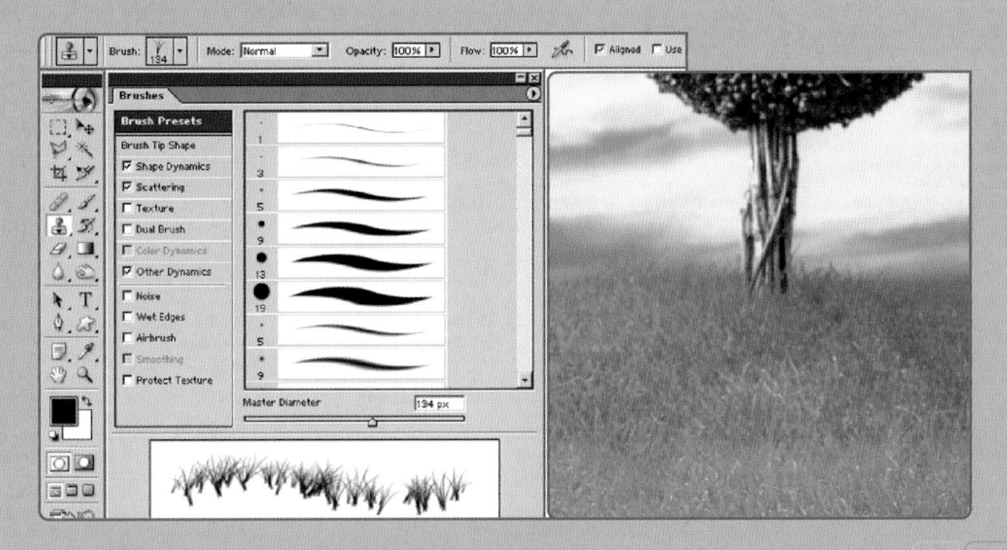

Create a new snapshot in the History palette and select the hill layer. Select the Burn tool with the Range set to Midtones and the Exposure at about 8 percent. Start to add shadows on those parts of the hill where you think they should go. Do the same for the other hill and the trees also. If you think that you've gone overboard with the Burn tool, go back to the snapshot and work through the shadow placement again until you're pleased with the result. Next, duplicate the tree layer, set the blending mode to Soft Light, and set the opacity to 50 percent for both trees. Merge each copy with the original layer, and blur each of the surreal trees with its respective hill using a 1-pixel radius to create more depth. Slowly, this world is looking more like it should, with some dramatic light in the sky and a surreal clean, empty, and yet somehow strange geometrical feeling that's suggested through the trees and the composition.

Make Set 1 visible and drag it over Set 2. Now it's time to make some adjustments. First go to the sky layer and drag it a little to the right. Then use Levels to darken the sky a bit more because, currently, it isn't dark enough. The mood of the image should be oppressive, indicating that deep silence created by the complete absence of any kind of music. I want to create this desired atmosphere using a dark sky among other elements. Lastly, select the Set 1 layer and scale the creature slightly from the bottom up.

Next, we'll change the tree at the right. Scale this too and position it more to the right.

In Set 1, activate the bodycrow layer and use the Healing Brush and Clone Stamp tools to create a seamless transition where the two parts of the body meet. Add some more shadow inside the body and also slightly darken the cage part inside the body. Build up your work in small steps until you're pleased with the way everything is looking. Again, use your creativity here. It's up to you how clean the transition is, and how much shadow and light you want to add to the body.

The fact that the cage now seems to float over the grass would not be all that unusual if you believe that the creature can fly, but I don't want to let the creature do that, so we need to lay it down on the grass. In Set 2, duplicate the green layer and drag the new one into Set 1 above the bodycrow layer to cover the creature. Expand Set 1, activate the body layer, and load the selection. With the selection loaded, change to the green copy layer and hit Delete. Now repeat this for the fiddle and cage layers. If you do everything correctly, you should be able to see the creature now.

Activate the green copy layer, select the Clone Stamp tool and the Grass brush you created, and start to clone the grass around the base of the cage to make the cage and fiddle appear as if they are in the grass. Once again, remember to keep changing the size of the grass and switch between the two brushes to get the best results. When you're done, select the Burn tool and add some shadows on the area of grass beneath the creature. You can see how powerful the Burn tool can be—use it like a paintbrush and add shadows where you think they're required and make them as intense as you think they should be.

The composition of the image is now complete; everything is in its place and looks fine. You could leave the image the way it is and it will look okay, but I'm still not pleased with it. I want to give the image another mood, and we can make this happen by trying to get all of the disparate components of the image that came from different sources to meld together in a common way; hopefully this will get rid of that patchy feeling and create harmony in the image.

We will achieve this using adjustment layers, blending, and other modifications. This is where you can take advantage of using sets—because the adjustment layers will affect the entire set—but you also have full control over each layer inside the set and their individual masks. Another powerful feature of adjustment layers is that you can use them without losing any information from the original image.

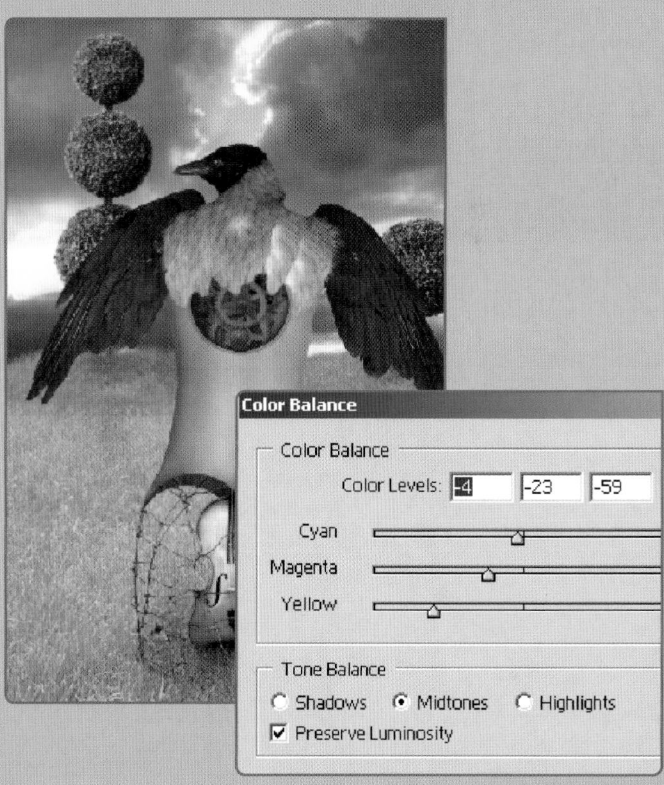

Before starting the adjustments, create a new snapshot in the History palette. Now go to Layer ➤ New Adjustment Layer ➤ Hue/Saturation. Set the Hue to 74, the saturation to 51, the lightness to +4, and then set the opacity to 60 percent. You can already see how that changed the feel of the image. Now all the parts in the image have some kind of harmony between them. The colors are much stronger and the contrast has changed. With one simple adjustment, you've brought life to the image.

However, you can still go further. Go to Layer ➤ New Adjustment Layer ➤ Color Balance and use the settings shown in the image opposite.

The image looks warmer now. The next step is to adjust the levels. Go to Layer ➤ New Adjustment Layer ➤ Levels and darken the image a little by dragging the center marker to the right. Use your own feeling to decide how dark you want to make the image. Now go to Layer ➤ New Fill Layer ➤ Solid Color and fill it with brown (#6F5F40). Now set the blending mode for the layer to Soft Light and the opacity to 40 percent to harmonize all the elements together.

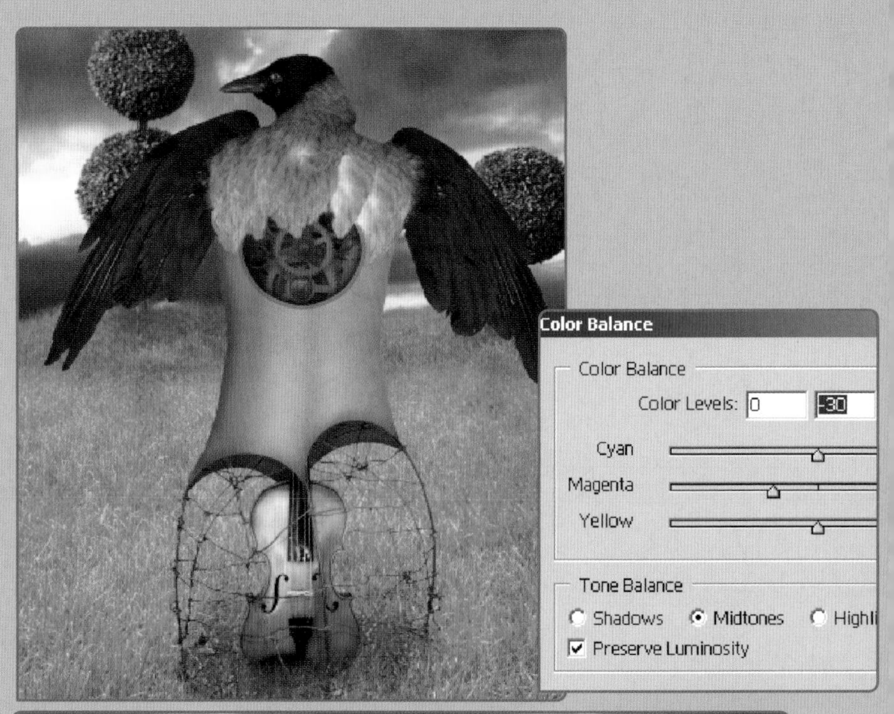

Now you have to do some more adjustment to individual layers of the sets to complete the work. Expand the two sets, activate the green copy layer in Set 2, go to Image ➤ Adjustments ➤ Color Balance and set magenta to –30. Do the same for the hills and the green layers.

Now let's add some more shine to the body and the fiddle. Go to the fiddle layer and make a copy. Set the blending mode to Multiply and the opacity to 30 percent. Do the same for the bodycrow layer and, via Image ➤ Adjustment ➤ Levels, lighten the bodycrow layer slightly by dragging the right marker to the left. Because this isn't quite enough, use the Dodge tool with a Soft Round Brush and a 10 percent Exposure to lighten the back of the creature and the fiddle. Now the image has the desired look, and you can clearly see the difference in atmosphere and feel between the two images.

The image still isn't quite ready; I want to try to make it even better. This time we'll use another method, one that is kind of destructive because we'll be altering the main image. Save the image and, starting at the last snapshot you made (or you could use `Snapshot1.psd` on the CD), create a new document and then close the main document. Be sure to also save a copy of your main PSD file as backup, because if you make a mistake at this point, your whole work will be gone.

You now have a new document called `Snapshot1`. Flatten the image, and rename the Background layer "main." Then, from the History palette, create a new document from the current state and perform the following operations:

- Select Image ➤ Mode ➤ Grayscale.
- Select Image ➤ Auto Levels.
- Select Image ➤ Adjustments ➤ Brightness/Contrast and set the contrast to +10.
- Select Image ➤ Mode ➤ Duotone and select Pantone 134 C from the Pantone Solid Coated palette.

Now go back to Image ➤ Mode ➤ RGB, select the image, and paste it via copy into the `Snapshot1` document. Drag it under the main layer and name it "color." Select the main layer and set the blending mode to Soft Light. Now activate the color layer and change the Color Balance (CTRL+B). With Preserve Luminosity and Midtones checked, set Yellow to –45, Green to +2, and Red to +20.

Check the Highlight button and set Red to –4, Green to +3, and Yellow to –8. Go to the History palette and create a new snapshot. Then merge layers (CTRL+E), duplicate the layer, and set the blending mode to Screen and the opacity to 45 percent. Add a vector mask and select the Gradient tool with the Reflected Gradient. Let just the middle part of the wings and the crow's head be lightened.

Flatten the image and duplicate the layer again, then add a Gaussian Blur to the new layer with a 2-pixel radius. Now go to Edit ➤ Fade Gaussian Blur, set the opacity to 100 percent, and the Mode to Darken.

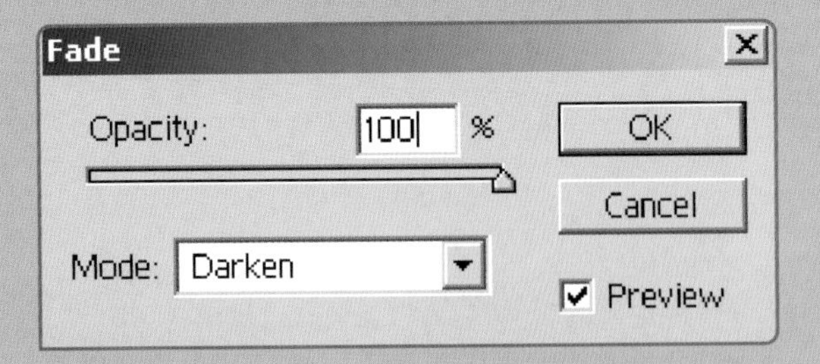

After that, return to the top layer, set the blending mode to Color, and flatten the image. If you feel that the image needs a little more touching up, feel free to keep editing it until you're happy with the result. My final touch-up steps were to darken the clockwork under the feathers slightly, to lighten those parts that remain uncovered, to darken the right part of the body, and to lighten the crow's eye.

This is the final look I wanted to create. Even though the method I used was destructive, I got what I wanted and achieved the correct mood. All the components of the image are now harmonized, and the image has lost that patchy look. It is colorful, but it also has a dark mood that supports the story behind the image.

Now we've reached the end of the tutorial. You've seen what you can create using basic Photoshop techniques, nothing fancy, and how you can achieve what you want to. Also, in the last few steps, you saw that, with Photoshop, you can use different methods to get the result that you want; this is also the case for the tutorial as a whole. I hope you can use this as a guide to your future work, because I am sure each of you will find your own way. One thing is for sure, Photoshop gives you a lot of great possibilities, but it is just a tool that depends on you. Your imagination is the main component in this kind of work. I have used the same techniques you've seen here in a whole series of images and have been pleased each time with the result; this is because I've managed to make them appear how I see those images when I close my eyes.

Of course, not every kind of image fits this look; that is why I use different techniques to fit the idea behind each image in order to make my thoughts understandable. You can see this in my different series—each one involves different techniques as the base and each has a distinct look as a consequence. But even when you use the same technique for a series of images, it's important to develop that technique, not just to use it as a template and run the danger of failing to express a certain idea or emotion through your image. Once again, it is all about your imagination and your ability to set it free. Get rid of logic. You don't have to make things look as they really are, but how they could be. Forget what other people say about it. It is what you think about, what you want to say, and what you can see that is important.

If you work a lot and experiment, you will be surprised at how much you'll discover. I hope this guide will help you go further toward developing your own personal techniques, style, and method of expression, and that it helps you create many wonderful works to delight our eyes.

3

“THERE IS A WAY TO MAKE DIGITAL ABSTRACTS EXCLUSIVE AND UNIQUE. YOUR WORKING METHODS MAY BE THE SAME AS EVERYONE ELSE’S, BUT YOU CAN USE YOUR OWN ARTISTIC SENSE TO PUSH IT FURTHER

PER GUSTAFSON
WWW.MODERNSTYLE.NU

Oil paintings, 1996

I first started experimenting with Photoshop eight years ago. I saw some magnificent websites and digital artwork created with this program, which inspired me. Ever since, I've been constantly jamming and developing abstract digital art. I've managed to make a living as a graphic designer, and I sell my digital art pieces so they can be used on record sleeves and promotional material such as posters, flyers, and business cards. Although most of my clients get in touch with me through my online playground at MODERNSTYLE.NU, I've also built a network of contacts from the years I've spent in the graphics community.

Because I began as a graphic artist and was not a designer originally, I've always painted and drawn. As a result, I found that the next step up for me from traditional oil paintings was graffiti art. The color schemes and development of style in this medium have always fascinated me. My interest in this type of art increased when I started experimenting with digital creations. It was my discovery of Photoshop along with the Internet back in 1996 that really changed my life into what it is today—juggling freelance projects and my urge to develop.

When I first began working with Photoshop, I had no idea where to start and had no tutorials available to me, so I explored techniques and all the tools that this program had to offer. Finding all the filters and tools was easy, but learning how to use them in a good way was much more difficult. My first experiments with Photoshop were attempts to copy other people's creations. If I found an image I liked, I tried to make it myself, but it always resulted in a worse looking version of the original.

I quickly realized that I couldn't copy anyone's image and then use it legally, so my next biggest issue was developing a personal style. I had time on my hands back then, and by practicing more and more in Photoshop, I quickly discovered new techniques that helped shape my art. I quickly learned that I had to choose from among the many tools to create a specific special effect. Even though I continued to be influenced by many online designers, I found my own rare style from learning to work differently from anyone else.

Per Gustafson, 2003

As I already mentioned, I have a passion for graffiti art. This type of art still has so many inspiring old-school artists who are still keeping it real, as well as new talents who shape new forms and styles. It seems to me that some of these artists also use a computer these days to create some elements and forms. I know a lot of these artists work as illustrators or designers, which could explain the current development and exploration of styles.

I furthered my interest in this kind of art by getting in touch with some of local graffiti artists. After learning their techniques and terms, what I saw in their art quickly changed. I started to appreciate details in their pieces that I'd never seen before, and I learned how much work went into a deceptively simple piece of art. I immersed myself in this area by spending time down in the harbor of Västerås where it is legal to paint, and where the city's graffiti hall of fame changes week by week with new artwork.

The strong colors the graffiti artists used also inspired me. It seemed as if they could produce colors just like that, whereas I spent hours mixing the same colors in oil just to get it right. This is probably one of the reasons why I both quit oil painting and never became a graffiti artist. Apparently I'm too lazy and I've found Photoshop so much easier to control.

My inspiration comes from many different sources—music, people, film. Whatever it is that's caught my attention is often shaped into something, and I try to illustrate it. My main source of inspiration is music. I can always depend on good music to help me visualize ideas in my head and transfer them to paper or computer. Other strong factors that stimulate my creative thinking are movies and special effects, particularly the environments in the new giant trilogies *Lord of the Rings* and *The Matrix*. I remember these environments in my own way, develop the ideas in my head, and sometimes use these as a thematic starting point. Tarsem Singh's *The Cell* (2000) is also one of my favorite movies. *The Cell* is both strongly unique and beautiful visually (but it has a pretty simple script and a lot of unnecessary violence, which is probably why it got such a small audience).

In addition to films and music, I've also been inspired by several artists. The artist Damien Hirst is one of these; I really like the concepts of dream worlds and highly abstract themes he introduces, along with his unique ideas. I also collect ideas from old surrealistic artists like Salvador Dali, but I am mostly just fascinated by their knowledge and skills. However, I can appreciate their delivery of emotions and expressions, which is similar to what I try to shape.

Above all, the artist who fascinates me the most is H. R. Giger. He introduces variety to his work, yet retains the same kind of distinctive style throughout all of his magnificent collection of paintings, furniture, sculptures, and music. What I think affects my work the most is these new twentieth century artists like Giger. I find myself collecting most of my inspiration and ideas from fresh artists, rather than older artwork from previous centuries. The old art is present, but new developing styles that are always changing offer new perspectives.

My art has three purposes: it is made for people to enjoy, it fulfills a self-perpetuating cycle by further stimulating my creativity, and I hope it helps other designers find their inspiration. So, it's all a magic circle and hopefully it fulfills all those purposes.

Dr Hoffman and his techno surgery team made him ready for the crazy Mecano style... But where is the "o"
Puppet, 1994, Sweden

Digital art is probably the only art form I've experienced since its birth. From when I started in this area, I've never seen anything else develop so fast. Prior to the Internet and online culture, print art led trends and fashion. But now, even some of the graphics you see on MTV or in certain offline magazines were developed first online and were popular there several years ago. This migration can probably be explained when you realize that older web designers might now be working in broadcast design, but it could also be that the power of the online design community affected established design outside the Web. Still, it's hard to keep a high level of quality in online design, because many designers produce the same thing.

Per Gustafson, 2003

The Internet has been a great inspiration and resource for learning for me and many others, but it also almost killed off some digital art forms because of its fast development and the rapid evolution of styles it causes. For example, the idea of the digital abstract developed very quickly. More and more people are producing this kind of work, and many designers do not perceive it as an art form. The design community has frequent discussions about this and, although I believe the digital abstract is an easy art form to reproduce, what you think depends on your own perception; what the viewer gets out of it is what really counts and determines whether it's art or not.

I consider myself a pioneer of the digital abstract and still try to develop this style to keep it alive. I think there is a way to make digital abstracts exclusive and unique. Your working methods may be the same as everyone else, but you must use your own artistic sense to push it further.

Per Gustafson, 2003

Per Gustafson, 2003

I discovered Photoshop (version 4.0, I believe) at school. I remember opening a sample image of a car and starting to play with the Smudge tool (which I don't use often today). I quickly found out that the program was number one for image work, so as I made my websites, I always had Photoshop open too. Through a lot of editing and practice, I developed my skills, but I thought that there was no future for me as a graphic designer without an advanced education in this area or at least some form of a qualification. Somehow though, this image manipulation has evolved into my profession today in quite a short space of time.

I can't recommend doing what I did, finishing school early and starting to freelance immediately, because the first few years of trying to make a living as a freelance designer are always a struggle. This is why having a strong education to lean back on is vital. Instead, use your interest in design as an opportunity to hone your technical skills while you are studying, and until you can see that it's possible to make a living from it in the real world, hold off on starting up your company.

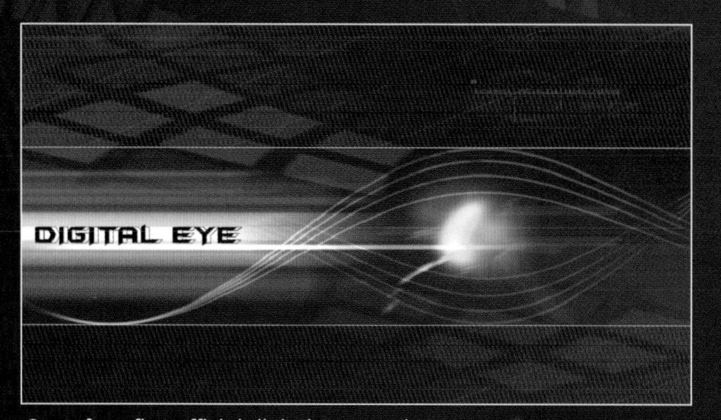

One of my first official digital art creations

At the same time I was developing my design skills, my friend, Kalle Everland, was studying media at the same Kantzowska Media Centre where I was. We both made our own websites and taught each other design techniques without realizing that this is what we would be doing in our future occupations. Three years passed at which point I had started a local design firm making websites. Kalle started work as a designer in Stockholm, then freelanced for a while, and is now located in London. It was Kalle who introduced me to the digital abstract genre, which he first saw produced by the artist Andreas Lindholm. Andreas was creating these giant digital art posters with Photoshop and 3D elements; these stunned me and made me want to create them too.

I began watching inspiring artists such as Andreas Lindholm without knowing exactly which elements of their work were created in Photoshop and which were pure 3D. I tried to make something that looked similar but entirely in Photoshop. This way I learned a lot and also managed to draw the 3D parts freehand with Photoshop's paint tools. I found that once I finally opened a dedicated 3D program, I could more quickly and easily realize my visions with a basic 3D symbol, thanks to all that early jamming in Photoshop.

I was quite late inserting 3D elements into my work, but when I finally did, it lifted me up to a whole new level. The reason I waited so long was because many people warned me about the steep learning curves associated with programs like 3D Studio and LightWave. After someone taught me how to use these programs' basic tools, I finally got a grip on them. As with many things, I really think that it's all about experimentation and practice, but to become a good 3D artist, you also need a lot of time, patience, and sometimes a manual.

Modern City series, Per Gustafson, 2003

I bought my domain MODERNSTYLE.NU and began to upload my work. I started by displaying my digital art in the form of downloadable wallpapers, the kind of wallpapers that later became part of a thriving online community thanks to places like www.deviantart.com and www.deskmod.com. These downloadable wallpapers increased the number of visitors to my site and fortunately also promoted my business. I believe I started with this practice at the time when interest for digital abstract desktop images was at its largest. The new artwork I made was regularly posted at news sites like www.designiskinky.net, www.halfproject.com, and www.k10k.net.

Although the search for inspiration is important, I value the search for motivation even more. It's important for me to have a life outside of my art; having a social side helps me be more productive and creative. Having this social outlet also helps refresh my mind and helps me get valuable critical opinions from friends. They provide the help I value most, the few people I know who can really give me great feedback and be honest.

Without such critics, I would have made far more mistakes. After working on a single piece of artwork for something like ten hours, I can only see it in one way. If I like it at that point, I can almost consider it finished, but by showing it to the people I trust, I can get feedback and ideas that I never thought of before. This helps a lot and saves time, as I often get locked into a piece of art and miss some details because I've been working with it for too long. I also help them out with their work, by swapping roles and offering them my opinion.

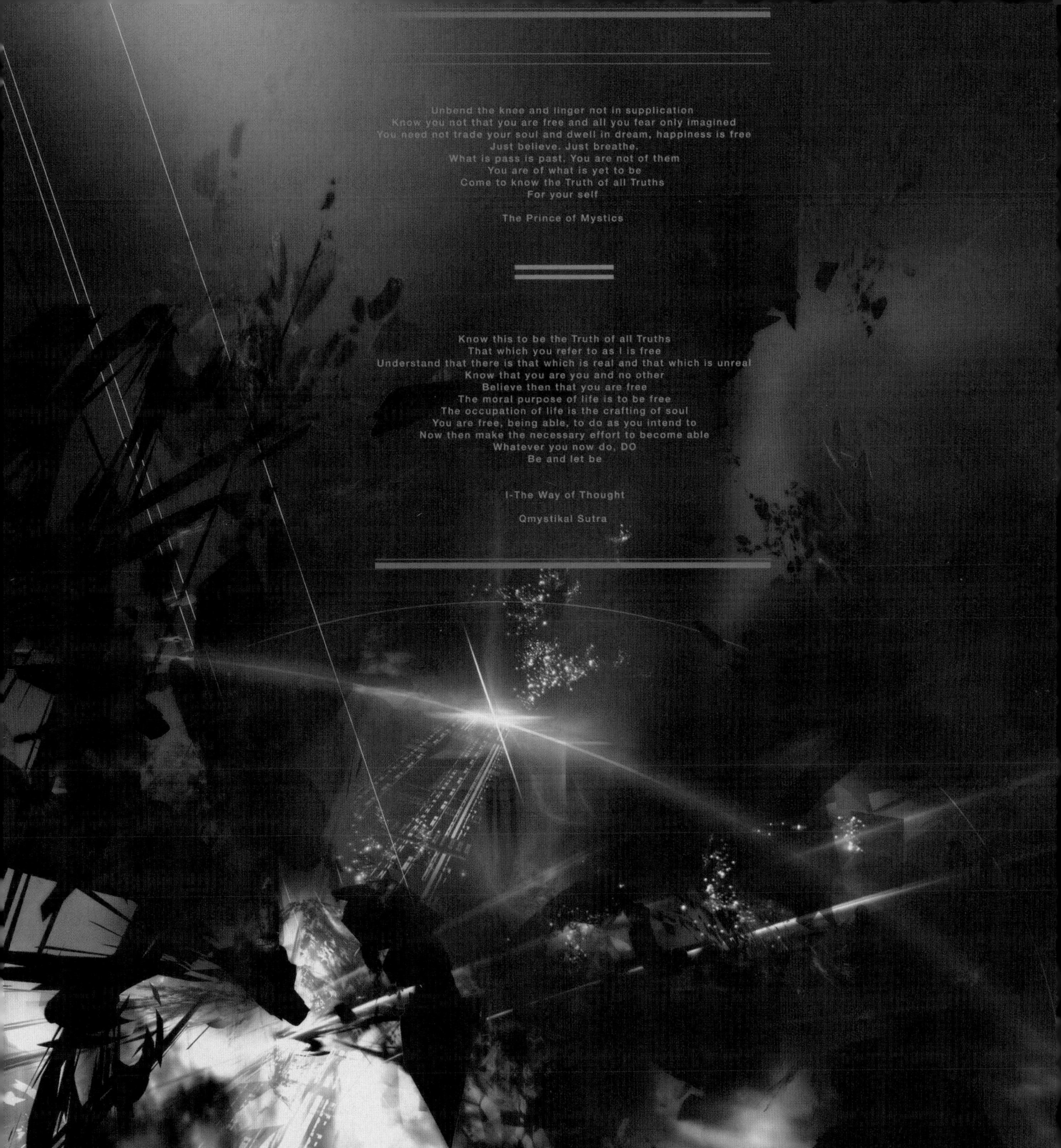

Unbend the knee and linger not in supplication
Know you not that you are free and all you fear only imagined
You need not trade your soul and dwell in dream, happiness is free
Just believe. Just breathe.
What is pass is past. You are not of them
You are of what is yet to be
Come to know the Truth of all Truths
For your self

The Prince of Mystics

Know this to be the Truth of all Truths
That which you refer to as I is free
Understand that there is that which is real and that which is unreal
Know that you are you and no other
Believe then that you are free
The moral purpose of life is to be free
The occupation of life is the crafting of soul
You are free, being able, to do as you intend to
Now then make the necessary effort to become able
Whatever you now do, DO
Be and let be

I-The Way of Thought

Qmystikal Sutra

"Truth of All Truths" poster designed for the spiritual health organization www.MaijJai.com, Per Gustafson. 2003

When I first started designing, I didn't know what I was looking for in a final image; I just sat there and jammed in Photoshop with a 800x600-pixel image. Today, I create the majority of my work at print size for commercial use offline. I don't have any standard dimensions but always work in 300dpi; the dimensions depend on the area I need to use or a client's specific demands. The quality and sharpness also increase if you shrink the image a little, so it's always good to have the original source with large dimensions. However, keep in mind that such large files require a powerful computer with a lot of RAM.

When working on very large client projects such as huge posters, I split the image up into sections. When I'm finished, I flatten the image and piece all these sections back together into one image. This is tricky and not something I would recommend. Buy more RAM or a faster processor instead.

One funny thing I've noticed is that many people think that there's no practice behind these images—that I was born with a pen in my hand. They're always kind of shocked when they see my oldest creations and notice that they aren't up to the same standard as my newer work. My artistic way of thinking has definitely helped me shape my own style, as I almost always draw some of the elements I've used in my previous creations into my new piece. But basically I think that anyone can learn what I know about the program and how it's used simply by hard practice.

People often ask how long it takes to make a digital art piece; I always explain that it depends on a lot of factors and can't just be calculated in time. However, I always finish what I've started because I consider this to be better than starting 20 projects and never reaching the goal with even just one of them. This practice of finishing what I start is a great way to control my work process, but the problem is that I am always working on at least three projects at the same time. I try not to accept more work than I can handle and, so far, I've managed to complete all the work I've signed up for.

digital vision's infinity2 series: Primecut, Per Gustafson 2002

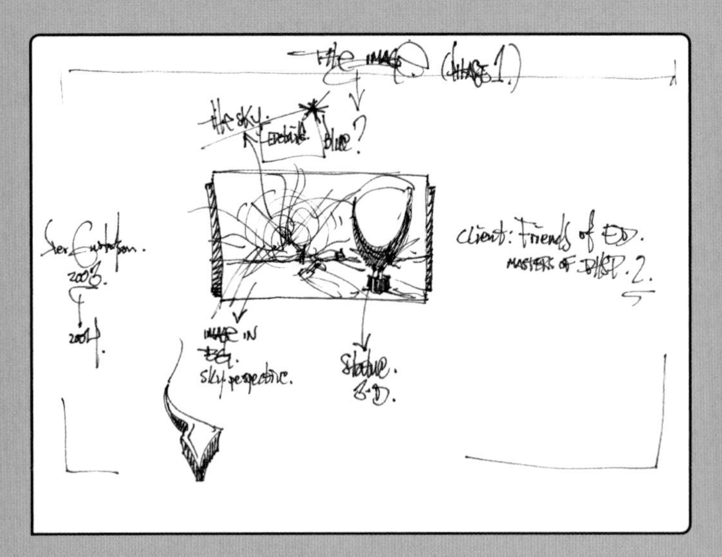

The process in which I shape a piece of art is best explained as the result of three phases: the mind phase, the construction phase, and the experiment phase. The mind phase is where I think out the concept or just the look of the creation. Sometimes I sketch an idea on paper, just so I can remember it all. If it's a larger project, this sketch is crucial; if I don't do it, I know I'll forget it (and the final image never turns out the way it begins life on the paper). The second phase is the actual construction of the image and its individual elements. The third phase is the most time-consuming, and this is where all the magic comes into play as I add the lighting and shape the image the way I really want it to look. I often add a lot of effects at this stage, especially lighting, which I may reduce later if I think it has been overdone.

Whether a project is business or personal doesn't make too much difference; I can usually follow the same process. Obviously I have more time to add elements or change the details in my personal work because I'm not restricted by a deadline, and sometimes when I'm working for a client, they have some pretty strict input on what they want. On the whole, clients have seen my earlier work and know what they want, so the development process is stronger in my personal work.

I start by thinking out a concept in my head, which I then develop, by drawing a basic sketch. After this, I usually render a 3D model I'm going to use in the image. I make a basic startup image and place some 3D elements in the right positions. Sometimes, at this point, I begin experimenting and twisting the elements to see if they can fit better somewhere other than where I originally placed them. As I've said, I'm often involved in several projects at the same time, which is why it's so hard to say the exact amount of time I spend on an abstract piece. I usually leave the image for a day at this point to get try to get some perspective and another point of view.

When I'm adding the lighting and focus, I can spend days or even weeks in this Photoshop work phase until I'm satisfied. At this point, I also make notes if I get ideas that I know will take a lot of time to establish.

As the image expands in file size, I usually merge some layers to decrease it. I also start saving the work file as a .002 and so on, so that all separate layers are saved in older versions of the piece, just in case I need them later on. Also, I crop the images during the working process to get rid of unused elements outside of the picture.

It's also important to remember to burn a safe CD-R in the event that your computer crashes (believe me, it's going to happen someday, and it's no fun to lose all your work). I've noticed, by talking to other colleagues, that it's pretty usual. It's probably because we Photoshop designers fill up all the scratch disks working with very large files and thus push our computers to their limits.

I often receive questions regarding my images from younger designers and feel an urge to share some of my knowledge in a large tutorial someday. Even though most of the techniques I use are controlled through years of practice, there is still so much more to learn. Of course, tools and techniques can be used in many different ways. Hopefully, in the following tutorial section, I'll give you a glimpse of what I mean.

I can't say that the way I work is the right way, but it's one way of making digital art. Hopefully, you'll see that what I talk about in this chapter is my personal method of working and, with a little experience with Photoshop, you'll surely discover other ways of achieving certain effects. A piece of advice is to skip the computer games and keep on jamming in Photoshop instead. That's what I've done so far and I've been lucky enough to turn a hobby into a business. Also, as I mentioned earlier, it's very important to have a formal education to fall back on one day, and to be honest, returning to study in a few years or continuing this business is a choice I still have to make. I've learned more in my spare time than I believe a school would have given me because of my interests and urge to develop; I've collected valuable experience, some programming skills, and design knowledge along the way. It's hard to find a design school that teaches in more than one specific area, so I think it is best to also have a well-rounded education in addition to a formal design qualification.

I also think that I made my choice of what to do with my life at too early a stage. With almost no clients and no experience, I started freelancing. I should have tried to get a full-time position instead. However, if I had done that, I probably would not have gotten to work on the great projects I've worked on and developed the knowledge I have today. I believe it's a big chance you're taking whenever you decide to go your own way. I'm not afraid of running out of work, but time will definitely tell because this environment is changing so rapidly. The only advice I can give to newbies is practice, practice, and never give up. As I mentioned before, you're better off finishing a project that might turn out badly, than starting on 20 new ones and never completing them. At least if you finish one you've tried, hopefully you've learned something along the way for next project.

In this tutorial I'll show you how to re-create an abstract digital artwork image from scratch. This will include adding image and lighting effects to the image (in the sky), transforming the light, and using layer effects to get a 3D element to fit into the image.

There are three source files on the CD that I use in this tutorial:

- `base_landscape.psd`: This is the basic image, taken by me in Sweden (summer 2001), of a landscape. We are going to try to integrate and duplicate this abstract statue and make the sky more spectacular.
- `sky.psd`: This will be used to make the sky in the piece more spectacular.
- `3d_statue_model`: This 3D statue was created in LightWave.

You can follow this tutorial using these images or you could use your own. No matter which approach you choose or what your final image looks like, you'll learn some new techniques that you can use in your next artwork in your very own way. This tutorial gives you some new perspectives and hints on the way I work in Photoshop, but it's not necessarily the only, or correct, way of creating the artwork. I see it a bit like special effects or make-up—I work with basic tools and effects, and if no one can point out what kind of filter or tool has been used, it's a part of a great composition.

Image effects

Let's start with the base image (`base_landscape.psd`). You can retouch this image how you see fit—for example, you might want to adjust the colors, contrast, and brightness levels. As I usually say, I'm a bad photographer but I'm much better at retouching. With photography, I usually make the colors brighter and sometimes I use a layer of color to minimize the sharp contrasts.

The first adjustment I usually use is Image ➤ Adjust ➤ Brightness/Contrast. I often make the image a little bit brighter and then follow up with the contrast to keep the image sharp.

Playing with these settings can make the colors more sharp, sometimes too sharp—the contrast between two colors can mess up the image. To smooth this out, you could use that color layer I mentioned earlier. You would do this by creating a new layer, filling it with a color, setting the layer effect to Color, and changing the opacity to something like 30–50 percent, depending on your own preferences. This layer can also remain editable as you work on the image; you don't need to merge it into the background base image. If you keep this colored layer above all the other layers, it'll give all the other layers a bit of color so that they fit better into the whole picture. I prefer to add this layer (if I decide to use one) as the last phase of the artwork.

To get white light to integrate into an image, you need to have a strong contrast. This will make the brightest areas, such as the clouds in this image, a very strong white. If the contrast is too low, your clouds will look a kind of grayscale, and the white light effects will look obvious and stand out in the layer above. To correct this, use the Eyedropper tool and click the brightest spot in the sky and check the RGB colors. If it's not 255, 255, 255 then increase the contrast a little.

For this tutorial image, I also used the Magic Wand tool to lighten up some parts of the sky. Click the sky with a Tolerance of between 10 and 50 depending on the size you want the marked area to be and then increased the brightness. Try it yourself and feel free to lighten up or darken certain parts to make a more mean and sinister sky.

By keeping the image in a separate layer, you can always go back and change the colors on the specific background image afterward. This is something I do to make it combine better with all the other colors of the 3D element, for example. A piece of advice: never decide the color of the finished product at the beginning unless you're working to a client's demands because it's a lot easier to control this aspect on the finished product, especially on a flattened image. I sometimes make several versions of an image if I'm unable to choose which one I like best, as in the shirt design for my label sonicnerve.com. In these images I adjust several layers before I flattened the finished result.

Image effects: The dream world of illusions

One effect I've learned is to create that dream-world feeling in an image. It's something I prefer to use last on a flattened image, but you can try it on the background layer. RIGHT/CMD-click the base photo layer and choose Duplicate Layer. Change the opacity of the top layer to approximately 45 percent and add Filter ➤ Blur ➤ Gaussian Blur with a radius of around 60 pixels.

You'll learn that this is an effect you can use in a lot of different ways; only your imagination sets the limit. This technique is something I like to experiment a lot with. You can, for example, change the blur effect, the opacity, or try it out on several layers, and much more.

The 3D statue

What I had in mind as I shaped this three-dimensional abstract statue (`3d_statue_model.psd`) was a futuristic metal piece, which is why I made it a little bit blue to get the metallic feeling and to break up the warm image with a cold color.

What I usually do with imported 3D elements is first edit the brightness and contrast. Here I work totally on feeling, just to get the same sharpness and dark areas that are in the background image. For example, you can use the Eyedropper tool once again to check the darkest area in the 3D element along with the darkest area in the image.

Now, to get the statue to melt better into the image, you can use the layer effects. What I've done in this image is duplicated the statue and used the Multiply blending mode on the new layer.

This amplifies the dark shadows yet retains the light areas in the symbol, so it looks like the sky itself is casting light on the statue.

This is a great area to experiment with, especially if you aren't familiar with the image effects. Some are useful in all areas like in lighting, backgrounds, and typography, so try these different effects whenever you feel like it just to see what they can establish in a basic composition.

If you now want to move or transform the statue, you should link both the statue layers so you can move them both at the same time. Select the top statue layer and then click in the empty square to the right of the eye in the lower statue layer. A chain icon indicates that these layers are now linked.

I rendered the 3D symbol almost exactly as you see it, but sometimes I like to twist it a bit in Photoshop. The best tool for this is definitely the Free Transform tool. Select the layer containing the element you want to transform and choose the Marquee tool. Right/CMD-click in the image and select Free Transform, then start scaling or rotating the element.

Right/CMD-click once again in the image and another menu appears. Choose Distort or Perspective and you can start working to get better depth in the image. This effect requires some practice and editing before you get it right, because if you make too large a perspective change, the element can look blurred and pixilated. Learn what you can or can't do by experimenting and editing.

Another way to twist an element is to use the different filters. I've tried some extra plug-ins but am still comfortable with all the standard filters Photoshop has built in. I don't feel I need any new "magical" plug-in. I'm very keen on learning the program from the ground up beginning with the basic tools and filters rather than resorting to a "one-click" trick with a plug-in. For example, the blur effects are endless when used with all the distort tools. You just have to use your creativity to come up with new ways of using them.

My opinion of a good use of filters is when you can't tell what filters have been used from looking at a composition. So, all the distortion tools are very useful but are still hard to hide. Take the Wave tool, for example; it can be very useful when you are trying to make waved light, but you will need to make a lot of adjustments and distortions to avoid it becoming an obvious effect.

At this stage, as you start to insert elements into the work area, you'll often find elements on a layer that cross outside the image; this is usually a good time to crop the image (especially when you use the Perspective tool and parts of a layer expand way outside this area). These extraneous parts increase the file size, so why keep them there? Keep this in mind and crop every time before you save the image.

Lighting

It seems as if I've kind of specialized in light; light is the largest element in my digital art. I use it in almost all of my creations, which are all made in Photoshop, not a 3D program. I could talk about this area for weeks, but here I'll focus on using light to spice up the sky.

First of all, I imported an image of a sky (`sky.psd`) that I drew freehand along with sections from a photo of a real sky. I created this sky planning to use it as an image in its own right, but that never happened. I discovered that it worked a lot better as a layer above the original sky in this background image.

To create this part of the image, I used the `sky.psd`, increased the contrast, painted above it all with a Photoshop brush, and then used the Perspective tool on the whole sky.

To smudge some parts out, I also used a little motion blur to make the sky look more alive.

I put this layer above the background image and used the Overlay blending mode to get rid of those sky sections that spread over the trees on the horizon. Once again, the Brightness/Contrast tool comes into play here. You could also try changing the opacity on your sky layer if you feel that the sky is too much.

Because I then wanted to lighten up some parts of the sky, I used the Lasso tool to select the part to be brightened. Fill a new layer of this area with white, and then add a Gaussian blur (I used a radius of 200 pixels) to smudge out all the sharp edges.

To adjust this bright layer, change its layer opacity until you get the perfect match. Also, if you want it to cover a larger or smaller area, simply use the Transform tool on this separate layer. You can then adjust the opacity after this extra step.

Now it's time to use the variety of lighting effects like glowing lines, cloudy effects, abstract light, and light explosions. I often improvise with these elements in each image to fit the special area. Now that I have some basic ideas and have experimented with the sky, I feel it is important to increase the brightest areas with some kind of explosive feeling and also improve the perspective and depth of the artwork.

Start with the Rectangular Marquee tool and make a wide line (9px) in the middle of the image. Fill it with white and select the Free Transform tool for this element. I first chose to rotate it and move it to the right. Then, once I thought it was in place, I started to duplicate the layer to create more lines, and transform them with a 15-degree rotation from the original line.

Now you should merge all the line layers into one layer, then use the Perspective tool to control the perspective of the lines, adding more perspective to get a better concentration and depth of the lines and the image as a whole.

If you now like this line effect, there's plenty of experimenting you can do here. For example, try duplicating this lines layer and using the lines in other areas of the image too. If you think the duplication is too obvious—that you can tell they're the same lines—then rotate them or twist them with the Distort or Perspective tool to make them unique. Here are the lines from the final image (most of the layers are turned off so that you can see the lines clearly).

One other little trick I like to use is to keep a duplicate layer in the same position as the original layer, and then just add a small Gaussian blur to one of these layers. This way you can create a glow from the lines, yet keep their sharpness, and you can adjust the overall effect with layers' opacity. This technique can be used for many different light effects.

To make the sky feel more alive, I wanted to illustrate lava erupting from a volcano somehow. I added a group of dots on a new layer with the regular Airbrush tool (soft round 100px) with a 100-percent opacity. I rarely change the Flow setting of the brush when making this kind of light because the glow wouldn't show up as well. If you want to make a softer light, simply change the flow to 30-percent opacity and choose a large brush. However, remember that for every click you make with the brush, the opacity doubles in the layer.

I then duplicated the dots layer and added a Gaussian blur to one of the layers. To get these dots to explode, I use the Perspective tool and focused these dots to one of the light areas of the sky image.

From here on, I experimented with these existing layers and effects. For instance, let's say you decided to start all over with this tutorial from the part where you first added the line and simply change the line to a circle. By doing this, you get a new lighting effect that you can try to integrate somewhere in the image.

When I leave the image and return to it a day later, I usually change the last details and then consider the work complete.

When I came back to this image, I decided to remove some of the lighting effects, because I thought there were too many.

I also decided to add some circle elements. You can draw these with the Elliptical Marquee tool and hold down SHIFT while you draw to constrain the shape to a perfect circle with a constrained aspect ratio. Holding down ALT while you draw allows you to let the circle grow out from the exact point where you clicked the image with the Marquee tool.

Right-click inside the circle and choose Stroke. I used 5px for the width of the circle and then made a second circle outside the first one with a width of 30px. To make the circles melt into the sky, use the Soft Light or Overlay blending modes once again.

Here, I duplicated these circle layers to make plenty more circles fill out the sky.

I also duplicated the statue and adjusted the color balance of the statues a little. What was supposed to be one statue became three in a row. To get the statue to look more natural, I also duplicated the statue layer and colored it completely black. I then adjusted the layer with the Free Transform tool to make it look like a shadow of the statue. Next, I added another Gaussian Blur to make it look more real, and repeated this step for the other statues in the image.

Final adjustments

The last things I do are flatten the image and then, sometimes, duplicate the layers to try to create the foggy, dream-world atmosphere. Then I adjust the brightness and contrast one last time, and make some color adjustments. At this stage, I also add a layer called color that sits right at the top of the image in case I want to use it in the specific image. Sometimes that's necessary and sometimes it's not. In this image, I used a red layer with an opacity of just 20 percent to get a better fade between the color and contrasts of the whole image.

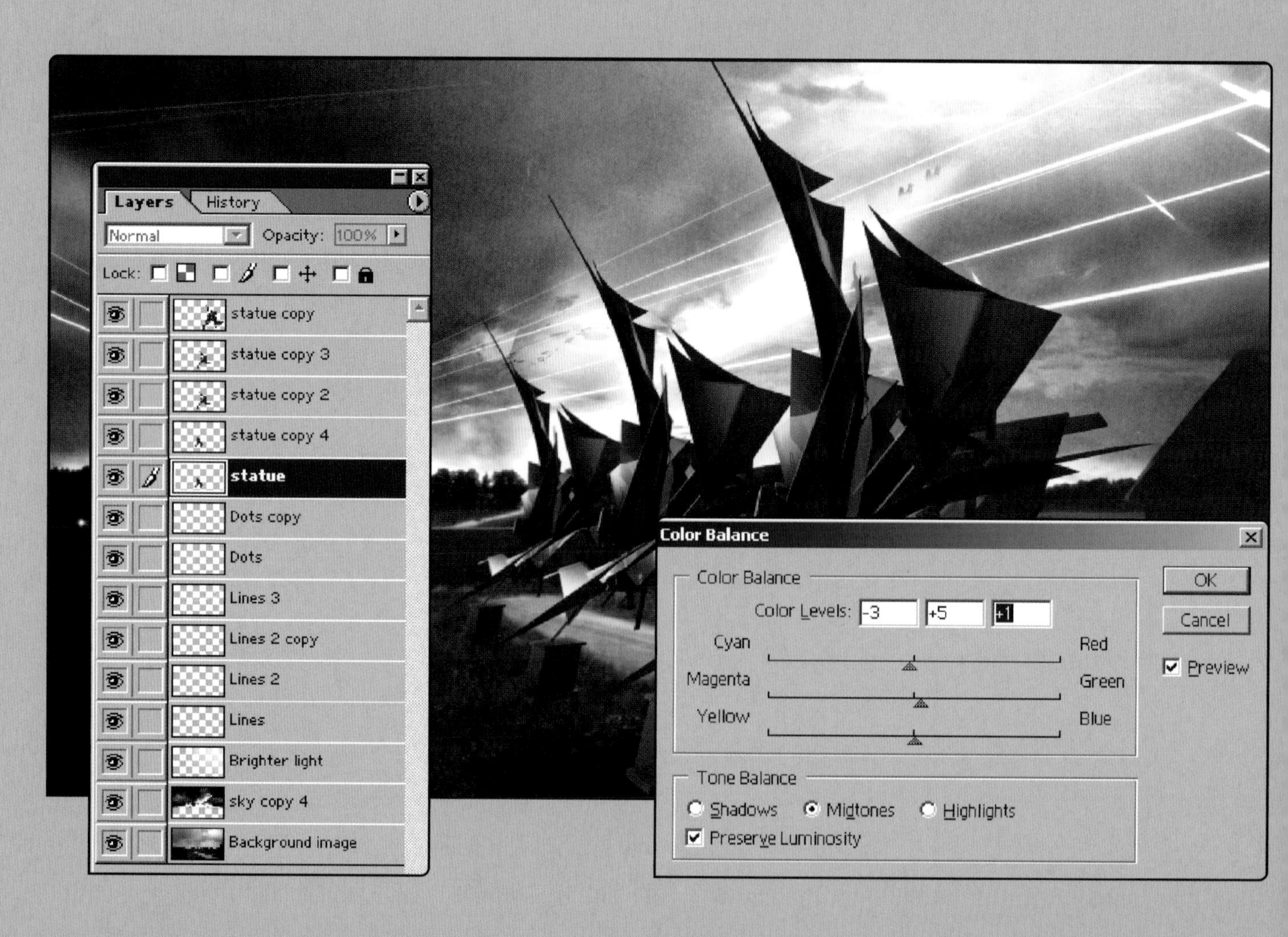

When I reviewed this image for the last time, I also found that I wanted the sky to be even more powerful so, before I flattened the image, I duplicated the overlay sky layer and decided I liked it better. I brushed some areas with the Eraser tool (brush size 100px) freehand so that a few areas of the sky were not darkened.

I believe this is where the tutorial ends. From here, how much further you go is up to you. I spent a couple of hours adding and removing light in this image to get a final result I was pleased with. So, by learning these effects, you can start shaping your artwork the way you want it. No one can tell you how to do that; doing so would be like saying, "teach me to sing like you," to Pavarotti. Either you can do it or you have to discover it on your own, sometimes with a little help along the way. I hope that this chapter is that little help and that it gets you started in Photoshop for real so that you can discover your aesthetic ability and start experimenting.

Every age will always have new talents; they will grow up and learn what you learned, but they'll learn it even faster. This is why I always try to stay on top of things by continuing to develop, by making sure I get better, and by finding new techniques and styles of creating digital art through experimentation. With an unlimited program like Photoshop, only your imagination limits you.

If someone had told me eight years ago that this digital art form would be my future career, I wouldn't have believed them. But, with a little insight, an interest in developing and exploring, and a passion for art, I managed to get here far more quickly than I ever thought possible. I haven't quelled my urge to develop and the creative possibilities with Photoshop are endless. With new versions and the new tools they bring, I can continue to expand my knowledge and change my perspectives and style along the way.

04 FOUNDATION

"WHILE IT'S CRITICAL TO KNOW HOW TO USE THE SOFTWARE
WELL, TO ME IT'S MORE IMPORTANT TO BE CONSCIOUS OF
PUTTING MY OWN PERSONALITY AND SENSITIVITY INTO THE WORK."
ALICIA BUELOW
WWW.ALICIABUELOW.COM

Photo: Jeri Jones

I tend to feel my way through the world, experiencing my surroundings and relationships in a tactile, sensual, and emotional manner. I sometimes have the sense that I am completely transparent—that others can see through me to all the darkness and messiness. The truth is, there is so much noise and distraction in the world, most people don't see through the layers unless something draws them in, something that stands out from the noise. My illustrations both reflect my own sense of feeling exposed and document the collection of visual and sensual experiences I gain from my environment.

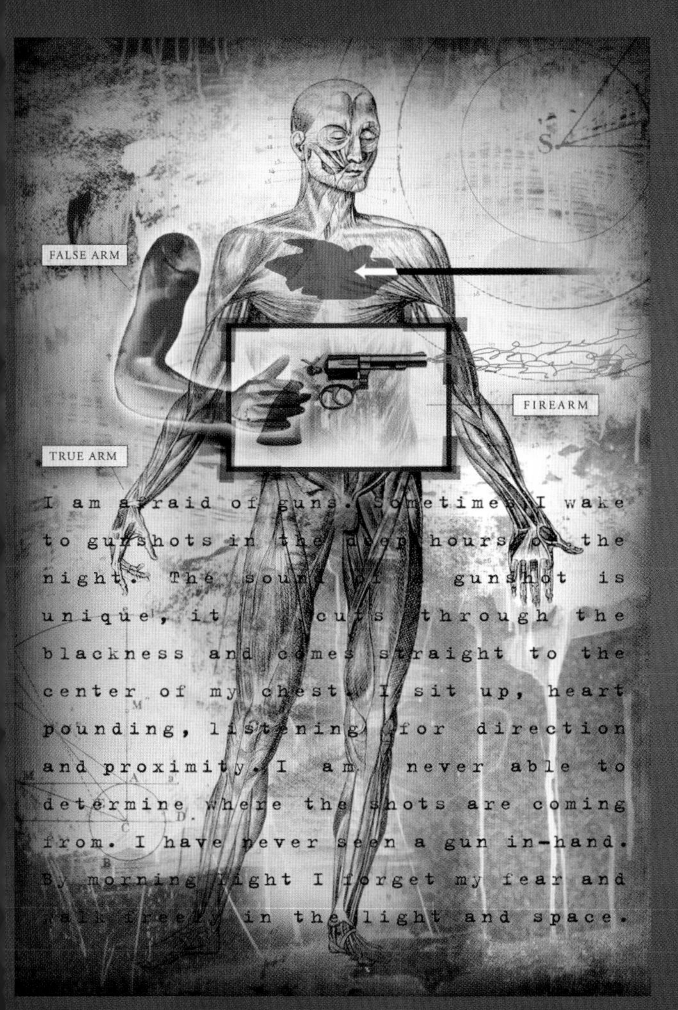

FALSE ARM
FIREARM
TRUE ARM
I am afraid of guns. Sometimes I wake to gunshots in the deep hours of the night. The sound of a gunshot is unique, it cuts through the blackness and comes straight to the center of my chest. I sit up, heart pounding, listening for direction and proximity. I am never able to determine where the shots are coming from. I have never seen a gun in-hand. By morning light I forget my fear and walk freely in the light and space.

"GunArm" ©2004 Alicia Buelow

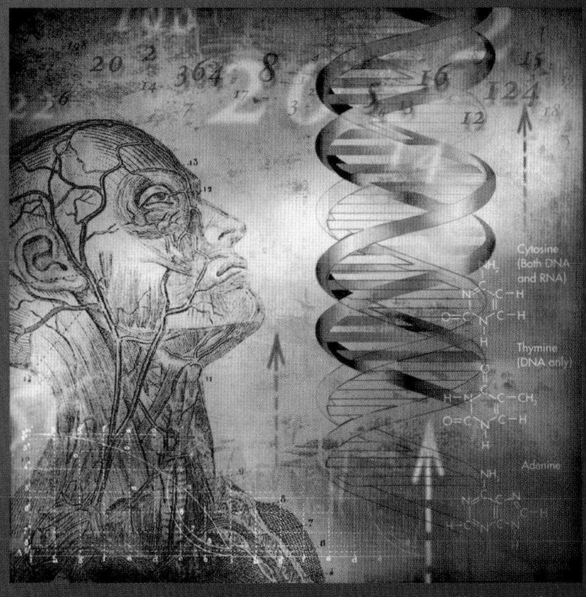

"Genetics," Managed Care Magazine ©2001 Alicia Buelow

was born in New York, I grew up in the heart of Silicon Valley, nd I now live in San Francisco. My parents are both originally rom New York City, where they met at the Bronx High School f Science. When I was very young, they moved the family, six f us kids, to the beautiful foothills of Santa Clara County, alifornia. With them they brought the culture, art, and ophistication of New York City, plus their own interest in cience and technology. They set the family down in one of the nost naturally beautiful areas of Northern California.

As kids we spent a lot of time outdoors, playing sports and exploring our neighborhood. On weekends, the family took trips to museums, galleries, the ocean, and the redwoods. At dinner it was not unusual for my parents to give us experiments and problems to solve, such as, "Why does ice break when placed in cold water?" and "What color is fire?" All of this fueled my fascination with science, nature, anatomy, and movement. The inclusion of these elements in my work truly reflects the environment of my development.

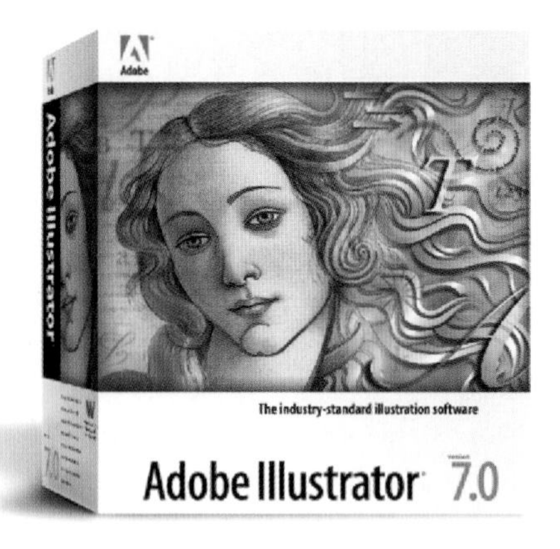

PageMaker and Illustrator package images © Adobe Systems, Inc.

And as we grew up, Silicon Valley also grew up around us. I was introduced to the computer when I was very young, although I didn't use it as a design tool until much later. In the Graphic Design program in college, my instructors forbid us from using computers to complete design projects because the typographic tools in the software were not very sophisticated as far as kerning, leading, and so on, were concerned. For assignments we would draw the type by hand or use press-type rub-down letters.

In 1987, during the last year of my Graphic Design degree, I was hired by Adobe Systems as an intern with the in-house art department. I didn't even know how to turn the computer on! They taught me how to do that, in addition to a few other things. At Adobe I was surrounded by an amazing group of designers, typographers, writers, and engineers. This provided me with a uniquely extensive education in design and digital printing. Because desktop publishing was brand new, the artists at Adobe spent many hours perfecting fonts, solving design and printing problems, and exploring new ways to use the software. Photoshop was introduced to the Adobe in-house artists in 1988, and I fell in love with both its technical and creative capabilities and began pushing it artistically. Photoshop 1.0 shipped in 1990. At Adobe I had the opportunity to design packaging images for Illustrator and PageMaker, and these packages represent the beginning of my illustration style.

Obviously, Photoshop plays a huge role in my process. Although I use it mostly as a tool to execute my ideas, I also find that I am *inspired* by its capabilities. I do need to be careful here. Though it is critical to know how to use the software very well, to me it's more important to be conscious of putting my own personality and sensitivity into the work. I shy away from effects and filters, using them subtly, if at all. I tend to use the blending modes and drawing tools rather than effects like beveled edges and lens flares.

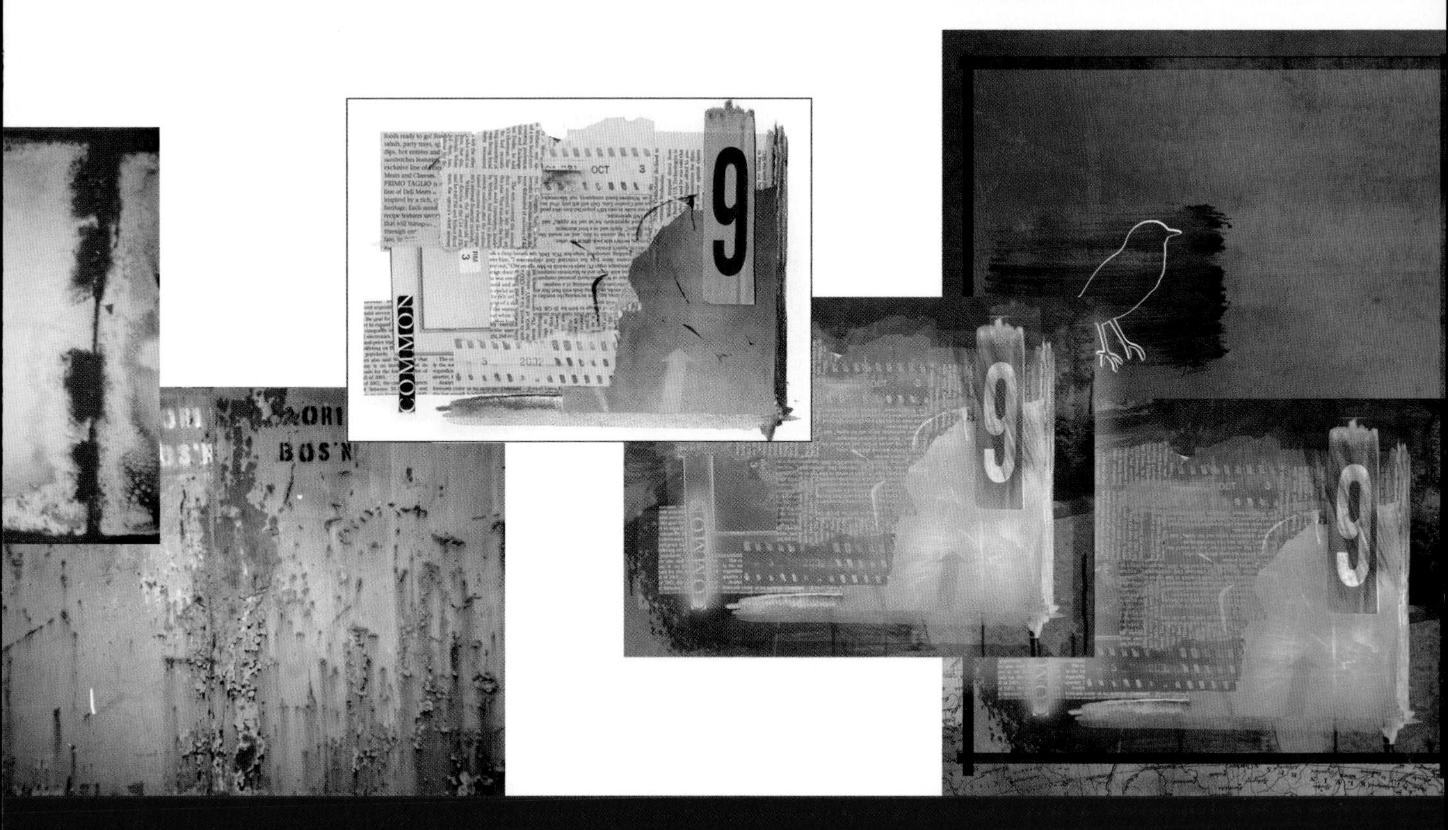

ly inspiration and influences are the things that surround me very day. As an artist, I think it is natural to be influenced by the isual environment and the work of other artists, especially by nages that suit one's own sensibility. External images always eem to seep in one way or another, even as a subliminal xchange. I feel lucky to live in San Francisco, where the liberal ultural atmosphere and expansive disposition provide a colorful ffering of material. In addition, I'm influenced by TV, film, the nternet, newspaper, and everyday life. I soak up this barrage of nages. Strangely, it never seems to be too much for me.

Vhen choosing images, I like to use photos and drawings that I ave made myself. I have a huge source library of photos, opyright-free etchings, and objects that I've collected over the ears. I create textures from traditional materials by painting, craping, drawing, and gluing imagery onto a surface. I also take ons of photos for source backgrounds. I live in one of the outer eighborhoods of the city, where there are many great old uildings with faded, peeling, and rusted surfaces. I scan the hotos and hand-made backgrounds on my flatbed scanner, hen add other elements and photographic imagery using hotoshop.

I believe that using images that I create, rather than using stock photography, yields a more unique work. Of course, if a client asks for subject matter that is difficult to obtain (i.e., blood cells or fiber optics) I go straight to the stock photo sites! All of the pieces I use in my collage are either copyright-free, of my own creation, or I pay a usage fee to a photographer. I try to be very sensitive about copyrights and usage rights.

My work can be described as photo illustration and mixed-media collage with a post-modern sensibility. Like many people, my life is a mixture of my experience of cultural, physical, and social activities, followed by hours and hours spent staring into my computer screen. There can be a huge contrast between technology and nature, but to me it seems that the two are becoming more integrated. We now use computer technology for very personal experiences such as viewing art, listening to music, and writing email. The line is blurring between technological and natural experiences. So, when I create my illustrations I bring everything with me—the influences of technology and nature combined with my emotional experiences and relationships. And all of this shows up in my images.

Adam and Eve, 1504 (engraving)
by Albrecht Durer (1471-1528)
British Museum, London, UK / Bridgeman Art Library

Philosopher in Meditation, 1632 (oil on panel)
by Rembrandt Harmensz. van Rijn (1606-69)
Louvre, Paris, France / Bridgeman Art Library

I've always been drawn to the Renaissance artists (for example, Da Vinci, Michelangelo, and Dürer) for their incredible craftsmanship and for the depth and richness of the oils. I am drawn to the color palette, sensibility, and pure beauty of that work. When I was young I spent hours drawing, surrounded by books with pages open to these artists. Even now I am known to incorporate images from the great masters into my work.

The following illustration is for a web magazine and is designed to convey the idea of a "New Renaissance" of technology. (And yes! I paid a license fee to use the portrait of Da Vinci in the background.)

Today, I am influenced by traditional collage artists such a Robert Rauschenberg and Joseph Cornell, and digital pionee like April Greiman. I love the typography and image-intensiv work of designers Vaughn Oliver, Neville Brody, David Carso and Tibor Kalman. I also love Doug and Mike Starn, who see to work outside of the narrative, asking the viewer to experienc it on an emotional rather than literal level. I still surround myse with books and imagery from my favorite artists.

"Web Innovators," New Architect Magazine © 2002 Alicia Buelow

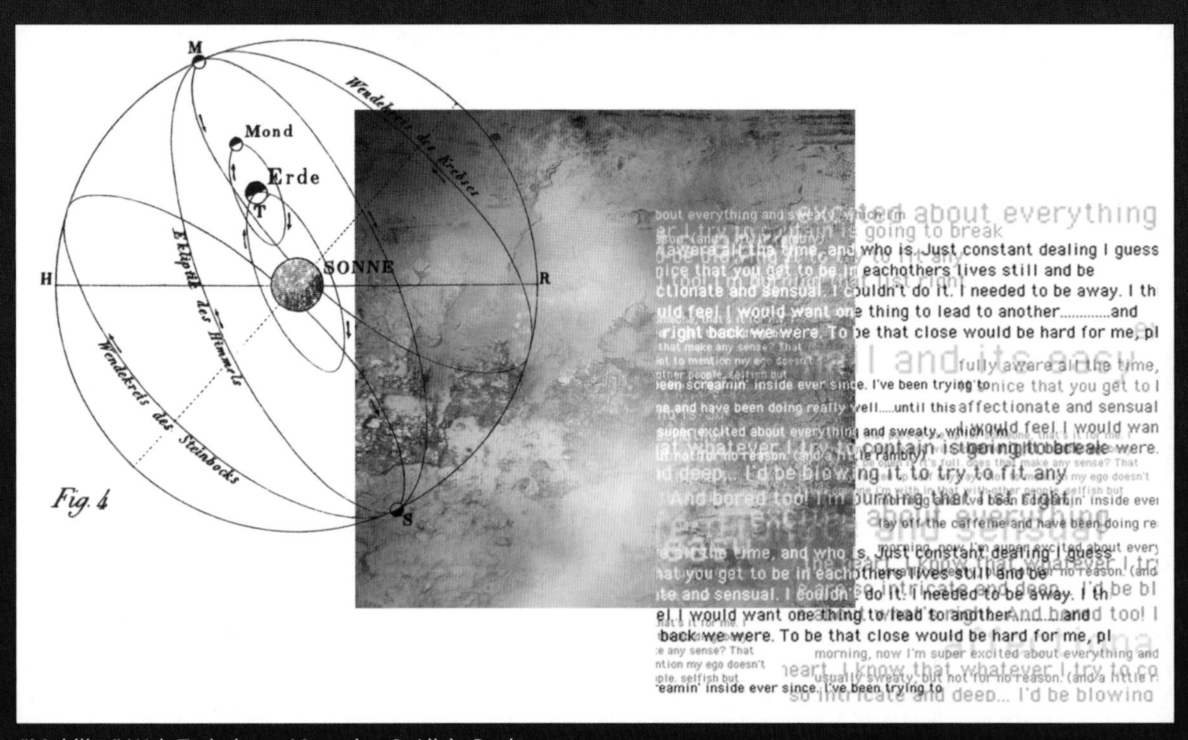

"Mobility," Web Techniques Magazine © Alicia Buelow

Many other artists also influence my work: Magritte, Picasso, Basquiat, plus today's graffiti and stencil artists; writers such as Gabriel Garcia Márquez and Isabel Allende; musicians Michael Stipe, Michael Franti, Paul Weller, The Roots, Radiohead, Jill Scott, Beth Orton, Marvin Gaye, Rickie Lee Jones, and more. This may seem like a wide spectrum of style and talent, but what all of these artists have in common is an ability to weave a tapestry, create a montage, which incorporates social, psychological, and emotional subjects into one successful artistic expression. This is what I aspire to do with my own illustration.

I build my images from the base of the subliminal, to the surface of clarity. I create texture and light in the images so the viewer can feel it on a tactile and intrinsic level. Almost everything I add to an image has some symbolic meaning, even if I seem to be using it as a simple texture. It is easy to get bogged down in the technical aspect of a project, so I consciously try to put a little bit of myself into every piece I create. I usually start with a background, such as a photo of an old building that I layer with a photo of clouds, and possibly another image of text from my own emails. I then add areas of light and shadow to the background using the Dodge and Burn tools to give the image depth. Then I begin layering the subject matter into the image. . . I work as I go, usually with no preliminary sketch. The deadlines can be very tight—sometimes only a week from start to finish—so I let the image unfold in the process. To me, the end result is successful if it solves the assignment in a visually unique manner.

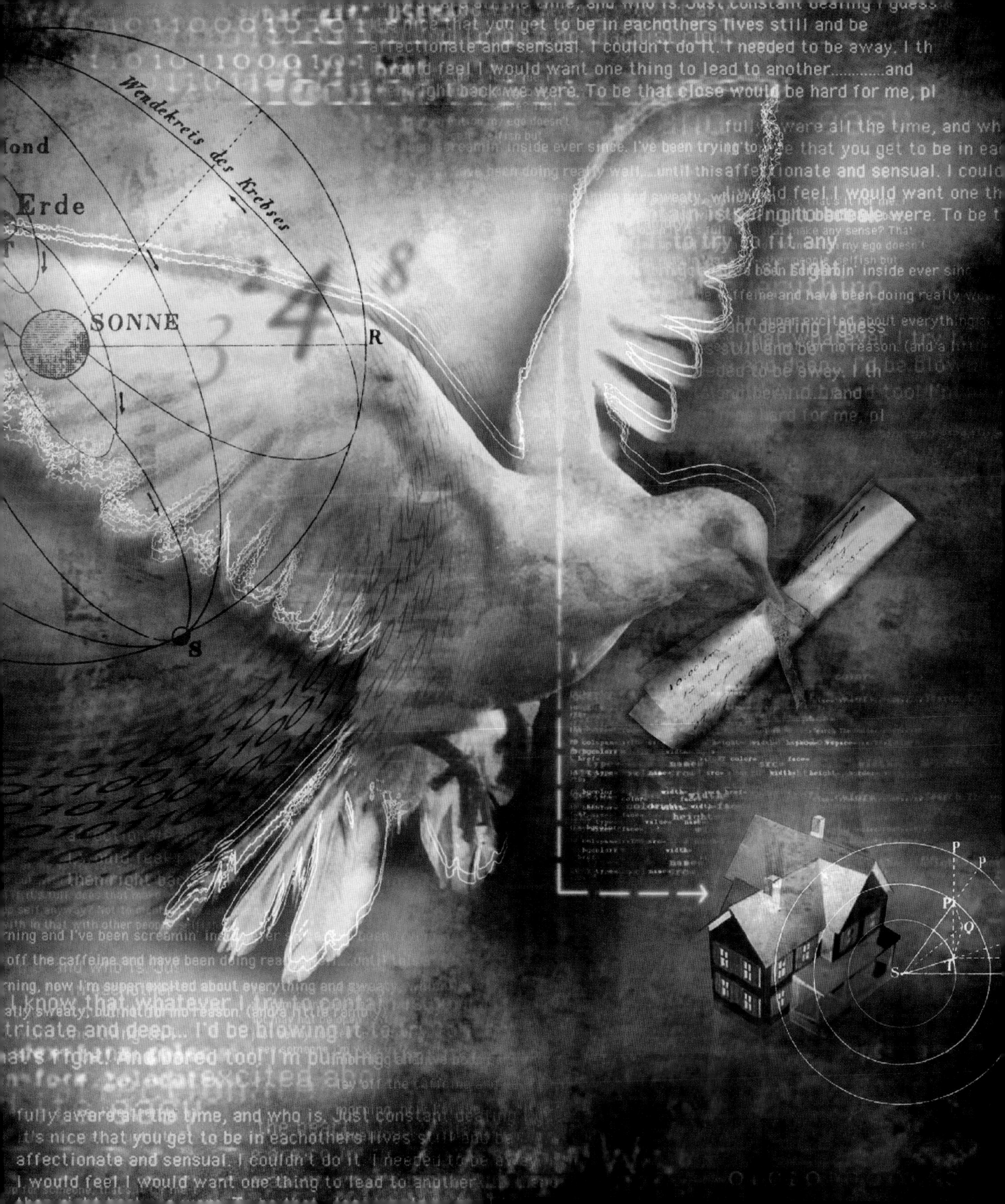

Wendekreis des Krebses
Mond
Erde
SONNE
R
S
it's nice that you get to be in eachothers lives still and be
affectionate and sensual. I couldn't do it. I needed to be away. I th
would feel I would want one thing to lead to another.............and
To be that close would be hard for me, pl
fully aware all the time, and who is. Just constant dealing I guess
it's nice that you get to be in eachothers lives still and be
affectionate and sensual. I couldn't do it.
I would feel I would want one thing to lead to another

I created this tutorial image (called *Ascension*) as a self-promotion piece. Although it has never been used commercially, it has definitely provoked inspiration for some of my other illustrations. This piece is a good example of one of my background creation techniques—the layering of many different textures and light to create a unique feeling in space and time.

I make images that reflect the relationship between science, nature, and emotion, as it is experienced in our daily life. I created this piece after doing some research into the symbology and mythology of crows and flight. I was impressed with the idea that different cultures place opposing meanings on certain objects and images, such as the crow. Some cultures say the crow represents wisdom, others say mortality or death. Birds and flight represent messengers between the sky and earth, gods and humans, or between the subconscious and awareness. I tried to create a piece that conveys the depth of these traditional concepts, while also including my own personal ideas and emotions. To me, the image represents my feelings of safety and security in being bound to earth, while at the same time my aspirations of reaching spiritual heights. I wanted to create the feeling of this simultaneous pull of gravity and the influence of a higher power.

I achieve the sense of depth in *Ascension* by creating a background layer of rough texture and combining it with an image of clouds. I then add a splash of light and darken the edges to enhance the feeling of depth.

To create the background, I start with a scan of blue watercolor paint on textured paper. I always scan my textures at 300ppi at 8.5"x11", the approximate size of a single page illustration. Because I tend to use backgrounds over and over again, I like to store these scans in my source library at a fairly high resolution. If my original scan is not large enough, I occasionally enlarge my scans (usually a big no-no). I only do this if the photo is inherently roughly textured or blurry; then I know I can get away with letting Photoshop interpolate the image. (When upsampling an image, Photoshop must invent extra pixels based on the pixels that are already present in the image, usua making the image appear more blurry as a result.) I've scal down the scan I've provided to 3"x3.43" so that the file size w be more manageable for this tutorial.

This watercolor scan has a great texture and nice value change but the blue and white colors are not quite right f the concept. For this image I actually wanted to start with rich gold color palette, so I use a quick trick for shifti the color spectrum. I open the watercolor background fi (`watercolor.tif`) in Photoshop and invert it (CMD+I). In o keystroke, I change the tone and hue to the opposite spectru

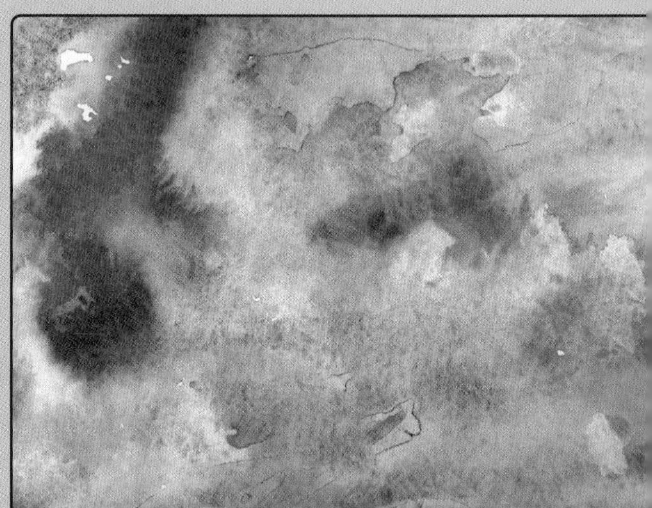

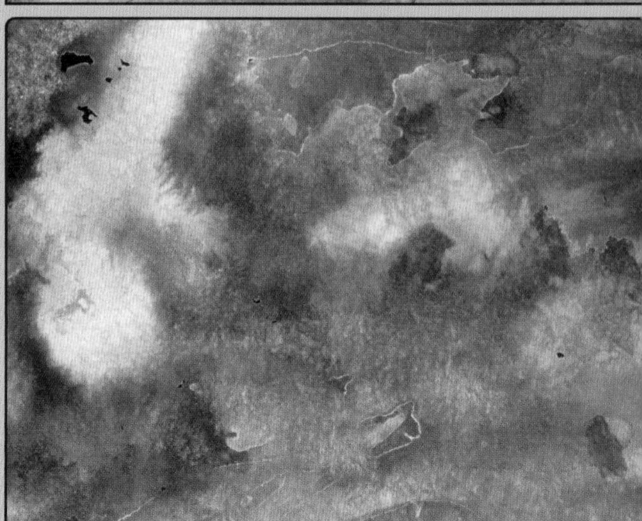

ext, I create a layer of clouds, which I will use to soften areas of the textured
ackground to give the image a greater sense of depth. I create the clouds
rectly in Photoshop using the Render Clouds filter. To do this, you can create
new layer and choose a new foreground color that matches the image, such as
old, then choose white as the background color. Choose Filter ➤ Render ➤
ouds. In the Layers palette, change the clouds' layer's blending mode to Hard
ght and the layer opacity to 70 percent. The Hard Light effect makes it so it is
most as though someone is shining a bright light on the image. Sometimes this
fect is too harsh, so I like to tone it down by decreasing the opacity of the layer.

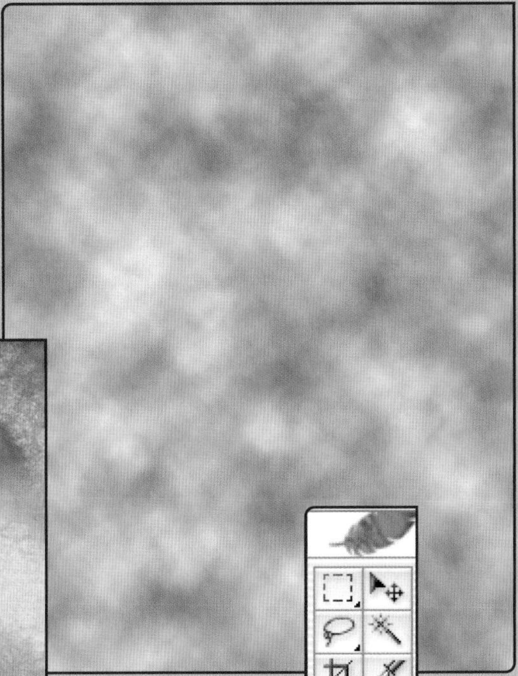

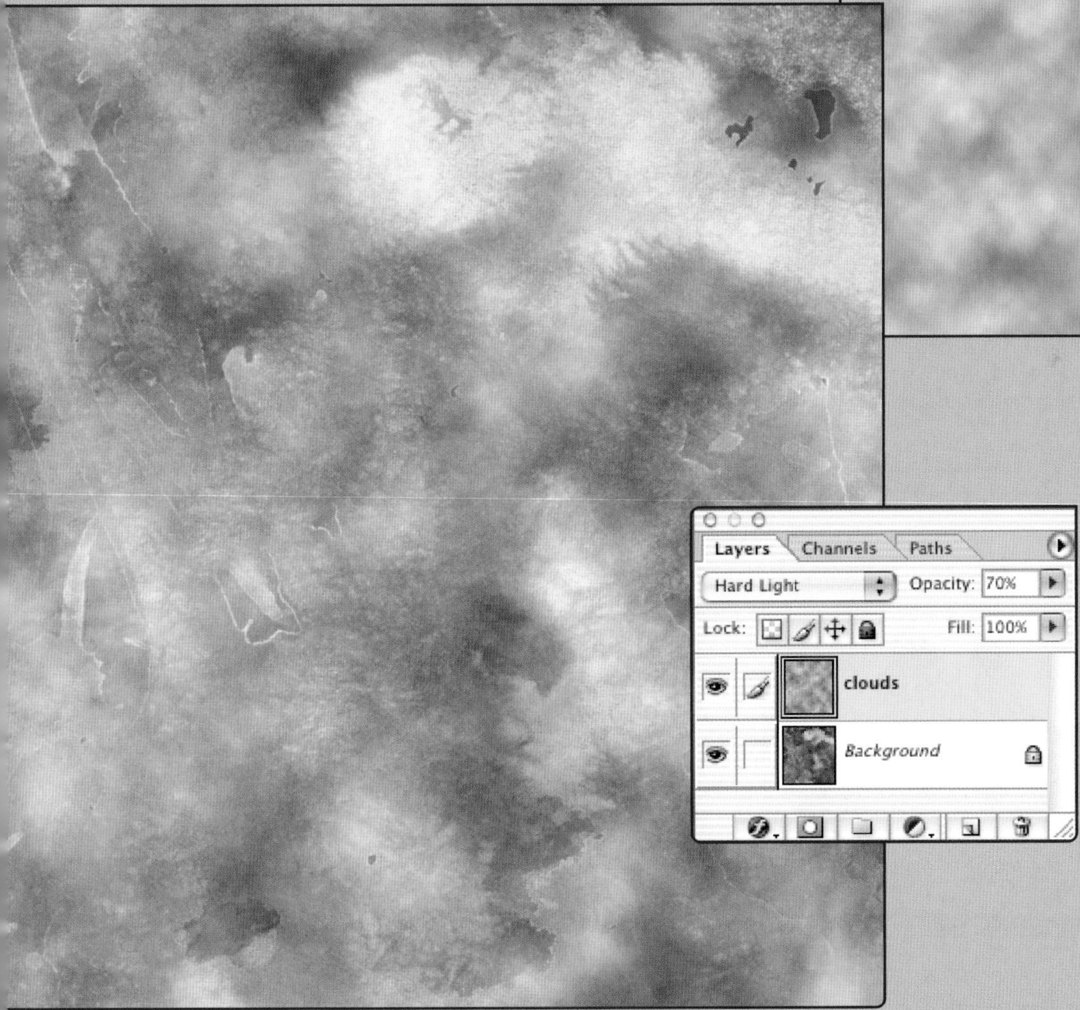

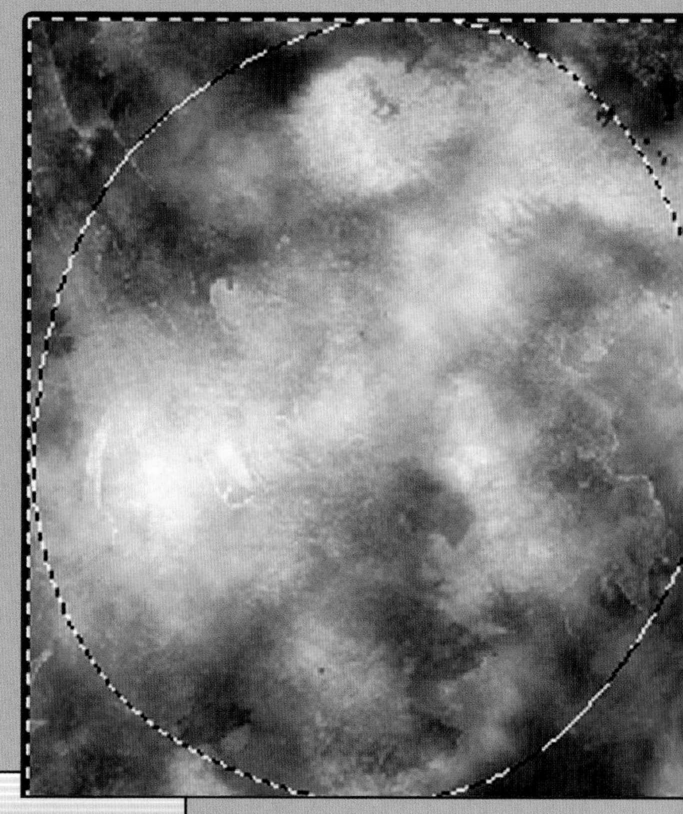

To darken the edges of the background, I use the Lasso tool with a Feather of 90px to make an oval selection in the center of the image. Then I invert the selection using a quick SHIFT+CMD+I so the outer edge of the image is now selected. Notice that by using this method of selection, I end up with a soft feathered edge toward the center of the image and a hard-edged selection at the outer border.

I then add a Levels Adjustment layer, sliding the Input values to darken the edges of the image. I repeat this same method, adding another Levels Adjustment layer to create a splash of light through the center of my image. By using an adjustment layer, I am able to darken the image without permanently changing the pixels of the layers below. If I decide later that I don't like the dark edges, I can simply turn off that adjustment layer.

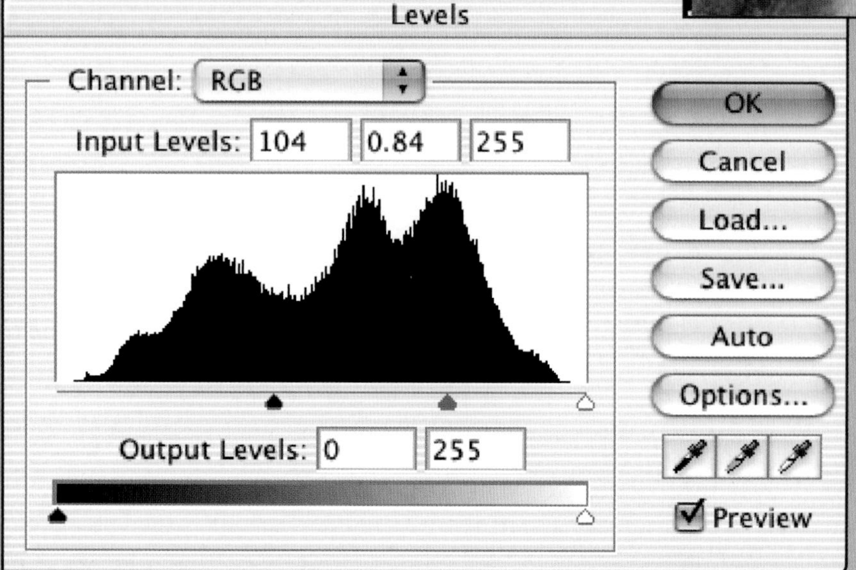

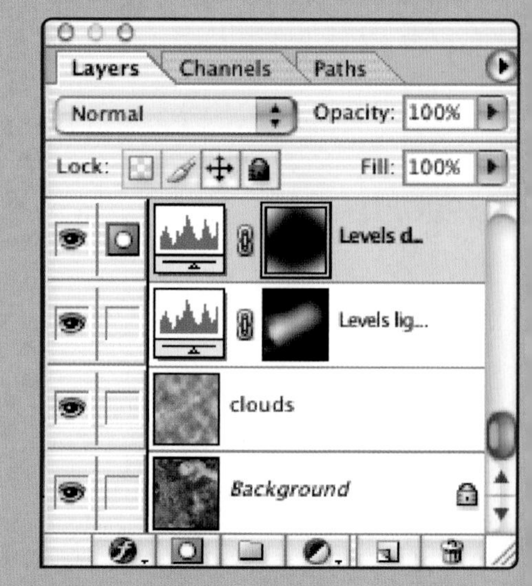

Vhen I am satisfied with the background olor and texture, I begin to add line art lements such as text and diagrams. The text n *Ascension* is simply a grayscale scan of my wn handwriting (`handwriting.tif`). It's nportant to me to have a bit of my own and in my images, whether it's a drawing or handwritten word, to truly create a unique iece. I paste the handwriting into a new layer nd set the Layer Blending Mode to Color urn, and the layer opacity to 90 percent. I lmost never leave a layer at 100-percent pacity. By allowing some of the background o show through, even slightly, the image eels more cohesive as a whole. I then add a ayer Mask and use the Brush tool to blend he script into the background. I've added a imilar scan of script in the upper-left corner s a sort of "second thought." I obliterate ome of the text so the viewer has to struggle bit to find the meaning. My intention is that he images pick up the fragment of thought /here the text drops out.

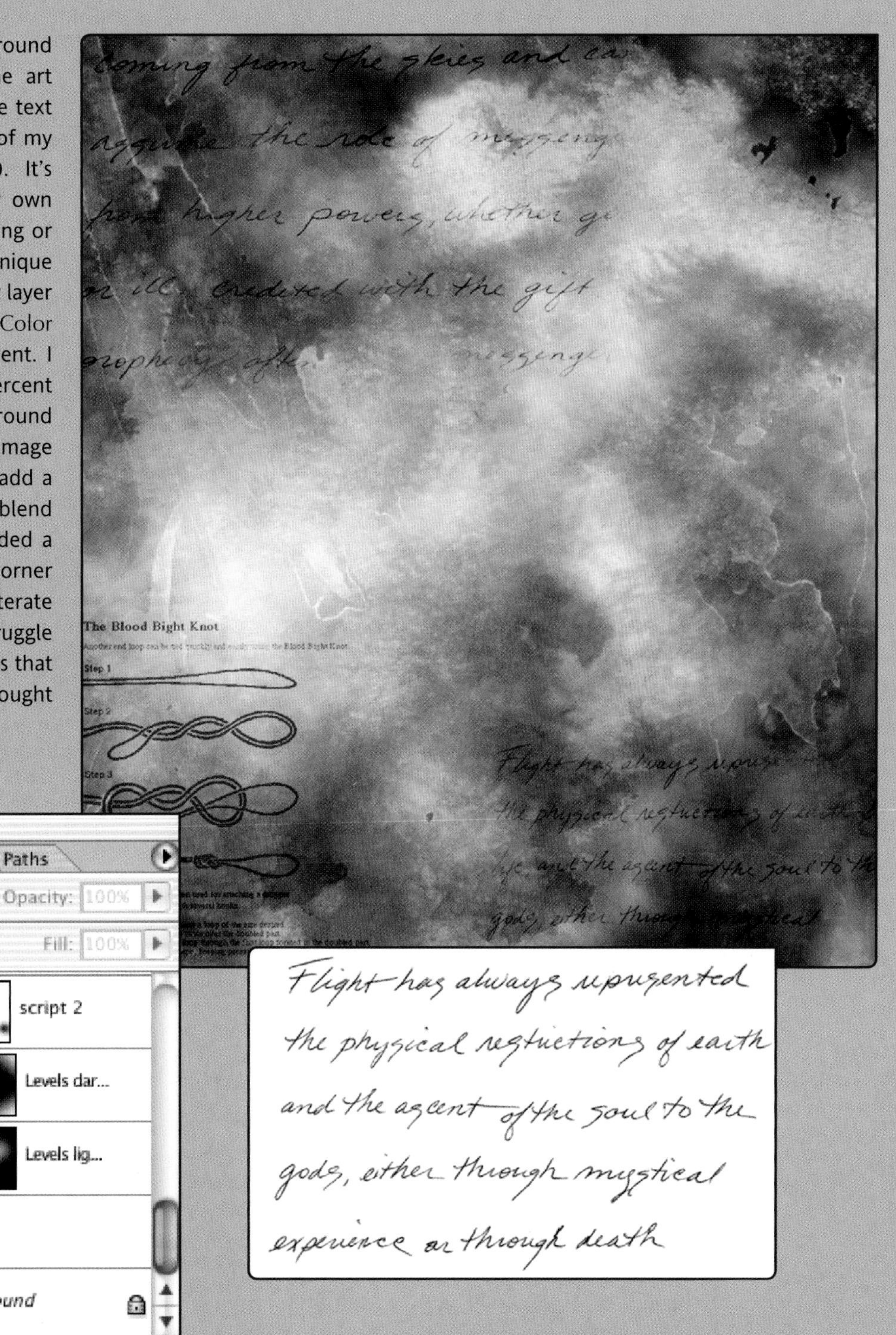

The crow itself is a composite of three images: a drawing of the head (crow_head.tif), a feather texture (crow_body.tif), and an etching of the legs and feet (crow_feet.tif). By compositing three different images, I am able to give the bird the stance and feeling that I want. This image is roughly composed, because it will be very dark and blended into the rough background texture. This stage of the image development is extremely forgiving, so I don't need to make precision selections or worry about the crow details. I am trying to convey the idea of age and wisdom, and the feeling that when the crow departs it leaves an impression.

Once they are composited (crow_composited.tif), I merge the layers into one, and then paste the crow into a new layer using the Color Burn Blending Mode, and an opacity of 85 percent.

Coming from the skies and
the role of
with the gift
The Blood Bight Knot
Another end loop can be tied quickly and easily using the Blood Bight Knot.
Step 1
Step 2
Step 3
Step 4
The Blood Bight Knot is often used for attaching a dropper
when fishing deep water with several hooks.
1. Double the line back to make a loop of the size desired
2. Bring the end of the loop twice over the doubled part.
3. Now pass the end of the loop through the first loop formed in the doubled part.
Flight has always
ascent of the soul to the
gods, either through mystical

To create the line around the crow I use another great shortcut. Rather than trying to trace the outline with the Lasso or Pen tools, I copy the crow to a new layer and use the Levels dialog (CMD+L) to create a high-contrast silhouette of the crow, sliding the Input levels toward each other to compress the grayscale. (The slider placement will vary with each image, as shown in the screenshot below.) The high contrast crow is a working layer, which I will trash when I'm finished with it.

Once I have a clean silhouette, I use the Magic Wand to select the black area of the crow. (Now I turn off the visibility of the silhouette layer.) While I have the marching ants encircling the crow, I make a new layer and use the Edit ➤ Stroke command to stroke the selection with three pixels of white. Instant outline! I use the Move tool to offset the stroke. To add more interest, I duplicate the stroke layer and offset it once again. Now I can trash that Silhouette layer (or save it to a channel for future use).

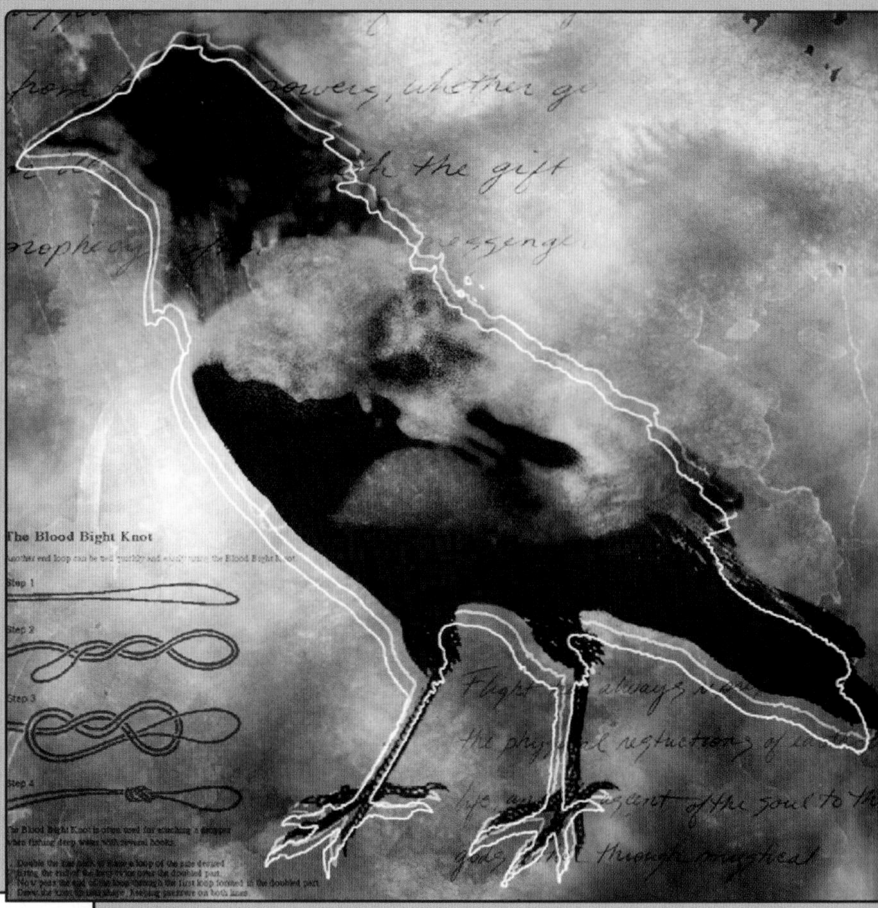

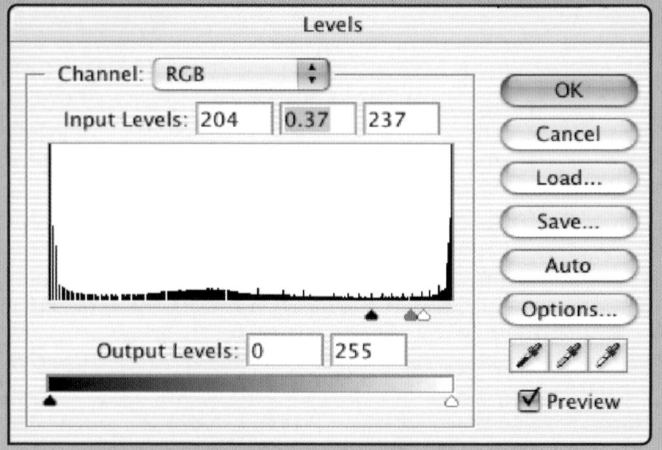

ow to give the impression of flight, I add wing (`crow_wing.tif`) as a light nprint in the upper-right corner of the nage. This helps further the idea of time assing, the feeling that the crow may be eady to leave and will leave a ghost of an npression when it does. I paste the nage of the wing into a new layer, and otate it to fit using Free Transform CMD+T). Then I add a Layer Mask and paint away" the areas I don't need.

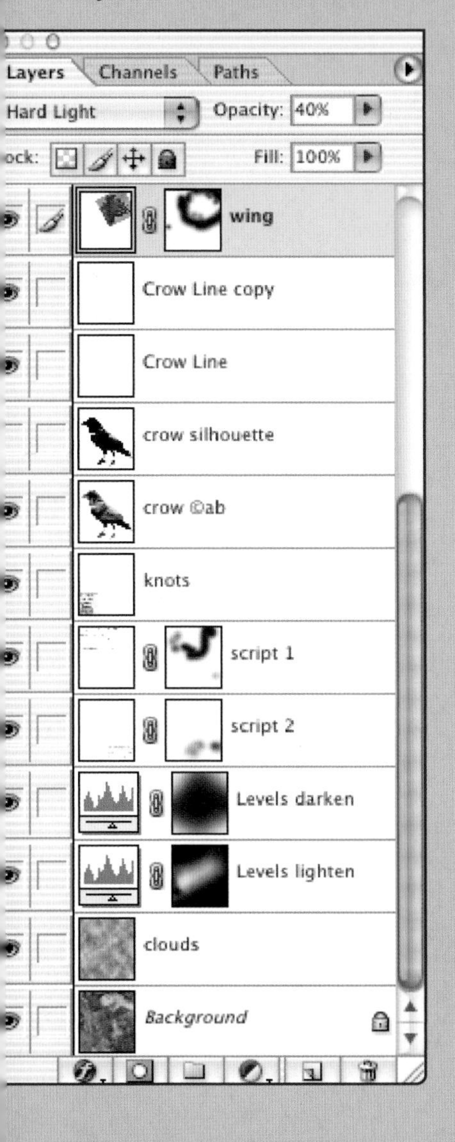

I like to incorporate hard-edged linework because it tends to look as though it is sitting on top of the image, giving the overall illustration a greater sense of depth. I chose the compass (`compass.tif`) and circle diagram (`circle.tif`) to represent structure, direction, and earth-bound ties. I open the line art file and invert the image (CMD+I) so the black line on a white background is now a white line on a black background. I copy and paste the line art into my layered file, then change the Layer Blending Mode to Screen. Because screening with white produces white and screening with black leaves the color underneath unchanged, the result is that the black background is no longer visible, whereas the white line remains visible.

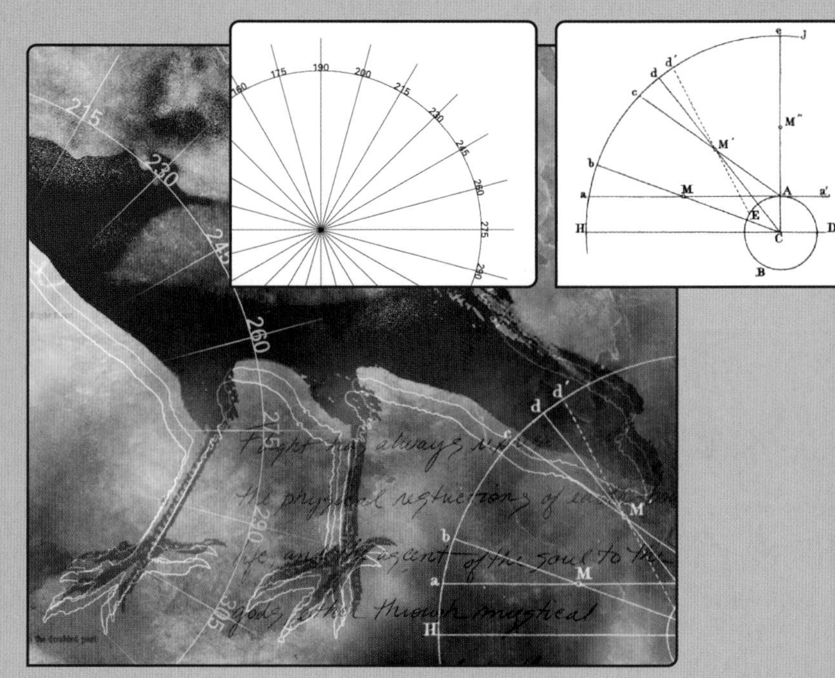

Finally, I add the type and give it a glow using Photoshop's Layer Styles. This is a great method for creating a blurred text effect without losing the editable status of the text. I use words in my illustration as both objects and as dialog. In this image, the "see past" text at the bottom that is placed over the diagram of knots asks the viewer to break earthly ties. The word "hope" sits in contrast to the ominous idea of the crow, and the number 13, conveys the possibility that the number 13 is lucky and a crow may actually represent faith, direction, and intelligence.

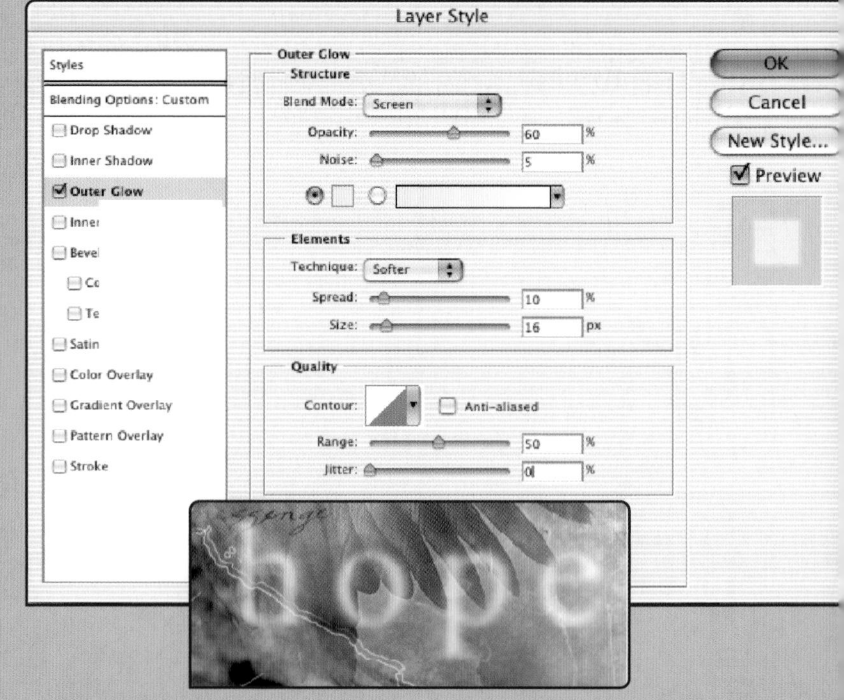

To create the first word, I choose a foreground color of light yellow, then click with the Text tool and type in the word "hope." After sizing the word to fit the composition, I add the Outer Glow Layer Style. Now I have a blurred edge but my text remains editable. At this point, for instance, I can change this word to another word and it will retain the blurred effect.

ıe last touches on my illustration are the hand-drawn ements. This image uses script handwriting, which provides e feeling of personal touch. And I've also added a simple nd-drawn outline around the number 13 at the eye. I didn't ally think about this as I created it, but looking back, I think it nveys the idea of blind faith, ignoring bad omens, and seeing ıck" in this typically fateful number.

create the outline, I create a new layer, choose a light color, d use the mouse to simply draw the box using the Brush tool th a roundness of 18 and an opacity of 70 percent. The box yer uses the Color Dodge blending mode. It's hard to find a od written description of the Color Dodge blending mode, ıt my interpretation is that Color Dodge basically brightens e light areas of the image beneath your layer. Here's a hint for ing this blending mode: Be sure that your stroke has some lor in it rather than using a stroke that is only white; you'll get uch more interesting blending effects. Even a slight hint of llow will make a huge difference.

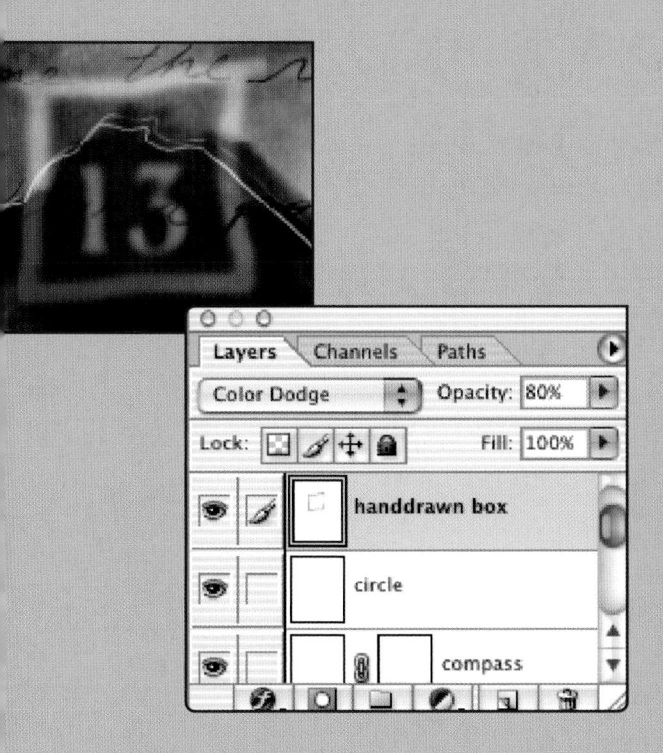

At this point, I'm satisfied with the image and am ready to call it final. When creating a collage, you may sometimes think it's difficult to find a stopping place. I stop adding elements right before the main image begins to lose its impact. In an image with many layers such as this, it's tricky to keep the visual balance. The nice thing about working in Photoshop is that I can keep editing the layers until I'm completely satisfied.

I am not sure where my art will take me in the future, but I'm definitely heading toward a darker, more dramatic, overall feeling. In the past, I didn't promote the more shadowy images for fear of scaring away clients. I kept these images to myself or showed them only as fine art. But now that I have a solid client base I have room to explore these darker concepts.

Because so many artists today are using Photoshop to create photo-collage style illustrations, I feel it is especially important for me to consciously continue to grow and develop my personal style. Sometimes it can be difficult to do my best work while under a tight deadline. I have to catch myself if I find that I'm cutting corners or copying something I did before. I really don't want to go that route, so I try to stay conscious of finding ways to keep my art fresh and new. Mostly, I want to create the images I love, keeping the quality and integrity as high as possible to satisfy my own sensibility.

“Ascension” © Alicia Buelow

ming from the

ume the role of messeng

13

powers, whether g

h the gift

messenge

hope

Bight Knot

can be tied quickly and easily using the Blood Bight Knot

Knot is often used for attaching a dropper
p water with several hooks.

back to make a loop of the size desired.
of the loop twice over the doubled part.
end of the loop through the first loop formed in the do
up into shape, keeping pressure on both lines.

Flight has always

the physical restrictions of earth

and the ascent of the soul to

gods either through mystical

05 BRAINBOX

The Past

If anyone asked me when I first realized I could be creative, I wouldn't know how to answer. I'm firmly convinced that creativity develops thanks to talent, experience, sacrifices, and most of all, curiosity. Curiosity that pushes you to know, to understand, to study, and to learn from your mistakes, from the past, and from expert and talented people. But I couldn't give you a clear definition of creativity because I think that it's articulated in so many places and it's meanings are so varied that it would be impossible to confine it to a single rule.

My passion for drawing began when I was a child from the need to draw my cartoon heroes on paper, first with uncertain and rude pencil strokes, then, as I wasted paper and ink, with a firmer style. At this point, I hadn't developed style yet because style is one of the highest goals for a creative individual, something that only comes with experience. But, I was beginning to have my own personal vision of reality, as if I could store, codify, melt, and transcribe information from outside onto paper.

So my great passion for drawing became a constant friend, and I was increasingly influenced by my TV heroes, TV serials of the 1980s, and the piles of comics I was accumulating in my room. Comics have been one of the greatest sources of stimuli and inspiration in my life. *The Amazing Spider-Man*, *The Fantastic Four*, *Batman*, *Superman*, *The Punisher*, and so on, really contributed to modifying my vision of reality and pushed me to find my style. Admiring the strokes, analyzing anatomy and the distribution of shadows, and understanding the ink job and the color quality, were all necessary tasks every time I bought a comic. All the information I collected added to the background knowledge and skills I was developing. It goes without saying that, at that time, due to my meager finances, I could count only on a few pencils, colors, pastels, and a lot of imagination as instruments; but these little tools still gave me the illusion of being a real comic artist.

With my first savings, I ordered some books—my first little manuals about the ABC's of drawing and art—which increased my interest in some artists' stories. After studying the history of art from ancient times until now, I understood that my attention was focused only on some specific artistic movements.

The Amazing Spider-Man, series #186, © Marvel Comics 1963

'heatfield with Crows, Van Gogh, 1890

ırtistic influences

enaissance manierism, portraiture, and Michelangelo's sculptures ıd affrescos (I hope Italians can forgive me. . .) are not for me ecause I've always found the effort to imitate reality a little bit edundant. I prefer artists who are able to give their own vision of eality, even destroying or spoiling it in the process, but those who ırn it into something so full of emotion and meaning that I can't elp but be fascinated by it. Impressionism became my passion, ıd Van Gogh with it—a unique artist in his genre whose influence as felt in two centuries. It's even tough to describe him as an ıpressionist because I can see the beginnings of abstractionism ıd futurism in his work too. He is so mystic and irrational and ıts so many feelings into his work that it's impossible to find just ıe interpretation of his pictures.

very artist should throw himself into his work, using lines and olors as expressive functions to try to convey emotion. This is hat Van Gogh's art taught me. His masterpiece for me is *'heatfield with Crows*, a picture that embodies the troubled ıd dramatic journey of Van Gogh.

Analysis and criticism of this picture are many and different: and this is where the fascination with Van Gogh's lies—his skill is in the suggestion of a certain feel that he puts in his work, and it is this that makes it unique. My first impression of *Wheatfield with Crows* is about the colors; in the gloomy atmosphere, the blue and light blue of the sky contrast with the yellow and orange of the grain field. This combination is so lively that it seems like fire, especially when compared to the road that crosses the canvas with subdued colors. Over this landscape, a bunch of black strokes portray a bevy of crows, so simple in their shape but so ominous and meaningful. The colors of the three elements—sky, field, and road—are discordant. The darkly colored sky can't light the landscape, which, in contrast, shows strong and luminous colors. That light can't come from anywhere but from inside, as if celebrating something beautiful and important. The never-ending, lonely road is the shameless statement of existence, with no point, without knowing where to go or what to look for. Van Gogh committed suicide shortly after finishing this picture.

The beginning of my passion

Metaphors and hidden meanings exude from every stroke and every element of the *Wheatfield with Crows*. I can see in the artist's autobiography, *Dear Theo: The Autobiography of Vincent Van Gogh* (Plume, 1995), that he used his skill to show spontaneously and deeply his feelings of disruption and frustration, and his experience of life.

I based this analysis on my belief that an artist must be able t relate who he is through his work using a variety of expressior that he considers his own, from comic to dramatic. I chose iron because it's the tone that belongs more to me and bette represents me.

nfortunately, even if I had learned techniques such as acquarello d acrylic painting, I would have felt that painting was not for me cause I was looking for something quicker, something more namic and accessible. This desire came true because a new orld of colors, graphics, and dreams soon unfolded before me: deo games.

was just like seeing comics moving, but not as a cartoon; I was w involved in something interactive and I could control the aracters' fates.

this point, the printed comics' imagery melded with the credible world of video games, and my longing to find tools that would enable me to make my drawings live from an esthetical and interactive point of view was whetted. The imagery that I had built up so far had traces of video game dynamism, lively colors, and a visual mood. These combined perfectly with the comic/dramatic/noir colors of the comics that had provided me with so many emotions and cues to polish my illustration techniques. To all this, I added my inner passion for trash cinema, B movies, pop culture, low-budget productions, and TV serials and films from the 1970s and 80s.

That universe of rounded fonts, plastic futuristic inventions, and Jackie Brown hairstyles was sneaking into me, and later, it became a key to my search for a style.

Meet Photoshop

At that point in my artistic development, I was clear in my mind on what to do (even though I was attending a school that had nothing to do with art) and, by a lucky chance, a PC appeared on my bedroom desk. Also, thanks to a piece of advice from a friend, I got a copy of Photoshop. So, my trip through exploring the potential of this new technological medium began and came to be a substitute for the traditional drawing tools. For the first six months, I used Photoshop 4 (the new version had just been released) and I quickly fell in love with the filters th made my drawings real (Lens Flare and Blur were my favor effects for re-creating real atmospheres). I used to scan r drawings into Photoshop and then polished them by getting of the pencil strokes. I added colors, softened them, and us many effects to make them similar to my comic's covers believe I made hundreds of files trying to obtain the quality the original covers.

POSEIDON
IS COMING!

Photoshop now

After a while, I realized that Photoshop could give me more, and I tried to work with photographs using selection tools, shading, hiding, and color effects. I found that as soon as you become more and more confident with the program, it becomes clear that Photoshop will allow you to do almost anything; you can take a blank sheet and fill it as you please—with a hand drawing, an old photograph, or a scanned shoe. With its brushes, you have dozens of different shapes to take advantage of. You can work with transparency on hundreds of layers, always safe in the knowledge that you can correct each mistake. Perhaps for a canvas artist this is sacrilegious, but for me it was great. This is why I was basically kidnapped by this tool.

I experimented more and more, each time trying to learn some tricks to speed up the workflow. Overall, I was trying to tighten the process from my mind work to drawing on paper to editing with Photoshop. With my increasing knowledge of the software, my experience with colors, formats, and other creative possibilities increased too. I really could work on a project in one, and only one, file with all the materials, experiments, and resources I needed (thanks to layers).

Also, with the Web, Photoshop became a good ally too, becau I could use it to create one file that contained different proposa for client presentations.

To tell the truth, what really impresses me about Photoshop that it's so versatile. You can create anything you have in mir and, if you can combine it with other design programs, it's rea the ultimate creative solution.

I use Photoshop in many ways. Sometimes I might scan any o object that I can turn into a texture, import a file from anoth program, choose a particular font, or simply export images f the Web. For me, Photoshop is at the heart of doing everythin

It may seem like a cliché, but over the years, I have learned th to fully realize Photoshop's potential, you must also have a we constructed concept and a pre-production paper project. On with all these elements and the knowledge of the software c you hope to reach the highest levels. As for all the time that h passed since I started with Photoshop, I can say that I'm co stantly experimenting with new techniques to try to fina achieve a style that accurately represents me.

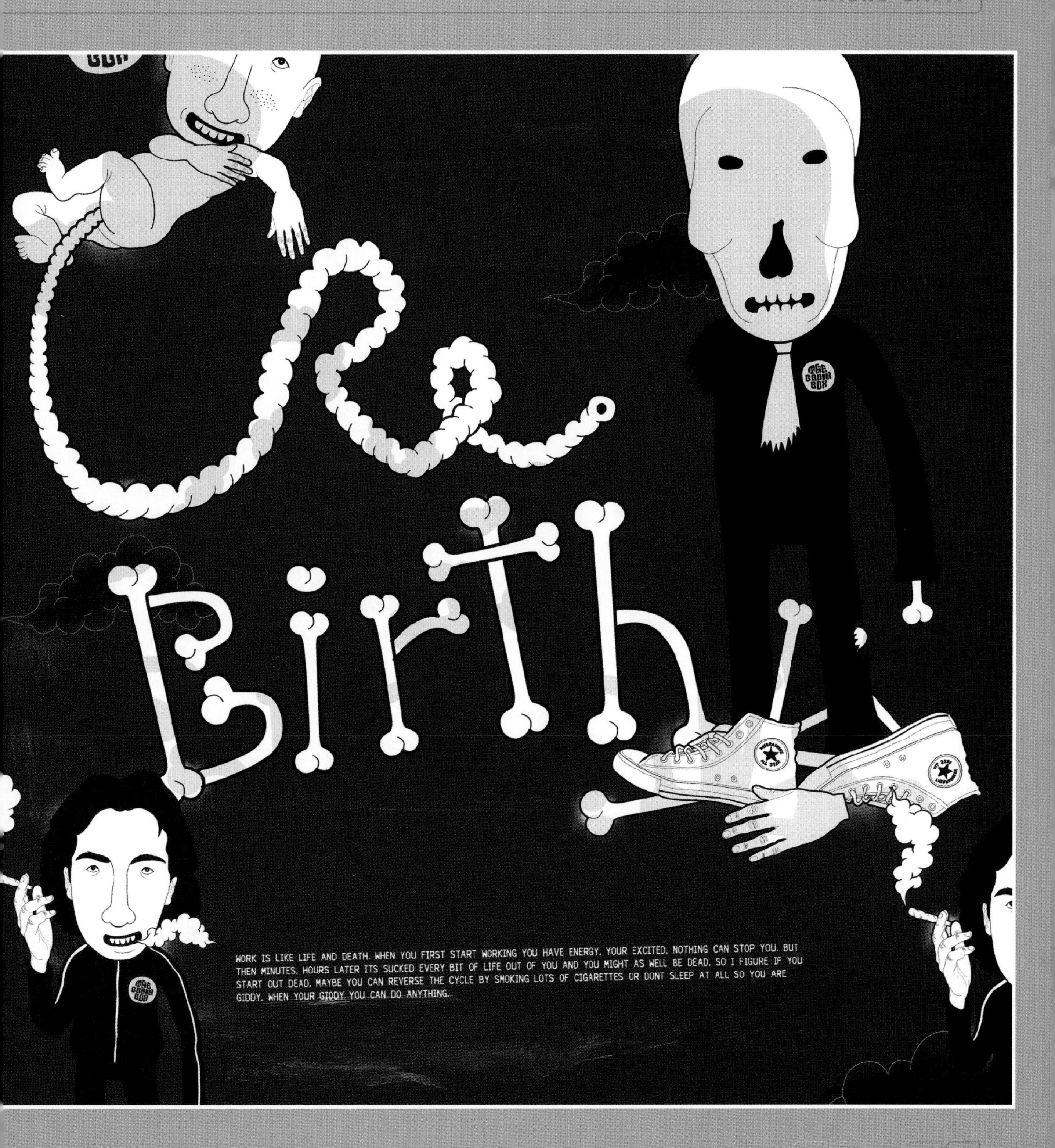
Re
Birth
THE DEATH BOX
WORK IS LIKE LIFE AND DEATH. WHEN YOU FIRST START WORKING YOU HAVE ENERGY. YOUR EXCITED. NOTHING CAN STOP YOU. BUT THEN MINUTES. HOURS LATER ITS SUCKED EVERY BIT OF LIFE OUT OF YOU AND YOU MIGHT AS WELL BE DEAD. SO I FIGURE IF YOU START OUT DEAD. MAYBE YOU CAN REVERSE THE CYCLE BY SMOKING LOTS OF CIGARETTES OR DONT SLEEP AT ALL SO YOU ARE GIDDY. WHEN YOUR GIDDY YOU CAN DO ANYTHING.

SOTO
"Spaceman in the trashcan". Acrylic on wood. 2002. For the Broken Wrist Project. Collection of James Hughes.

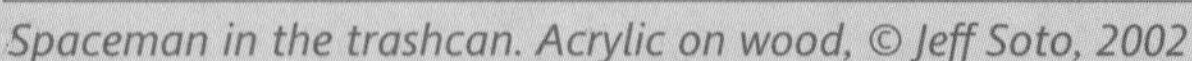
Spaceman in the trashcan. Acrylic on wood, © Jeff Soto, 2002

Missy Mojo Magazine © Tim Marrs, 2004, www.timmarrs.co.

Online inspiration

The arrival of the Web gave me access to a huge database of artists, styles, and resources. From 1998 to today, I've seen many Internet trends follow one another and then finally disappear. But among the thousands of sites that I have discovered and visited, I consider some to be great sources of inspiration and of the highest artistic value. I'm talking about those sites that have been able to keep a new and innovative attitude, those that have always surprised me with the works they have edited. I'm referring to those where, from the final Photoshop result, you can trace the meticulous and precise preparations that makes the concept first class. It's a bit like Van Gogh: emotions contained within colors and shapes.

Miika Saksi (www.non-stops.com) impressed me with his skill foresee styles and the coherence and beauty of his works, whi are in a Nordic style with a bit of punk mixed in. Jeff So (www.jeffsoto.com) is a great artist whose style is unique; uses an incredible mix of elements from comics and TV create original work.

Tim Marrs (www.timmarrs.co.uk) is an English illustrator wh find very fascinating. He has a mix of styles—no doubt influenc by the 1970s and 80s—but with a fresh approach.

mone Legno, http://tokidoki.it, 2004

nese are the main artists who constantly influence me and who spire my growth in this profession, but I could list some others: atrick Sundqvist (www.supershapes.com), James Widegren www.idiocase.com), Simone Legno (http://tokidoki.it), or Joost orngold (www.renascent.nl). These artists can show how notoshop possibilities are infinite.

They show that beyond their techniques is talent and a will to make artwork that is moving and meaningful from their own vision, each one absolutely different from the others and the original. All I've discussed so far in this chapter has helped me find a personal style and my own way of working, which will be exemplified in the tutorial in the second half of this chapter.

The image I chose for the tutorial is the poster for a trailer that was shown in Venice during the ceremonies for the reopening of the Fenice Theater (December 2003).

The title of the image is "A Reconstructed Future," and it tries to present the spirit of the short film—an interpretation of musical theater as a source of universal harmony that shapes matter from its own grace and evolutional importance. This film is basically about the battle between the present and the past, the values and the horrors of our times, and between culture and modernity. When the film was shown at this venue, it was a work-in-progress and I could see only the trailer and many hours of footage. (You can view this trailer at www.mimic.it/nmop/futuroric.mov.) I had to come up with a design concept without the final version of the trailer to view, so I couldn't just rely on the images because they could have changed by the end of the work. So, to produce the poster, I used illustrations, frames from the video, typography, and hand drawings. These individual files are all included in the materials folder in this chapter's source files on the CD.

Why I chose to use Photoshop

I had many reasons for choosing Photoshop to create this image. First, it was a matter of time. I only had a day to make the poster and the quickest tool for combining all I had in mind was Photoshop. Another reason was a practical one: with Photoshop, photographs, scans, typography, drawings, and colors can all be controlled in the same program.

I also had to think about a concept on which to base my creation. I was present while the trailer was shot, so I knew the theme and the main message of "A Reconstructed Future" quite well. I just had to choose a style to link it to the playbill. My idea was to avoid the classical frame from the film or a photographic patchwork, and produce something more elaborate and more in-depth. I wanted to create an imaginary context (possibly with the hand drawing technique) where the audience could find the key elements of the film, such as music, the city of Venice, metaphors to the theater and to love, and the skater as the main character.

decided to focus on a part of the playbill leaving some empty ›ace for the reader to complete using their imagination (they ›ight imagine the colors of the Venice landscape, for example).

he first step was gathering the material. I scanned a white ›eet of paper, took some frames from the film, and took some ›hotos (such as the sky) with my digital camera. I also used a ›seful tool for drawing in Photoshop, a graphic tablet (such as Wacom tablet), which creates a more realistic brush stroke ›an when you use the mouse. I created some parts of the ›age with other software (the skater and violin EPS files were ›ade in Illustrator), and then imported them into Photoshop.

›, our base will be the scanned sheet of paper and the ›ements created outside Photoshop and brought into it ›kater.eps and violins.eps). These have already been ›nported and positioned in the fenice_start.psd on the CD.

he resolution for this file is 200dpi CMYK; I chose this res- ›lution to maintain the original quality of the film trailer (shot ›ith a digital video camera at 720x576 pixels) and so that I ›ould print the file afterward. Initially though, when I was ›orking with the image for the first time, I used RGB mode ›ecause I had to work with a frame from the film; I then turned into CMYK later.

›et's get started. First, I want to create the back of the image as photographic patchwork, based on the photos I took in ›enice. The first thing to do is to make all existing elements ›visible except for the Background layer (which contains a ›canned piece of paper).

Now open `Venice1.jpg`, `Venice2.jpg`, and `Venice3.jpg`. Copy and paste these three images into your working PSD and name each new layer as follows: "venice1", "venice2", and "venice3".

My initial idea was to create a landscape, a horizon made o buildings, bridges, and boats, which could convey a strong an sudden Venetian atmosphere. To achieve this, I decided to lin three different photos I took in Venice. Let's see what come out of this.

ıow have to reduce the images in ze in order to place them next to ıch other and create a landscape. ı do so, make the Venice2 and enice3 layers invisible, then ·lect the Venice1 layer. Use the ee Transform tool (CTRL+T), ıaking sure you click the Maintain spect Ratio icon in the tool ɔtions, to resize the image by ɔout 50 percent. I want to place ł three images side-by-side, so I timate that they'll need to be ɔout half their current size; in the ıd I chose 46 percent for this rst image.

epeat this same process for the enice2 and Venice3 images, ıaking them smaller. Position ıem next to each other, as you ın see here:

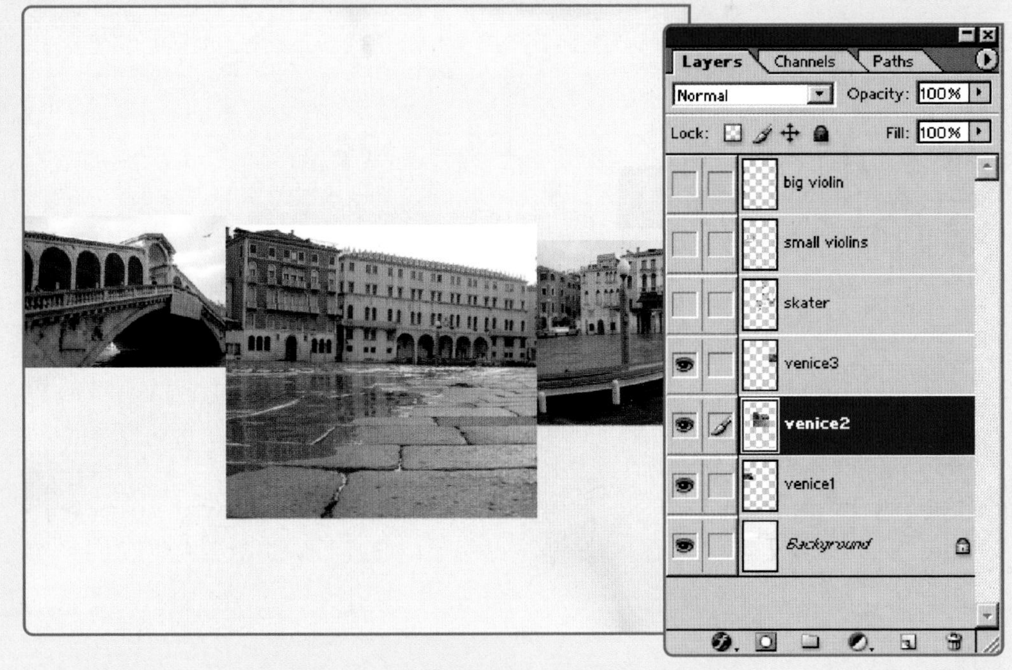

ow that the patchwork is done, I ave to trace the borders to eate the drawing effect (you ıay wish to link these Venice yers once you're happy with ıeir position).

Open a new layer to draw on and call it "sketch". Lower the opacity of the three Venice layers to 30 percent, so that you can easily trace over them. I want to sketch the outlines of these photographs onto a different layer to create the look I'm after.

I select the Brush tool and choose a hard-edged 3-pixel brush. This size of brush ensures that the result is quite like the borders of the skater and violin, which helps keep the effect unified across all parts of the poster. Of course, you could use other brush dimensions to see different effects on the image.

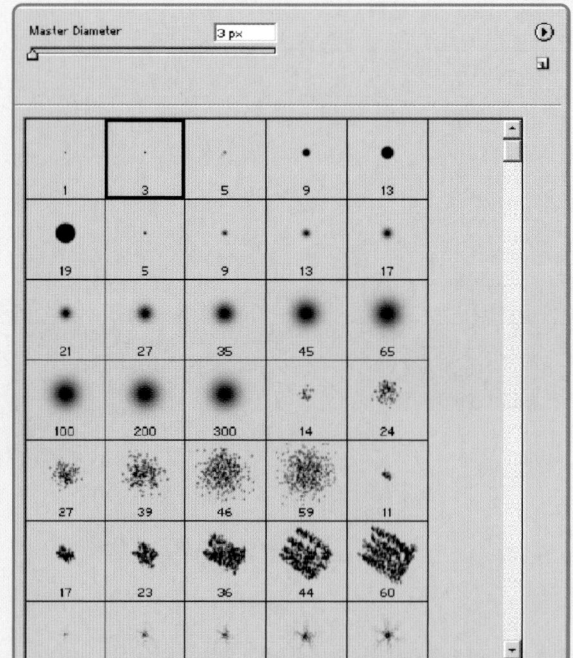

Now working on the sketch layer, begin tracing the bridge at the left of the patchwork with your brush, working your way over the main outlines of the photo patchwork (possibly with the help of a graphics tablet, if you have one) until you get a result like the following image.

lso, because the skater layer will be bove the completed patchwork in the nal sketch, I don't want too much of ne sketch of the buildings to be visible hrough the skater's trousers, but it's K to be a bit loose here. So, keep hecking the visibility of the skater layer r temporarily reduce the skater layer's pacity during this sketch process so hat you don't needlessly trace behind ne skater. It's important to always use he Zoom tool in order to be as precise s possible when tracing the borders, nd also because, when you're working n large images, you can see the extra etails that aren't visible at 100 percent.

chose to hand draw on this copy to try o convey a comic-like appearance and nood, to give a smooth, less technical, tmosphere. This way, all the pictures of ne pages will have a harmonic and imilar movement.

ontinue to draw over the rest of the atchwork with the Brush tool. Once ou've finished tracing the whole atchwork, delete the three Venice ayers containing the source photos. low you can see how the composition s developing.

Rename the Background layer "paper" and insert a new layer above it called "skater shadow". Select the Lasso tool and draw a shape beneath the skateboard to create a shadow, as if the light is shining down vertically onto the skater. The Feather for the Lasso tool is 0 pixels. To give a more realistic effect to the shadow, I could have used the Gaussian Blur filter (you then have to find the best focusing).

However, I chose the Lasso because my picture didn't need ar particular zooms since there's no photographical realism, an since the shape of the shadow needed an irregular look with handmade style. If I had wanted a realistic result, I would hav chosen two alternative solutions: setting the Lasso tool's Feath option to a number above 0 (to regulate the zoom options); c using a Feather of 0 and then working with the Gaussian Blu which helps better control the zoom.

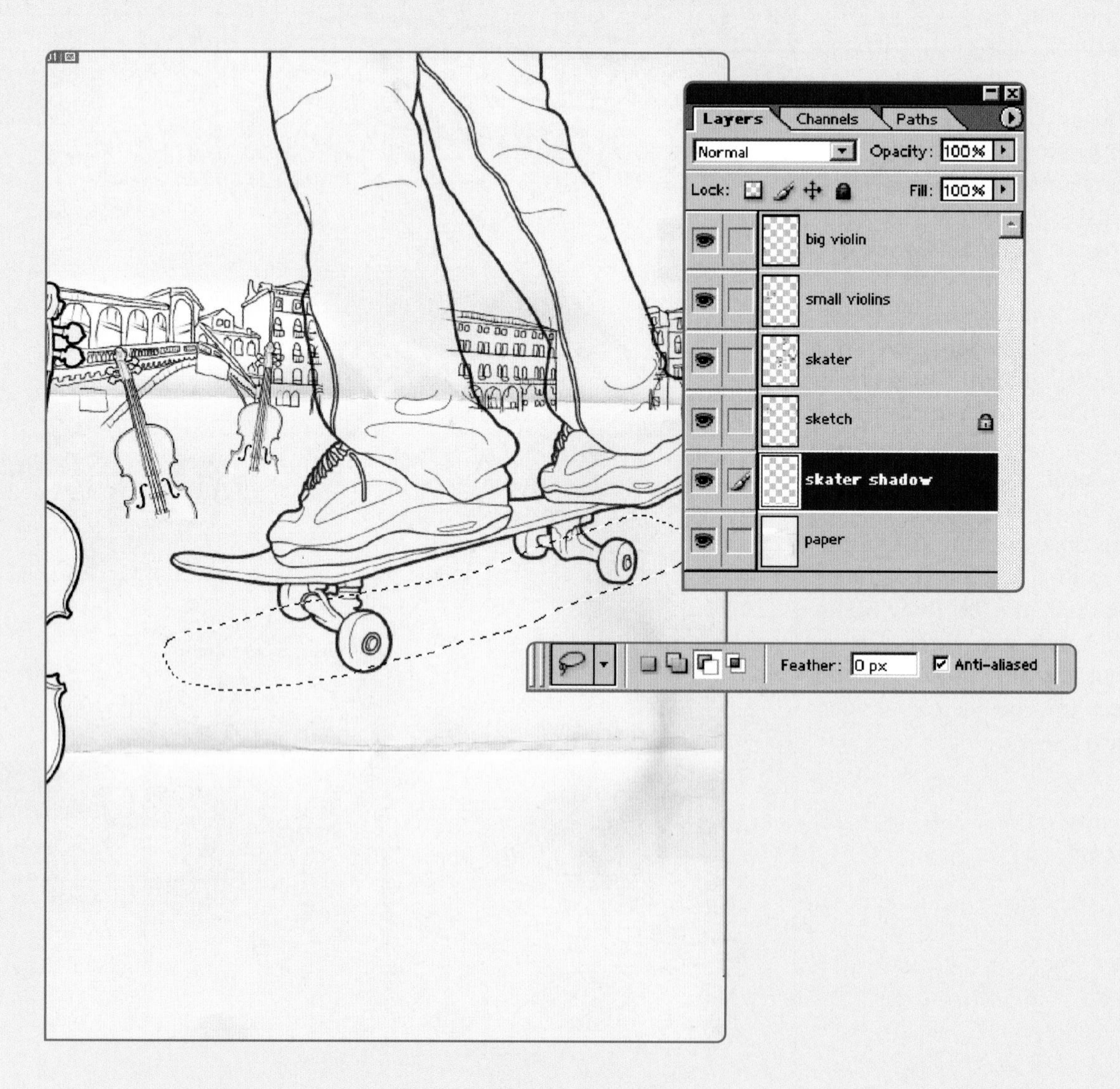

ow it's time to put the color into the shape. The color must be ght and match the comic look of the whole image. The shadow ust add an element of depth to the picture, but it doesn't ave to catch the audience's attention too much, so it's better select a light color rather than a dark one at this point.

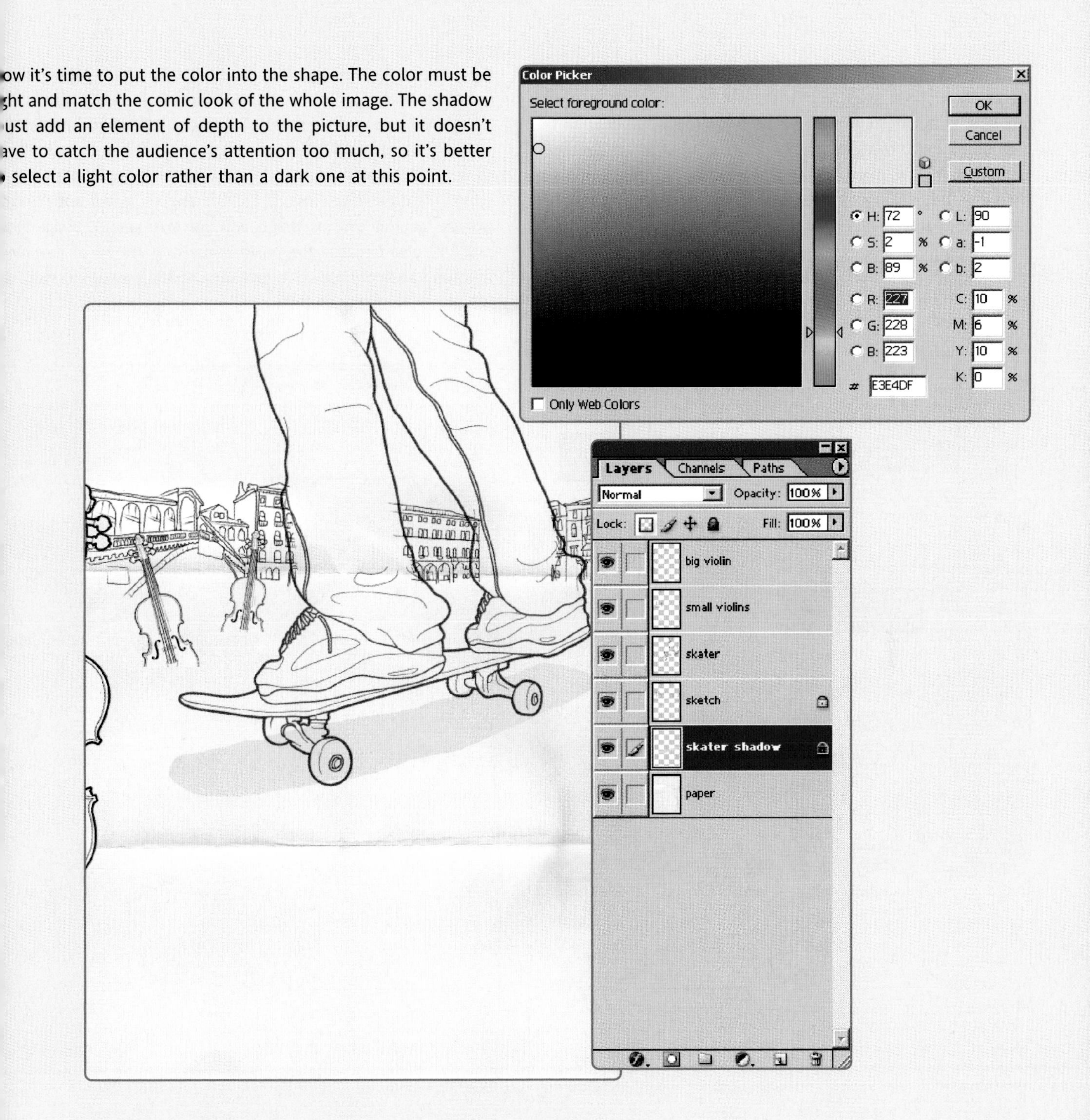

The next thing to do is create the sky over the Venice drawing. Open `materials/sky.jpg` from the CD, and drag it into your working PSD file, immediately above the paper layer. Call this new layer "sky". Position the sky image in the top center of the composition and make the rough selection shown here using the Lasso tool. It doesn't need to be too precise, just enough to help you divide the sky from the Venice drawing.

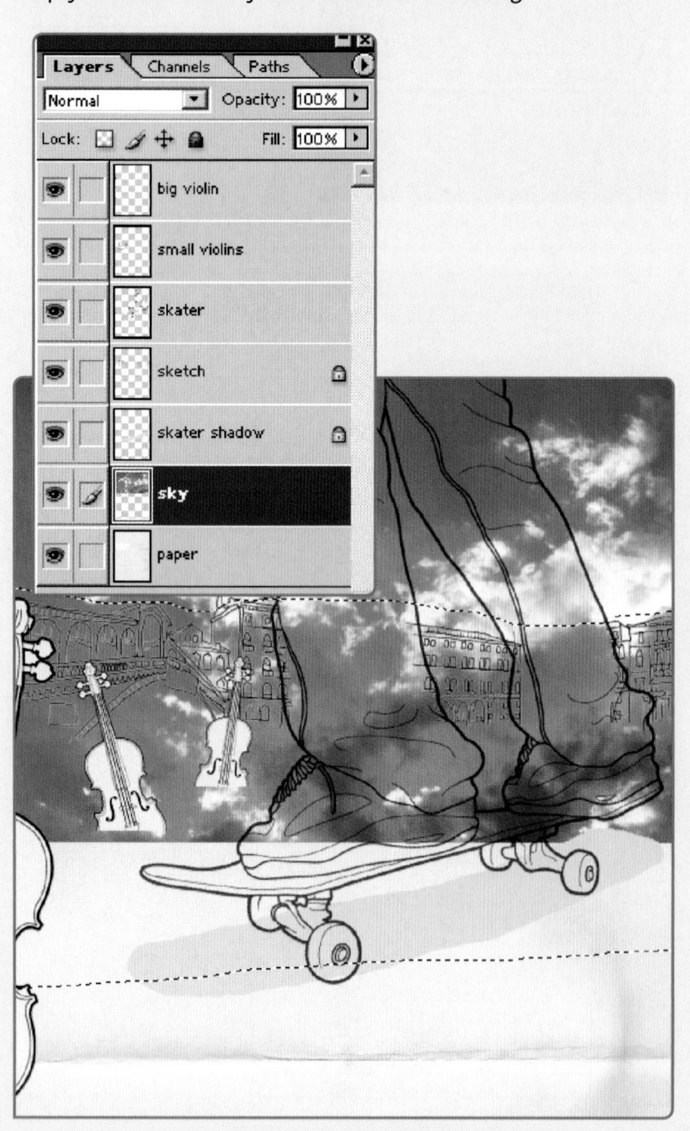

Go to Select ➤ Feather and choose 10 for the Feather Radiu value. Now choose Edit ➤ Cut. The image of the sky is now we positioned and of the proper dimensions. The larger the Feath Radius, the larger the smooth zoom will be. My choice allov the sky photo to spread and melt with the base underneath. you try and use a less strong Feather Radius, you'll see that th border of the photo image will be less smooth and mor evident (also because the basic image is made up of just blac lines and a white base). If the base included a photo as well, th result would surely be different.

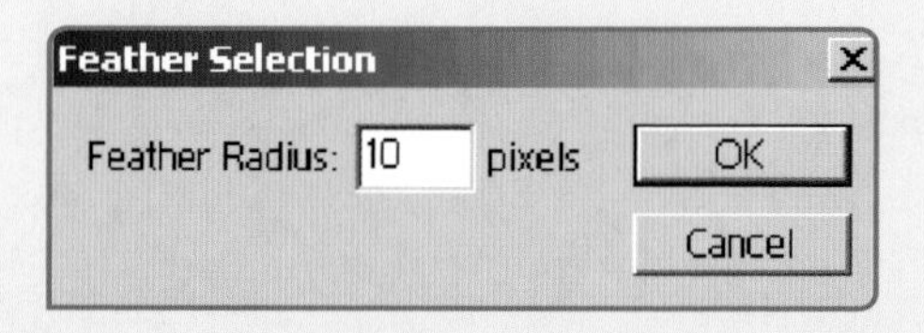

ne sky is still too predominant in the image, so I have to find solution to give a stylistic coherence to the whole piece. The sult I'm looking for is a harmony between the elements, ustrations, and the photos. By the end, I only want a few ements to contrast with the rest of the image, which should e smooth and elegant.

Reduce the saturation of the sky in the Hue/Saturation dialog box (CTRL+U) down to –50. In the Layers palette, change the layer blending mode from Normal to Pin Light to get the result shown here. These layer blending modes can give an original touch to your images. By experimenting with and using these filters, I can often find visual solutions I've never thought about before.

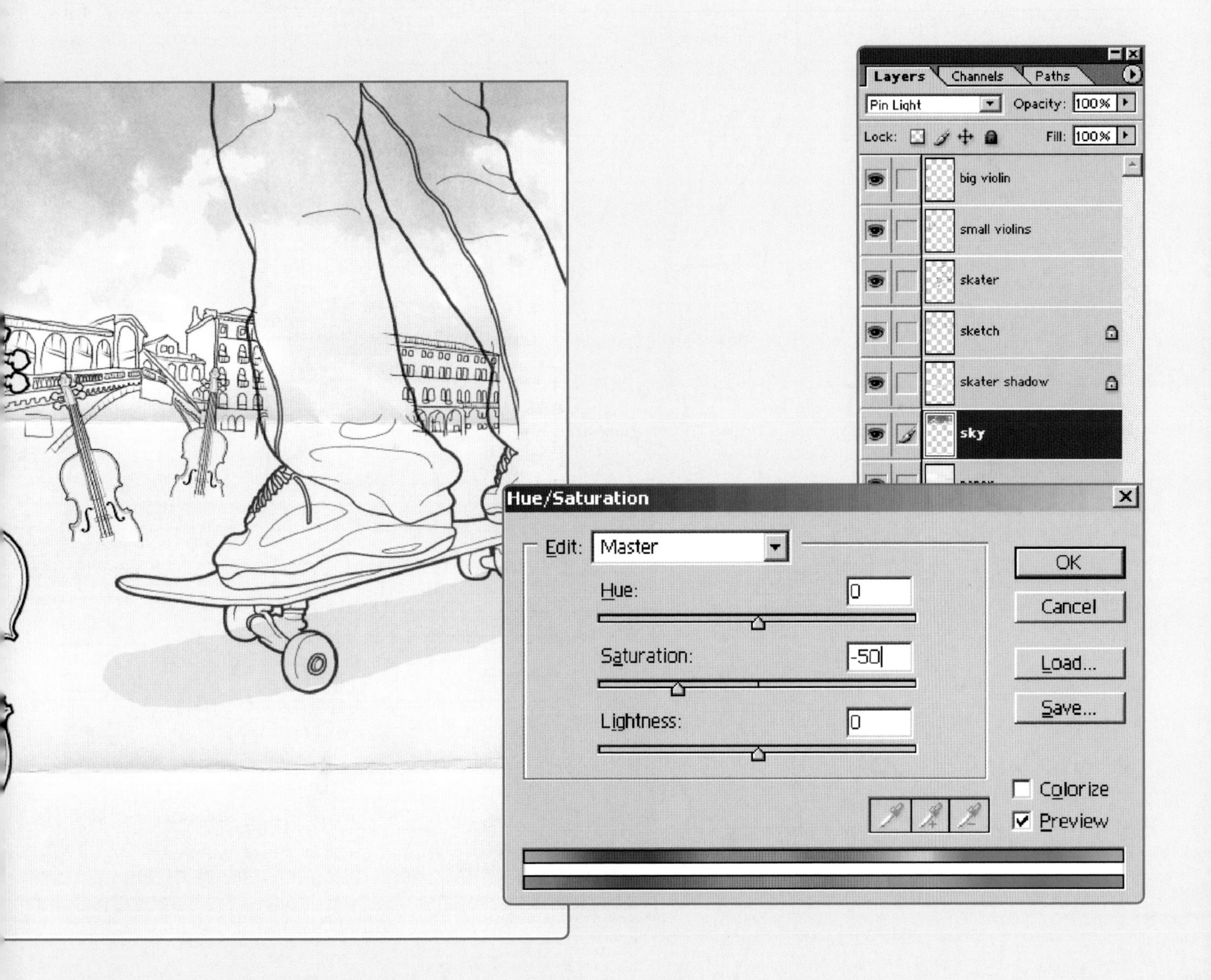

Change the opacity of the sky layer to 80 percent. Now duplicate this layer and change the opacity of this sky copy layer to 60 percent. Next, in the Hue/Saturation dialog box (Ctrl+U), make sure the Saturation is 0 and change the Lightness to –5. By duplicating this sky layer and by making the changes, we have made the clouds less colored and more in tune with the context.

And now for the skater's legs. Select the skater layer. Choose th Magic Wand tool (W) and set the Tolerance to 1 in the to options. Then select the jeans area, which will be used as a bc for the next sequence of steps. I decided to use this area of th skater because it lies in a central position within the image.

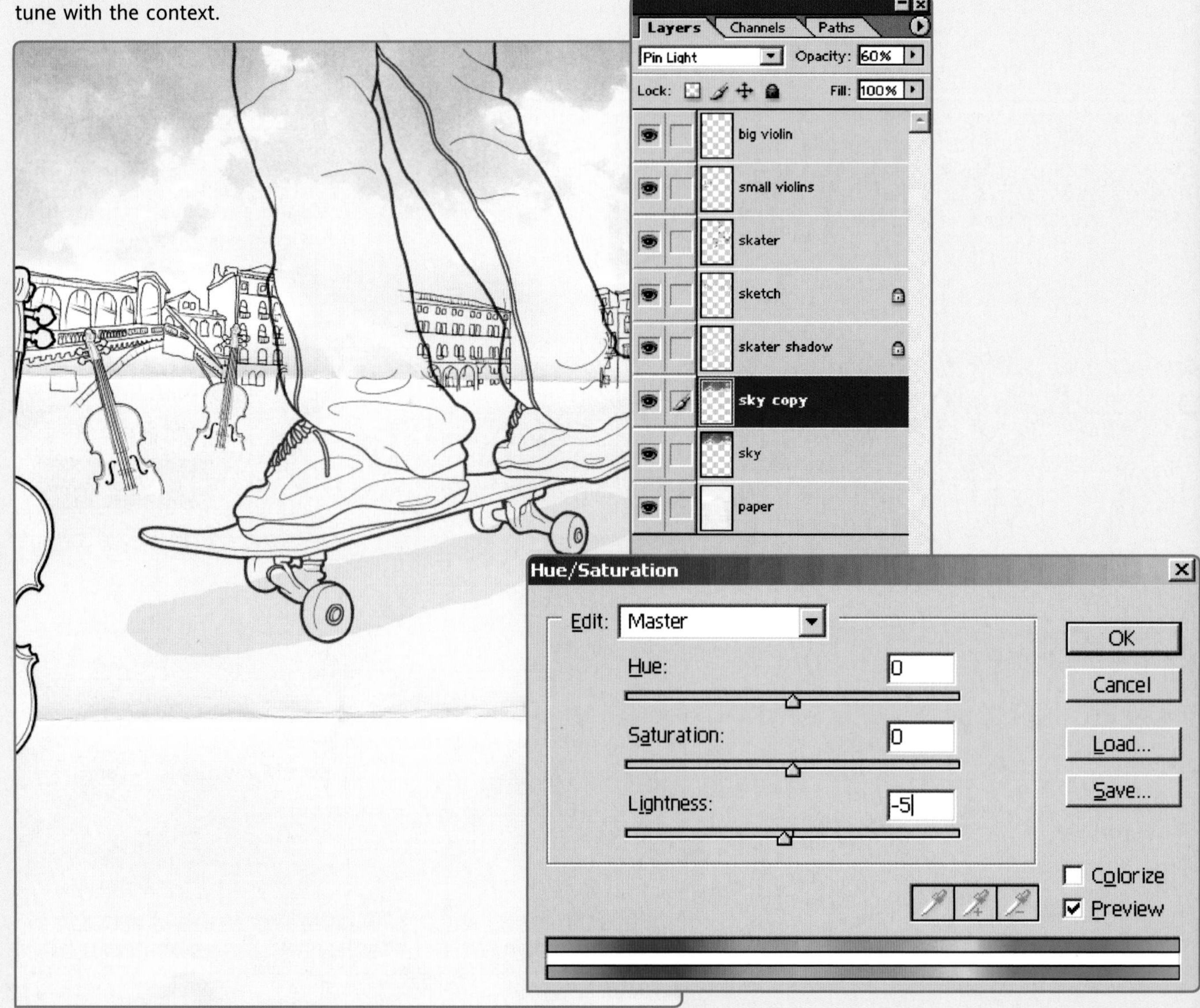

ou can keep holding SHIFT while you select to build up multiple lections. The Magic Wand tool is very useful when the lection doesn't have to be too accurate, and thanks to the olerance setting, the precision is acceptable anyway. If you ant to create perfect selections here, then you would be etter off using the Pen tool.

You're going to be using this selection frequently in this tutorial, so it's a good idea to save it now for later use. Go to Select ➤ Save Selection and save it with an appropriate name.

Without closing the selection, create a new layer called "pants" beneath the skater layer. On this new layer, go to Select ➤ Modify ➤ Expand and increase the selection by 1 pixel. Fill the selection with a color using Edit ➤ Fill. The color itself doesn't matter at this stage since the pants layer will be edited further later on.

Now make the pants layer invisible and create a new layer called "sketch pants" above the pants layer. Using the Brush tool (B), paint with rough strokes inside the selection. Set the brush Opacity to 40 percent, and while you paint, vary the brush sizes.

For example, I started by painting the trousers using a brush siz of 19 pixels, then 13 pixels, and finally 9 pixels, to re-create pen tip effect.

The best technique to obtain a realistic brush effect is t alternate the brush's size four or five times with a low opacit level. For example, try opacities around 20 percent and brus dimensions from 10 to 60px. This way, every brush decrease the transparency with an effect of fresh paint.

ow let's work on the photographic elements that will fill the ousers. Let's begin with the right leg. Working on the pants yer, fill it with a solid gray color.

ow open `she.jpg` and `he.jpg`, copy them, and place them n new layers called "she" and "he" immediately above the pants layer in your working PSD. With the Lasso tool set with a Feather of 20px, remove the top-left corner of the he image so that you can melt the two images together. The feather helps create a smooth and delicate blend where the two images overlap.

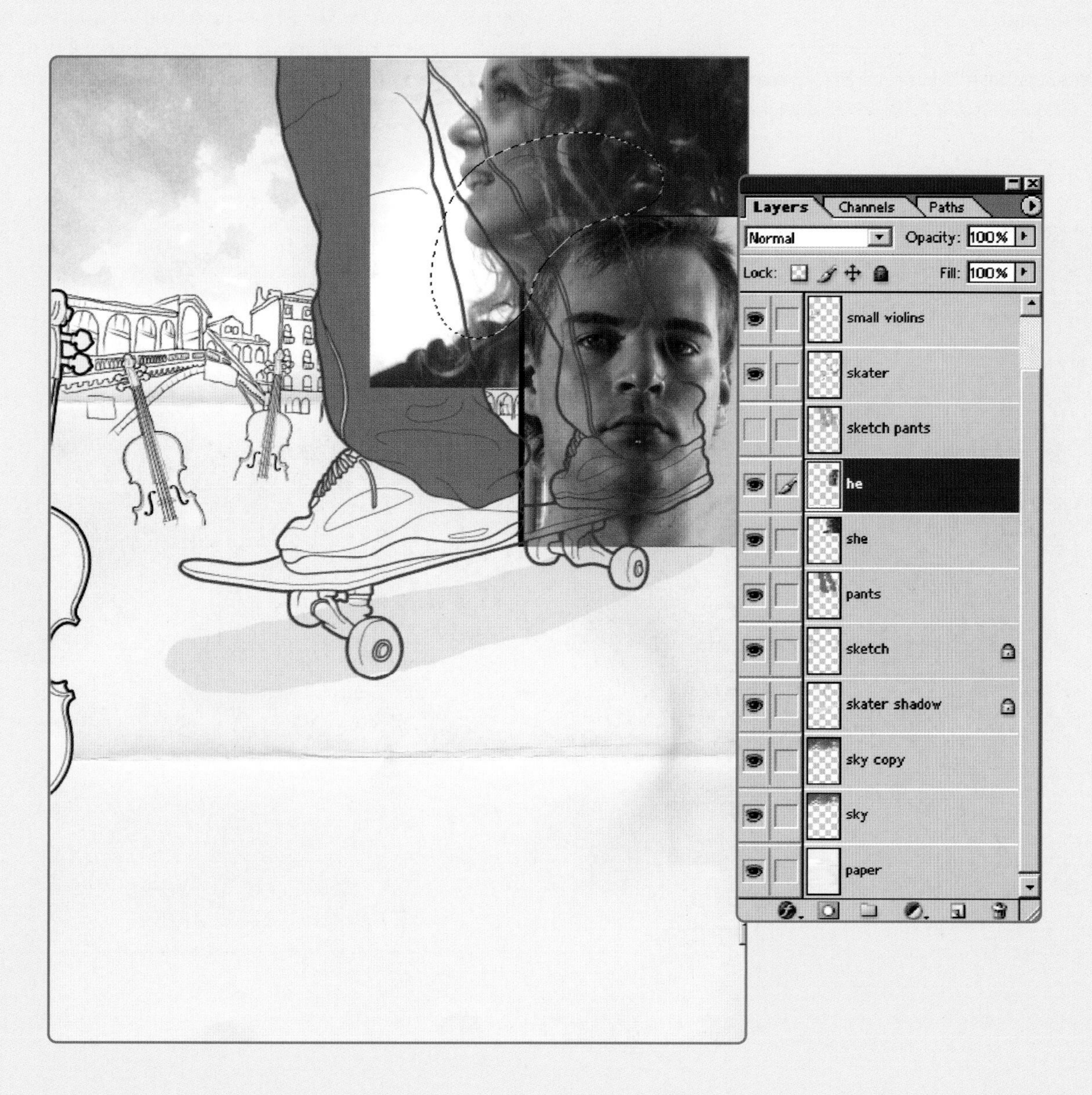

Merge the he and she layers together (select the he layer and go to Layer ➤ Merge Down), and call this merged layer "couple". The object now is to get rid of the areas of the couple photo that are outside of the right trouser leg outline. Select the skater layer and use the Magic Wand tool to select the right leg of the trousers. Expand this selection by 1 pixel (Select ➤ Modify ➤ Expand).

Leave the selection active, select the couple layer, and choose Layer ➤ Add Layer Mask ➤ Reveal Selection. There you go.

We absolutely need masks to work effectively with Photosho Thanks to the masks, you don't have to cut images accurate every time. You can create selections and place images insic them without using difficult procedures. Here, the result creat a spot in the image that tells the story of the movie; this portio tries to give the audience a preview of the relationship betwee the two characters. My aim is to create an impression of th possible feeling of the movie, to convey some sort of emotio (love, homesickness, pain, tension, happiness, etc.) with the tw images.

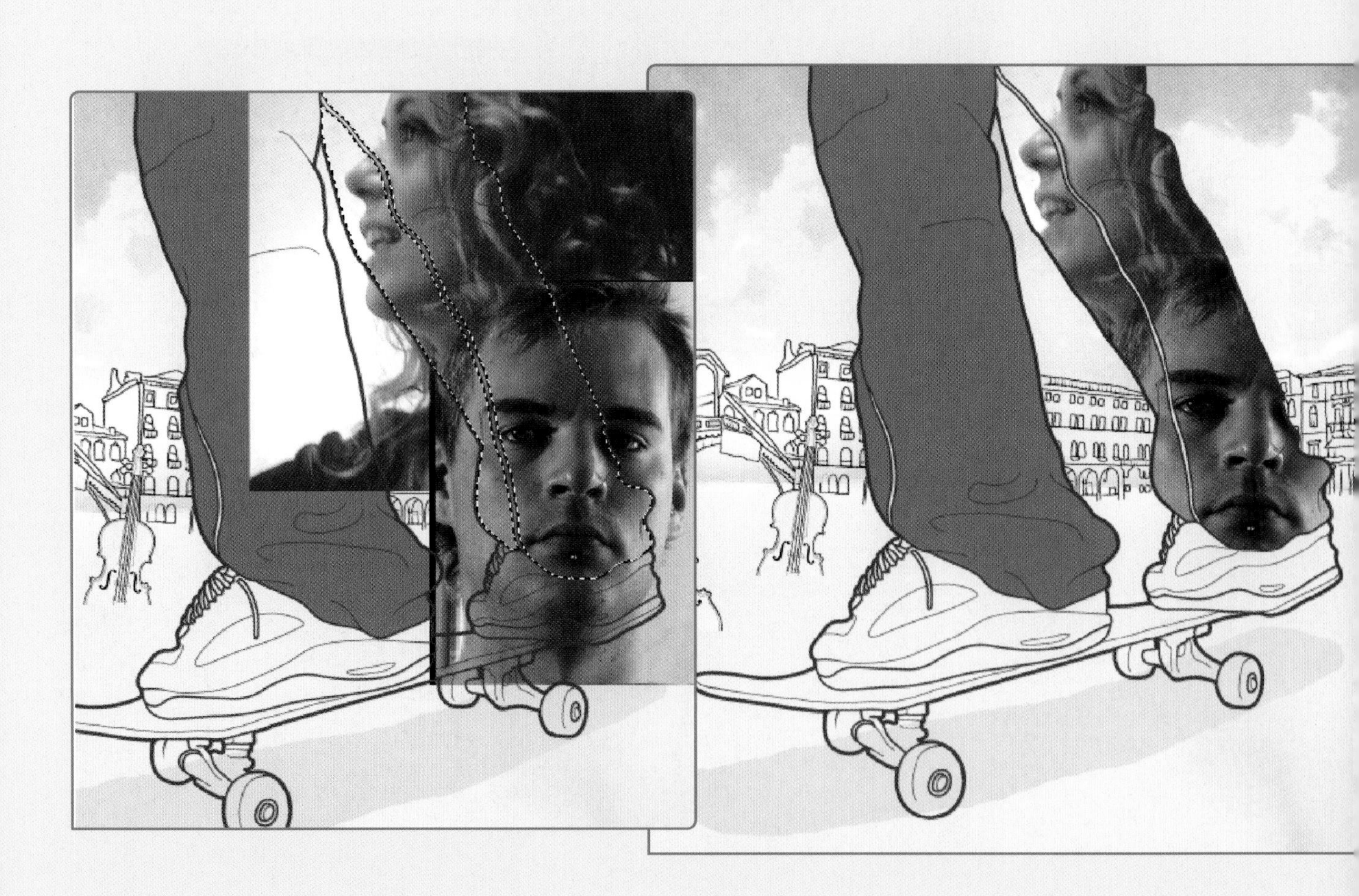

ow repeat the same process for the skater's left leg, but this me, use the source file `fenice.jpg`. First, copy it and edit it the proper spot. Add the mask to this layer as well (I called fenice) using the same method of masking as you did for the ouple layer, which ensures that you create the mask for the left g only.

Now that both the right and left images inside the legs are ready, let's try to create a unique visual sense for the couple and fenice layers using duplication and layer effects.

Select the fenice layer and switch the blending mode from Normal to Soft Light. Then duplicate this fenice copy layer and edit the levels (CTRL+L), as shown in the dialog box in the image below. The use of levels helps create a good contrast between the dark and light areas of the image. By editing the levels at this point, you will find it easier to then add luminous effects that work on the light parts of the image.

I want the current image to have a unique color different fro white or black. I chose the green color in this step because i similar to the general color of the photographic work of t other leg. Use the Hue/Saturation controls (CTRL+U) to ma the fenice copy layer look like the image below. Ensure Colori is checked when you're modifying the colors.

l the polishing you do to the image depends on the look and e mood you want to give to your composition. You can just periment with colors, saturation, and opacity, or you can use e filters to find your own solution, perhaps even the one that ou had in mind from the start.

t this point, I always try to experiment to find new solutions, ich as duplications, and changing just a simple layer blending ode to see what results.

For this work, I am going for an unsaturated, luminous, and plain effect at the same time, using just a small group of colors.

Now it's time to edit the couple layer. Use less saturation (–25) in the Hue/Saturation dialog box and change the blending mode from Normal to Soft Light, and then duplicate the layer twice.

Select the sketch pants layer and fill it with a strong yellow color using Edit ➤ Fill, not forgetting to check Preserve Transparency in the Fill dialog box. This yellow color will help give a luminous effect to the whole image.

Move the sketch pants layer above the pants layer, change t sketch pants' layer opacity to 50 percent, and change its lay blending mode from Normal to Luminosity. Now change t lightness of the pants layer to –25 in the Hue/Saturation dial box (CTRL+U).

y working on the sketch pants layer (editing and duplicating it few times), I'll get a handmade effect on the photographic omposition of the trousers. This way, I can create a link etween the playbill illustrations (the landscape, skater, and olins) and the photographic composition. In the next few eps, we're going to work on the sketch pants layer in different ays; in particular, we'll work on its position and its levels to make the effect we want for the image more evident and lighter, but without being too strong for our composition.

Duplicate the sketch pants layer and put this copy under the skater layer. Change its blending mode from Luminosity to Screen, and its opacity from 50 percent to 25 percent.

Duplicate the sketch pants copy layer. Change the opacity from 25 percent to 15 percent and the layer blending mode from Screen to Normal. Above this, create another level called "gradient". Choose the color and select the Gradient tool (G). In the Gradient tool options, select the Foreground to Transparent option and draw a vertical gradient on your image. I choose light color for the gradients to once again increase the luminou impact of the image. Also, thanks to this gradient, a feeling bottom to top directional luminosity is created. All this work useful to obtain life from the images.

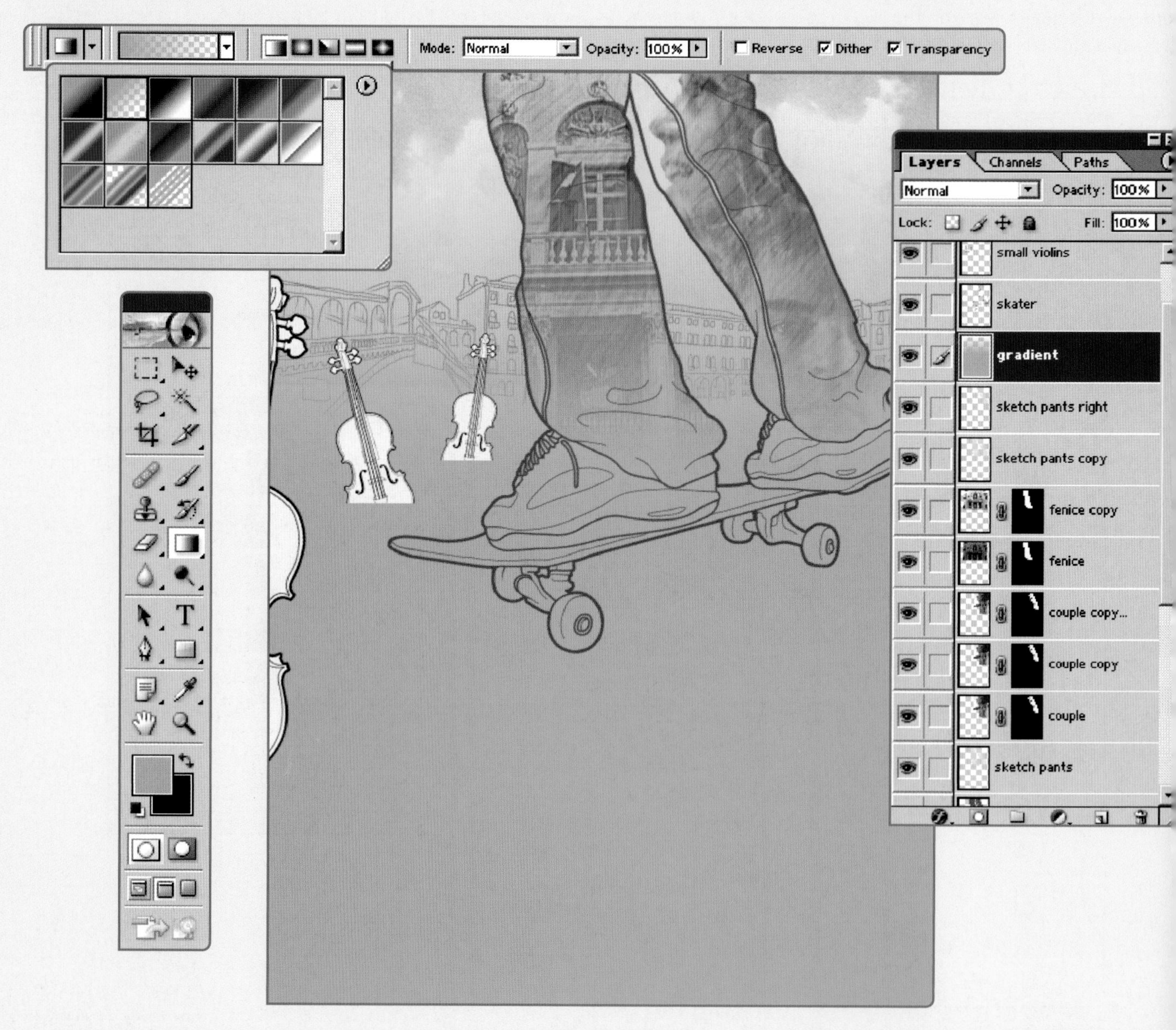

ow select the pants layer and load your pants selection that u saved earlier in the tutorial (Select ➤ Load Selection). Now u have the selection available to create a mask in the gradient yer. On the gradient layer, make the mask using Layer ➤ Add yer Mask ➤ Reveal Selection. Also change the blending mode om Normal to Hue.

After all these steps, I've got a handmade effect for the photocomposition. As you can see, there is a color difference between the left and right legs. Let's try to make the colors similar to create a well-defined visual spot.

Now to melt the colors, duplicate the pants layer and put it under the skater layer. Fill it with a dark blue color and set the layer blending mode from Normal to Saturation.

Duplicate this layer, fill it with a lighter color, change the opaci from 100 percent to 50 percent, and change the blending mod to Color Burn.

ow that the colors inside the legs are similar, let's move on and eate a texture to make the images appear rougher to fit in ith the idea of collage and sketch. Open `texture.jpg` from e CD, copy and place it in your working PSD just below the ater layer. Use your pants selection to create the same layer ask like you did for the gradient layer (Layer ➤ Add Layer Mask ➤ Reveal Selection). Also change the blending mode of this layer mask from Normal to Linear Light, and change the opacity to 40 percent.

To underline the contrast of the image in the right leg, duplicate the couple layer.

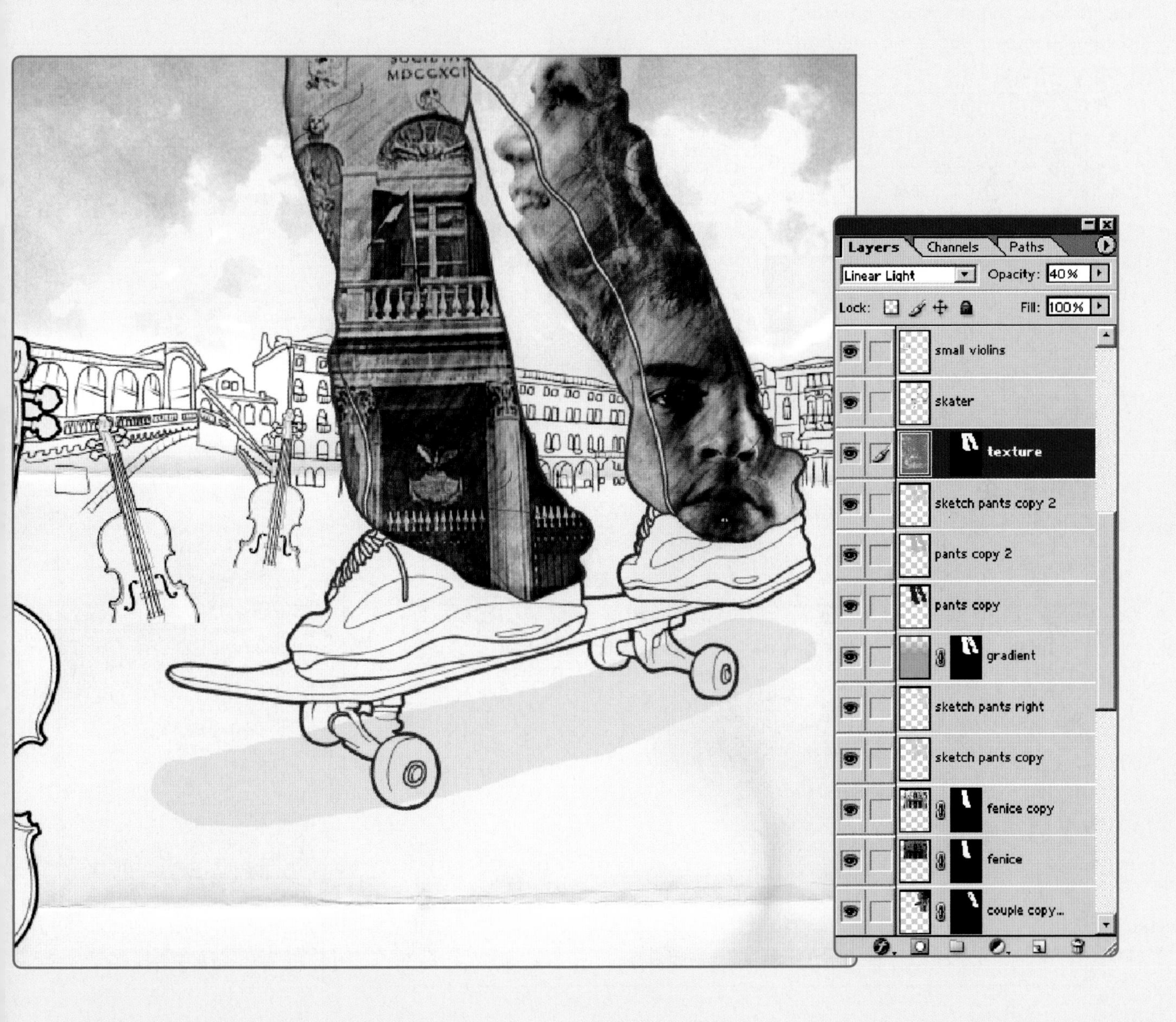

Using textures is one of my favorite processes. The effects are really interesting and you can achieve all sorts of them. For example, you can make an image look older (using a texture made of sheets taken from old books) or brighter (using a metallic texture, for instance).

Now let's add something to make the image a little brighter. Create a new layer above the sketch pants layer called "light".

With the Lasso tool, create a selection with Feather set at 2 percent. Fill the selection with solid white (Edit ➤ Fill).

As you did with the texture layer, make light a layer mask usin the saved pants selection. Change the layer blending mode fror Normal to Screen, and the opacity to 80 percent.

'eate a new layer right at the top of
›ur Layers palette called "light2".
gain, create a selection with the Lasso
ol, but set Feather to 30 percent this
ne.

ll this selection with a light
ay color, and change the
ending mode to Hard
ght.

epeat this process for
ıother new layer called
ight3" under the skater
yer. This time I create two
tle selections with the
ısso tool.

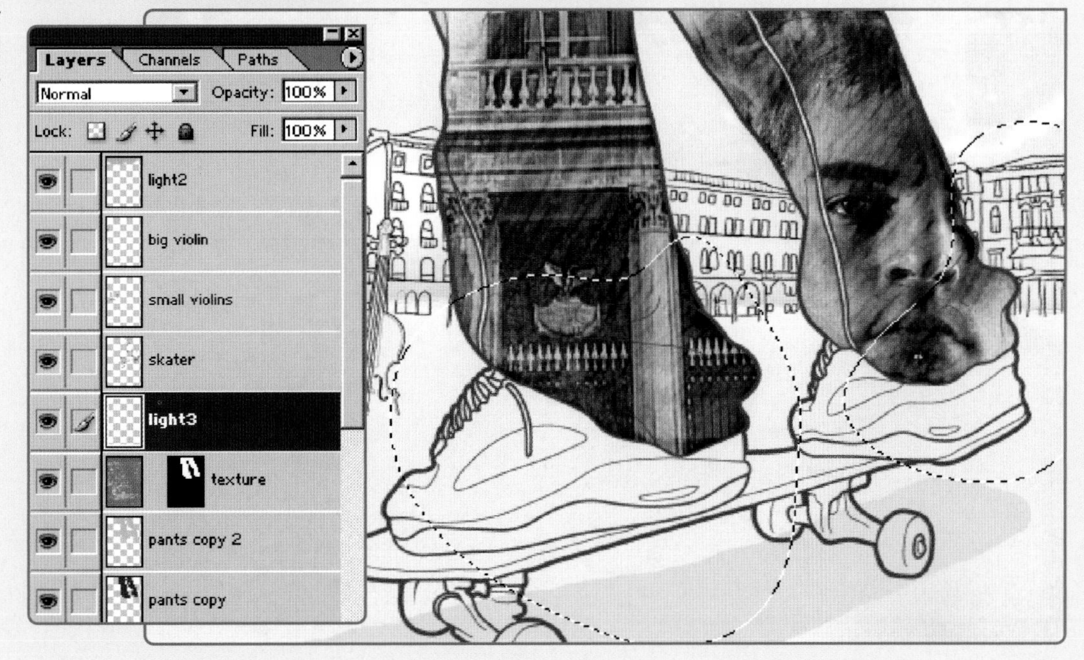

Make a layer mask using the pants selection, as you've done previously, to get the result you can see here:

Now it's time to increase the image luminosity and to strengthe some effects (i.e., the handmade effect of the composition).

uplicate the sketch pants layer, placing the copy beneath the xture layer. Change the blending mode from Luminosity to ue, and decrease the opacity to 35 percent. Select the pants yer and, using the Hue/Saturation dialog box (CTRL+U), ecrease the Luminosity to 35.

Now we'll add some lighting effects to the image using a simple gradient. Create a new level called "glow" above the light2 layer. Select the Gradient tool (G). Create a yellow foreground to transparent gradient and change the gradient type to Radial in the tool options.

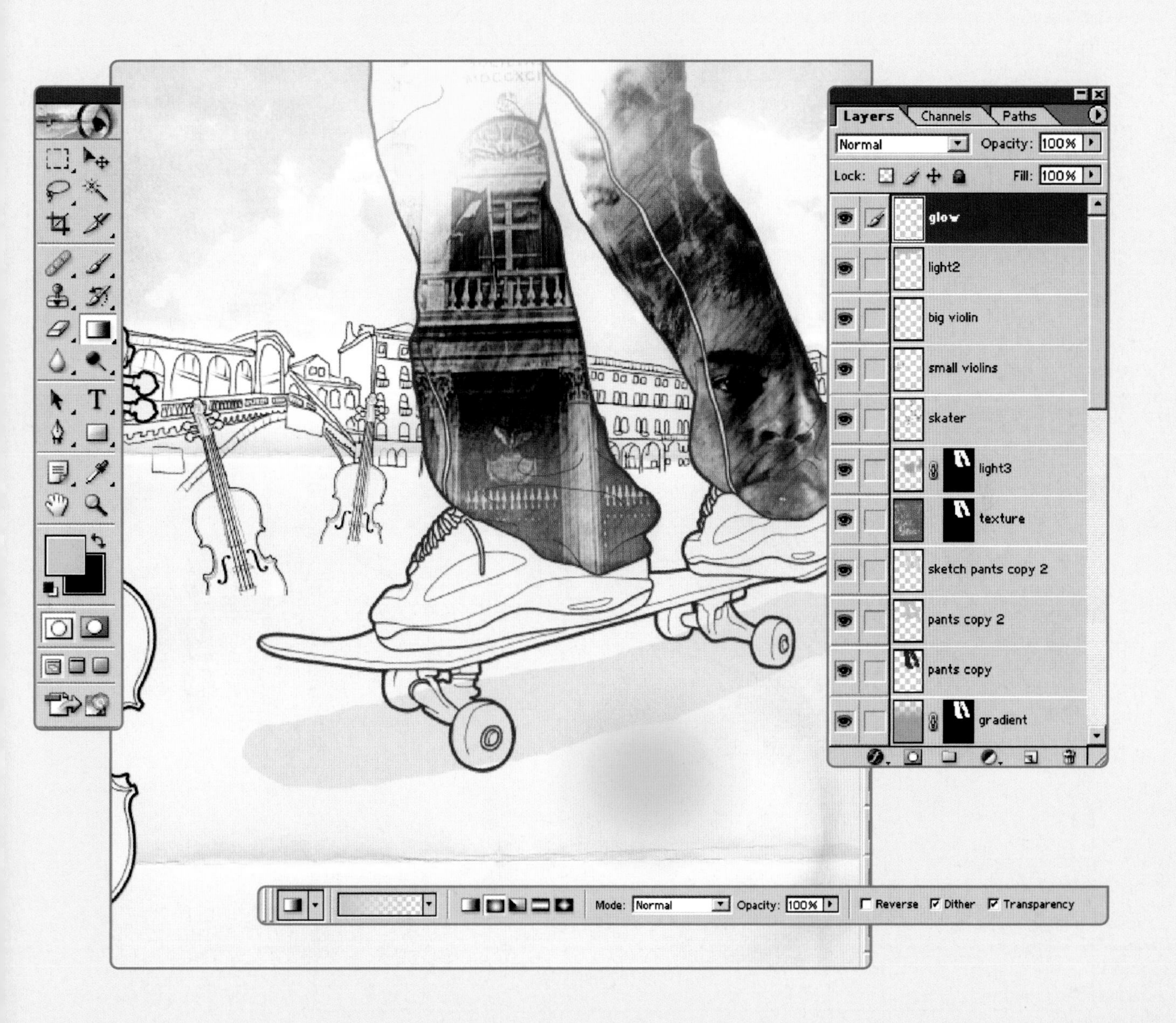

Change the blending mode from Normal to Linear Dodge and place the gradient in the image where you would like a luminous point. I duplicated the layer in order to have many luminous points scattered around the image. You can change these lighting effects using different gradients, textures, or opacity settings. Decide what looks best in your work depending on the material you need and the main effect you are trying to achieve.

The lighting and imagery is complete. As you can see, the imag has a large space at the bottom to both the left and right of th image. These areas have been intentionally left blank so that nc too much of the poster is filled with imagery. This leaves spac for an imaginary horizon, the logo, and text.

o it's now time to work on the composition of text and logos for ie poster. The title, the largest piece of text is "Un Futuro icostruito" (A Reconstructed Future). One solution for displaying iis is to place the three words on solid color blocks, so go ahead nd create three defined areas where the text will be prominent. reate a new level called "text base" above the light2 layer and raw three rectangular selections with the Rectangular Marquee ɔol (M).

Fill this selection with a light green color, and change the layer blending mode from Normal to Multiply. Now add in some text for the poster on a new layer called "text" above the text base layer. I put the main title in block capitals and all of the background information in a smaller size.

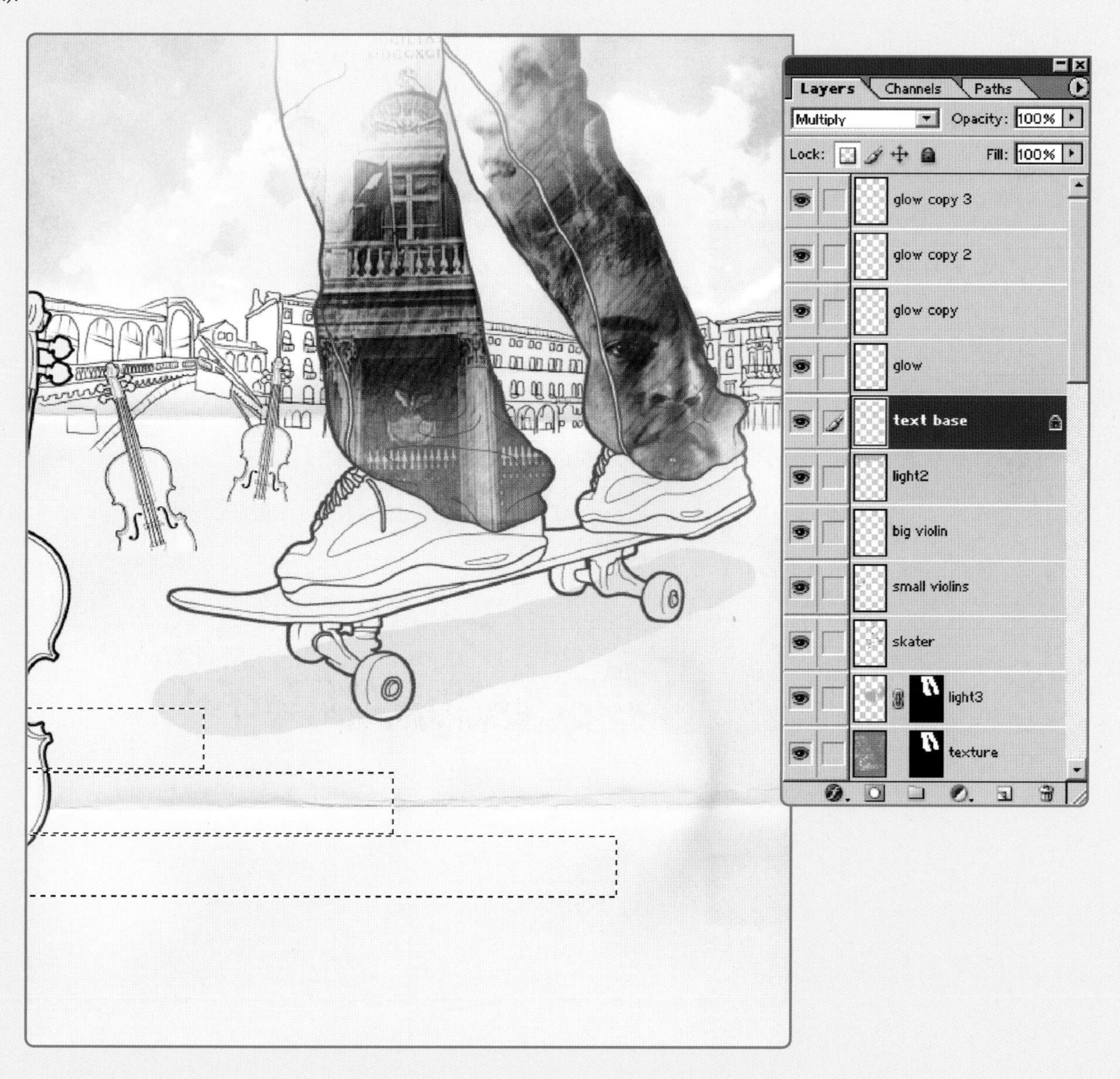

The style I used for the text helps create a harmony with the image style as well. The alternation of bold and regular characters and a little magnification give the text a raw feel, perfectly matching the general style of the poster. I also added three small logos on a new layer called "logos".

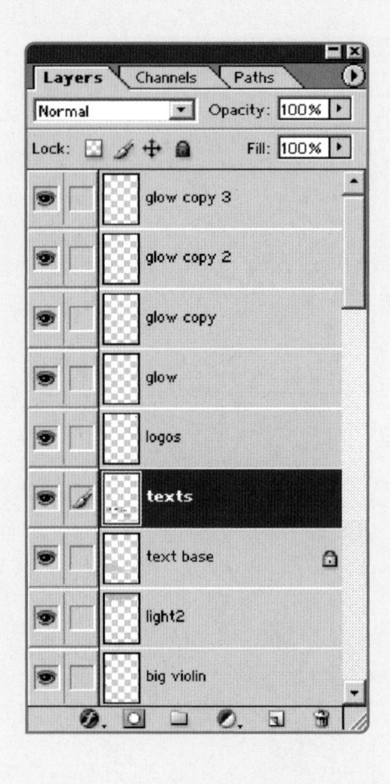

ıally, I decided to make the sky more intense. I did ıis by duplicating the sky layer and changing the ending mode from Pin Light to Overlay. Next, I ıplicated the texture layer, changed its opacity to 70 ercent, and changed the blending mode to Saturation.

; I said before, duplicating levels and experimenting th the available filters can increase the tone of your ıage. Once you've finished your image, try to work ı the overall levels and you will see that sometimes ou can reach outstanding results.

ıe last thing to do is convert the image from RGB to MYK because this is a poster destined for print nage ➤ Mode ➤ CMYK Color). Now the file is ready r printing.

ecause I had to produce this piece in a single day, I ıly focused on creating a well-balanced and pressive image. I needed to combine different visual ements in one program in a short space of time. It oes without saying that if I had had more time, I ould have certainly come up with a better idea, or I ould have polished the images with more accurate fects. But, for me, the greatness of Photoshop is in its otential to create great work even in a short neframe. If I had had to hand draw, scan, set, polish, ıd erase the borders, it would have taken three times e time it took to create this poster in Photoshop. All e procedures to create the poster are simple ıotoshop procedures that, if mixed well, can produce ıtstanding effects even with a few tools. If you pay tention to the lighting, typography, and color choice, ou've already accomplished a considerable part of e work.

think that there are 100 ways to reach the same sult, that everyone develops 100 procedures in their wn work field, and there are 100 solutions for each ea. It doesn't matter when we reach those solutions ıt how we reach them.

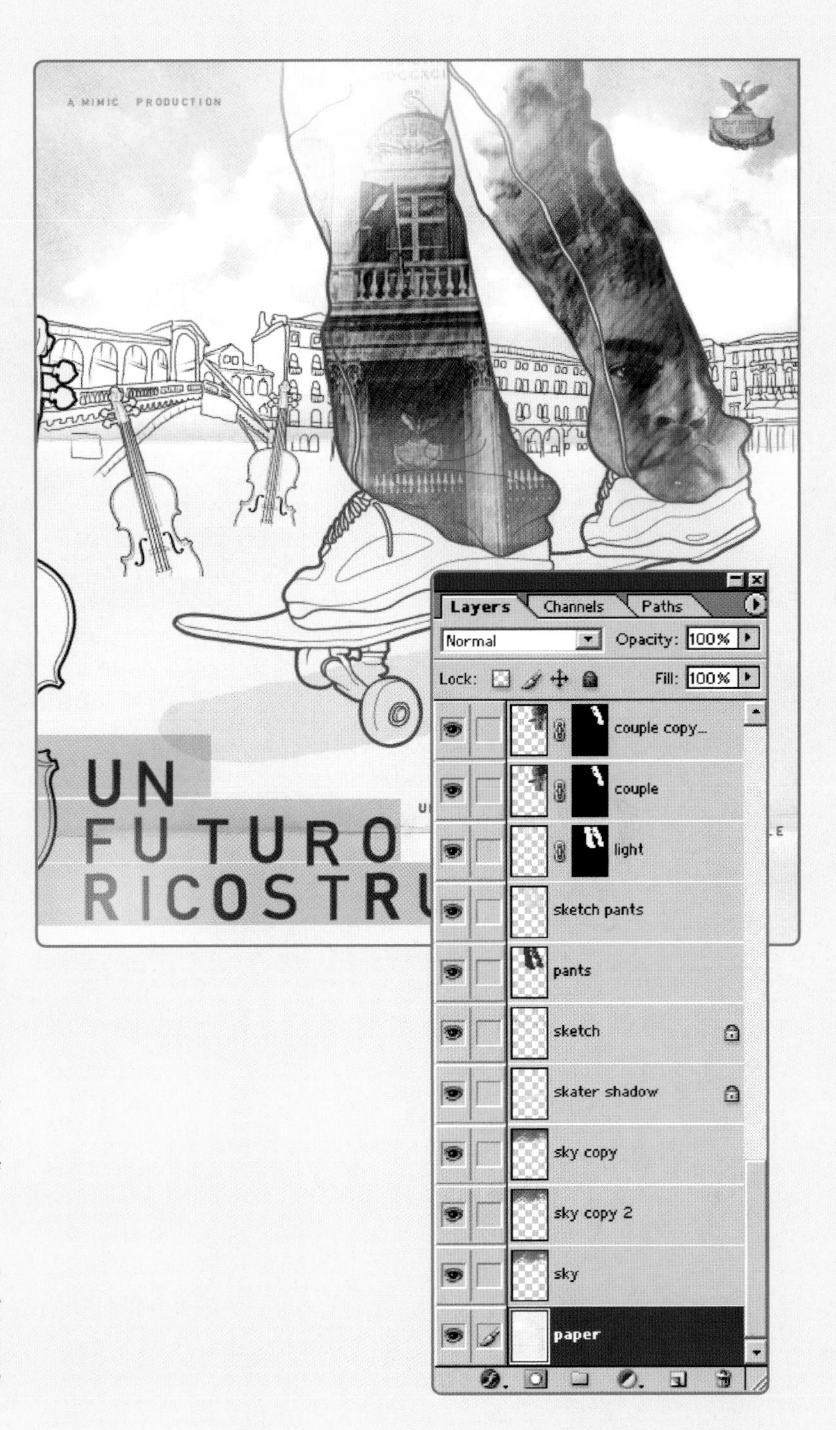

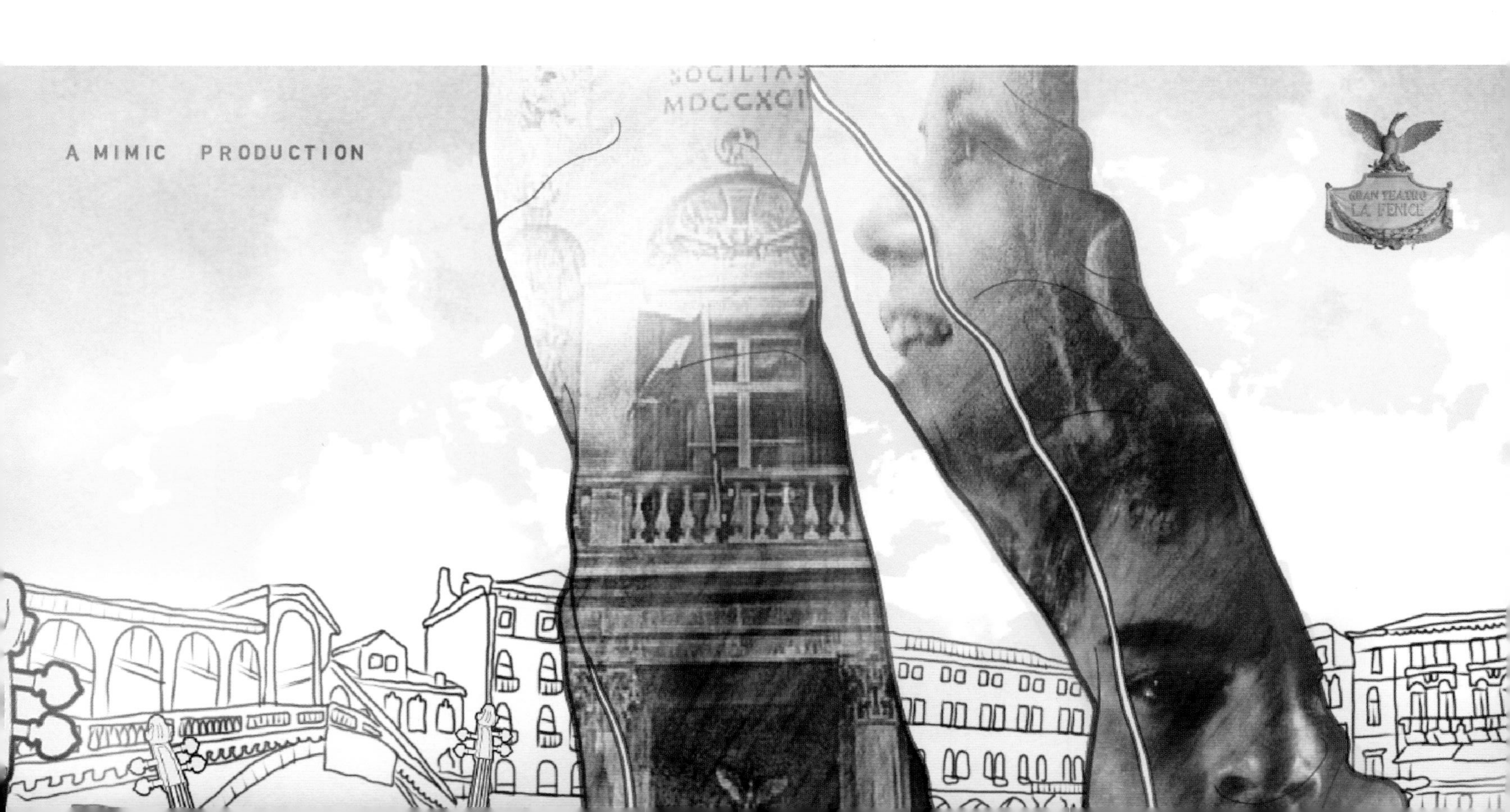
A MIMIC PRODUCTION
MDCCXCI
GRAN TEATRO
LA FENICE

UN FUTURO RICOSTRUITO

UN FILM SU CIO' CHE L'AMORE RENDE MISTERIOSAMENTE POSSIBILE

A RECONSTRUCTED FUTURE

UNA PRODUZIONE MIMIC DIGITAL CONTENTS

SCRITTO E DIRETTO DA LORENZO MIGLIOLI

CO DIRETTO DA LUIGI TUFANO

CON GIULIO PESENTI ED ELISA ALLORO

CON LA PARTECIPAZIONE DI

ATTILIO TONIOLO, LORENZO MIGLIOLI E

CATERINA VIANELLO

PRODUTTORE ESECUTIVO: ANDREA TONIOLO
DIREZIONE ARTISTICA/SUPERVISORE EFFETTI SPECIALI: MAURO GATTI
EFFETTI SPECIALI: PATRICK SUNDQVIST E JAMES WIDEGREN
DIRETTORE DELLA FOTOGRAFIA: FRANCESCO VITALI
OPERATORE DI RIPRESA: VALERIO PELLICIOLI
FONICO: PAOLO FERRARIO
SEGRETARIA DI EDIZIONE: CATERINA VIANELLO
TRUCCO: VALERIA CHESSA
MUSICHE: MAXIMILIANO "MOG" FACCIO
MONTAGGIO: LUIGI TUFANO
RESPONSABILE TECNOLOGIE DIGITALI: LORENZO MANFREDI

BARCA PER RIPRESE: BRUNO BELLINI
TAXI SU STRADA: ATTILIO TONIOLO
TAXI SU ACQUA: MAURO VIANELLO
ELETTRICISTA: MASSIMO RIATO

06 GRUNGE

PERHAPS IT IS THE SHOCK VALUE, BUT I WOULD RATHER HAVE THE VIEWER CRITICIZE MY WORK THAN JUST PASS OVER IT.
JASON MORRISON
WWW.DUBTASTIC.COM

Origins

My background in art reaches as far back as my memory. In fact, my earliest memory of venturing into anything artistic is in second grade, when I created my own Transformers and Go-Bots using green Staedtler professional templates. In elementary school, we were given a choice of either going to band or art class, and it was not a difficult decision for me to make. I was able to develop and nurture my creative side throughout elementary school, middle school, and into high school, where I enrolled in as many art classes as I was allowed. In college, my initial goal was to obtain an art degree; however, when I was confronted with the thought of becoming a "starving artist," I altered my plan; I finished an associate degree in art and then moved on to get a bachelor's degree in business. My last years in high school and my development in college helped me forge an understanding of art, composition, color theory, and so on, that has helped my digital work to no end. In high school, I racked up accolades such as "Art Student of the Year," was voted "Most Artistic" as a senior, and was nominated for Governor's Honors two years in a row. I had made a lot of progress, but still had a long road ahead.

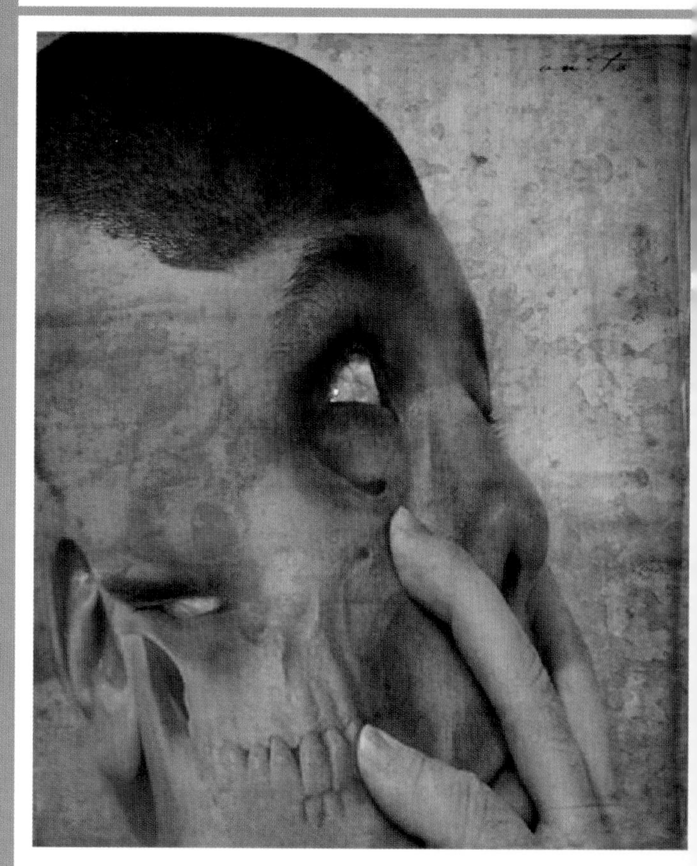

It was during a special project in college that I was first exposed to digital art. The project involved self-portrait work with a photograph that we had developed during a previous project. My experiments were merely that—experiments. They consisted primarily of very tacky filter usage on the photos I took. Even though I had absolutely no idea what I was doing and applied the effects just for the sake of applying them, it was still an eye-opening experience because it was the first time I had done anything along those lines. I can remember submitting a notebook full of some of the worst "photoshopped" images the world has seen to date.

Candid Strangers

It was this exposure to the digital world that, when combined with my love of art and computers, resulted in a beautiful marriage. From there, I began to look into creating a website for myself, mainly to portray some personal information and to provide a small showcase for the earliest of my digital experiments, before I would even call them art. This showcase became yet another launching pad for the work that I am doing today.

Displaying my work on the Web, and more important interacting with others on bulletin boards, really brought th "critique" element back into my artistic process, and I quick realized how much I had missed it. The bulletin board componen also resulted in many lost hours of endlessly searching an viewing other's artwork, wondering how in the world the produced a certain effect. I quickly latched on to the dark themed images and sought to define a certain style as my own

Chapter 14

hat style was one born out of several inspirational areas and ne that I quickly came to enjoy. I have a great deal of respect or anyone with true artistic abilities; however, the darker and irtier images that are twisted and contorted typically hold my nterest much longer than other types of art. For me, there are o emotions or reactions when I look at a painting of a mountain tream, horses running wild in a field, a sunrise, or any other imilar scene; this is why I create the type of work that I create. erhaps it is the shock value, but I would rather have the viewer riticize my work than just pass over it, not even giving it two econds' thought. When I sit down to create my images, I find nyself utilizing the dirt and grunge along with certain darker nemes to create not only the image that I wish to create, but a eeling or reaction in the viewer. I want them to look at my work nd wonder what was going through my mind that would have aused me to create such an image. I want them to argue, iscuss, feel, and live. Art should conjure up emotions, not just ook good hanging in a frame in a living room.

he end result has been Dubtastic Design Labs (www.dubtastic.com), ny personal site, which has been online and kicking for several ears now. Everyone wants to know where the name "Dubtastic" ame from. When I was in college, my friends and I all had some eally crazy nicknames for each other. For those of you who sten to hip-hop, you should be familiar with the group EPMD, ut more so, one half of EPMD—Erick Sermon. Erick Sermon carried the title of "E-Double the Green-Eyed Bandit" and I always thought that was rather clever. Soon after, I became "J-Double the Brown-Eyed Bandit." Of course, that was much too much to say in any sentence, so it was shortened to J-Double, then to J-Dub, and then finally to just Dub. The first domain name I registered was just my real name, but I wanted to incorporate my nickname somehow into the domain and the identity of the site. Dubtastic just hit me and that was what I registered. I thought that it would be different than a lot of the other popular graphic domain names at the time and would be something that people might remember.

Since then, I have watched as traffic and bandwidth consumption have increased along with my artistic skill set. Through this site, I have been able to not only help promote my own work, but also help other aspiring artists. The sharing of resources via the Web is a great way for artists to share with each other, which is why I try to publish any and all resources that I can through my site, such as the brushes and tutorials. I remember scouring the Internet looking for Photoshop brushes to use in my work, and at the time, it was difficult to locate them. With the Internet the way it is today, you will find it very easy to find many tools to use in your own work. I am pleased that Dubtastic has not only developed into a growing portfolio site showcasing my work and ability, but that it is also a site that is deemed helpful and is bookmarked for its resources.

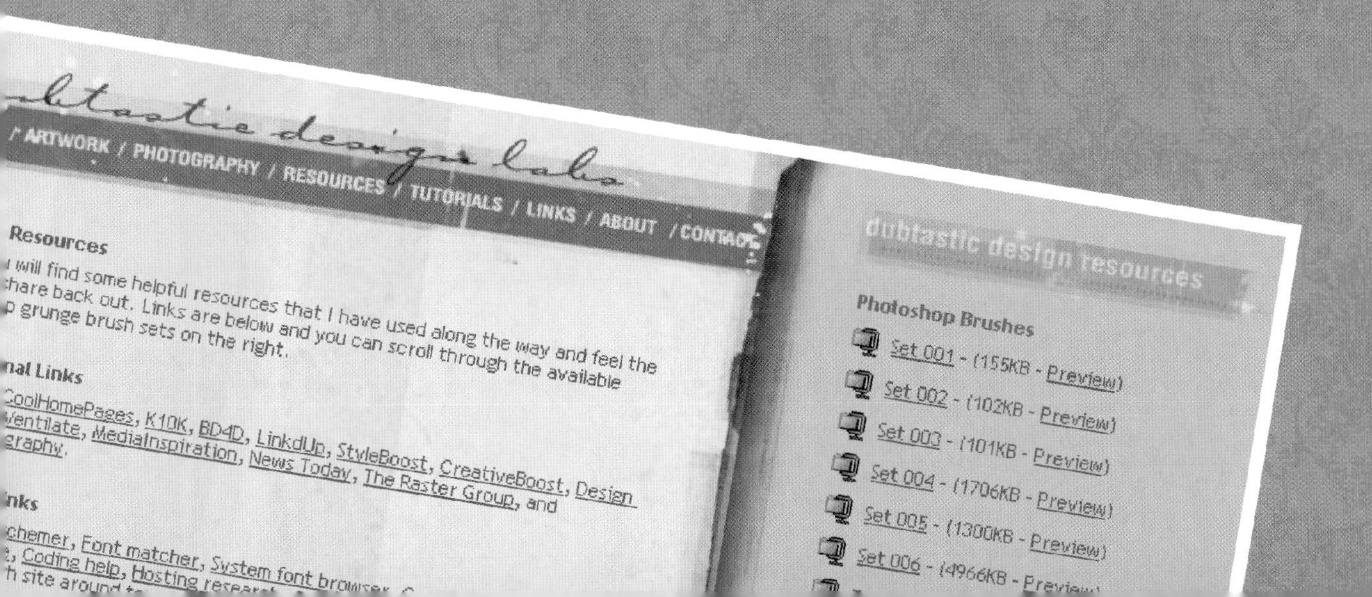

Those that inspire

Art history bored me to tears. Granted, studying the works of artists past gave me a better grasp of where art once was and how it developed over time, yet very few artists interested me. If I were confronted with selecting a "traditional" artist whose work I found intriguing, I would more than likely have selected an artist from the Impressionist or Surrealist periods, though naming one would have proved a difficult task. This isn't to say that those who came before me possessed little ability or talent, as certainly only the opposite is true. In fact, in college, being exposed to many different media gave me a greater appreciation for these older artists. However, my primary inspirations lie in modern artists—those who are still actively producing work.

As far as modern artists go, what can be said about Dennis Sibeijn (www.damnengine.net) that hasn't already been said? I first encountered Dennis through his posts on the bulletin board at www.designsbymark.com; he gave me new inspiration with his unique style. At the time, I was still a digital art infant, and I was in awe of his work—mainly because of the thoughts that drove his creative process, but also because of the high quality work that he was producing. Dennis displayed powerful and thought-provoking work that was way above a vast number of other artists, and his desire to create and produce was inspirational. If I remember correctly, it had become quite popular to use 3D applications to create random shapes and vividly colored images, which never appealed to my artistic side. Dennis's work offered a refreshing alternative to that, one that I hung on to.

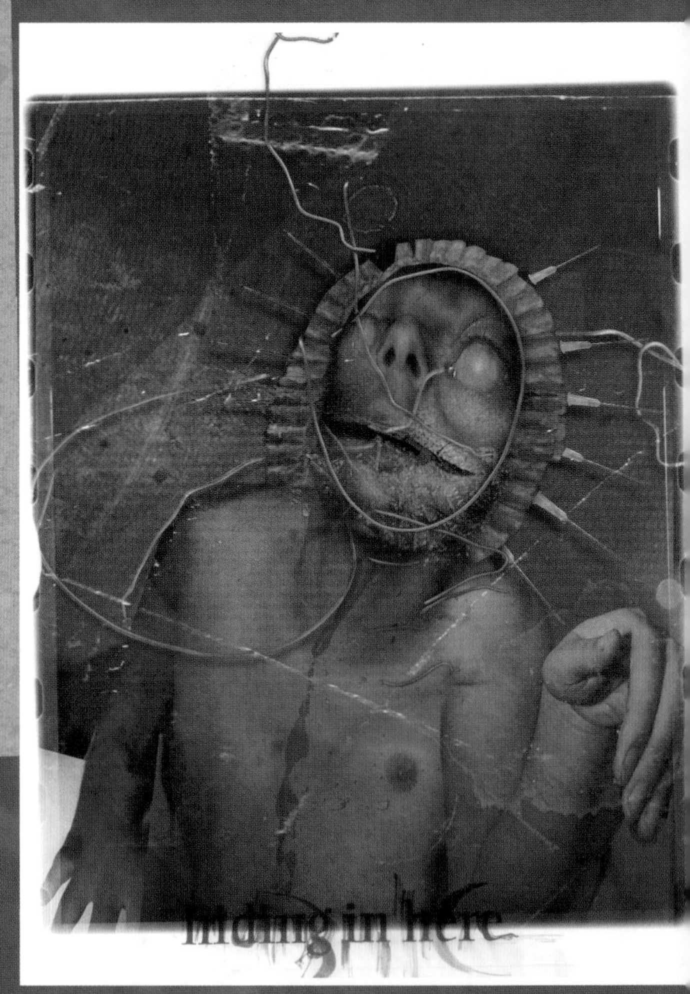

Hiding In Here by Dennis Sibeijn www.damnengine.ne

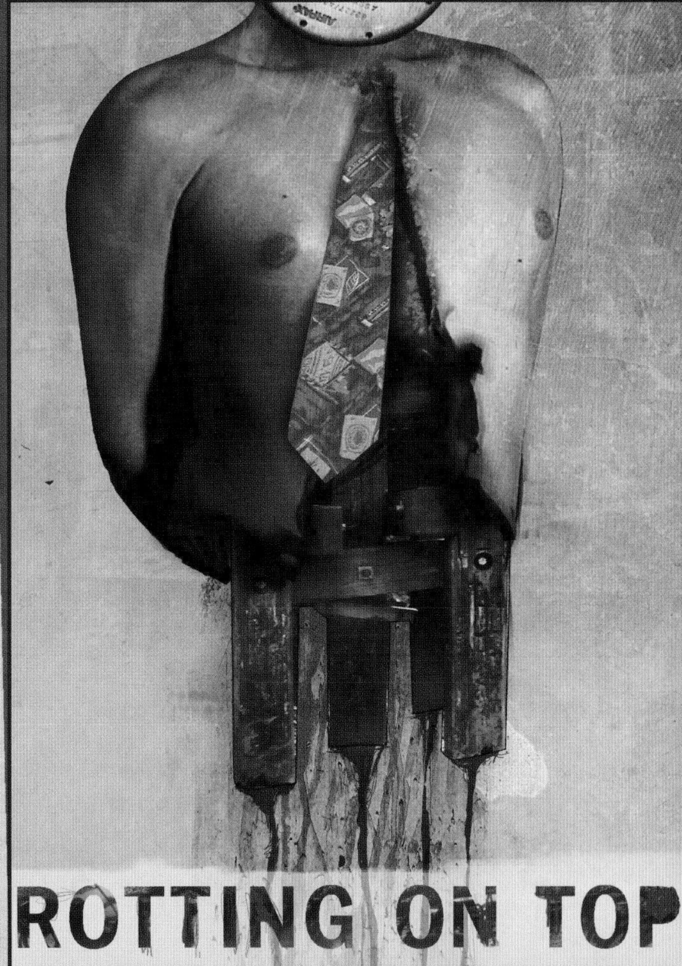

Chairman by Dennis Sibeijn www.damnengine.net

believe one of the things that attracted me to Dennis's work, nd one of the reasons that I found his creations so well put ogether, was his use of typography. Many times, his images ould not even contain a title or text anywhere in the image, llowing the image to speak for itself. Even when he opted to nclude type in his work, it was never an afterthought but always ffectively and seamlessly integrated into the image. In fact, it ecame another component in the image and not something hat sat on top of the work obstructing the message. This ecame a model, if you will, for me and how I use certain omponents within my work. One of those components is runge, which I will be discussing later, and how it should be just nother component in your work and not a dominating factor hat overpowers the image.

ince that time, Dennis has continued to produce fabulous art s well as inspire many other artists. His combination of hotography, 3D elements, and wonderfully contorted ompositions provided a needed push for the work that I really anted to do. I had grown tired of still life shots, painting of utterflies and rainbows, and happy little animals. Dennis was ne of the artists who helped paved the way for others to reate a different style of work, and to do it effectively.

Evergreen by Chris Arlidge www.steeldolphin.com

St Michael, digital painting courtesy Chris Arlidge www.steeldolphin.com

My interaction with Chris Arlidge (www.steeldolphin.com) has been another source of inspiration for my work. At first glance, it might be difficult to see how Chris's artwork has influenced mine, because the majority of work on display in his portfolio is not something that would typically be classified as grunge. When I first "met" Chris, it was via a bulletin board, and right away it was clear that the guy knew what he was talking about. His talent and skill level was one that I wanted to strive for. Chris held a certain mastery of compositions, colors, and several design applications that has always been a source of inspiration for me.

The inspiration I draw from Steel Dolphin is two-fold. First, Chris's creativity seems to know no bounds, and he is certainly not limited to using a single application to produce his work. With each new work, I am consistently impressed with his overall grasp of design and art. Without knowing it, Chris has instilled a desire in me to increase my knowledge about more applications, to learn how to take my art to new levels with more tools, and to learn how to improve the overall presentation of all of my work. These are all elements in which he excels.

Secondly, by getting to know him, I've come to benefit from h critiques of my work, which have helped push my work eve further. Having access to a resource such as Chris—where I ar able to show him progressions of my work or even the fin product, and receive a very honest and knowledgeable critiqu from an industry professional—has proven invaluable to m creative process.

As my work evolves and grows, I find myself wanting to mov my talents into new areas. One of those areas has been digit painting. I am currently planning to bring my darker theme work and grunge element playkit to the forefront an incorporate them into digital painting. Chris has more tha ample experience with digital painting, and again, has mastere it in a way that makes me have the greatest respect for him.

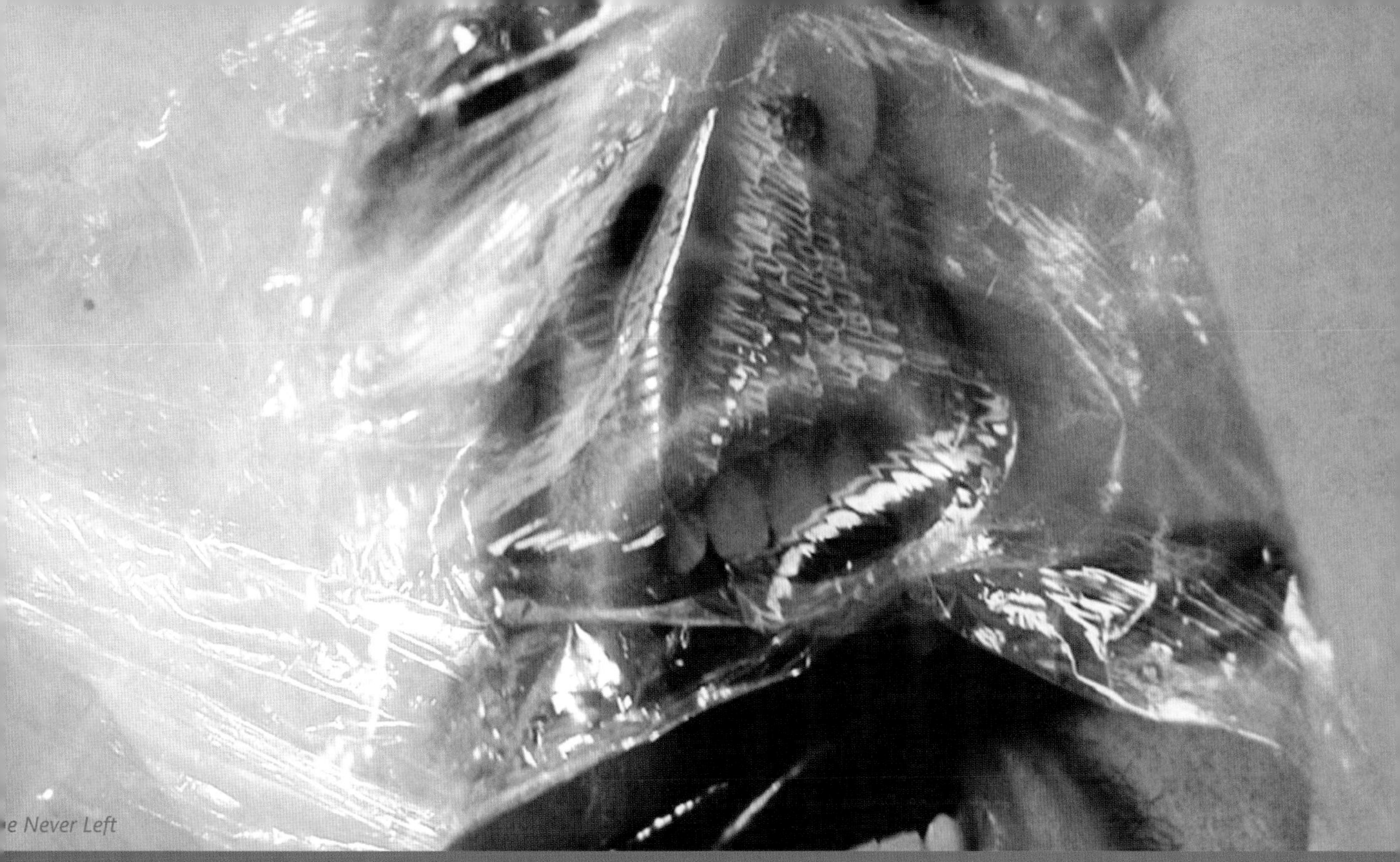

e Never Left

ne other major source of inspiration for my work is in my ind, or more specifically, my memories. I've found that eping an old photo album and journal nearby produces some eative results. First, by flipping through a photo album, I've und that I can access various memories. For instance, I might member a special vacation I took with my parents or mething not as positive, such as a family member getting sick. o matter what the emotion, it is great to latch on to it and use as a catalyst for my work. When I find myself in a creative rut, metimes it's not as helpful to look at other artists' work as it to look within and focus more on my own emotions and oughts. OK, so you might be thinking to yourself, "Why is ost of your work dark then? Are your photo albums filled with ally bad pictures?" That is not the case at all; however, I do n across an occasional bad memory or two.

r example, take the image you see here, entitled "She Never ft," which was affectionately inspired by an ex-girlfriend. hile flipping through some stacks of old photos, I came across few pictures of her and the hair on the back of my neck mediately began to stand on end. By just looking at the otograph, I was immediately reminded of feelings and notions that had been buried away in the recesses of my mind. I was able to take a bad memory and use it to my advantage; the result was this creation. Many have asked me why I titled it the way that I did, because when you first glance at the image, it appears to be just a mangled face. That is actually me—mangled, in every sense of the word—when I think of that certain ex-girlfriend. In our relationship, I felt distorted, disturbed, restricted, suffocated, and unable to speak. Seeing a photograph of the ex conjured up those feelings, feelings that never really left, hence the title of the image and the meaning behind it. The entire image might have been lost without stumbling across those photos!

A journal is a great idea for any artist. Some of my best ideas did not come about while sitting in front of the computer waiting for ideas. They came about while I was out driving to the store, visiting with friends, or eating at a restaurant. Carrying around a pocket journal or sketchbook and pencil may sound awkward to you, but the ends will justify the means. If you can quickly make notes or even simple sketches that you can bring to the computer later, you will find that you will not lose any of your best ideas.

Methodology

When first approached to author a chapter of *New Masters of Photoshop: Volume 2,* my reaction was one of shock combined with happiness. Soon, nervousness set in and I began to wonder how I would begin to effectively communicate the process that I follow to produce the type of work that I create. In fact, I was unsure if there actually was a method to my madness. The invitation alone caused me to sit down and really evaluate how I work. Grunge is often an element that's not defined in a certain way, created in a set process, or, more importantly, always the same within each image. This might be why I've never had a grunge tutorial on dubtastic.com.

Before I get started creating one of my works, the most important questions I have to ask are "What am I going to create?" and "How will I apply the grunge in the image?" Never open Photoshop with a blank canvas and just fill the white space. If it has a purpose, message, theme, or reason for being created, your work will have much more power and presence, especially when compared to something that is blindly created for the sake of filling up the canvas.

The reason that I mention the question of how grunge will b applied in the image is simple. Grunge effects are too oft misapplied; so much so that the grunge itself takes over a becomes the focal point of the artwork. Any time a compone of the work becomes the focal point instead of just another to used to convey the overall message, the artwork has failed some degree or, at the very least, has become less effectiv Grunge is a great tool to use, though, because it can effective cover blemishes in blending and other problem areas witho calling attention to them. The trouble occurs when it's used much—such as when it is used as a dominant texture overlay that when you first look at the image, you begin to think mo about the grunge than what the artist was feeling when th created the image. One of the reasons that grunge has co under fire is because its popularity and use on the Internet h resulted in a stereotype—that it is used simply to cover up t lack of proper blending and general lack of Photosh knowledge with textures and dirt. The grunge work has beco almost synonymous with "horror" or "dark" images, a although some of these labels are justified, some artists o there effectively use grunge; labeling their work as meaningle and "covered up" isn't warranted.

Next, you need to consider the title of your work and how th title will become a part of the image, if at all. I have seen ma excellent images that became too distracting once their ti was placed in or on them. If the visual you are creating powerful enough, allow it to stand on its own and leave the ti off. However, if the title or text you wish to use contains so required meaning to your message, then by all means, inclu it. Just because you are creating art with Photoshop does n automatically mean that you must include text on the image. you opt to use text, consider your composition, colors, a overall look and feel before you place text in it. Of course, go into detail on this later in the chapter, but I'm telling you t now to get your mind around the initial concepts that I w cover in the tutorial section.

›w that I've addressed those issues, it's time to tell you about me resources you can use to create your work. Some of my st resources include textured photos and custom Photoshop ushes. As one of my sources of inspiration, Dennis Sibeijin, l tell you, it's best to have your own library of images to work th. I know for a fact that one of the reasons the artwork oduced at Damn Engine is of such high quality is that Dennis in total control of all of the stock photography that he uses his work. To create this collection of images, you will need a gital camera; such a camera quickly becomes a valuable tool stead of something that would be nice to have. To get started eating your library of grunge and dirt textures, I'd recommend king a walk one afternoon and taking random shots. Some of e best textures that I have returned to time and time again are essed concrete, bricks, dirt, and mud. If you don't have access a digital camera, then you should be able to locate several lpful stock photography resources on the Internet that have ample supply to get started. Here are just a few sites that are lpful:

- **Abnormis:** www.abnormis.com (I have uploaded some of my personal photos and textures here.)
- **DeviantART:** www.deviantart.com
- **B-STOCK:** www.stock.b-man.dk
- **Imageafter:** www.imageafter.com
- **stock.kriegsnet.com:** http://stock.kriegsnet.com
- **R3 Stock Photography Archive:** www.stock.reh3.com
- **morgueFile:** www.morguefile.com

fore you use any stock photograph that you download from e Internet, it is vital that you read all the fine print on the site u want to download from. Often, the owner of the image quests that you use the image only in a certain type of work doesn't want it to be used commercially, so be sure to uble-check prior to using it; it could save you quite a bit of ssle in the long run.

Next, a nice selection of custom Photoshop brushes would be in order. Again, the Internet is a great medium for sharing and finding resources. Here are numerous places that I would label as Photoshop brush heaven:

- **vbrush.tmp.layout:** http://veredgf.fredfarm.com/vbrush/main.html
- **Nocturna.net:** www.nocturna.net
- **.ABR—Another Brush Resource:** http://anotherbrushresource.com
- **Adobe Studio Exchange:** http://share.studio.adobe.com
- **Angryblue:** www.angryblue.com
- **Open-Minded.org:** http://open-minded.org
- **jeffsdigital:** www.jeffsdigital.com
- **Dubtastic Design Labs:** www.dubtastic.com

Of course, I'd always encourage you to create and use your own library of resources, which will only help to build your individual identity. I have one caution about using other brushes—many brush sites have become quite popular, and thus recognizable in your work. Therefore, if you just blatantly use them without any modification, people are bound to recognize them. This isn't a major design no-no, but it's better that people associate the work you create with your own style, and not someone else's resources. I realize that sometimes that's easier said than done, because you don't always have the time and ability to create every single resource and tool that you use in your work. But it is something to strive for. The following tutorial will give you an idea of just how wonderful a healthy brush library can really be.

Now that you're armed with some additional tools and resources, and hopefully now that you have a special idea in mind, you're ready to begin creating.

Finding Me

Creating and using grunge: Hellraiser

Since my site has become more and more popular, one of the most frequently asked questions I get is how I create "the grunge effect" that is a constant in much of my artwork. Up until now, I have not offered a detailed explanation of the process I follow when creating such images. As I mentioned earlier, it's difficult to pin down a specific and exact process that I follow every time. Grunge has many variations depending on the image you're working with. It's important to understand that there are numerous ways to accomplish this effect. For the purposes of this exercise, I'll be going over the basics so that you understand how to create the effect and how to properly implement it.

In the past, my work was just experimental, so 72dpi and a average size of 800x600 pixels was plenty. As I progressed, found that a higher resolution image and higher quality produ became more of an issue. If you plan to sell prints of your wor I recommend that you work at higher resolutions to yield larg and higher quality prints. That being said, I worked with a image size of 2500x2000 pixels (8.333"x6.667") and 300d resolution for this tutorial. Depending on your desired fin print size, you may choose to work with a larger file. In son cases, I work with 300dpi files at 4500x3000, but I have scaled down for this tutorial for the sake of those who might not hav the memory to handle such large files. Some of the pho manipulations tend to result in hefty file sizes so, be caref while working with some of these files—these images mig require more and more of your computer's disk space as yo get closer to completing the image.

·t's get started. Much of my photo manipulation and grunge ork relies heavily on distorted images and textures. Contrary · popular belief, this isn't because it is the trendy way to proach graphics, but because it ties into the meaning of my ork. Also, in much of my work, I use photographs of myself, if u haven't yet noticed. I do this because it adds a personal mension to my work and it also frees me from acquiring ermissions from someone else to use his photos in my artwork.

r this tutorial, I've provided a base image that we'll begin th. Open `Hellraiser-Dubtastic-Start.psd` located in e Morrison\Hellraiser folder on the CD. This base image is a otograph of me, and is technically comprised of two photos. s I said, my work almost always requires a distorted figure, so is is the one we'll start with. The goal of this image, if it is not vious from the title, is to convey pain, angst, struggle, and so n. I envision our final image as a "tortured soul" of sorts who presents a feeling I had when I was younger, a feeling that all did was cause trouble. So I will allow those emotions to be the eative catalyst here.

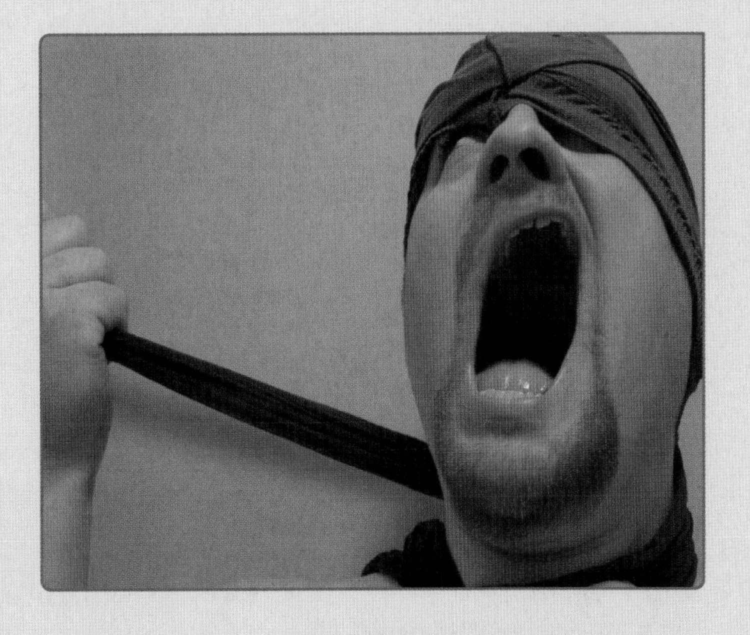

r the sake of moving right into the guts of this exercise, I've ready handled distorting this photograph for you. The mouth d proportions of the head have been disfigured. I have also odified the skin and teeth colorations, rolled the visible eye ack into the head, and distorted the nostril area. For those of u who might be wondering how the distortions were done, I lied heavily on the Selection and Eraser tools. First I'd bring a lection of the face into a new layer, and then use the Eraser ol to blend it into the base image. You might also wonder why e image appears to be weighted so heavily on the right. First, chose to move it right because it makes for a dull composition have the image centered and, secondly, I wanted to leave me room in this layout for the image title, which we will add ter in the exercise.

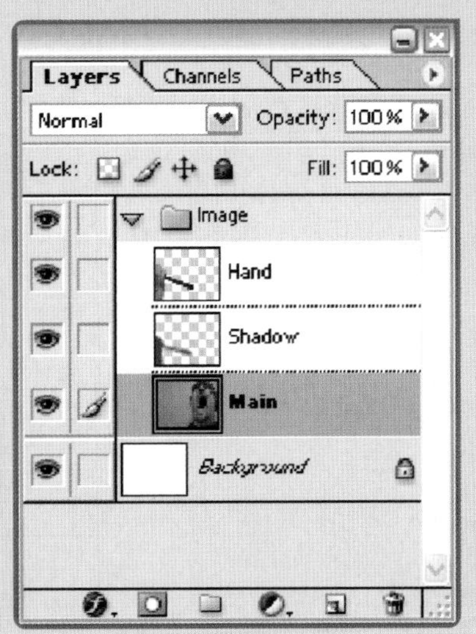

otice that the starting PSD file already contains a folder with ree layers. The Background layer contains the bulk of the cal points we'll be working on. The other two layers hold the cond photograph and an added shadow that helps maintain e lighting of the piece. The image is disfigured enough that it's bvious that the face is not average, yet the strain on the figure ere needs to be emphasized.

With this in mind, we'll use a similar technique to the one I used in the *Candid Strangers* image (shown earlier in the chapter): we'll incorporate nails. As with my use of grunge, I receive numerous questions on how I added the nails into the skin of the face to make them appear like they do. The first step is to find a decent photo of the nails; despite the abundance of stock photo websites, you may find it difficult to locate images to fit a theme like this. In these situations, a digital camera proves invaluable, as you can set up the environment you wish to create and photograph it from any angle with any lighting to fit your purpose. For instance, the nails in this photo are actually small nails you'd used to hang pictures on walls. To create this effect, I wrapped some leggings around Styrofoam, arranged the nails in the formation I wanted to see on the face, and then photographed them using the macro mode on the camera. I removed the surrounding elements from the nails in Photoshop, isolating them so that they would be ready to use.

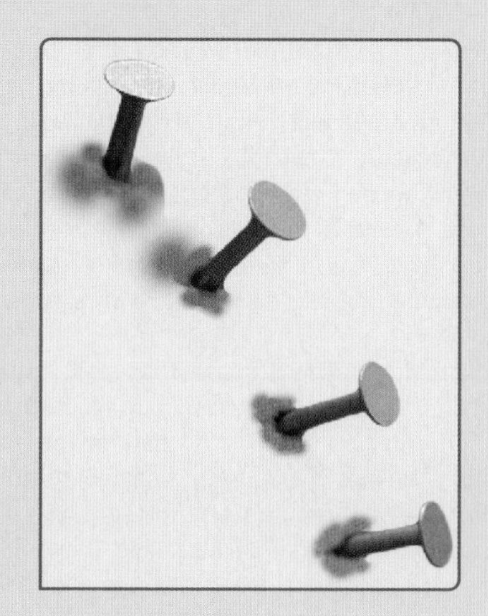

Open `Resources/Exercise-Nails.psd` from the CD, select the Nails layer, and paste it into a new layer at the top of our Image folder. Rename the new layer Nails. By now, you'll notice that the roughness of the edges and the colors don't exactly match. This is perfectly acceptable and will be addressed soon enough. One of the greatest characteristics of grunge, and also one that takes a lot of criticism, is that it covers up minor defects, such as this mismatched color and nonexact blending.

ɛmember, grunge should not be used just to cover up mistakes · to take over an image; the focal point here is the figure, so ccurate blending is key. To begin this blending process, zoom in n the nails area, and select the Smudge tool and a smooth ounded brush (I used the Soft Round 17 pixels brush).

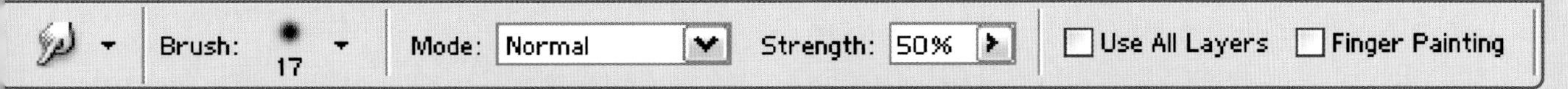

mudge the areas around the points where the nails enter the in. Click and drag from the top nail down and *away* from that ail. This gives some additional stress marks and makes the nails at much more believable when the final image is complete.

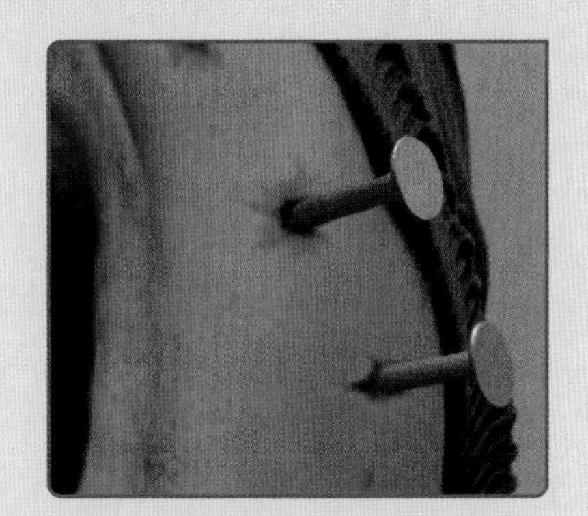

ext, let's add a bit more detail to the entry points because you ever see clear inserts such as these. Open `CarpetGlue.jpg` om the Resources folder on the CD. You need to select just a ortion of the photo, specifically the seam of the carpet.

Courtesy of www.free-image.net, 2001

opy your selection and paste it onto the chapter image over ne of the nails. Place this new layer above the Nails layer and ame it Cuts. Next, we need to convert this layer from color to lack and white. Use Image ➤ Adjustments ➤ Desaturate to esaturate the layer, removing the color. Lastly, change the lending mode in the Layers palette from Normal to Overlay. ou should now have a rough colored patch over one of the ails.

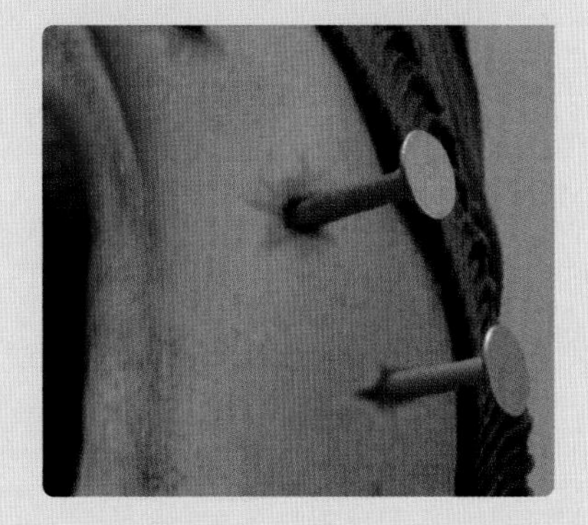

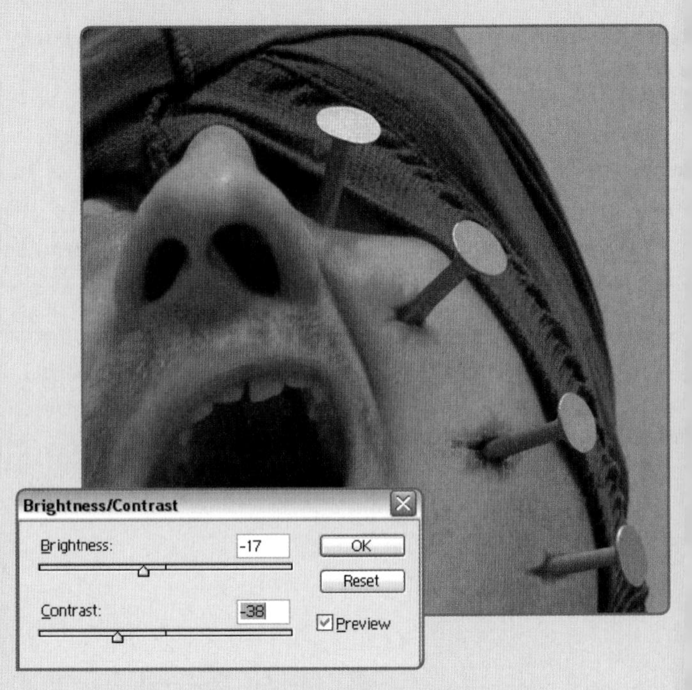

Now you'll need to use the Eraser tool. Select a small rounded brush and trim away the excess of the carpet so that there's a healthy area around the base of the nail that represents the scar. Once you've done that, it would be good to make one final adjustment to the cut area by adjusting the brightness and contrast of the layer. Select Image ➤ Adjustments ➤ Brightness/Contrast and adjust the layer so that it fits a bit better with the skin and nail.

Repeat the previous steps for each of the other nails, keeping in mind the lighting, blending, and realism. To coincide with the Hellraiser theme, it would make sense to duplicate this effect on the other side of the face (the main character in the *Hellraiser* movies, Pinhead, has nails all over his head). Given the foundation image and the fact that he isn't bald, duplicating the exact Pinhead effect isn't an option. Instead, we'll do something similar here; we'll just duplicate the effect on the left side of the face using the same techniques and resources we used to create the nails on the right side. It is important to note that when you're creating the various cuts and entry points, you should use different selections for the carpet glue image, rotate it to fit the shape of the face, and adjust the brightness according to the lighting in the area you are working with.

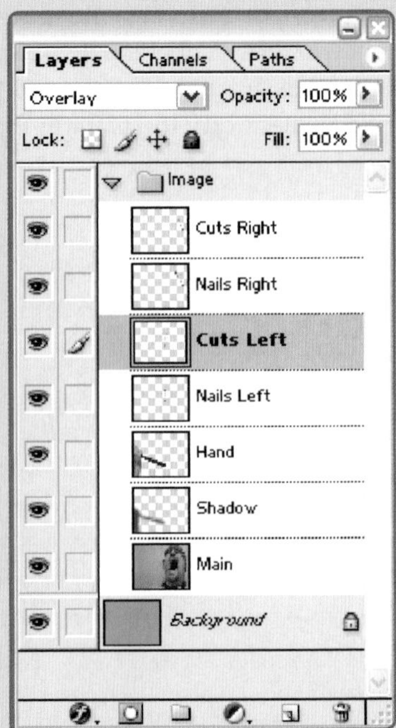

While doing this, it's a good idea to keep your layers organized in case you want to edit nails and components again later. I renamed the original Nails layer as Nails Right and the original Cuts layer as Cuts Right. While adding the nails and cuts to the left side of the face, I created their respective layers as well. After all that, we're ready to incorporate the grunge into the image.

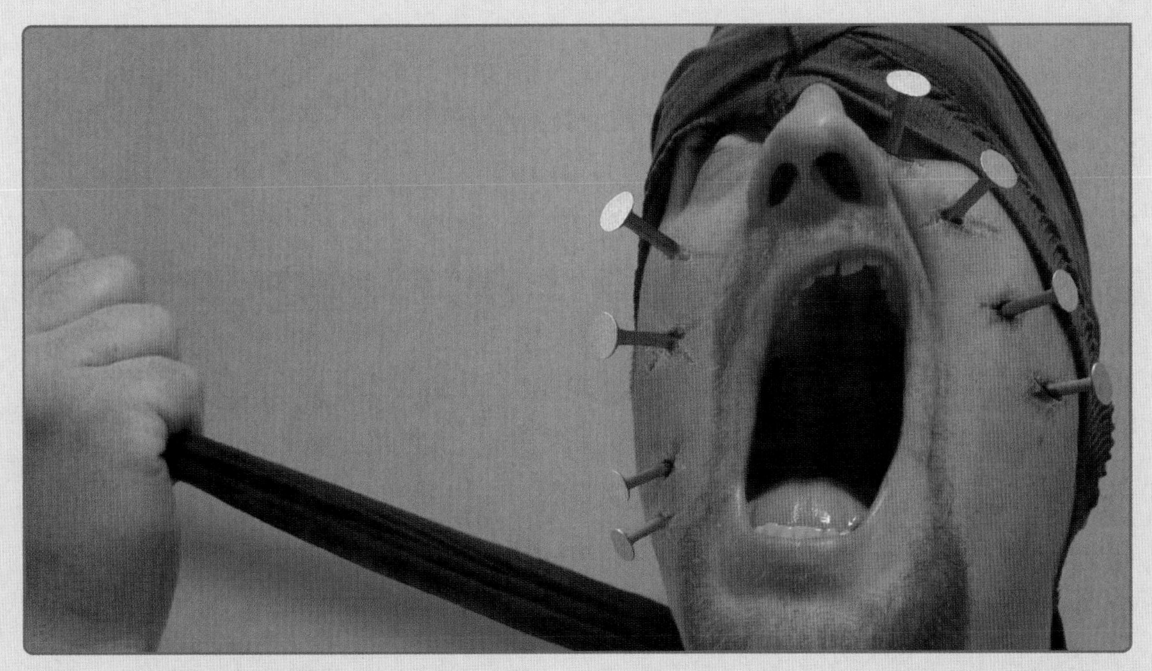

always enjoy using a slightly saturated color in the overall ıage when I'm applying the grunge. This is a personal ·eference of mine and isn't, by any means, a requirement to ove on to the next step. However, I wanted to mention it mply because I have always included it in my artwork. ·pically, these types of images are darker in nature, and given ıe title of this image and the meaning behind it, I think this ·fect works well and gives the image an additional visual push. ·y steps for doing this are quite simple and easy to follow, and feel that such treatment adds a certain component to the ork.

rst, select the entire image and then Edit ➤ Copy Merged. ext, paste the selection above the other layers and name Base. The layers that we've created so far will not be required ıroughout the rest of the exercise. However, as a practice, maintain all of my layers to make future editing and ljustments easier if they are required.

Duplicate the new layer and change the blending mode for this new image from Normal to Soft Light. Make the Base layer (the new layer that you just pasted in) active, and desaturate it to remove the color (Image ➤ Adjustments ➤ Desaturate). This gives the image an effect I enjoy and wish to work with.

Open the `Dubtastic-Texture-01.jpg` from the Resources folder. This is a photo of some dirty concrete in an old parking garage where I used to work. (In fact, I've included six textures to use if you wish to deviate from this example). Select the entire texture image and paste it on to your working image, making sure it's the topmost layer. Rename this layer Texture 01, desaturate the image, and change the blending mode to Overlay. You might need to stretch the image to cover the entire canvas, depending on the size you're working with. If you do need to stretch the layer, use CTRL+T and transform the size of the Texture 01 layer. Next, select the Eraser tool, pick a smooth rounded brush, and change the Opacity to 50 percent.

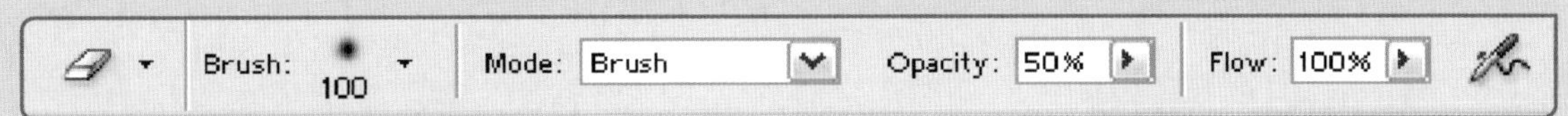

Trim away the Texture layer over the figure's head and body, bringing it more into the focal point. The result should be similar to this:

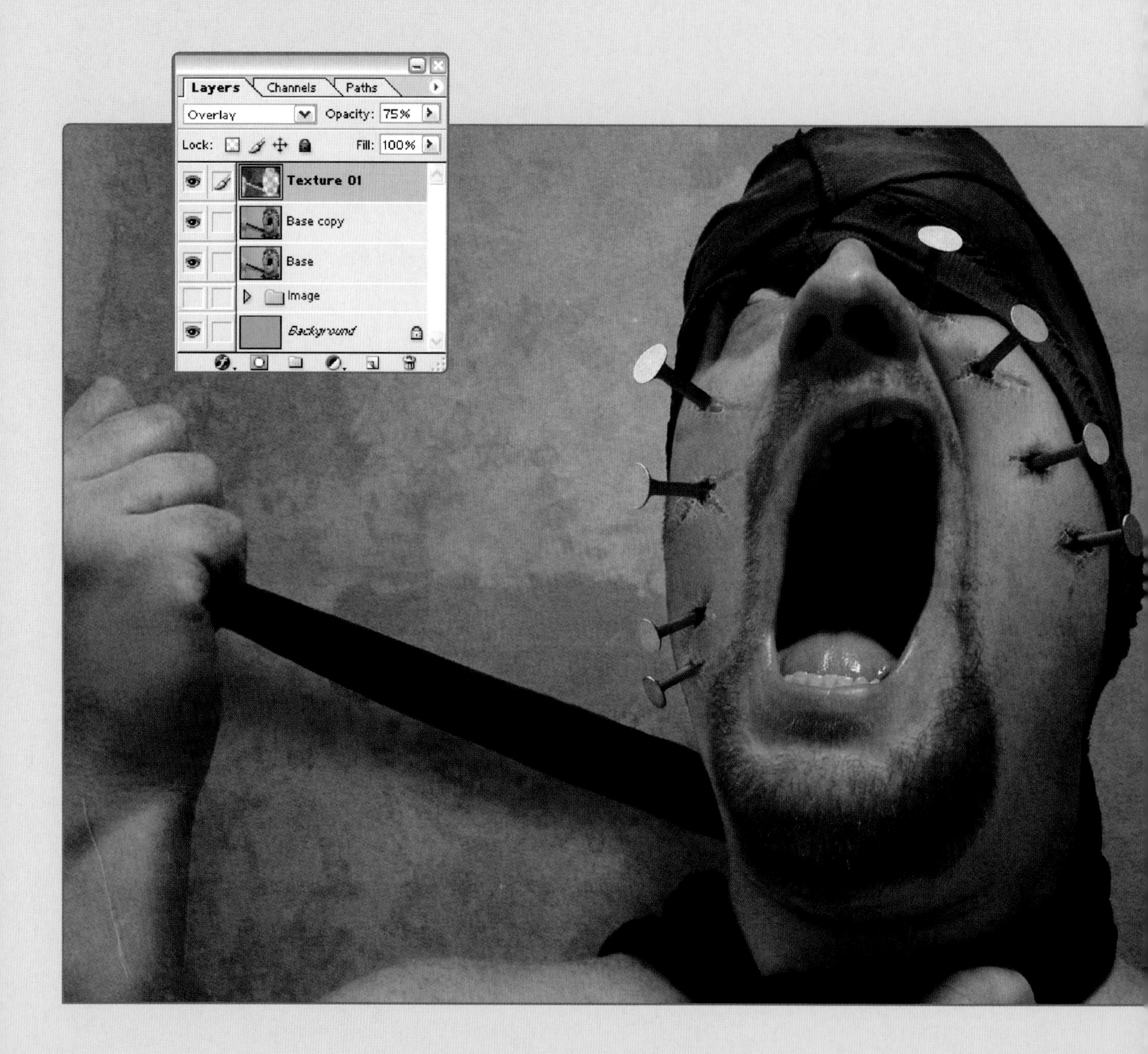

ne more textured layer should be just right. Getting the right 'unge effect requires a lot of build up. By that, I mean building xtures upon textures, adding, erasing, and experimenting. 'hen I create my images, I am rarely satisfied with only one xtured layer, so I opt to use several, as in this image.

pen `Dubtastic-Texture-04.jpg` and follow the same steps described for the first texture layer. Place this new layer above l of the other layers, and name it Texture 02. As with the first yer, desaturate this one and change the blending mode to Soft ght. With the Texture 02 layer active, CTRL+click the Texture 01 yer to load it as the selection, and invert the selection TRL+SHIFT+I). Now just press the DELETE key. This will easily trim vay the texture from the figure, as we did before. You still may want to go back into the Texture 02 layer with the Eraser tool; using the same settings as before, you can trim away the edges just to be sure.

Notice here that the Image folder is still present, only the visibility is turned off. This is merely my way of preserving some of the previous layers, while hiding them from view. As the image stands, this folder could easily be removed without affecting the image.

Here is where the exact steps to follow become a little blurred. Although the end result of adding grunge might be quite obvious, there never seem to be exact steps that you can follow the same way for every single image.

Now we're going to use some custom Photoshop brushes to add additional grunge effects to the image. You could sample from the selections I mentioned earlier in the chapter or create your own. Creating your own will give you control over the effect, yet using brushes created by others saves time and trouble.

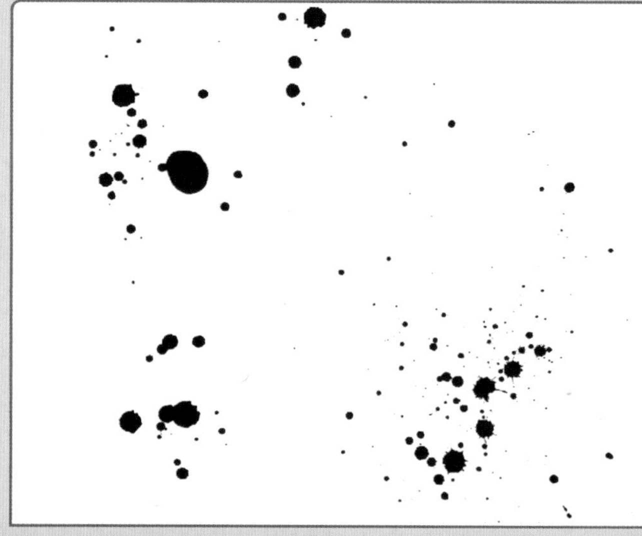

If you want to follow along with my example, load `Project-GrungeBrushes.abr` into your currently installed Adobe Photoshop brushes. The first one we'll use comes from Shiver (www.open-minded.org). It's called **Open-Minded Brush – 01**, sized at 1496px, as shown here:

Create a new layer on top of all the others and name it White Grunge. Make your foreground color white and randomly use the brush once or twice throughout the image. Feel free to use several types of brushes, sizes, and placements to add to the image. When done, change the blending mode of that layer to Soft Light and then change the opacity to 40 percent. This will help blend the brushes into the image so that they appear to be seamless.

Each time I add a different brush or texture, I always do it in a new layer, controlling the blending modes, brightness, and other aspects until I'm happy with it. By using layers, you can easily remove any unwanted additions without affecting the rest of the image.

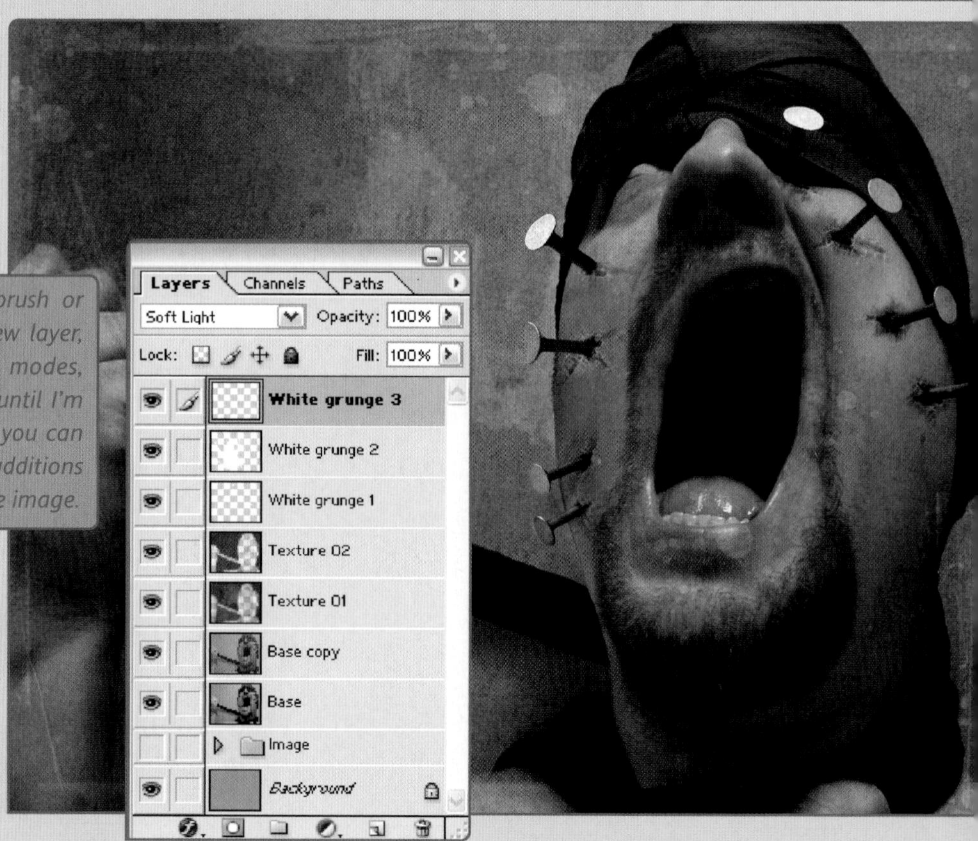

otice the three White Grunge layers in the Layers palette. ie brushes I used were gathered from Shiver (www.open-inded.org) and the Adobe Studio Exchange (http://share.udio.adobe.com). Technically, the exact brushes I used don't atter in the sense that experimenting with various brushes sults in very similar effects. I'd encourage you to experiment well rather than follow my brush steps exactly. Try different ushes, distort them, create your own, and make the image ours!

member the earlier reasons why I said the grunge style has a d reputation? One of those is color usage. Many grunge ages are simply dark and disturbing, yet, how interesting ould it be if more vivid and lively colors were used? This image d theme seems to call for that, and rather than use a clichéd d or other color that might be associated with the "Hellraiser" image, we'll take a different route. The image has a lot of red and pinkish tones. A great contrasting color here would be green, and to add even more impact, let's make it a bright green. Create a new layer called Green above the White Grunge layers, select a very bright green from the Color palette (I used #31E718) and fill the new layer. Now, with the Green layer active, CTRL+click the Texture 02 layer. Invert the selection (CTRL+SHIFT+I) and hit DELETE to remove the selection. This should trim out most of the green from the figure. If not, use the Eraser tool to trim the rest away.

Pretty rancid, right? Change the blending mode on the Green layer to Soft Light and drop the opacity down to 40 percent. Doing this will allow the color contrast we need, yet still adhere to the image's theme.

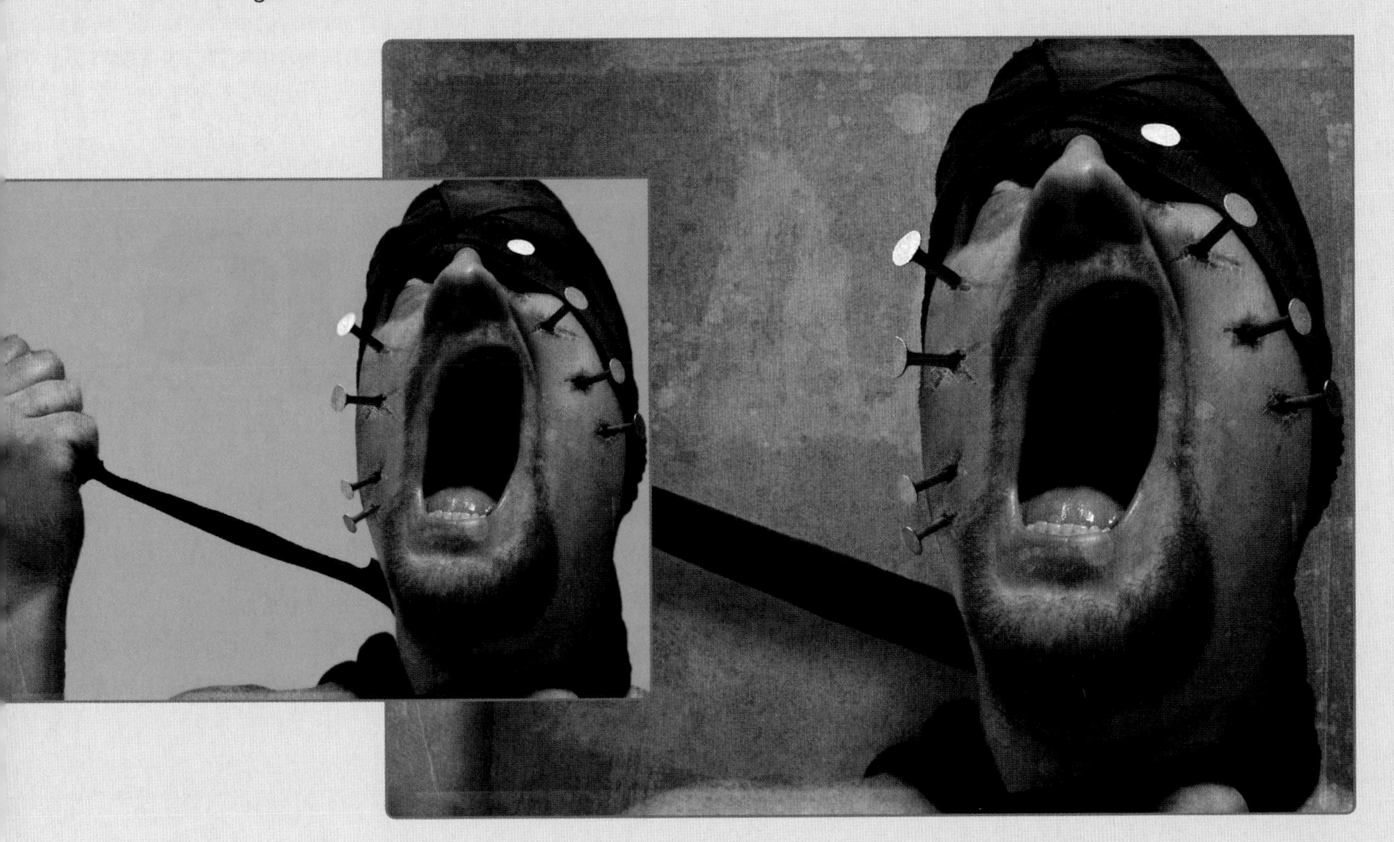

Now that the image is created, it wouldn't do it justice to throw any old text on top and call it a day. This is where many digital artworks can be made or broken—by the text and title.

Distressed fonts and type

Now that you have a properly grunged-out image, you need the proper type effect to accompany it. An endless supply of font foundries and websites offer just about every style of font you could want. Many offer grunge, distressed, and other similarly themed fonts readily available for download. Here are some helpful sites:

- **Chank Fonts:** www.chank.com
- **misprinted type:** www.misprintedtype.com
- **Cape-Arcona:** www.cape-arcona.com
- **Deviant Art:** http://fonts.deviantart.com
- **Angryblue:** www.angryblue.com

However, in the creative process, being unique and definin your own style are always factors to be considered. With tha said, sometimes it isn't enough to download a font and use it i your work. What you need is the ability to take existing fon and apply effects to them so that, in essence, they becom yours. For this example, we'll use a simple font.

Create a new 800x400 image (for this example, I have the d set at 300 and I've also used #E1DDD7 as the background color Select the Type tool, use Arial Black, size 24pt, and then typ BREAKING TYPE in block caps. Right+click the layer and sele Rasterize Layer. This gives us the ability to modify the typ beyond what the Adobe type engine allows.

Now that we have our rasterized type layer, it's time to break and really modify it. One of the first steps is to rearrange an transform the letters to get them out of that nice neat straigh line. Using the Selection tool, select one or two letters at a tim and then rotate them (Ctrl+T) just a few pixels in eithe direction.

BREAKING
TYPE

ɔw, hopefully you took a break earlier, investigated some of those eat brush links, and now have a hefty library of your own. In case u haven't, you can use one of the supplied brushes from 3rush's collection(http://veredgf.fredfarm.com/vbrush/main.html), ed at 565px, named **VBrush Brush – 02**. It looks like this:

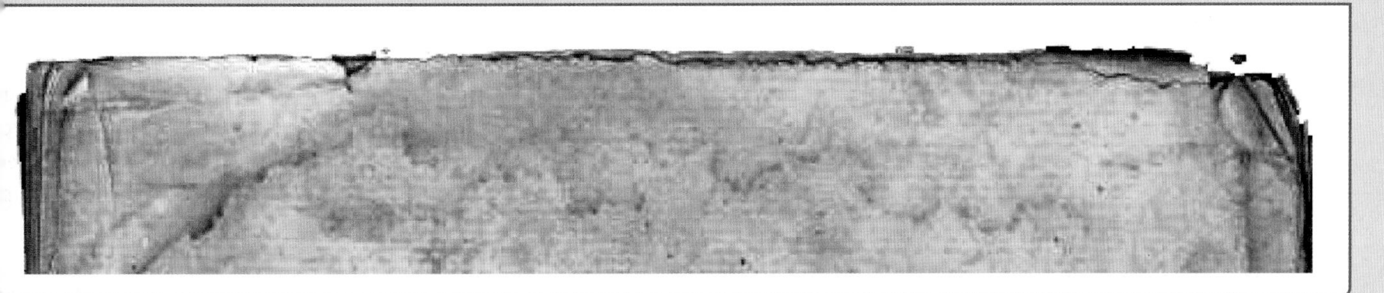

ith the Eraser tool and this brush, erase portions of the text in e middle. (Note that if you're continuing this from the evious step where we modified the image, you may need to ange the brush opacity from 50 percent back to 100 percent.) member, there isn't a right or wrong way to do this. After you ck once to erase the type, you might notice that it doesn't ally erase much; this is because of how "thin" the brush tually is. You may need to click several times in order to hieve the desired effect, or have portions of the text moved.

The next step is simple—probably more so than you thought. We'll use various brushes on various places of the type, to break it up and create discrepancies between the letters. It's important to use combinations of soft-edged brushes and hard-edged brushes to create even more differences in the text.

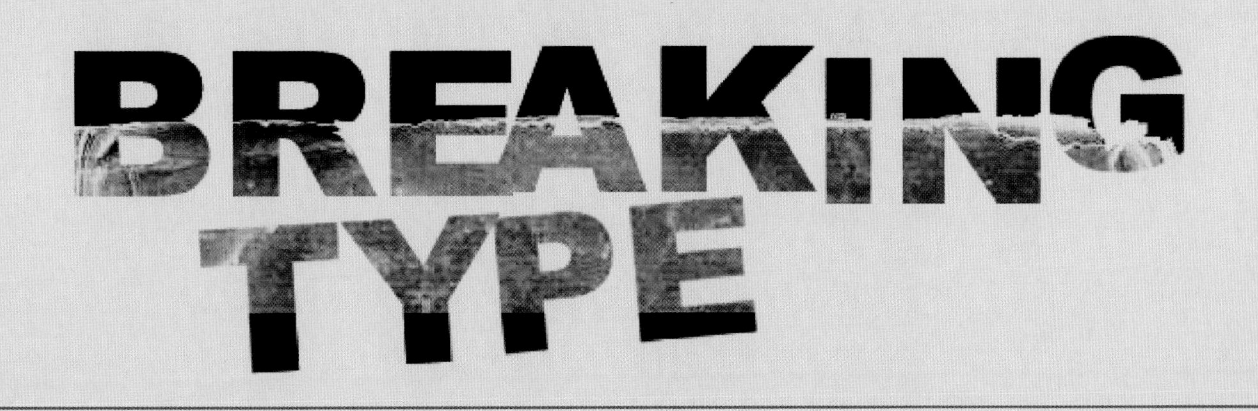

Use the **Angryblue Brush - 01** brush (by Justin Kamerer of www.angryblue.com) included in the brush set on the CD. I've added some inkblots to the text. You see, another great thing about grunge and this type of work is that it calls for organized disorder, chaos, and somewhat illegible type. Allow the viewer's mind to re-create the text, give them a hint, a teaser, something else to draw their attention. Just because you are using text within an image doesn't automatically mean that every single letter has to be 100 percent legible. In fact, that can be very boring and clean-cut, which doesn't fit in with this chapter at all. Take a few minutes to experiment; remember to utilize your layers as you experiment.

You can further complicate matters by introducing a background to the image, again using brushes or textures (brushes would be easiest). Using **VBrush Brush – 01** sized at 651px, select that brush and resize the master diameter down to 445px. The brush should look like this:

reate a new layer under the ext and Black Grunge layer hat you created, and name it ase Grunge. Click once to lace a rather dark blemish ehind the text. Now, using he Eraser tool, select the **Brush Brush – 02** sized at 12px. It should look like the ollowing image:

sing that brush, chisel away at the dark blemish by clicking andomly on the background grunge layer. Here is the image as have it, using various different brushes along with the Eraser ool to remove portions of that background layer.

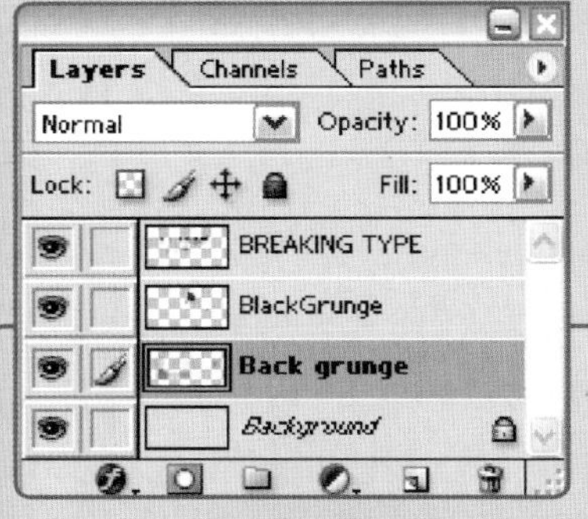

If you wish to explore my completed file, feel free to open `BreakingType.psd` from the Resources folder on the CD to see how it was created. Coming up with a step-by-step guide on how to use grunge in any precise manner is a difficult challenge. The options you could choose when creating and breaking down an image are limitless (which might be why there are not more instructional guides available). The most important thing you have is your imagination, and it should be used to its full potential to explore any and all possibilities with this type of image.

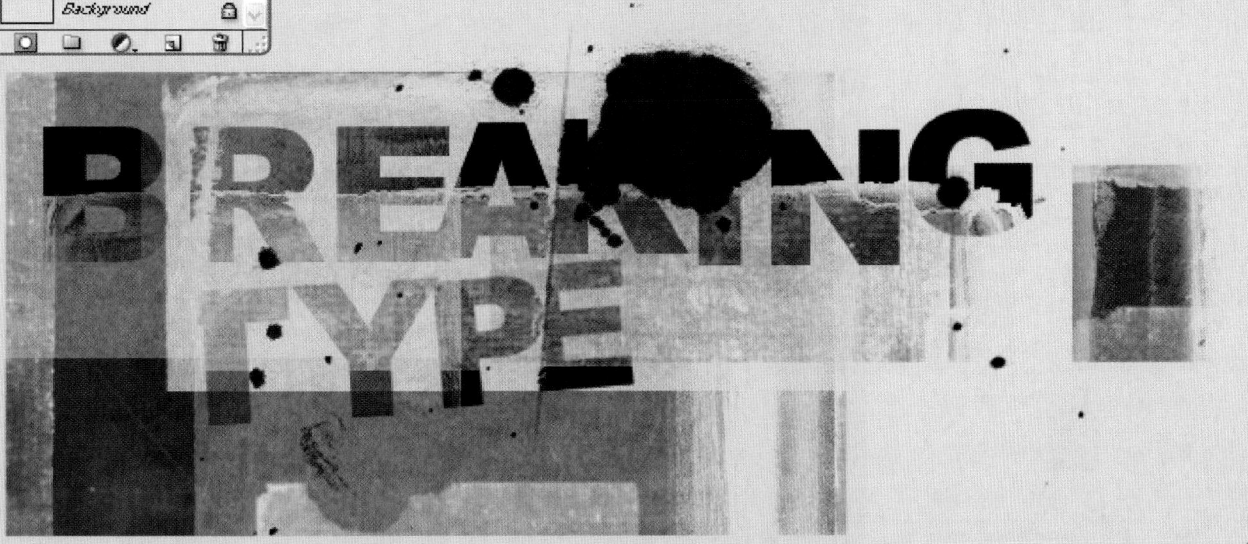

Finalizing

Now that you know how to incorporate a little grunge into a basic font and how to put your own little twist on it, let's bring the two together using the Hellraiser image that we created earlier.

Go back to your Hellraiser image. It was intentionally created "right heavy" for several reasons, as mentioned earlier. From my point of view, this is something that I wish more digital artists would consider. By placing the text in an inappropriate location you can throw off the composition entirely. Also, if the text, like grunge itself, is not properly developed into the image, it can cause conflicts.

First, create a new folder above all the other folders and nam it Title. This is where the work for the title text will be done. Th font for this title is Carpenter ICG (if you don't have it, it's in th Resources folder on the CD). With the Type tool selected an Carpenter ICG at 36pts, type the word hellraiser in lowercas Place the font close to the upper-left corner of the image.

Now, just like we did in the Breaking Type discussion, right-clic the text layer and select Rasterize Layer. Change the blendin mode on the text layer from Normal to Soft Light. Granted, th font is on the thin side, so working with it will be a little mor difficult compared to something as thick as Arial Black. Usin one of the VBrush paper texture brushes (any will suffice) tri portions of the title away.

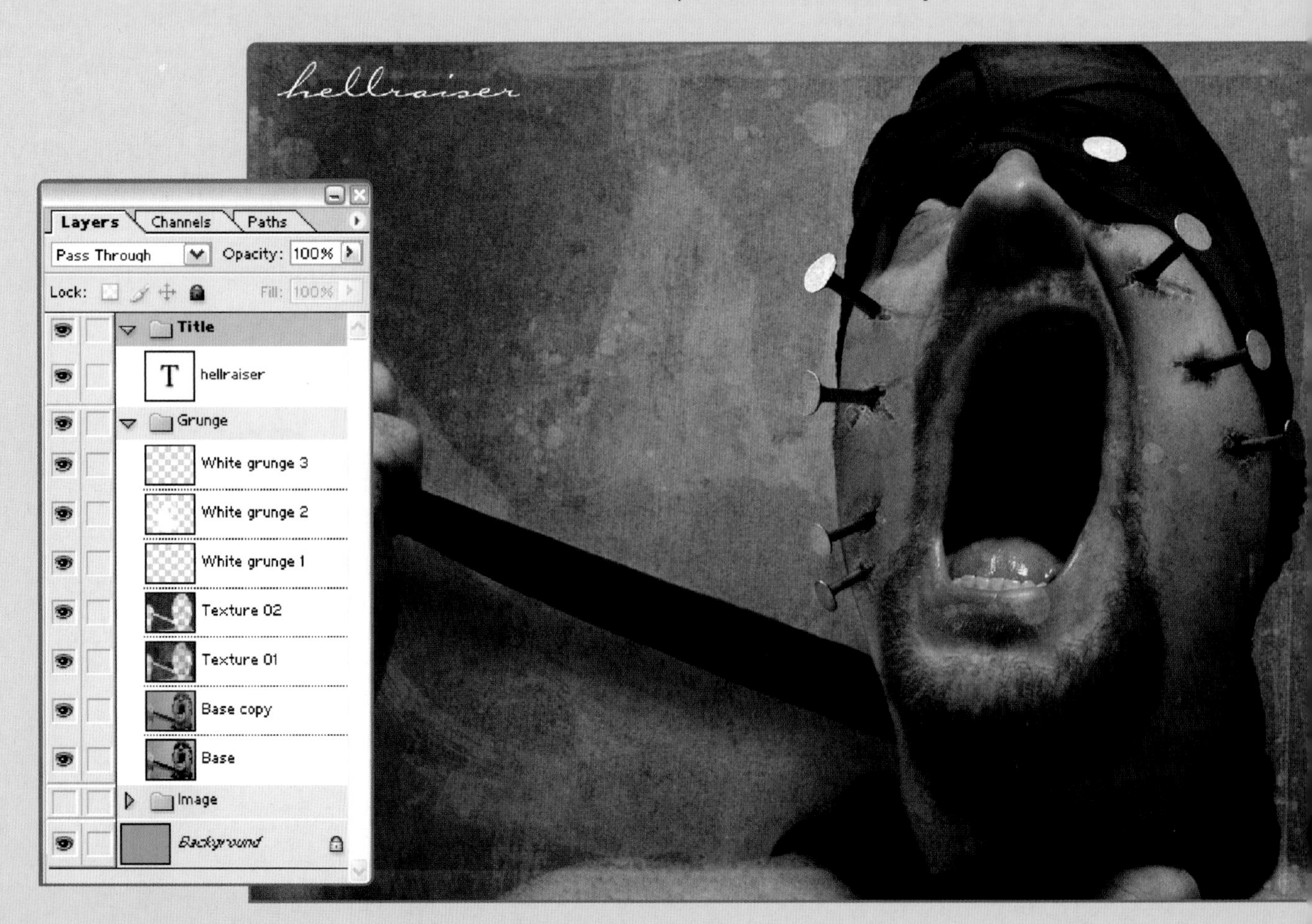

xt, create a layer under the hellraiser layer and name it Title
unge. Set the blending mode to Screen for this layer. Select
e Brush tool and then select **Open-Minded Brush – 02**, sized
859, which looks like this:

w, sample a color from the figure's forehead using the
edropper tool. You should be looking for one of the colors
at appears purple. This will help tie in the font area with the
st of the image, while allowing it to stand out enough to be
ticed. I sampled the color #38282C. Create one brush
pression behind the text on the Title Grunge layer.

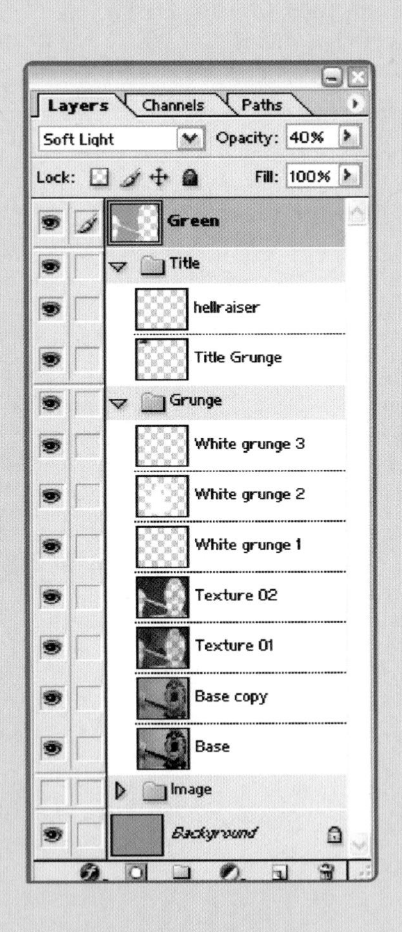

This is a minor change, but the image title is now sitting on top of the green background when it should actually be sitting under it. Open the Grunge folder and drag the Green layer above all other folders in the Layer palette.

As simple as that may seem, that is really all there is to it. When you consider the endless number of fonts and brushes that are available, you can easily see how vast your options are when you're creating this type of work. Lastly, if you're curious about any of the layers or steps, the unflattened file is `Hellraiser-Dubtastic-Final.psd` on the CD.

̣onclusion

ɔpefully, you've now had a better glimpse into the world of unge and, more importantly, learned some helpful tips on ɔw to apply it effectively. When you study math, it is a given at 2 + 2 = 4, yet when working with grunge, you can use so any different methods to accomplish a certain effect. This is hy it's difficult to outline definite steps to achieve these fects. Earlier, when I mentioned experimenting with various ushes, you might have chosen different brushes, layer ɔacities, blending modes, or colors that resulted in quite a fferent final image. You might have felt that the mood of your age would have been compromised by introducing the green ɔlored layer and have opted to leave it out. You might have lt that you wanted the final image to be even darker and more visted, with a larger build up of grunge, dirt, and textures.

r me, the workflow is quite natural, yet I rarely follow the me steps with every image. As a result, conveying such steps an audience was more difficult than I thought it would be. I ijoy seeing what different colors do for the image, what fferent brushes do for the textures, and what different iotographs do for the effects that I want to achieve. ɔmetimes I even stumble across a look that I prefer even ough it wasn't intentional.

One of the most important things that you should take away from this chapter is not solely the techniques, nor my defense of the grunge style, but how to effectively use it in artwork. Grunge has many opponents, but I feel that it is not so much of the style, as how the style has been used. Remember to stay focused on blending and creating as natural an environment as possible. Consider lighting, colors, and composition, and how those things work along with the grunge elements to make a powerful piece. If you choose to ignore color, you will most likely end up with just another boring, dark image. If you ignore the composition, viewers of your artwork will not look at the image and will just move on. By covering your image with text, you confuse the viewer with mixed focal points. It is vital to your artwork that you utilize your tools and incorporate components just as they are: components as part of a whole. By overdoing text, color, composition, grunge, lighting, and the like, you will, in turn, take the power away from the message you are trying to communicate.

Now go experiment and create!

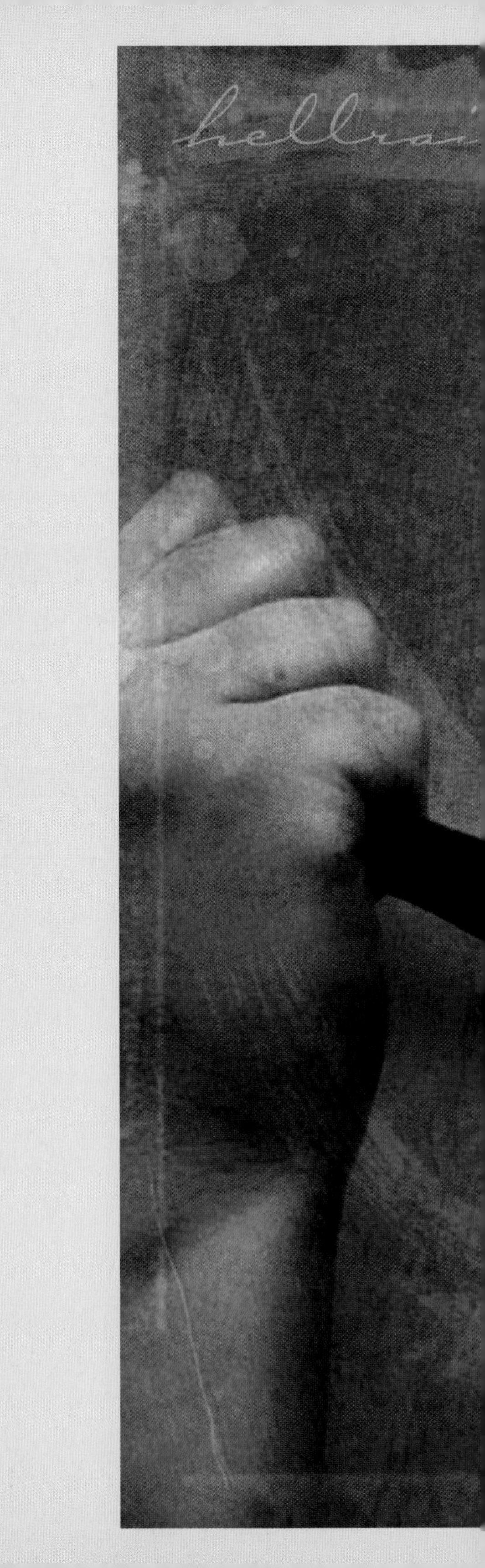

07 CONSTRUCT

"THE ONLY LIMIT IS YOUR IMAGINATION."
COLIN SMITH
WWW.PHOTOSHOPCAFE.COM

To be quite frank, writing my chapter for the first volume of *New Masters of Photoshop* was one of the most difficult things I have ever done. Writing about technique, style, theory, and other things I already know is not so difficult. The challenge comes when you are writing about something you don't know. When I sat down almost three years ago to write about what inspires me, I had a startling revelation. I didn't know myself as well as I thought I did. Sure, I could have winged my way through a few pages and called it a manuscript. I'm not built that way, however, and am one of those pesky people who feels the constant need to bear my soul. I guess that's what drives us as creative people—imagine art with no soul. I mean, think about it for a moment. Poetry, music, visual art, all smoothly calculated without any personal involvement from the author's heart. I think the result would barely deserve the title of art. People feel the need to be moved by all forms of art.

So, for me, the long journey began. It was time to search r soul, and I found myself asking the questions I had never ask before. No one but me could answer these questions. Wh moves me? What excites me? What involves my mind, body, a spirit to the point of inspiration?

For me, inspiration is directly related to imagination. It all begi in a very private theater. This theater of the mind only h seating space for one. As artists, we are on a mission communicate what we have viewed in this theater to the rest the world. I say a mission, because as an artist, this is not a jo it's a compulsion. The limited tools that we use help us produ our art, whatever its medium may be.

I have to see what I am going to do in my minds eye. Nine percent of the design is in the mind; the rest is simply t mechanics of reproducing this vision. Photoshop is the tool choice for me because it offers me the freedom to produce ju about anything I want.

lastery of the tools is not mastery of design; it's merely the ·arting point. Whether you choose Photoshop, Illustrator, or a) tool doesn't matter; these are still tools and they do not ave minds of their own. No magic tool will create a design for ɔu and, if it could, it would be hideous, because it lacks the uman element.

nce my imagination is inspired, I can lock myself in a room ɔr days. Heck, feed me bread and water and I am happy as ng as I am in the zone. It's like a game, a challenge to eproduce what you see in your imagination. When I say eproduce, I really mean come as close as your current skill vel will allow you. Anyone who says they have arrived is a liar. /e are always growing and learning, straining to move forward, ressing for a destination that's impossible to reach. The tracks ıat we leave on our journey are interpreted to the rest of the orld as art. Sometimes we blaze a new trail and leave a fresh et of footprints. More often than not, however, we travel on a ath that someone has traveled before.

ıere are two main types of work: personal and commercial. ıe former is where a lot of the new trails will be blazed as we xperiment. Most of my personal work is based on different xperiments. The latter, is where we travel down the well- ·aveled road, where it is most difficult to find inspiration. The ıallenge often lies in the mindset of the client. At least here the US, clients prefer to use the tried-and-true designs ather than risk experimenting. This is part of the reason why mericans glean a lot of their inspiration from places such as urope where the mindset is a little edgier, more willing to take few more risks. Of course the work is then run through a ultural filter so that it is relevant to the audience. As a gross eneralization (there are many exceptions), a lot of European yle would be a bit plain for the flashy American mindset. This ame flashiness can be interpreted as gaudy to the European ıindset. That's why it is very important to know your audience.

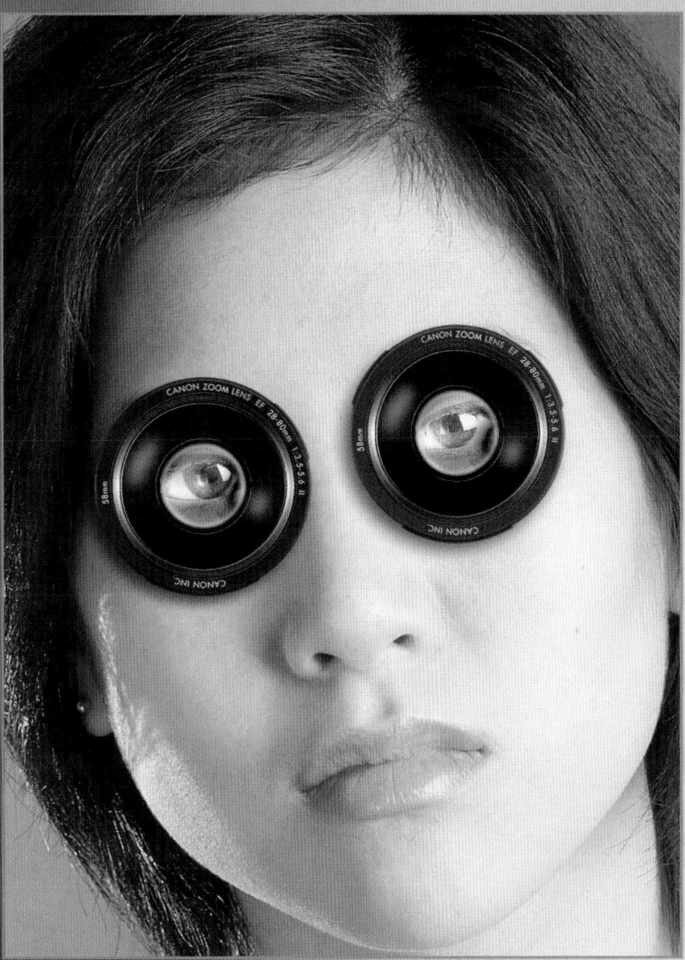

Past history

The past is the foundation that everything springs from. This is our reservoir of learning. The way we see things is based on our experiences and things we have learned. Our societies and cultures are based on those that have gone before us.

I spent almost nine years working for *VOICE*, a monthly magazine. First I was the production coordinator, then the designer, and finally the senior editor. I look back and wonder how I designed that rag. I had lots of ideas, lots of zeal, but my knowledge was lacking desperately. This really was my training ground where I honed my techniques and skills. I started with the first version of Photoshop available for the PC. As each new version of Photoshop was released, I couldn't wait to purchase it—putting up with the bugs was well worth the journey of discovery. I guess I grew as Photoshop grew, learning the new features and adding them to my repertoire of the mechanics. Obviously, I wasn't just using Photoshop; a lot of page layout was involved too. Laying out all those pages caused me to have a great respect for typography.

The ease with which typefaces can be obtained and shee number of styles that can be thrown at them has caused a voi in the design world. Typography is an art in itself; learn to lov and respect typefaces and all your designs will suddenly com to a new level. I have seen so many wonderful designs ruined b bad use of typography. A lack of understanding of typograph is a dead give away that the designer lacks experience.

What I have discussed falls under the category of mechanic —things you could teach a robot. I am not diminishing thos things. If you want to be a good designer you must learn them How can you break the rules if you don't even know what the are in the first place? Without the basic skills, even the stronges idea will be interpreted weakly. On the flip side of the coir having all the skills in the world is still not enough. Think of th skills as a car. Depending on your level of skills, it could be a For Escort or a Ferrari. A Ford and a Ferrari have one thing i common. Without fuel neither is going anywhere. I see inspiratio as the fuel that feeds the imagination. When this fuel is mixe

my time on that magazine was my training ground for the
ıechanics, then a one-year stint as the creative director at Villa
ne (www.villaone.com), a multimedia company, was my training
round for process. My very first project was to salvage a failing
esign project. The website was for an organization that owns a
ımous art deco building and the client had already rejected three
esigns from as many designers. I spent the next two days doing
esearch. I studied Art Deco, both the era and its styles. I
iscovered that the Art Deco period was partly celebrated by
ıdustry and travel. I learned the shapes and colors, the origins,
nd the reason for this revolution in art. I found this research
ıscinating. While pouring over books and articles, my reservoir of
nowledge was filled, but more importantly I found inspiration
nd excitement for the project. I would not even attempt to claim
ıat I am an authority on Art Deco with a mere two days' learning.
ut the result was enough understanding and inspiration to
hoose the right shapes, colors, and fonts to present a winning
esign to a delighted client.

he lesson I learned here was a valuable one. Before rushing off to
laze new trails, it is valuable to be aware of the trails that are
ready there. The past is a strong source of inspiration. Don't just
nitate what you see, that would be called ripping. Rather take what
ou see and push it a bit further and put your own twist on it.

/hile on the subject of the past, I would like to mention music.
lusic is so powerful. You can hear a song, and within the first few
tanzas, be taken to another place in time. It may be a song you
aven't heard in years, but all the memories and emotions come
ooding back. Perhaps it reminds you of a person, a place, or an
xperience. The music that you listen to is very important while
ou're designing. Music creates atmospheres. It may be rock, hip-
op, trance, jazz, or classical. Each style will put you in a different
ood, a mood to design a different style. A solid library of MP3s and
good set of headphones can be one of the designer's best friends.

Rights: Friedrich-Wilhelm-Murnau-Stiftung; Distributor: Transit Film GmbH

Present

Perhaps I am a strange creature; I design for a living and then, when I want to unwind, I fool around in Photoshop. The designs that I use to unwind are highly experimental. For instance, I created *Frozen Journey* in an attempt to freeze a moment in time, a moment that I could easily forget or miss. I wanted to capture what is passing through my mind in an instant. This moment is called the present. So often we are distracted by the past or future that we forget to enjoy the moment. When all is said and done, the moment is the only part of time that we can change; it is our opportunity to act. The past is gone and tomorrow never really comes, it is always today.

What impact does the present have on inspiration? Have you ever noticed that yesterday's inspiration will not carry you through today? The present is the container that inspiration lives and breathes in. So you have designer's block? You're dried up and uninspired and have a looming deadline. What to do? The truth is that you have no clear picture in your imagination. You have no goal to run to and therefore it's natural that yo don't feel like running. What you need to do is jump-start you creativity. I left the lights turned on in my car a little while ag and all the power drained out of my battery. I needed to g somewhere—it was an emergency. I took another healthy ca and pulled it up beside my tired car. I then attached jumpe cables from the live battery to the dead battery. The powe from the good battery flowed through the cables and provide the much-needed boost for my engine to turn over and my ca jumped into life.

In comparison, a valuable resource for inspiration is othe designers. Creativity and enthusiasm is contagious. If I am draine I talk to other designers and once again catch the spark fro them. The design community is a place of synergy and inspiratio Places like the forum at my site (www.photoshopcafe.com) an friends of ED (www.friendsofed.com/forums) are full of peop who are overflowing with creativity and ideas.

frozen motion

Life's breath is a journey... travel like a moving tide,
Flow in a lazy meander... flurry in a runaway ride.

Scenery rushes by... links us all to each other.
Stop, smell the roses... rush past in a blur of color.

Pause, smell the air... Time suspended, as frozen dew,
look around and see... beauty hidden in the view.

Journey

PAUSE

Watching other artists and designers work is also a way to awaken the sleeping inspiration inside you. When I look at the work of such designers as Andreas Lindholm, Jens Karlsson, and Eric Jordan, I become inspired. These designs feature a technical style that draws me in and causes my imagination to be stirred. For other people, it may be dark art or classic art that stirs them.

Other places of inspiration for me are books, magazines, and movies. I find it very difficult to sit through a movie and not feel the desire to run out the door to my computer and begin to design something.

With so many images flashing before my eyes and though rushing through my mind, the movie theater is a greenhouse fc inspiration. If you don't have time for a full movie, head over t www.apple.com/trailers and watch a few movie previews. Ther is something about movies that fuels my imagination. A goo film will create an imaginary reality. This imaginary reality is place where all kinds of ideas are just waiting to be discovere I personally love the science fiction and historical genre because they involve the imagination so heavily. Movies such a The *Matrix* trilogy, *Star Wars*, and *The Lord of the Rings* cann help but fuel the imagination.

INIT SEQ.
PLEASE BE SEATED
JOYRIDE TAKING OFF

G FRC eq 239
NO POPCORN SERVED
DURING LANDING

IC

IA

IA

IC

IE

IE

IB

STATUS: OK
IB

STATUS: OK
IB

IDIOSYNCHRATIC

DX02

ENTER DESTINATION HERE

ATMSPHR SECURE
COUGHING ALLOWED

ONLY VALID REASONS
WILL BE ACCEPTED

ACHTUNG
MISUSE OF ALIEN VEHICLE
IS NOT RECOMMENDED

SYSTEM: OVERIDE
SYSTEM: OVERIDE
SYSTEM: OVERIDE
PHOTOSHOPCAFE.COM
REACHING FOR THE STAR
BY COLIN SMITH A.K.A. KIWICOLIN

Another source of inspiration may be surprising. It involves doing something totally different that has nothing to do with design at all. I am presently running my own firm (www.pixeloverload.com) and spend many hours in front of a computer. I have to juggle many different projects as well as deal with the commercial aspects of the firm. Sometimes giving my mind a total break from design is the best way to refresh my thinking.

One of the things I enjoy is scuba diving. Picture floating through the water weightlessly. You are in a giant kelp forest at Catalina Island, you look up, and your eyes trace these massive growths all the way to the glowing surface. Reaching ahead, you part the kelp with your gloved hands to witness a shaft of light that reaches all the way to the bottom where it illuminates a patch of golden sand. Suddenly, a school of fish cuts through the beam of light. Their scales flash as they reflect the light. The school ripples and turns as a living mass. It is a different world under the waves, and for a moment, you have just taken your mind off design, but as a result, your imagination has been filled with wonder. Art is not the source for art; it is the result of a mind inspired by a fueled imagination. Sometimes it takes something totally different from design to inspire. Get a life, get a hobby!

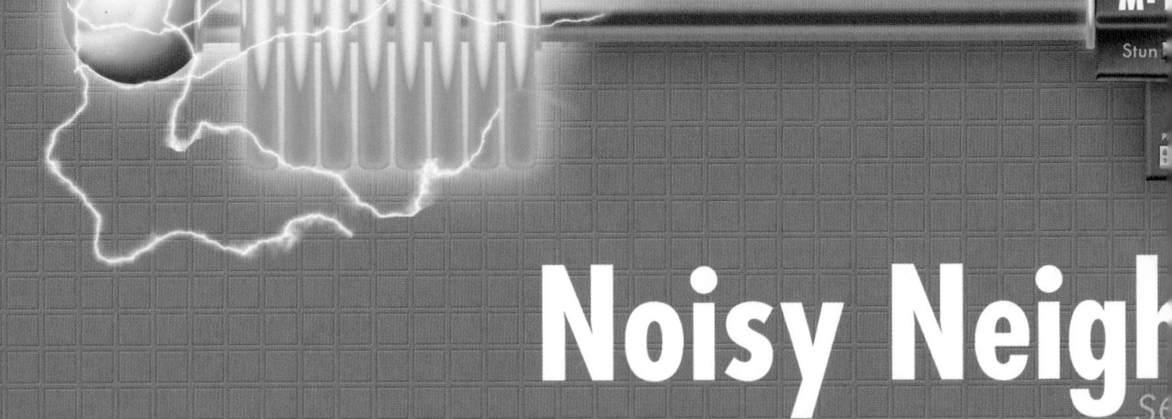

Noisy Neigh

Se

I am best known for my photorealistic renderings that I have drawn totally in Photoshop. I really enjoy looking at an object that is sitting in front of me and interpreting it in the way that I choose. I try to make it look as realistic as I can. Perhaps this style should be called neo–still life? Perhaps there is a name that already exists for this, but my objects are rarely alive; I prefer mechanical objects. I don't know why, they just fascinate me.

My roots in this kind of art actually come from building models when I was younger. I used to spend a great deal of time with these plastic miniatures. I would painstakingly paint all their minute details. I was never satisfied with how they came out of the box, so I would fashion them how I wanted, sometimes cannibalizing parts from other models. At other times, I would create the parts myself, or carve them up and make them do things they were not intended to do, such as making the doors of cars open, and so on. I would treat them like real objects and slowly build them up to make them as real as possible. Then I would create the surroundings for the models and build environments out of papier-mâché, matchsticks, and other things I could find lying around. Perhaps this kind of activity helped me develop the patience to work on something bigger, something that couldn't be accomplished all in one sitting.

I don't use scans, third-party plug-ins, or any illustration software for my images. Why do I choose to make it so difficult on myself? It's the challenge. When I come to each section of the image, I have a puzzle to solve. I can pull from my past experiences and apply a technique I've used before. A lot of the time, I will not have a canned technique for a particular effect. I will usually have to experiment and invent my own technique. This is the part that I love. It's the challenge, the discovery. When I approach a photorealistic project, such as my guitar that we'll look at in the tutorial, I don't look at the image as a whole. I break the image down into separate parts. Some of these parts are tiny and some are complex. If a part is too complex, I break that down into smaller, more manageable parts. It's like getting inside the object and breaking it down into easier chunks. Instead of the entire image, I'd rather look at the piece that I am working on currently and make that as realistic as possible. This can be tedious and difficult at times, and it requires a lot of patience. It's important to resist the temptation to rush and skip over things. When this temptation rears its ugly head, it's usually a sign that it's time for a break. When all the parts are assembled, I will have a very realistic object with plenty of detail.

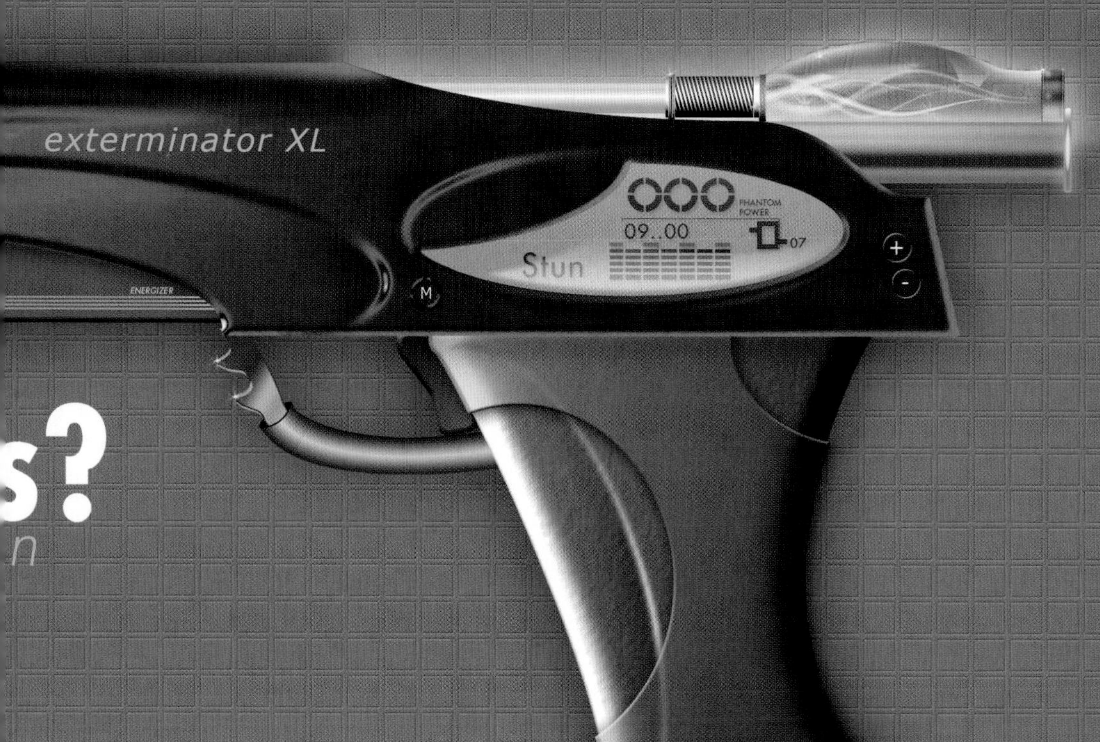
exterminator XL
PHANTOM POWER
09..00
Stun
07
ENERGIZER
s?
n

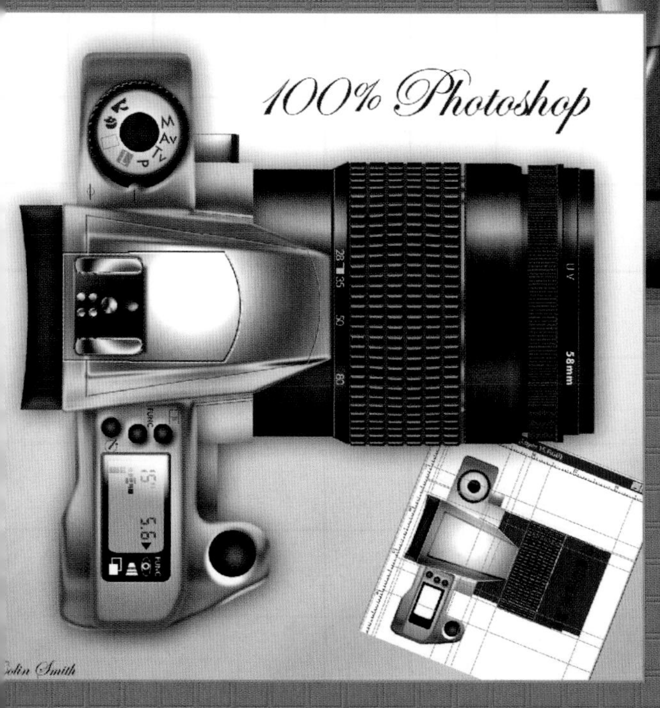
100% Photoshop
58mm
UV
olin Smith

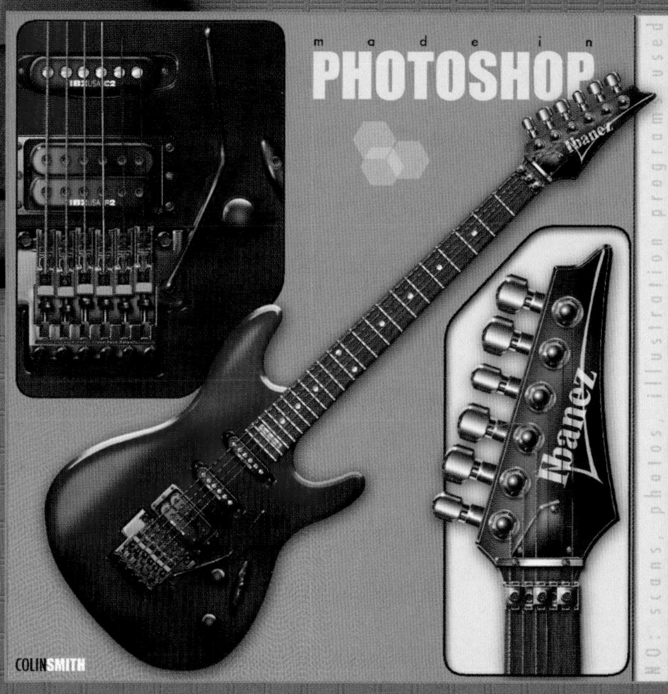
made in
PHOTOSHOP
NO: scans, photos, illustration programs used
Ibanez
COLINSMITH

We're now going to take a look at my guitar image. This image took many hours to complete and consists of hundreds of layers. My goal in creating this piece was to leave out no detail and shoot for ultrarealism. This was really a digital still life project. For reference, I placed the actual guitar in front of me. I prefer to work with real objects instead of photos because I can hold the object in my hand and turn it. This way I can find the optimal angle and lighting for each part. The lighting on the final image is actually a combination of different lighting situations, I found that certain light worked better for the paint and other lighting showed the metal better. The important thing was to have a believable light source for the finished project. To do this, I made a final sweep of the image where I added all the shadows and specular highlights.

With all the techniques involved and the complexity of this image, it would be impossible to show you all the steps I used to create it. This kind of a tutorial would fill the entire book. Instead, I'll walk you through the creation process and you ca see how I approach an illustration. My advice to anyone startir out with a photorealistic image for the first time is to take slow. Don't attempt to create a complex object and then g frustrated and cut corners. You are better off beginning wi something simple and making a really good job of it.

The first thing I did was create the body of the guitar. To mak the shape, I used the Pen tool to create a path. The good thir about paths is that you can adjust them until you are happy wi the shape. Paths will also give you the cleanest edge wh compared to any other tool in Photoshop because they a based on vectors.

I then filled the path with a simple color, which will make easier for me to identify the shapes later. This is something I c all the time. Often I will create the shapes first and then add th depth later on in the image.

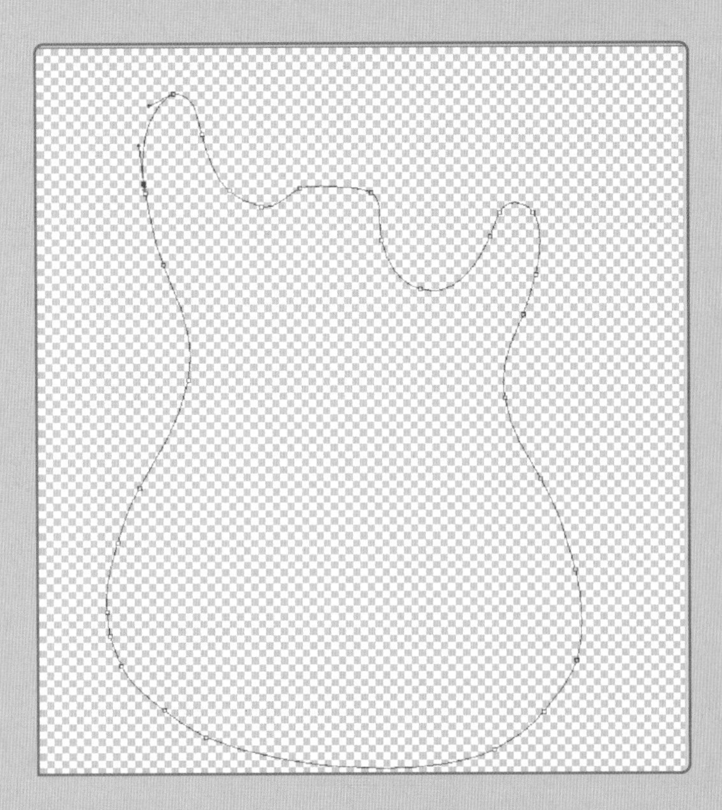

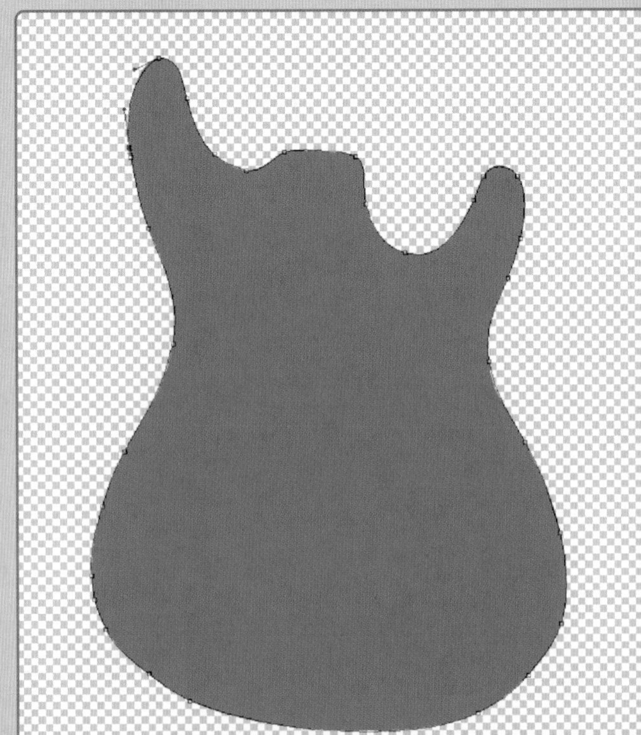

then transferred the shape to an alpha ıannel so that I can combine it with filters ıd create better depth later on.

ısed an airbrush to build up the depth. What ım doing here is creating what I call a "depth ap" (or bump map in the 3D world). I am inking of depth as I add the shades of gray. 'hite is the highest point and black is the west. By using an airbrush, I build up the erall map. I use a Wacom tablet for my ading because it enables me to use the essure sensitive tools in Photoshop. If you ın't have a tablet, don't worry, you can still eate something similar with a mouse. (I used e silly trackpad on my laptop for my camera age. In case you're wondering, the trackpad the thing you put your finger on, and it is a t lower on the food chain than a mouse.) If u are using a mouse, then make a selection ound the shape and choose a huge brush d paint around the edges with only the ge of the brush inside the image. This is a eat way to produce a smooth blend without tablet.

ɔw choose Filter ➤ Render ➤ Lighting fects. This filter is like the 3D engine of otoshop. By using the alpha channel as a xture channel, it's possible to create some ry realistic depth. I've found that the best ay to use this filter is to click and drag the ıints on the light. By doing this we can ange the angle and intensity of the light.

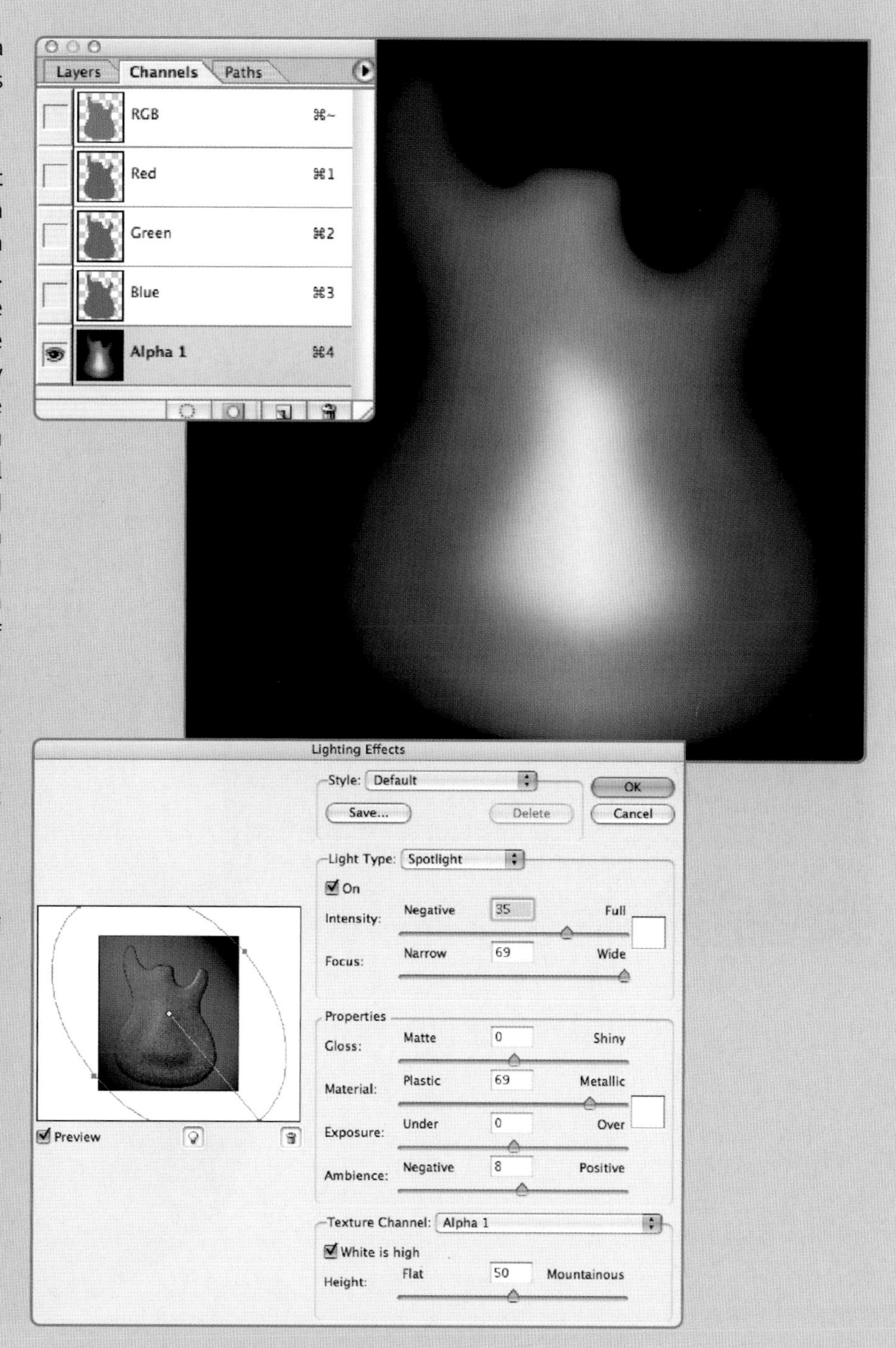

Here is the layer with the lighting effects applied. I love working like this. It's like a metal cast. The cast needs to be trimmed and smoothened out, but I approach my illustration as if I am handling solid objects. I find that this kind of approach keeps me focused on realism.

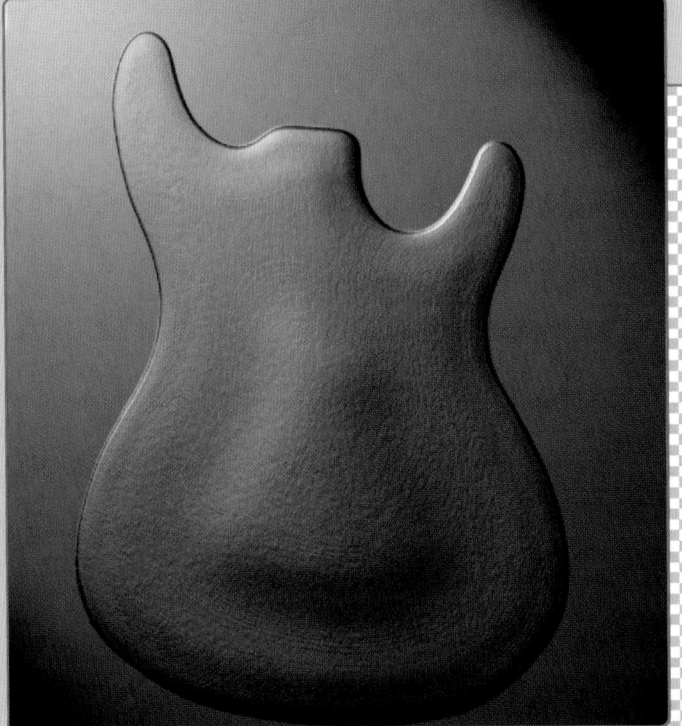

Here is the image after trimming and smoothing with som blurs and a bit of noise. The blurs remove any unwanted textu and banding. However, there are drawbacks with the availab levels in the alpha channel. Even with 16 bit in Photoshop C we are still left with only 256 levels of gray with the alph channel in the lighting effects filter, so the gradients are n that smooth. (Big hint if any Adobe engineers are reading this

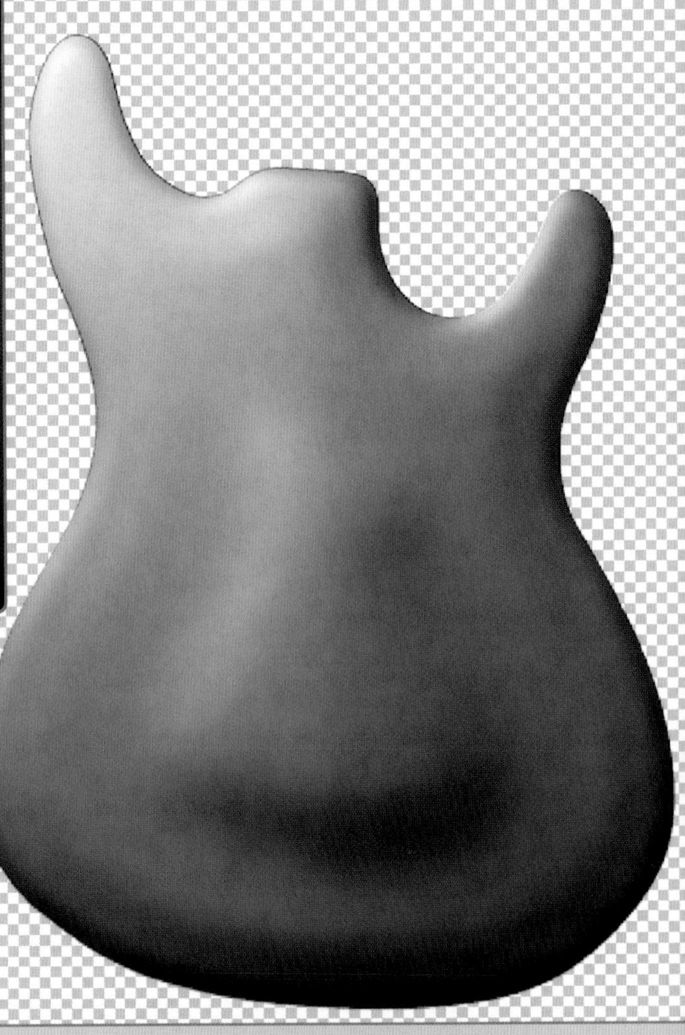

next added the base color with a slight bevel o complete the raw body. To be honest, I ever used to use the layer effects that come ith Photoshop for my personal art. I think hat the quality has improved to the point vhere I now use these styles for quick bevels.)f course, I always modify the settings and arely keep the factory ones. I still supplement he effects by using the airbrush and other echniques. Most of the time, I still prefer to nake the shadows manually because of the ne control that I can't get from the layer ffects. I still don't use any third-party plug-ins or these types of work. I will use plug-ins, and nything else that saves time, for my commrcial work, because time and budgets are lways an issue with these projects.

lext, I used an airbrush to add more coloring nd lighting to the body of the guitar to try nd create the effect of reflections in shiny aint.

enlarged the canvas size and added some uides to help me work. The guides show the pproximate positioning of the pickups and ridge of the guitar. Notice too that I have sed the Notes tool (N) to add notes. Because may be several months before I complete n image due to my other commitments, I nd it important to make notes to remind nyself of what I am doing and what I plan on oing next. When you are working on this ind of image, you are always faced with nique challenges—how to create each effect nd make it look realistic. Every image I create eeds an effect that I may have never created efore, which means that it requires some hought and creative problem solving. When I olve the problem in my head, it's a good idea o make a note of it before I forget.

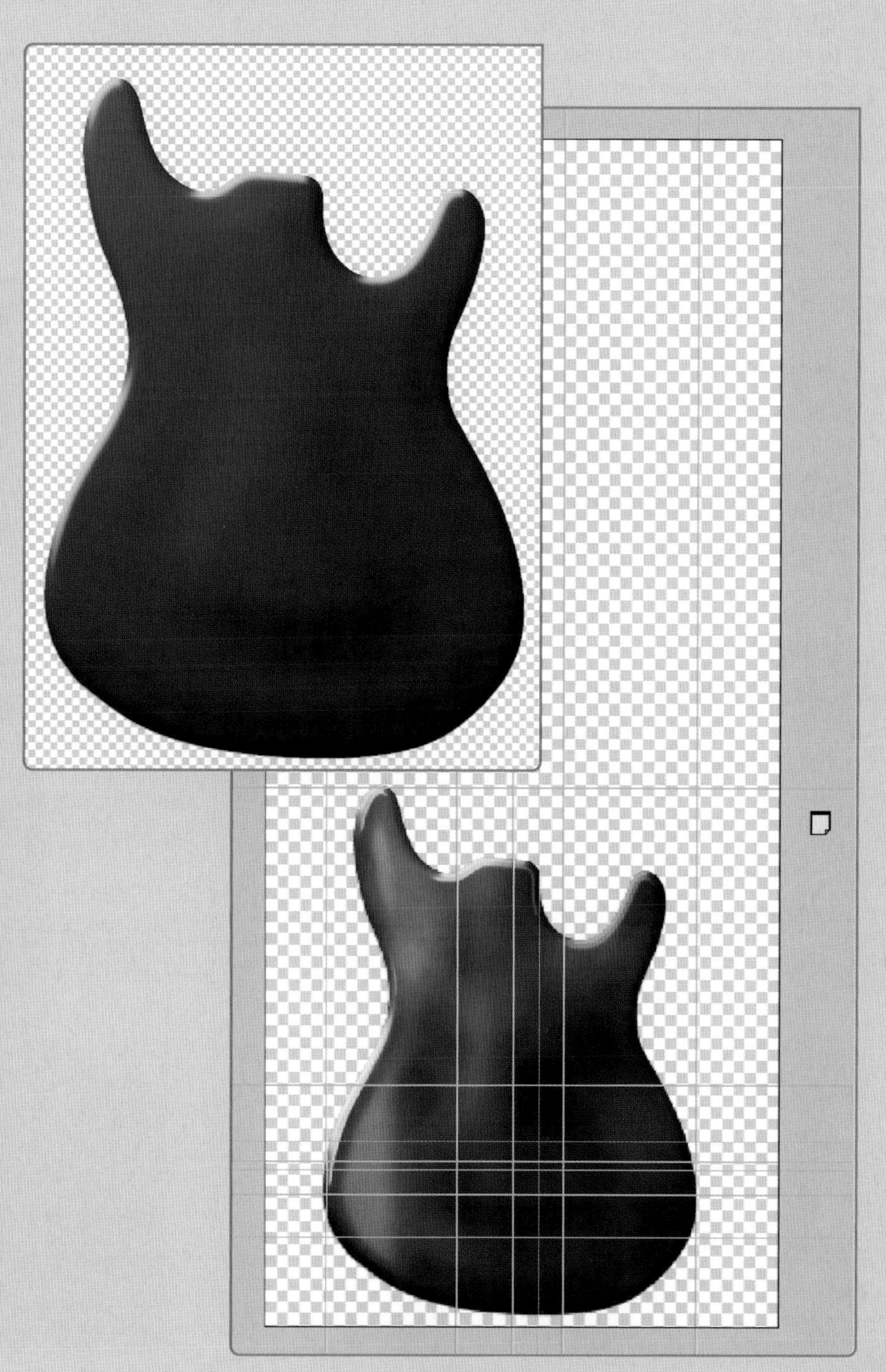

The next task is to create the shape of the neck and position it. Create each component in a new layer set and use new layers as often as possible. This adds to the flexibility of the image. You'll see later on why it is important to be organized even this early on in a piece. Layers can add up quickly.

I textured the neck out of wood. To create the wood, I adde noise and a motion blur. Next, I edited the Hue/Saturatio (CMD+U) to help produce the coloring I wanted. To get it jus right, I duplicated the texture layer and then changed the dup licate's layer blending mode to Multiply.

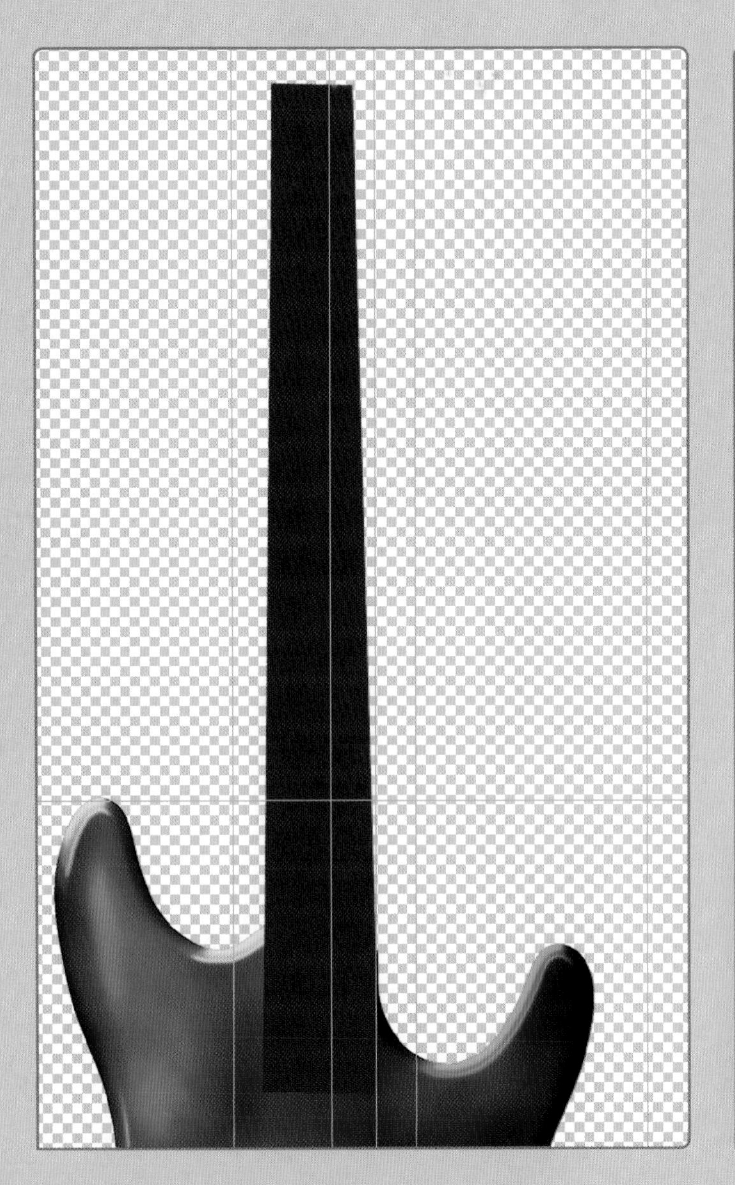

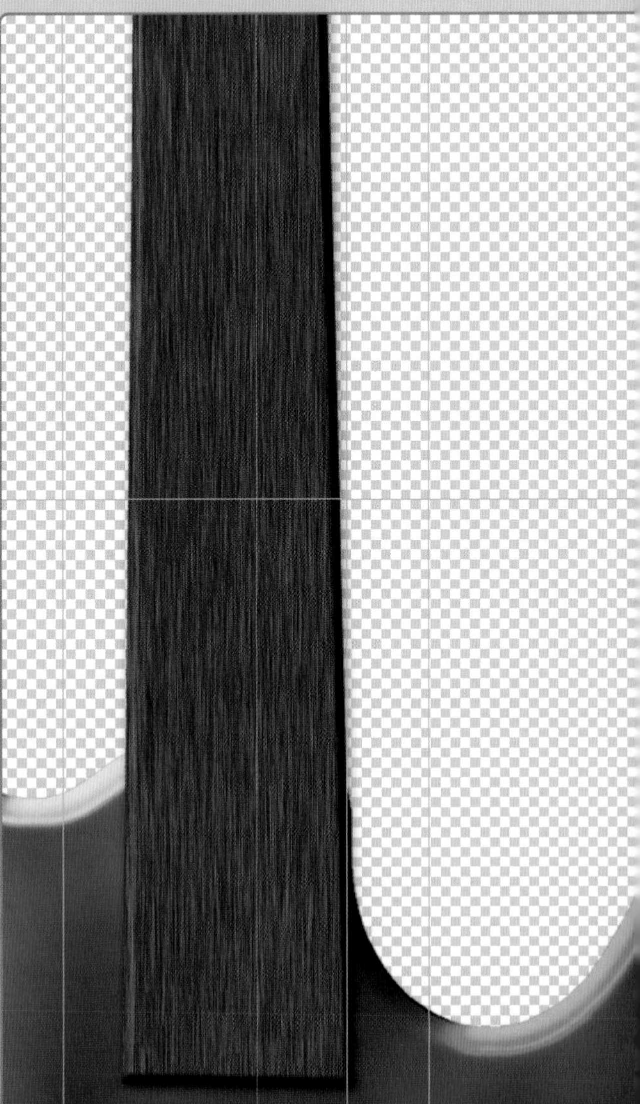

xt, I created the headstock shape with the Pen tool and filled with a solid color. While creating shapes, I tend to use a ferent color for each. This makes it easy to identify the parts the image if I ever need to backtrack.

To get the exact bevel on the edges, I used a bevel layer style (the double ring setting) and created a custom gloss contour. I found that this was a perfect time to use a layer style because the gloss contour creates the exact shaped bevel I need.

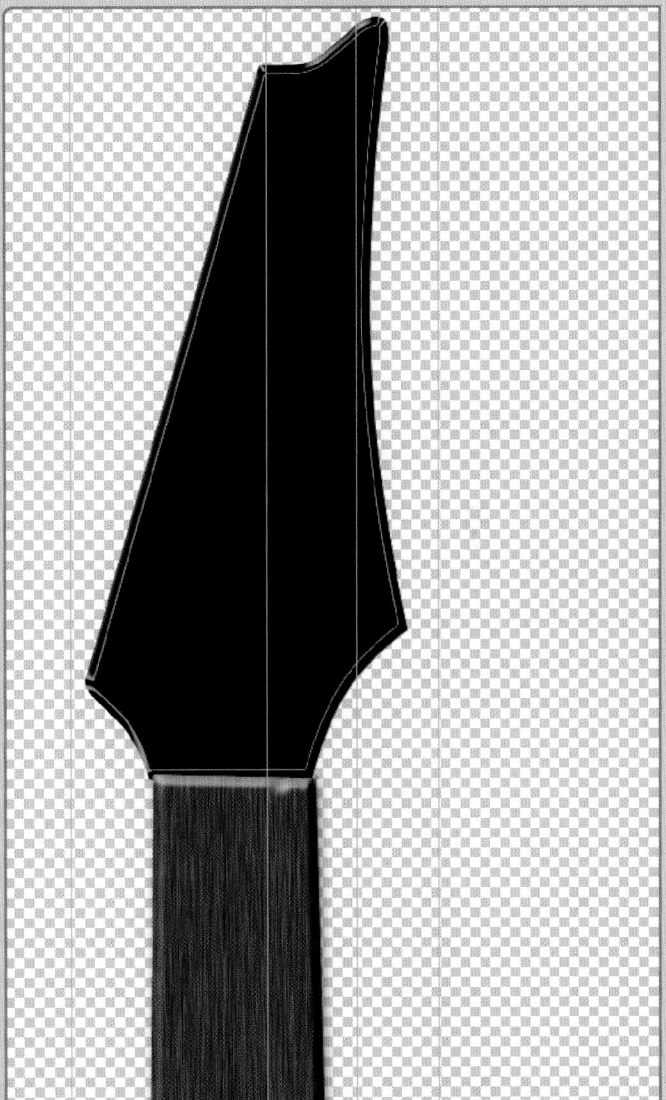

Once again, I used an airbrush to create some highlights and began to add some detail.

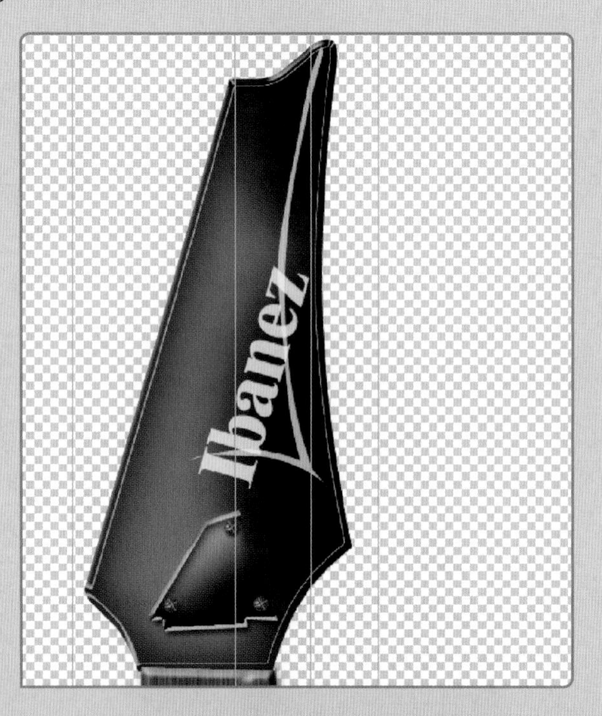

We'll now look at the posts on the headstock. Notice that the shapes are built up starting at the back and working forward. First of all, I made the washer with the Elliptical Marquee tool (M), a bevel layer effect, and a little airbrushing.

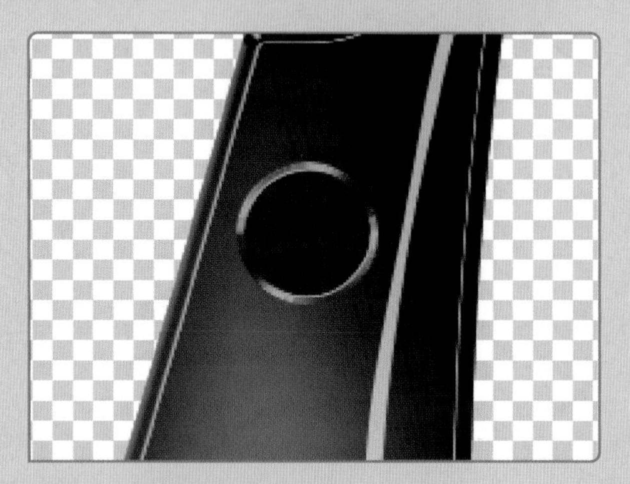

Next, I formed a nut using a circle and then cut away at it wi the selection tools. I used layer styles and mainly airbrushing create the depth and bevels.

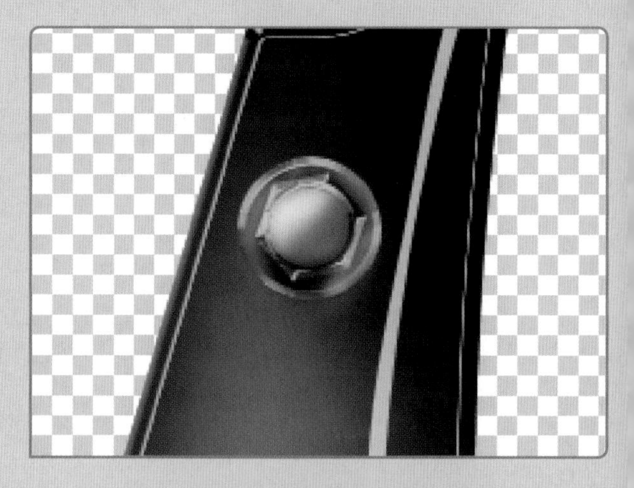

I used a radial gradient to create the round top of the posts.

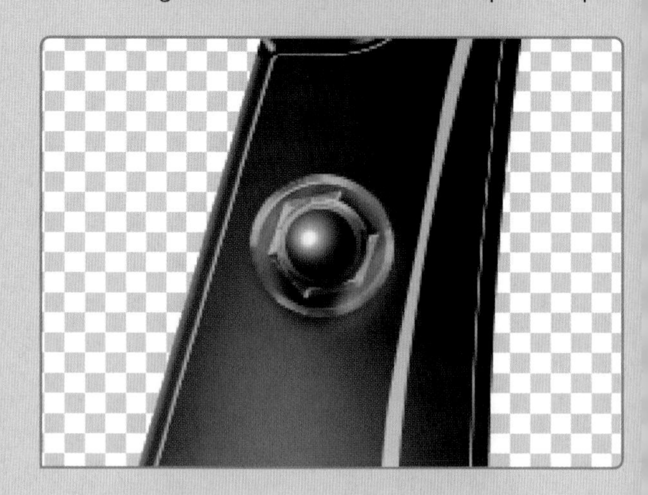

ow it's just a matter of grouping the post into a layer set and ıplicating the set five times to create the other posts on the ·adstock. This is the beauty of digital. We don't have to redraw ıch part. Sections can be reused, and this saves time and also ·oduces consistent results. A particular challenge in this step as placing the string posts. They had to be pretty much right ı, because the strings will eventually meet with them and, if I as off, the whole image would be off later on. Guides and rules e useful for precise placement.

Next I created the tuning pegs and the nut. To create the pegs, I used gradients and selection tools. To add a bit of variety, I rotated two of the pegs. I only had to create a single peg and then modify it for each of the other five.

Now it's time to create the frets. The tricky part about this is getting the spacing right. Frets are not evenly spaced; as you move further up the neck, they get closer together. There are two ways you can do this: create all the frets and then keep moving them until it looks right, or actually take out a ruler and measure the spacing between the frets on the guitar. Either way you choose is fine, as long as the result looks correct.

I used the curve shown here to create the correct texture of the frets, so they would look like shiny steel. I applied this as an adjustment layer to all the layers in the frets layer set. Also, the frets will always be highly reflective on a well-used guitar. I first created all the frets and then positioned them by eye. I would have loved to have used the Distribute tools, but each fret is a different distance from the previous one. It's this kind of detail that makes the difference between a believable image and one that looks right apart from that small part of you that thinks "something seems off."

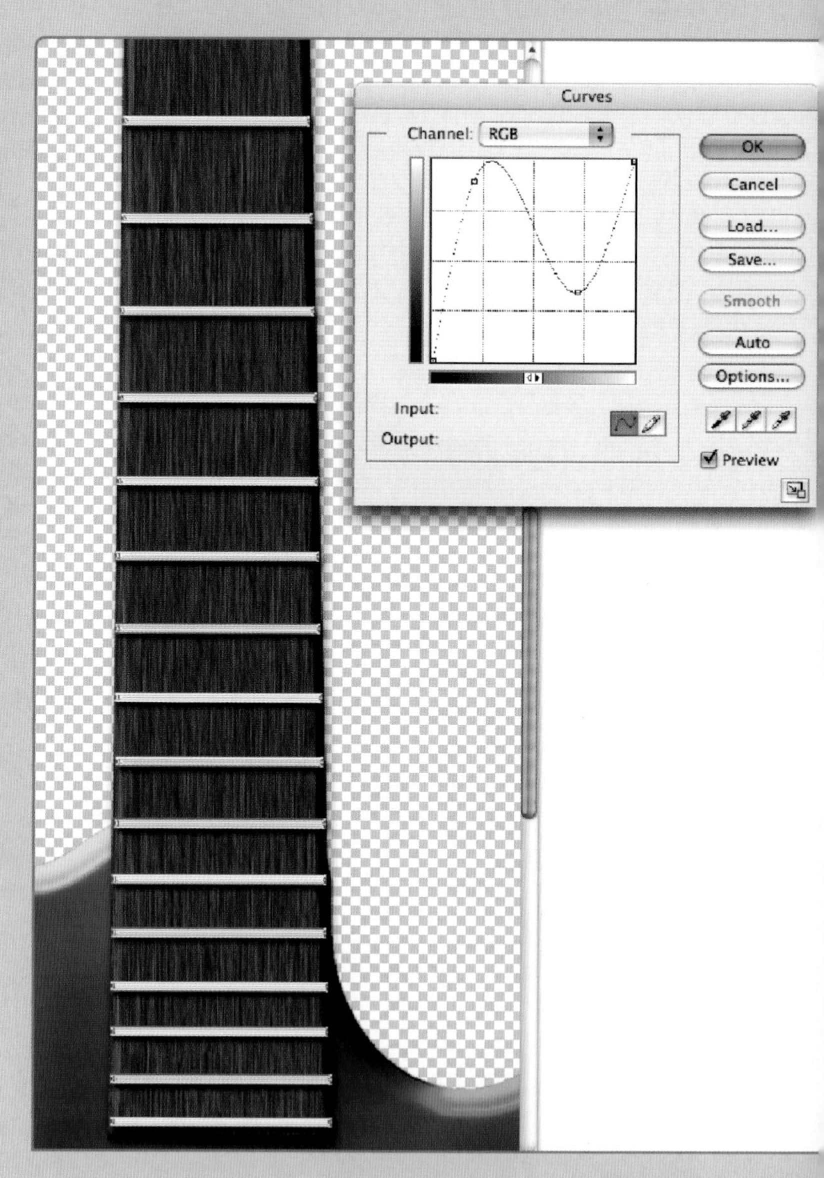

sed the Elliptical Marquee tool (M) with a little bit of airbrushing
add the inlays (the dots on the frets). Also notice the Layers
lette and see the adjustment layer I applied to the set.

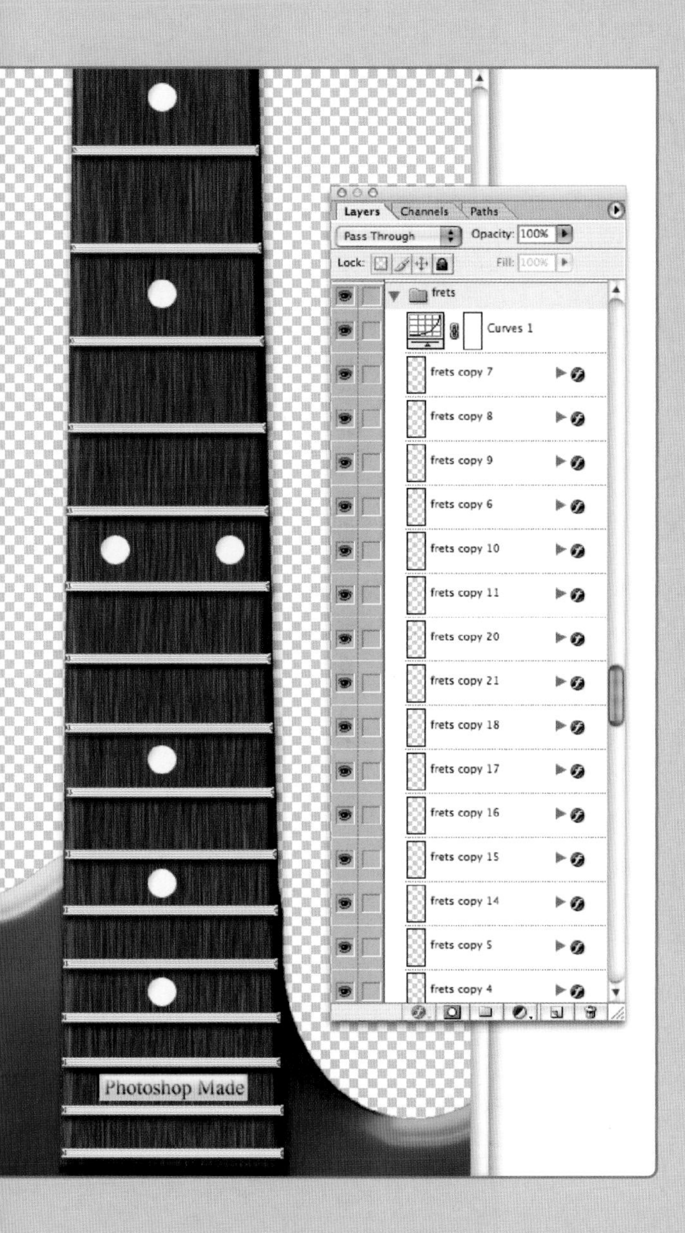

Next I added the strings. I used the Line tool (U) at varying widths to create the strings. It's essential that the spacing is exact at this point because this will affect the rest of the image later on.

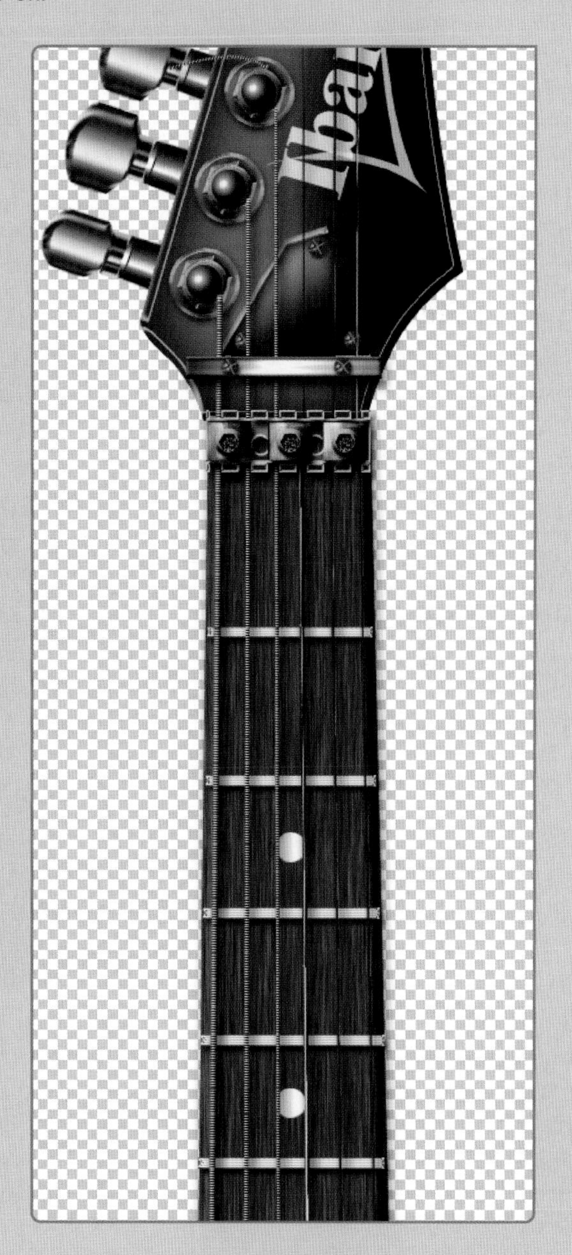

Now that the strings are in place, you can see that they now provide a good guide for the bridge (the bridge on this particular guitar is known as a Floyd Rose bridge). Creating this bridge was a mammoth task in itself and took several sittings, as illustrated by the Layers palette. Each part was fashioned and then it was all put together, just like when a real guitar is built. You have to have a lot of patience to work this way, but the results are worth it.

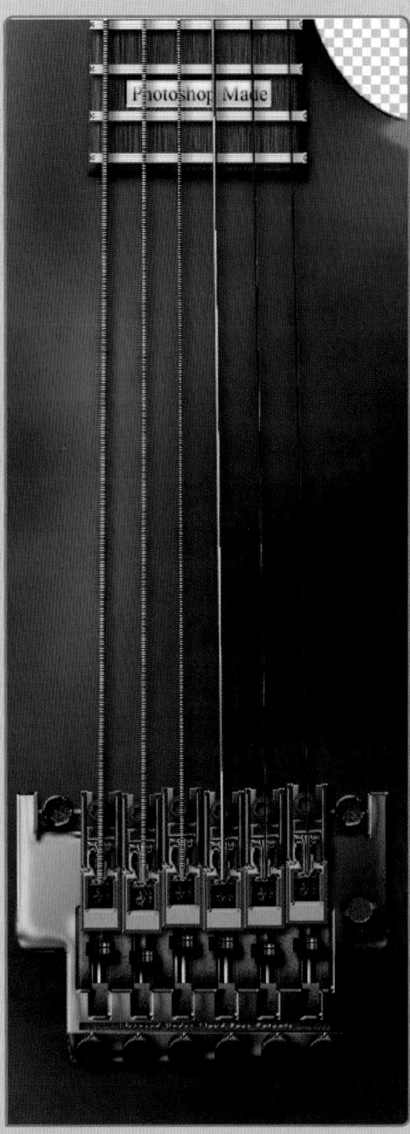

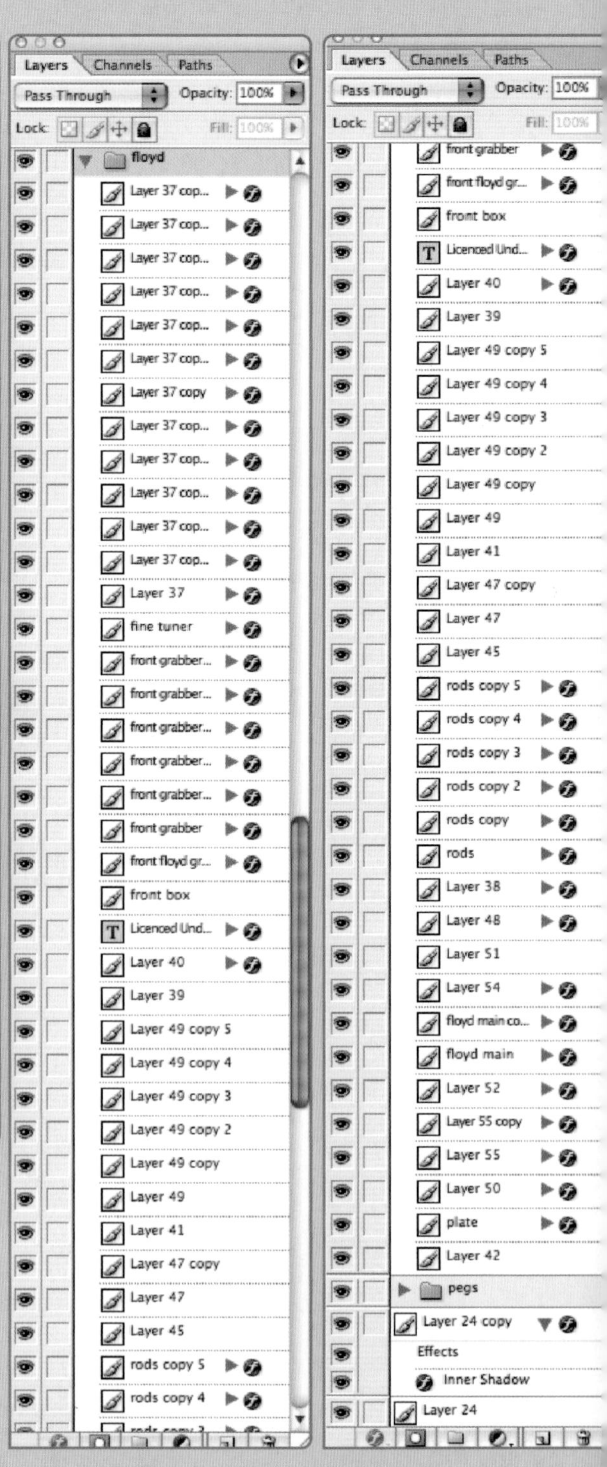

When I'm working, I name all the layer sets and key layers with meaningful names, but it would take too much time to name every layer. (I probably created upward of 300 layers through the course of this project, and many were merged as I worked through.) Because I don't take the time to name every layer, I am very careful to use layer sets and keep each layer in its correct set, otherwise the image would become a mess to manage.

ow it's time to make the cutouts for the pickups that sit nderneath the strings on the body of the guitar. I used the hape tool to make the pickups and trimmed them with lections. What I do is create a basic shape such as a rectangle. hen use the Marquee tools and make selections through these apes and delete them. I know I could use the Pen tool for all these shapes, but sometimes it's quicker to just create shapes d cut chunks out of them. My personal rule of thumb is if the ape has mainly straight edges, then I use shapes and the arquee/Lasso tools. If it's an irregular shape with wavy curves, en I use the Pen tool. Of course, use whatever tool you are mfortable with. Notice that I have also used an airbrush to etch out the highlights of the whammy bar in this image.

e'll now build up the bridge pickup. The first thing I did was eate the frame. I created some screws and embedded them ing a pillow emboss. You can find more information about eating objects such as screws and chrome in the book I authored with Al Ward, *Photoshop Most Wanted 2: More fects and Design Tips* (friends of ED, 2003). There are also me tutorials available on my site (www.photoshopcafe.com) well as some video training CDs (www.photoshopCD.com).

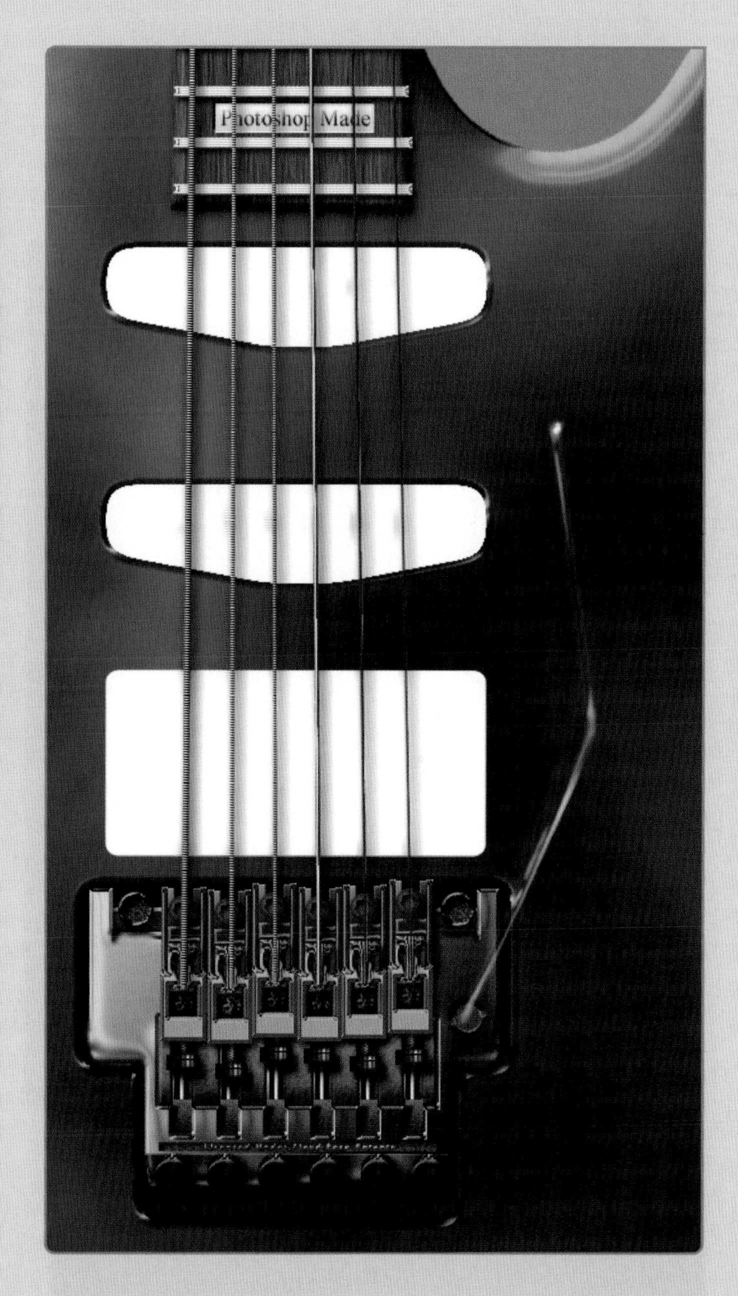

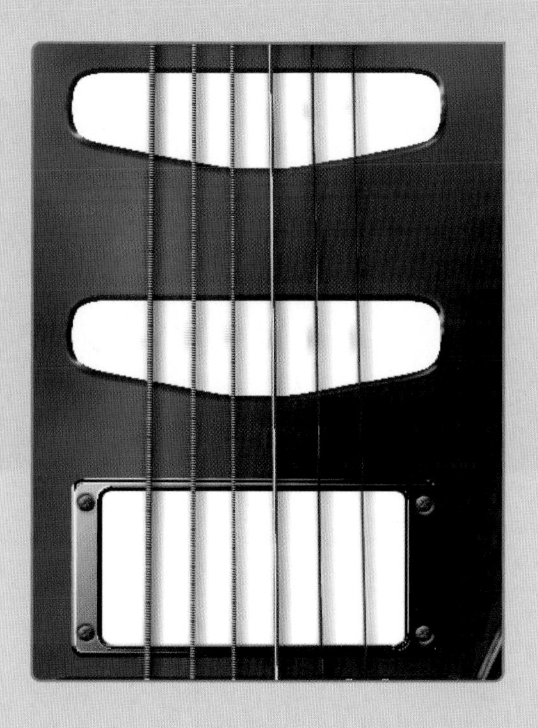

For a final touch, go over the image and add shadows where appropriate, taking into account where the light source is. I've added tiny highlights using the Airbrush tool.

Here is a view of the Layers palette showing all the collapse layer sets, there are well over 300 layers used in this image. If I hadn't used layer sets and naming on this image, it would hav been very difficult to organize.

\nd here is the final guitar image:

'inally, I took the guitar and created this layout to lisplay it. Realizing that few people would have the hance to view it at full size, I created the layout so that he detail could be seen even at small dimensions. I also hose a color and layout that would not distract from he image. Some people make the mistake of creating layout that competes with the object they are lisplaying. It must have worked, because I was lucky nough to win a Guru award at Photoshop World for his image and was also a finalist at Macworld.

y now, you will have noticed that I am very obsessive bout the details. I guess I got used to working this way rom building models as I grew up. I would even neticulously paint the parts that would never be seen. : adds to the total effect more by affecting my mindset s I am working. I feel like I must handle the image with are so that I don't break it. Silly I know, but if you have ver built models you will know what I am talking bout. At times, I hold my breath as I apply a brush- troke, feeling a bit like a surgeon with a scalpel. As trange as it sounds, even though I am the one creating ne image, I treat it with respect. It's almost as if I am orrowing the image from some unseen realm and, if I m patient and treat it with enough respect, I will be ewarded with a good result.

have mentioned the word "patience" many times. This ind of art is not for everyone; it is for the patient. ometimes only a small piece can be done in a single tting. When I feel the urge to skip ahead and take hortcuts, I know that my work for the day is over. I ave enough pressure from deadlines everyday running y design studio. When I am working on a commercial roject, I understand the deadlines, the goals, and the sponsibility to get the design right and done on time. Vhen I am working on private projects, there is no ush, this is my way of relaxing, so I find great peace nd clarity of thought as I work on these pieces.

m a d e i n
PHOTOSHOP
COLIN SMITH
Ibanez
IBZ USA C2
IBZ USA F2

08 BRUSHWORK

"DIVERSITY AND BALANCE ARE JUST AS IMPORTANT IN LIFE AS THEY ARE IN ART."

SEUNG HO HENRIK HOLMBERG
HTTP://HENRIK.CGCOMMUNITY.COM

When I was first asked if I wanted to participate in this project, I was terrified. I was afraid that my thoughts, or "story," would not come across as I intended, and that I would not be able to express what was going on inside my head all those years ago. I was afraid that my story would not be interesting enough to write about or, more importantly, to listen to. How do you go about writing an interesting and informative, yet personal, essay on inspiration alone?

Inspiration and motivation are key elements to success in your efforts, regardless of the subject matter. You find inspiration wherever you go, every day, and perhaps where you least expect it. This makes it so much more fun to explore. I am hoping that reading this chapter might help you just a little bit on your way, inspire you, and hopefully motivate you to create your own artwork.

Whole image painted freehand in Photoshop using a Wacom tablet
© Seung Ho Henrik Holmberg 2002

Growing up in a small Swedish city where contemporary art was very limited, dare I say next to nonexistent, I had to find art nfluences wherever I could. We didn't exactly have world-renowned art galleries or museums like the British Museum around the corner. We could not compete with the Tate in London or Le Louvre in Paris. Mind you, we did have a pretty decent library where I'd go and borrow books for bedtime reading.

The library was a nice red wooden building that looked something like a red barn with white corners. There was a box directly outside the building where you could return books when the library was closed. Sometimes I'd go to the library by myself and bring all kinds of books home. When I was finished, I'd return them, always on time. When you entered the building, the children's books were placed on the left-hand side, whereas the novels and more sophisticated books could be found to the right. Walking those aisles, looking up at all those books, created a strange feeling of humility inside of me. The work and knowledge that went into filling those shelves made a lasting mpression. I was able to feel a true sense of admiration and awe that I wish every kid got to experience. Not only kids, but everyone. I truly hope that this legacy continues to work its way through generations to come, that we, in our modern day with easy access to the Internet, still have some spare time to spend

I probably didn't know it at that point, but today, ten or so yea later, I guess, in a way, I've realized that that's where my fire c creativity was lit. I remember reading one series that consiste of four books. In Swedish the title is *Hjältar och monster p himlavalvet*, which translates to something like this: *Heroes an Monsters of the Heavens.* Written by Maj Samzelius, these boo have a nice and simple approach to Greek mythology—th gods, their stories, and their adventures. The books have sever separate stories tied together, all of which are narrated by grandfather who is telling stories to his grandchildren. Th stories revolve around the signs of the zodiac, where each sig has a related story. Those were some of the best stories I'v read. As a result of these stories, I developed an interest i Greek mythology at an early age and tried to learn as much a I could. Wherever I came across stories told of the gods, I' listen, whether I found them in games, books, or films. Th stories were intriguing, exciting, and imaginative, and ofte violent. I guess you can compare these stories to modern da fantasy novels like *Lord of the Rings*, but to me, reading abou Zeus, Athena, Dionysus, Oedipus, Hercules, and all the other was a far superior experience to any other fantasy novel I'v read. The stories of the gods left me wondering if there was a truth to them, if these stories had actually happened the wa they were described. Granted, the books weren't a sophisticated as Tolkien's by any means, but they were enoug

ther than the library, there was a small bookshop located on e main street of my town. Here, you could find simple art pplies, limited to drawing materials, and some children's ooks. I particularly remember spending my saved money on a ries of books by Enid Blyton called *The Famous Five*. Blyton is obably the most famous British children's writer of the ventieth century, with around 700 titles published. The umber is hard to confirm, but it gives you a general idea of ow prolific she was. Her books continue to sell well, even day. Some might seem old and outdated today, especially with e attitude displayed in her stories that could suggest an most sexist attitude in the way she portrayed the characters nd their relationships to each other. (Toward the end of the 950s, librarians would refuse to stock Blyton's books on the ounds that children would not read great works of literature. is had the opposite effect, resulting in even more books. fter some negative response from the press, Blyton allegedly ated that criticism from someone over the age of 12 didn't ally count.)

ne series puts friendship, stories, and mysteries in focus. *The mous Five* tells the story of four young kids and their dog; ey solve mysteries by utilizing their cleverness and wit to oid danger. This series was written in such a way that you ould be hooked once you picked up the first book and you'd ever let it go until the children were home, safe and sound.

nese two series of books—*The Famous Five* and *Heroes and onsters of the Heavens*—represented the kind of literature I ad. Reading definitely did create a spark of creative thinking, ut as far as direct artistic influences go, I had other sources of spiration that are more accessible and easier to understand. If u're young and want to become an artist, especially in the tertainment industry, you might want more than a few ildren's books as inspiration.

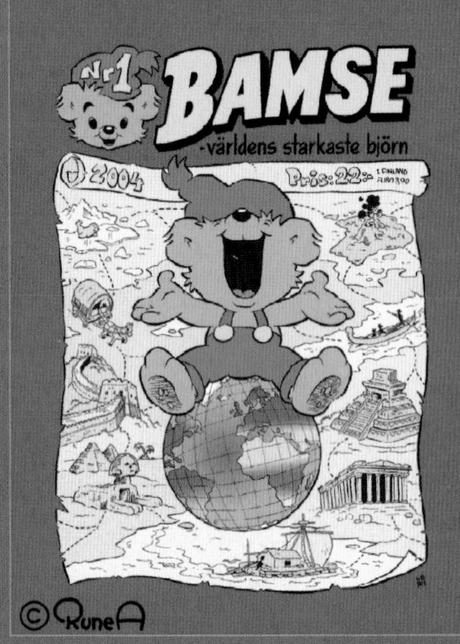

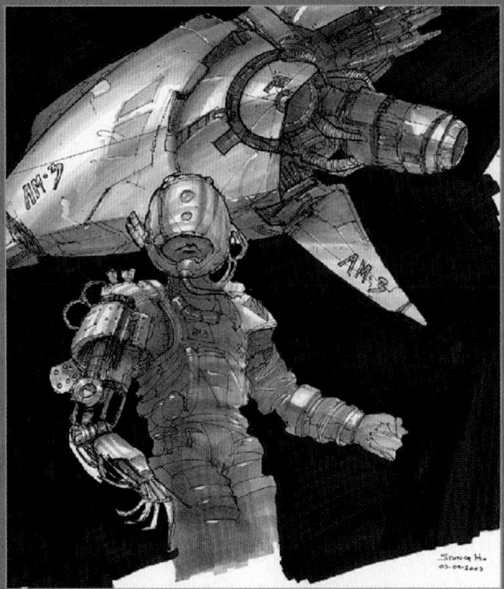

Copyright Rune A, used with permission.

One of my strongest influences as a kid was comic books. They were not very expensive, so I'd get some new ones every month. I'd have a limited amount of money from my parents, so prioritizing proved essential. Of course, this is where I put most of my money. Looking at my artwork today, I can see a vein of symmetry and simplicity. Sometimes I am even overpowered by a feeling that my artwork is childish. Whether it's a legitimate conclusion or not really depends on how the viewer chooses to look at it, but I won't deny that most of my earlier inspirations were all simple.

One source of inspiration was a Swedish comic called *Bamse*. It told the story of a friendly bear, Bamse, his family, and his friends. When he ate grandma's honey, he gained a huge amount of strength in a matter of seconds. In fact, the honey turned him into the strongest bear in the world. Anyone else who tried to eat the same honey would get a stomachache and wish that they'd never touched it. The world in which Bamse lived was a simple and stylized one, with characters portrayed as various animals, ranging from bears to turtles, rabbits, and hedgehogs. Humans and animals would have coexisted and lived in peace together in this world, had it not been for t wolves. These foul creatures always tried to create troub wherever they roamed. All the character portraits were cle with well thought out identities and characteristics. This com had a down-to-earth approach in the way it described t characters and their interaction with the world—there w always a clear moral that couldn't be misinterpreted. At hea it was a story about good and evil, friendship, humanity, a humbleness towards your peers. Nothing was ever impossible achieve. The friends would do anything to help each other o when facing trouble.

Clearly this wonderful comic was a huge source of inspiration me. Perhaps more so than I'd like to admit. Not only have t morals of these stories affected my outlook on life in gener but they are also reflected in my artwork. It's getting less a less obvious as I grow older and find other influences, but I s recognize the playful spirit of the comic in my pictures. Lin shapes, and colors are sometimes what connect my artwork today with my childhood influences.

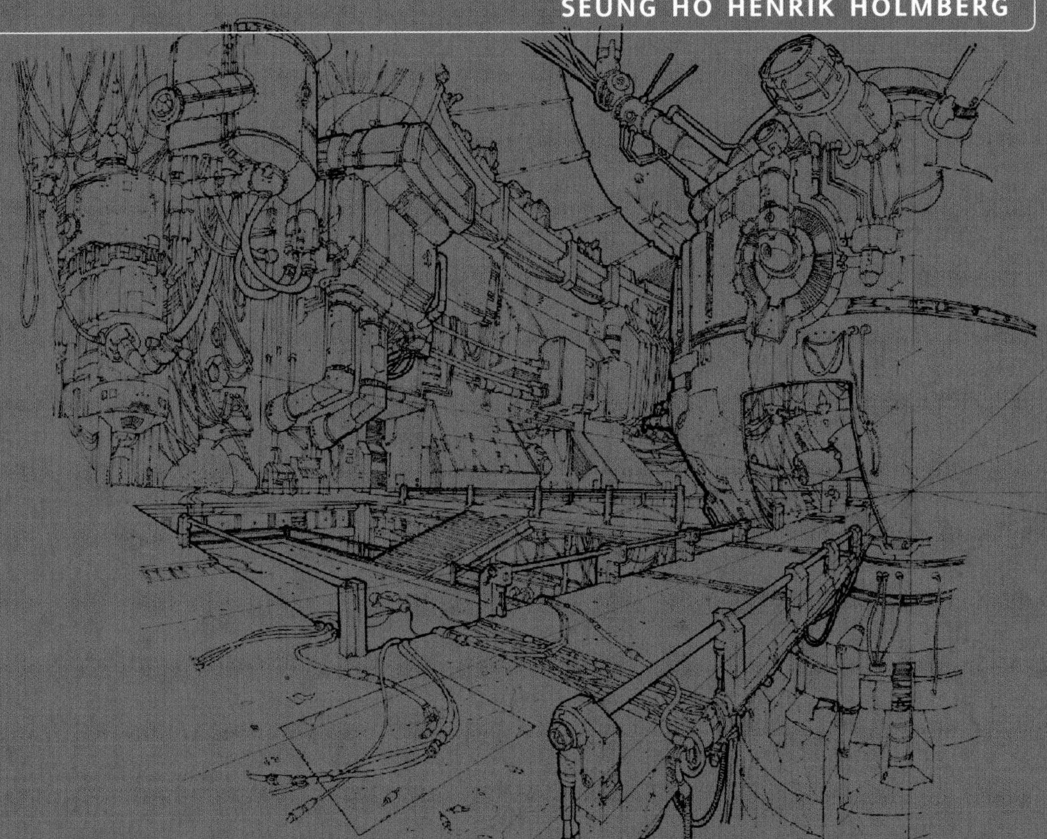

other huge source of inspiration was video games. I could
k forever about how they influenced me as a young aspiring
tist." Because I grew up playing the Nintendo Entertainment
stem, I found it easy to relate to the artwork on display in
ese games. Although the games themselves look outdated
day, with their minimal resolution and bit depth, even with
ch limited resources, they evoke an aura of magic and
eativity. Whenever I see those games mentioned today, I get
nostalgic and recall the memories of endless game play.

ch game was nicely packaged in a box, with a printed cover
ustration. They didn't always represent the games accurately,
t they were indeed nice to look at. These illustrations,
gether with the occasional purchase of a games magazine,
ould represent the majority of my graphical influences. It was
e coolest art I could think of, especially those with heroic
aracters like Link from the Zelda games, Samus from Metroid,
Megaman. I would grab a cover, a pencil, and lie down on the
oor with huge rolls of paper in front of me, drawing at any
portunity.

The composition, the way they looked, the way the artist tried to capture the essence of the game was what intrigued me. Very often, you could see covers where the main character struck a cool pose with lots of robots and enemy fire blazing in the background. That was all I needed to get inspired. At every occasion I drew, I'd end up with meter after meter of my paper roll filled with doodles. Spaceships, robots, machines, characters, and monsters all mixed together in an indescribable mess. My doodle didn't have much of a structure, a thought process, or a goal other than the pure joy of creating art.

As I mentioned earlier, inspiration and motivation are essential in order to obtain your goals. In today's busy art world, where you are working long hours and constantly fighting tight deadlines, it's easy to get tired of it all, to stop creating, and eventually to extinguish the "fire" inside. I have worked with great artists who have stopped creating personal art because they don't feel inspired anymore. If this is a result of getting more comfortable and lazy, I can't tell, but what I do know is that such great artists don't lose the fire easily.

People get inspired by different things; some things work for me, some don't. I'd like to use this opportunity to touch on creativity blocks—how I get around them and manage to not only keep working, but keep motivated to improve my knowledge and practical skills too. Please bear in mind that the following comments and speculations are my own thoughts—they may not be true for you. They are merely an artist's thoughts on how to deal with everyday life when pressure starts knocking on your door.

As an artist, you might sometimes experience a slow period where everything you lay your hands on disappoints you. It can seem as if the artwork is teasing you, smiling and enjoying its sole purpose of making you more and more frustrated. Like a cat sinisterly playing with a mouse. When you pick up the pen to draw, it feels heavy, your lines end up shaky, or your confidence isn't what it normally is. I'm sure all of you reading this have experienced it more than once. You ask yourself if you are the only one who can't draw. The person next to you can keep up with the pace; s/he seems so inspired that you can't do anything other than simply stare in awe. I'll say this to make you feel better; you're not alone. Creativity blocks can be devastating for artists, especially when we're facing a crunch period at work where we have to finish a bunch of drawings or paintings in a short amount of time. It's bad news when we feel not the least motivation to finish, we can't focus, and our minds wander. What's even worse is that we might get burned out. Whenever that happens, our first reaction is exhaustion. We simply can't work any more no matter how fun we find the projects. To prevent this, it's important to find a balance.

The most influential artists I have ever worked with are tho who are not only good at what they do for a living, but also many other things that occupy their spare time. These artists a not satisfied with the merit of being great artists, they a inspired human beings in all aspects. Some of them are gre speakers and musicians, some are great hockey players, cyclis writers, poets, sculptors, photographers, and so on. You c categorize many, if not all, of these activities as "art" or at lea art-related. It doesn't matter exactly what it is you choose to c the important thing is that you do something that doesn't rela to work. Personally, I've come to recognize that the importan of diversity and balance in life is as equally important for yo art as the art is itself. Working out, writing, or just relaxing w friends is a great way to keep sane.

Upon getting my first job in the art field, I had doubts abo whether or not to pursue a career in that direction. 3D wo drawing, and painting had been my passion for a long time, a I was facing a situation that was unknown and somewh intimidating. Having played games, and having watched film and animations since childhood, the temptation to throw mys at it kept growing stronger. However, creating art full time w something I was very concerned about. The line betwe interest and duty would be erased, blending into an inseparab relationship I did not desire. What made me choose the art pa was ultimately my motivation to improve my painting skills a to find myself. I had low self-esteem, and identifying myself my art was a way of escaping as well as a way of getti accepted. When you're young and insecure, you need a spa where you can feel comfortable and welcome—a pla to belong.

I remember the early years of my life when I used to play with Lego. I would sit for long hours, in what seemed like a meditative condition, forgetting everything around me. Building all kinds of weird, colorful, and technical creations all day long shaped my childhood and the way I work even today. That's where I developed my understanding for object composition and how objects work in 3D space. The models I made were not always functional; they often started out as badly drawn figures with no anatomy at all, or sculptures made with clay that had already dried out. I'd work hard to make the structure of a model work and look the way I wanted. If something was wrong and it didn't work, I'd take a break, and go do something else for a while. Coming back with a fresh mind and a new approac[h] is what seems to work best for me. After all, if the key doesn['t] fit the keyhole, it's probably not the right key.

In a way, you can almost say that not painting has made me [a] better painter. That it is actually taking breaks that helps m[e] learn the most, much like how muscles grow when you ar[e] resting after the actual workout. Sometimes I feel I don't pain[t] enough or work hard enough. But when these feelings start t[o] pop up, I know that my rest is important just like an athlete's and that's what keeps me motivated.

course, improving coordination and hands-on skill takes a lot practice, but what's more important is to stay inspired. An inspired artist will not create. Finding this inspiration, and ing able to turn it into motivation, is more important than ything else. I have met people who come from a humble ckground with limited resources or basic conditions, and they ntinue to motivate me, forcing me to stay inspired.

What ultimately makes me continue to grow as an artist is the way I live my life, the people I have had the pleasure to meet, the images and places I've had the opportunity to see, and the feelings I've experienced. I'm searching for a balance where I can coexist alongside the creativity, and not be overwhelmed by it or my everyday life. Thus, my artistic identity is equally shaped from the artistic influences I had as a kid, and the emotional pulp called life.

So why is it that Photoshop is the tool to use for painting? After all, you could have drawn the picture, scanned it, and colored it in with any software available. Or you could simply have taken several photographs, put them together, and read a book, all before dinner. I choose Photoshop primarily for three reasons.

First, I've been using it for a long time and feel comfortable working with it. It's like when you try to adjust to a new habit—just keep doing it and it feels natural the longer you stay with it. The speed comes with experience, and I haven't found any other software with the same speed and flexibility working together in a peaceful harmony.

Second, Photoshop is a very capable piece of software when it comes to blending modes, layer management (including adjustment layers), and alpha channel support. Blending modes can seem random at first, but once you learn what they do, they give you great flexibility. Also, the addition of adjustment layers makes life easier; it's as simple as that.

Finally, the brush engine is superb (albeit a bit slow). The fact that you can create brushes makes it so much easier and interesting to work with, and it also increases the "fun factor" when you're starting out and learning how to paint.

I love to paint beautiful things that evoke emotions inside, feeling of attachment to what I'm painting. It's one of mar things that drives me to create. For this tutorial, I wanted t create a beautiful painting of a temple with an interestir landscape and a sense of magic in the air. I was drawn to th challenge of painting this particular piece because it's a pictu for a personal project that I've been working on for a while could feel the story evolve and develop into somethir interesting as it progressed. It's difficult to explain in words wh "interesting" is, though I'll try to explain what's going on insi my head as we paint. The story of this project revolves arour many different locations, and this is one of them.

What inspired me the most to paint this was a couple drawings I did recently. The drawings look like something fro a Chinese city, but also with aspects of the Chinese countrysid The place I had in mind was the famous Guilin City. It's bee called South China's shining pearl and is known all over th world. Guilin City has been said to have the finest scenery und heaven, and looking at the landscape it isn't difficult to see wh Sometime in the near future I hope to go there and experien this mythical and inspirational place.

the following tutorial, I will show you a few techniques and ›s on how to maintain a simple and effective workflow, thout losing too much flexibility. Because most of my current ›rk is done on a laptop with limited hardware resources, eed is crucial and everything has to be optimized. The chniques I'll show you here are how I work in a real vironment, both personally and professionally. Having said at, it's important to keep the layer structure as simple, yet en, as possible (for example, when working with clients who mand quick and drastic changes). Most of the techniques re are fairly generic, so you can apply them to any other age you work on. Although some will be more specific than hers, the tutorial will rely heavily on straightforward painting owledge. Don't worry if your painting ability isn't too vanced. I'll try to break it down into small steps. The tutorial made up of four sections:

- Getting started
- Painting clouds
- Sketching
- Painting the image

rhaps you'll get more curious about digital painting and feel ger to try it out after you've read the different sections. Let's pe that the end result is interesting enough to make your gers itch from curiosity and easy enough to follow so that u can get started immediately.

tting started

ere are a few things I'd like to recommend before starting s tutorial, all of which are optional, but which will make life sier for you in the long run.

st, it's important to have a graphics tablet. Without one, you'll ve a hard time following the steps demonstrated here. Any and, size, or color will do. I would recommend (hopefully thout sounding like a salesman) a Wacom Intuos 2/Graphire 3 aphics tablet size A5 (6x8) or similar. They are easy to find in ›res and the price for the A6 (4x5) ones is affordable.

It's hard to see and estimate values accurately if settings are too dark or too bright, so you will need a good balance. Adjust your screen brightness and contrast so that white looks white and black looks black.

You can debate this forever, but there's no right or wrong way to set your brush parameters. I like to set Opacity and Flow to 100 percent, with Other dynamics turned on, which enables pressure sensitivity. These are the minimum settings for all my brushes.

Set up a few brushes for sketching. A couple of round hard-edged brushes set at low spacing (which prevents lines from breaking into streaks of dots) and some custom ones are enough for what we're going to do. Creating custom brushes helps get some texture into an otherwise flat looking image. Feel free to create your own. Experiment with the scattering and shape dynamics options to create interesting effects. Brushes can look something like this:

It's also worth learning some of the more important hotkeys, which will be used frequently throughout this tutorial:

- B: Paintbrush
- X: Toggle foreground/background color
- L: Lasso tool
- SHIFT+L: Cycles through lasso modes
- CTRL+E: Merge linked or merge down if no links (layers)
- CTRL+G: Group with previous layer
- CTRL+SHIFT+G: Ungroup
- SPACEBAR: Hand tool
- ALT+Eyedropper tool: Hold ALT when using the paintbru for color picking
- CTRL+J: New layer via copy
- CTRL+H: Hide/show extras

Find a window layout that you feel comfortable with Photoshop. Most of the work we'll do here is painting. T Paintbrush is the main tool for creating the sketch, so recommend that you set up your screen so that you can eas access Paintbrush settings, colors, layers, and channels. Y don't want to spend too much time traveling back and for with your pointer across the screen. If you paint all day lor you'll appreciate an optimized layout. Essentially, you want much space as possible for your painting while still being ab to select tools quickly. This is the setup I normally use:

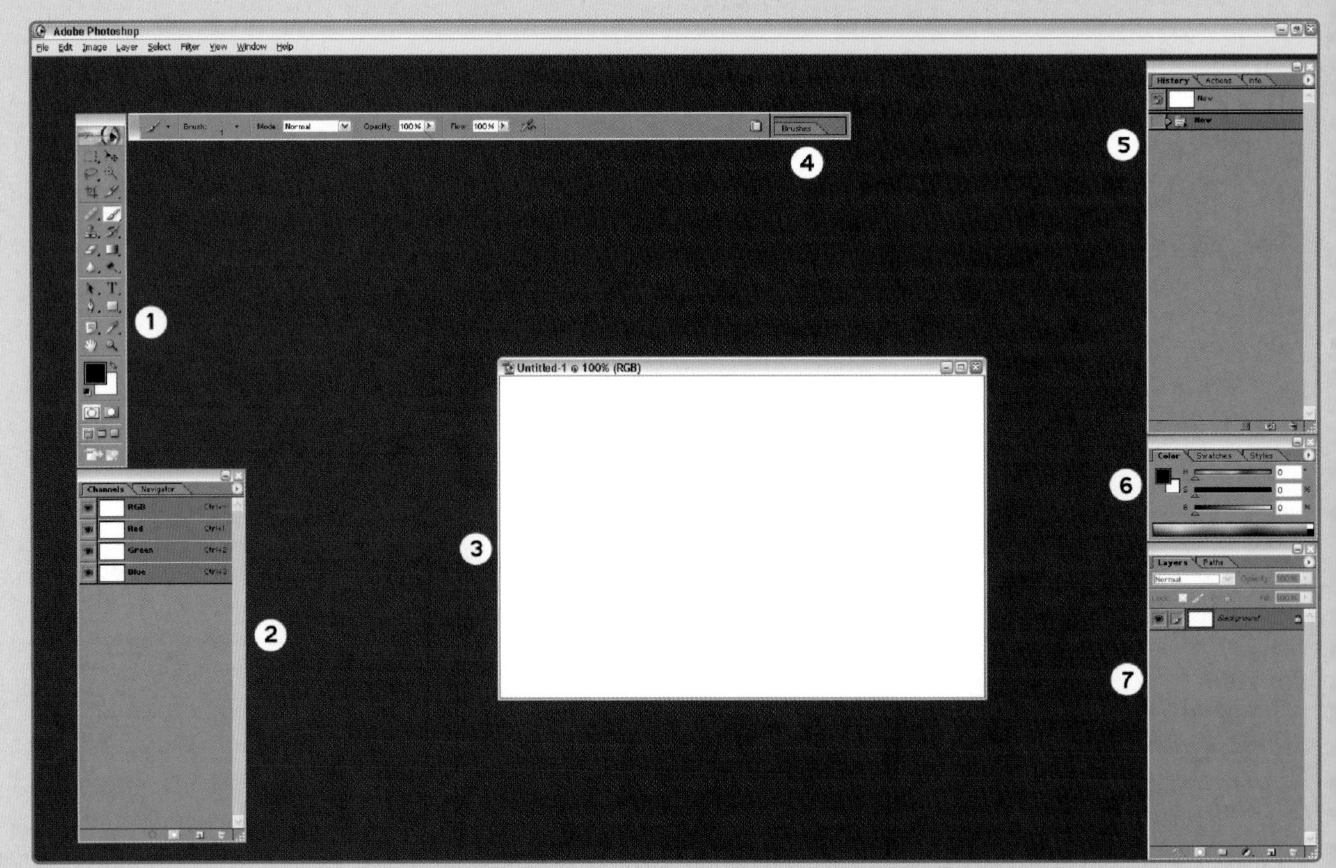

- **Toolbox:** I've placed this at the left. We'll mainly be using the Brush tool.
- **Channels palette:** We'll use this for painting through channels and to create masks.
- **Sketch:** Where we paint our image.
- **Brush settings:** We'll use these to create various brushes.
- **History palette:** Set your number of history states in Edit ➤ Preferences ➤ General to a minimum of 10. The more undo levels you have, the more memory Photoshop uses.
- **Color palette** (with set foreground color button): Clicking the set foreground color button brings up the Color picker so, if you clicked the same button in the Toolbox, you'd have one on both sides of the screen for quick color selection.
- **Layers palette:** We'll use quite a few layers; so giving this box some extra space provides an overview and makes it easy to manage them.

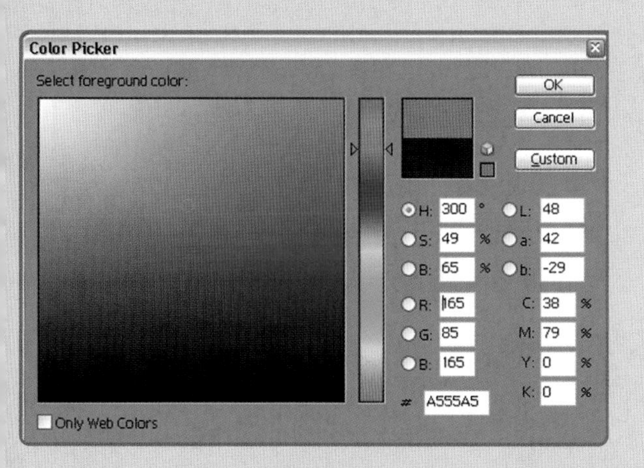

t your screen resolution as large as possible. If you're using a to 21 inch screen, I recommend 1600x1200. If you're using a aller screen, set the resolution to no less than 1024x768.

As a rule of thumb, work with your image at a higher resolution than your target resolution. If you plan to use it at 600x400, for instance, you should work at least twice as big as your final image. Open up a new RGB window, size 1200x800. I wouldn't go higher than that for a very quick color key like this. However, when we start the final painting, we'll go even higher, up to 3 to 4 times larger than the intended target resolution. The reason for this is so you don't have to zoom in several hundred percent with very little control over where your pixels end up. By working at a higher resolution, you gain more control and accuracy so you can see what you're painting. It's difficult to see what the image looks like when all you see is a pixellated chaos.

Painting clouds

Before we start, I'd like to share a few tips on how to create realistic clouds quickly. This will take about 20 to 30 minutes depending on how much detail you choose to render. The first steps are important because they describe the overall design of the shapes. The later steps focus more on detailing. Clouds are quite tricky to paint, because it's easy to overestimate values. They have very subtle value and hue changes that are sometimes difficult to nail.

Try to be as accurate as you can in the earlier steps without rendering details. Use a big fuzzy brush with a decent amount of scattering; it should look something like the image below. The fuzziness helps achieve a nice texture as well as make blending easier, because the center of the brush is more opaque than its edge.

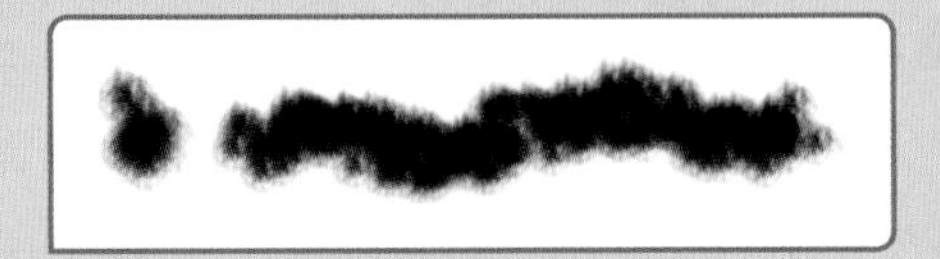

Open up a new document at around 1000x700 pixels and display the document at 100 percent. Exact resolution isn't that important here; the important thing is that you can fit the whole image on your screen at 100 percent without needing to pan around a lot (preferably not at all). As this will be just a sketch, speed is crucial whereas accuracy is not.

In the images here, you can see the progression of building up the clouds in six steps. You can also see the layer order with two paint layers—sky and clouds—and two adjustment layers grouped with the cloud layer. Separating the two layers makes it easier for you to redesign the clouds without touching the sky gradient and also to make adjustments to them individually.

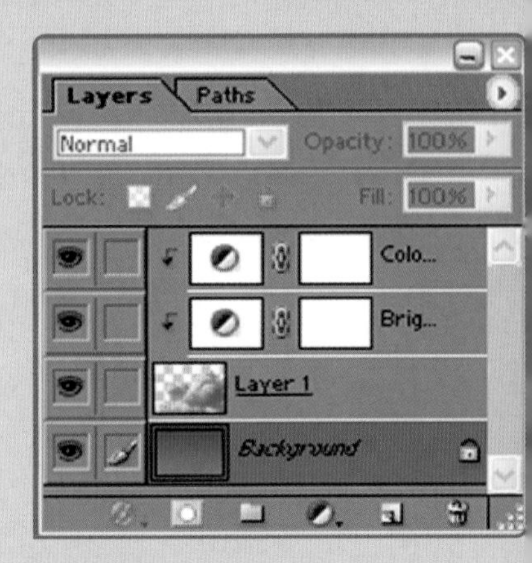

ck two blue colors, one slightly darker than the other, and eate the gradient as shown in picture 1. This will be the sky ıd bottom layer.

reate a new layer and block in a solid shape for your clouds. ke this opportunity to experiment with your custom brush, ıange its size, and place the clouds on the sky. Paint and erase ntil you're happy with the look. Don't use pure white 55,255,255) at any point, stay approximately 5 percent lower value. We'll use adjustment layers later to punch the whites.

hen you are done with this, figure out where you want the sun hit the clouds; which side is in sunlight and which is in adow? Get the overall design to look good and balanced (as ıown in picture 3). Where the sun hits the surface is where our brightest areas should be. The thicker the cloud, the arker the shadow side gets. Keep values close here; work with ght and darks and no details, just shapes.

ontinue painting the shapes and create a solid bright outline silhouette the clouds (picture 4).

ne fifth step is where you stop adding new features and start fining what you already have. Zoom in to 200 percent if you eed extra detail. Start smoothing hard edges/high contrast eas by picking a color and letting the scattering brushstrokes end your patches of paint together. Use very little pressure ith the pen to get as smooth a transition as possible. Using rge, soft-edged brushes will make the cloud lose its texture, so ork with the scattering brush as much as you can.

ne smallest details are created in picture 6. Use the Eraser tool define a nice edge for the clouds, and try to vary it so that it as both soft and hard edges, making it look more dynamic and teresting. Add a Brightness/Contrast adjustment layer and oup it to the cloud layer. Adjust it so you achieve a nice and ch look where the brightest parts—the edges—can hit white. se a color balance on top, linked to the previous one, for color djustments. You might want the highlights to receive some ellow light.

Sketching

Because we have no predefined design for this image, let's enjoy the process of experimenting with Photoshop. I chose to make this entire image digital, partly because it's a Photoshop tutorial, but also (and perhaps more importantly) because it allows me to quickly visualize my ideas in color without going through the process of scanning and coloring separately. Photoshop is a great tool for fast sketching; keeping the image size small while doing so ensures a fast screen update. In the initial sketching stage, we'll quickly throw some colors in and start building a structure to see how composition and values work together. Simply put, this is no more than a digital sketch.

OK, let's start. If your screen is big enough to display the entire image, zoom in to 100 percent. If not, I'd go for 50 percent. The following images show the progress of a rough painting. They don't have a lot of detail, but merely give me ideas for the final version later on. What I am searching for here is mainly the composition and colors. If you try to copy these images, a good idea would be to set a time limit for yourself on how long to spend on this stage. Adjust the time so that you think you can get close to what's shown here. Perhaps 60 to 90 minutes is a good target.

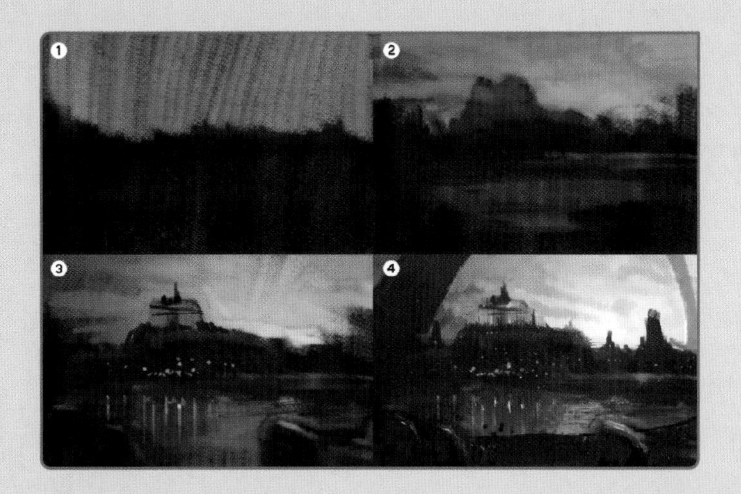

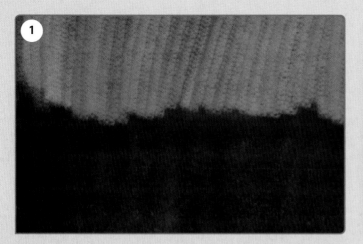

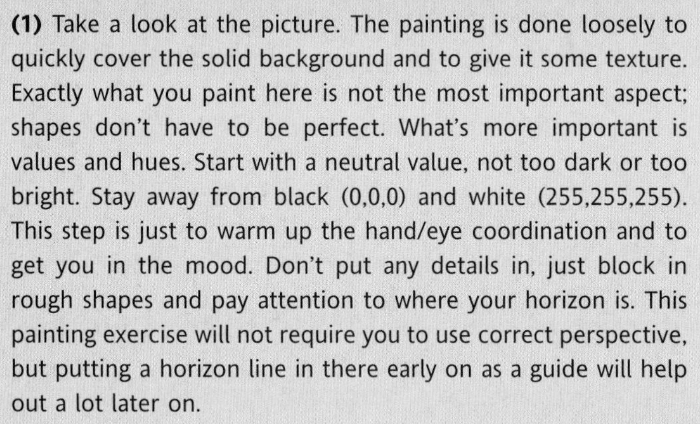

(1) Take a look at the picture. The painting is done loosely to quickly cover the solid background and to give it some texture. Exactly what you paint here is not the most important aspect; shapes don't have to be perfect. What's more important is values and hues. Start with a neutral value, not too dark or too bright. Stay away from black (0,0,0) and white (255,255,255). This step is just to warm up the hand/eye coordination and to get you in the mood. Don't put any details in, just block in rough shapes and pay attention to where your horizon is. This painting exercise will not require you to use correct perspective, but putting a horizon line in there early on as a guide will help out a lot later on.

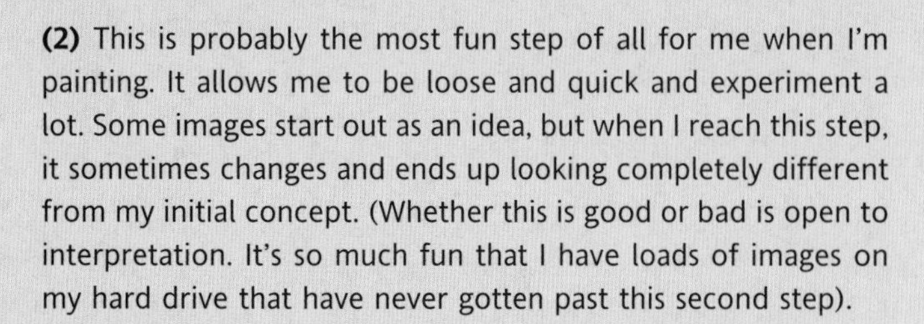

(2) This is probably the most fun step of all for me when I'm painting. It allows me to be loose and quick and experiment a lot. Some images start out as an idea, but when I reach this step, it sometimes changes and ends up looking completely different from my initial concept. (Whether this is good or bad is open to interpretation. It's so much fun that I have loads of images on my hard drive that have never gotten past this second step).

Rough in some large masses of color to suggest basic form. T to get your values and hues down without using layer zooming, or erasing, to get a sense of what you are painting. didn't have a specific idea in my head at the point, it was all ve generic, so being loose and staying away from details helpe From the rough masses of color, I try to find interesting thin to work from, almost like a piece of clay where the model "hiding" inside, waiting to be found.

Don't overestimate values; keep them close to each other. You darks should still be well above black, and your bright par (such as the sky) should be darker than white. I find it easier t work this way, where I keep the value range tight at th beginning, but allow myself to use a wider range later in th painting process. You can start suggesting where the sky is, th trees, water, and castle, and so on. Use broad shapes and pic colors accordingly.

Because we're working digitally, we don't need to use the Erase or even Undo. Nothing can go wrong. Just keep painting an use ALT for color picking. If you're not happy with how th painting turns out, keep painting on top of it over and ove again until it works. Play around with various brush shapes, an use this opportunity to really experiment and find a way t paint with big brushstrokes. Stay away from details for now– you don't want to get carried away. Make sure you are happ with your rough layout before going further in step 3.

) When you are done with your rough image, you can start fining the more important details and cleaning up rough ges. This step is where you take your concept further and sh things in the right direction. Don't get tempted to render e smallest details just yet, but keep it simple, focusing on nat's important and in direct focus. In my picture, the portant area is the castle and the small points of light rrounding it. I also felt that the reflections in the water will lp sell the image. You can put some effort into "cleaning up" me of your bigger shapes.

sh your sky up a bit in value, making it slightly brighter. Make re values are still pretty close to each other so that you don't ve to keep pushing darks/lights around.

Work with hues and subtle value variation in dark areas to make things look a little more interesting. You can saturate your colors and work them into the picture. Stay within the values and work with warm and cool hues. If things look out of scale, or if the castle looks like it's too close to the viewer, there are a few things you can do. First, check the scale of the castle; is it too big in relation to the image borders? Second, is the big shape that defines the castle too dark or too bright? If it looks too close, then it's probably too dark in value. Work some of the sky color over the castle and see if this helps. If your values and composition look okay, there's one more technique we can try in the next step.

(4) In order to make objects look proportionally large in an image, a few things need to work: values, shapes (with defined edges), perspective, and composition all need to be accurate. So, what else can we add? Well, there's no way to know the size of things if there's nothing that actually describes its scale.

A perfect example is this: imagine a tall skyscraper in a city. If you want to render such a building with the above criteria (values, shapes, and composition), all you would have is a tall box. It wouldn't look anything like a skyscraper, and why not?

What you need is some kind of reference to describe the size of the building. Texture, windows on the side, antennae on th roof, cars in the street, people walking, trees, clouds in the sk soccer fields, and so on, are all references that put everythi into the same world and space. The small details are wh describe its size and its surroundings. You can't avoid addir these details. Objects have to be rendered accurately and wi all the above criteria in place. This is what you should add he in step 4.

etails need to be relative to each other in order for us to nderstand what's going on. The human brain needs to ationalize, which is why you can't tell the scale of the block in nage A below, whereas it's more obvious in image B. Touch up hat's left of your image in this step; spend a few minutes to et the castle, points of light, reflections, and clouds to look ice. I used a color balance adjustment layer for the yellow/red rade. Using the highlight settings here makes the brighter areas op, which adds a nice bright hazy look to it. The big arc was dded for extra interest, to create a touch of unearthliness.

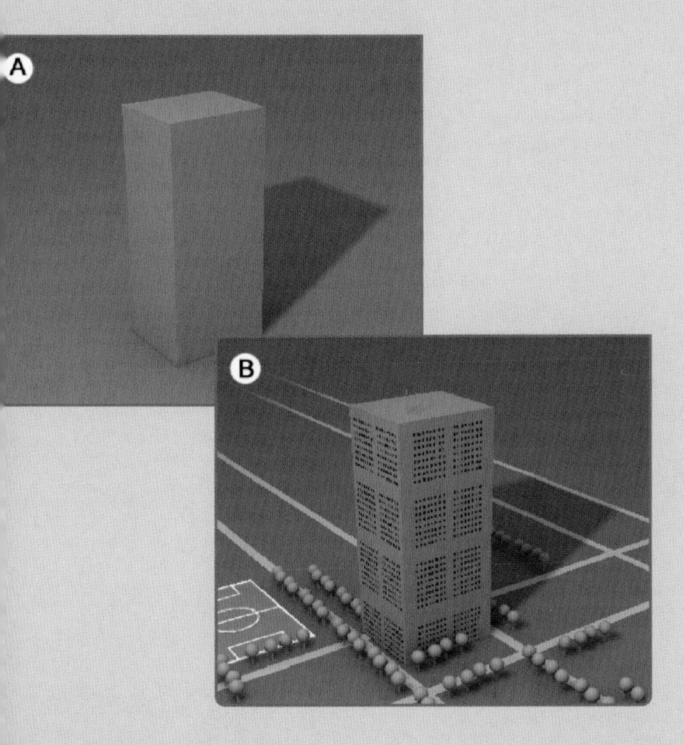

ainting the image

ow that we have a rough concept sketch, let's start painting ne image proper. The approach to this image will be exactly ke the quick sketch, with the same steps, only we'll work at a igher resolution this time. We will also utilize a few other tricks ıch as adjustment layers and blending modes.

Why work at high resolution?

Working at a high resolution gives you more control over brush strokes and helps you get more detail into the picture without having to work zoomed in, where it's difficult to see what is going on.

The sharpest edges you can get with brush strokes in Photoshop are by default anti-aliased (unless you are using the Pencil). This means that when you draw a line, it isn't 1-pixel wide, but often 2 pixels wider than the stroke itself, one on each side of the stroke in all directions. When you're working at low resolution where you don't have a lot of space, these extra pixels take up a lot of room, especially if you're working with brushes as small as 1 pixel. With two more pixels for the anti-aliasing, it's a lot. If you work at three times that resolution instead, when you reduce the image down to 33 percent, the 3-pixel brush is now 1 pixel. In the following image, you can see a soft edged brushstroke at 100 percent, as well as the same brushstroke reduced to 25 percent. Notice how the edges sharpen.

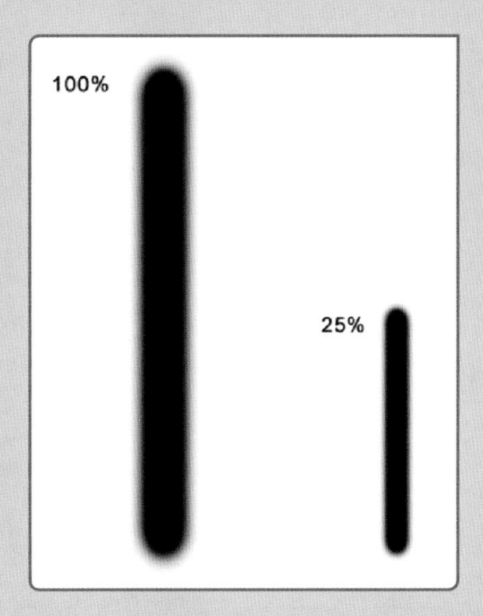

The real advantage of this is that you can be rougher when painting, because brushstrokes will shrink proportionally to the image reduction. You don't have to push pixels around like a puzzle; you can focus a lot more on the image. When you reduce the magnification, edges get sharper and details get smaller. You could utilize this technique in the above example with the skyscraper's windows and other very small details where accuracy is necessary.

The bad thing is that the bigger you go, the more power you need. If you work with layers, the file size gets large quickly and performance/speed drops. You need to find a balance here on how much speed you can sacrifice, but I recommend that you don't work any bigger than you need to. If you work on an image with no layers and draw a 10-pixel brushstroke quickly, there shouldn't be any delay. If it doesn't update immediately, reduce the image size until it does. Now let's get started.

Open up a new document, approximately 4000x2700 pixels.

Because of how we'll adjust the image through adjustmen layers, and to have optimum control, it's important to organiz your layers. Create three sets with one layer in each set. Nam one "sky" and create a gradient. This will be the sky.

Call the next layer "clouds". Separating the sky from the cloud allows you to add adjustment layers to them individually.

Call the top layer "paint". This will be the general paint laye where most of the work is done. If you've read through th "Sketching" section, you'll have a good grasp of the process.

Throughout the tutorial, make sure you paint on the paint laye unless you are painting clouds. Start by blocking out your majo shapes on the paint layer. Paint simple clouds on the cloud laye Don't worry about structure, perspective, or making mistakes because you can simply paint over these. Focus on making th shapes with somewhat accurate values. The first step is just t cover the canvas and to create a foundation to build on.

lean up some of the rougher shapes and add some interesting hapes to make the mountains. Organize your values to get a learer sense of scale (as mentioned in the "Sketching" section). dding a few strokes in the sky helps.

the perspective is off in the previous image, improve it here, naking it as correct as possible. I didn't use any drawn vanishing oint, because the building as well as the trees and mountains the far distance are located on a single plane. It will be easy o make the picture without it, because we won't paint any bjects that require that level of accuracy. However, try to be recise when you draw your eye level, using the bottom of the emple as a guideline. Don't cheat on this one.

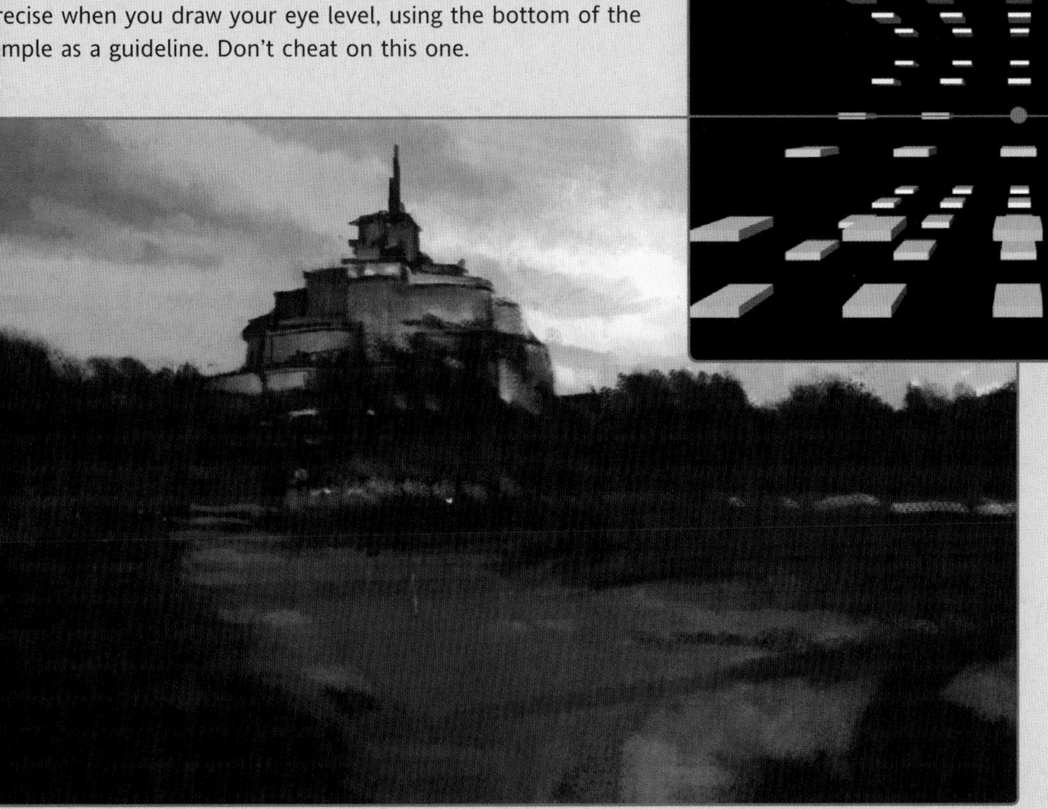

Briefly, the *eye level* describes a point in space that you're looking at right now. Place this point on a horizontal line, and everything placed below this line will be seen from above. Everything placed above it will be seen from below. When you move your eyes, you move your eye level. The following picture illustrates this:

At this point, I've established the final layout/composition. It feels okay to place the temple slightly off center. This is our point of interest, so we'll make sure it reads clearly. If you don't have the patience to paint everything in the picture, render the temple in detail and leave the other shapes rougher as you move further away from it.

Our shapes are still rough, the clouds are barely reading, but I can tell how far away things are now (the relationships and scale of objects in the image). When painting at this point, work on the overall impression, not the specifics. It's still a little early to render detail. The overall impression is essentially made up of four things:

- **Structure:** How things are drawn and the anatomy of things. For example, if you intend to draw a circle but draw an oval instead, that's a bad structure/drawing.
- **Composition:** The relationship between objects; their size and position in space, for example.
- **Values:** Light and dark. The sky needs to be lighter than the mountains. Clouds need to be darker than the sky but lighter than the ground plane. This image has a fairly simple value layout. Be sure to separate values generally– don't let the sky get as dark as anything on the groun plane (with the exception of the lights we'll add later Don't let anything on your ground plane become as brigh as your sky. When the sky is reflected in the water, it lose its intensity and has to be darker. To simplify, use tw values for now: dark for the ground plane, and light fc the sky (with clouds).
- **Color:** Hue and saturation. The image is quit monochromatic with few colors, but it uses a wide rang of saturation levels, especially in the darks. Don't ove saturate the sky and make it too blue, as this will create disharmony because everything else is red. A desaturate blue works well and you might even want to go mor yellow or red later.

ext, start to clean up the edges of the mountains to get a nice ad on their shapes. You don't want them all to end up on the me plane. You can achieve a sense of depth by making some them smaller and pushing them back. In reality, the further vay from the eye an object is, the less contrast it has. An ɔject in the far distance can never be as dark as it can when it close up—atmosphere prevents this.

art organizing the shapes that form the temple and make the chitecture read clearly. Don't put in any small details such as indows and spotlights just yet. We'll save this until the end hen everything else is in place.

ext, clean up the ground plane. The reflections of e temple and mountains in the water might need me work. Note that reflections in water have less ntrast than their source. To determine how long e reflections should be, think of it like this: water a reflective plane or a mirror. The distance etween an object and mirror is the same distance that from the mirror to the reflection. The water ane is the turning point in which everything is irrored, so the base of the mountains should nnect to the base of its reflections. The following cture illustrates this:

Now it's time to give the clouds a makeover. Work on the cloud layer only (switch to the paint layer if you need to work on the ground). Using a big brush, lay down a fairly flat layer of paint for the clouds.

Detail isn't necessary at this point; focus on making the design look interesting. You have to make a deliberate decision here on whether you want the clouds to be subtle, to stay in the background to break up the simple gradient, or to be more exuberant and almost compete with the temple. I chose the latter, but feel free to choose any of these options.

Don't worry if the hues or values in relation to the sky are not accurate. You can correct this with adjustment layers later on. However, do try to keep values within the shapes accurate, as this will be harder to fix afterward.

ep refining the clouds. Imagine the sun shining through the ouds at the right making an intense rim on the clouds. The nter of the cloud is the darkest and the rim is the brightest. e'll brighten up both the sky and the clouds later, so don't paint anything other than the clouds for now. Watch the values within the shapes and don't make them either too contrasty or too flat, but use a wide range of values to get rich detail in them. It helps overall scale.

To help the environment's scale, you need to add a few more things to push this. We'll start by adding some rock texture to the mountains, so that they have the look of foliage-covered mountains, very much like the mountains in Guilin. A few patches of stone texture, somewhat lighter then the foliage, will help break up the texture nicely and give you the extra distance. Don't over estimate these lighter values. If you go too high, they will start to compete with the main focus, the temple. If you go too dark, they will not read against the darker values, so you need to balance them.

Creating a subtle value shift in the foliage gives you a nice texture. Hit the top of the trees with more light than the bottom, but be careful not to create too much contrast here. Darks in the distant mountains have to be separated from the darks in the ground and trees closer to us.

The sky is still quite flat and doesn't have the impact I'm looking for. The addition of an adjustment layer helps to correct this.

We're getting close now to finishing the image. Add a visibil mask to the cloud layer. This layer enables you to paint throu a mask to hide and show certain parts of the layer. The sky distracting and very busy with all those clouds. Use X to swit between black and white to paint through the mask. 1 percent black hides the layer and 100 percent white shows t layer at full opacity (assuming the layer opacity is set to 1 percent). There are 255 levels between black and white, so using the whole range for subtle clouds that almost disappe against the sky.

ow add some subtle lights around e shoreline. Paint these lights on a parate layer from the background, it makes life easier if you want to dd some glow effects or add/remove ghts later.

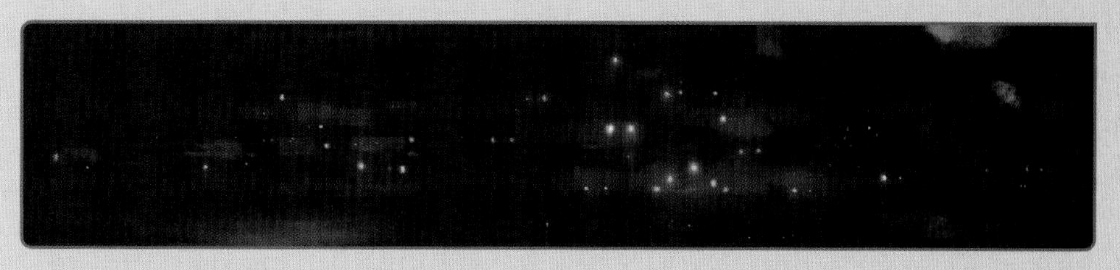

reate a nice layout for the lights, but don't use too many, as ou don't want them to be completely overwhelming. Distribute em with the highest concentration at the base of the temple, if this is the entrance to the pathway leading up to the big uilding.

make the glows nicer, duplicate the light layer and apply a otion Blur effect to create vertical streaks. Set the blur Angle 90 degrees and adjust the length and intensity until you're appy with the look of it.

Also use the layer opacity for additional control.

A good idea is to copy your layer with all the lights and try different things with the copies. Motion blur is one of them, but try blending modes such as Overlay too. I merged my layers, copied it, and flipped it to create the reflections easily. If you merge all the light layers, you should have a layer that includes all the lights and their reflections that looks something like this:

It might seem like a huge leap from the previous step to the final touch-ups but, in fact, 95 percent of the work is complete, and you only have adjustments left to make. There's no more painting other than a few masks. If you have a tough time following along with my image exactly, don't panic. A lot of the work is done by putting adjustment layer over adjustment layer for which there is no exact formula. I tend to use so many adjustment layers in the end that it's hard to keep track of them all. If one small spot needs more red, I use an adjustment layer to correct it. If an area needs to be lighter, I add another layer. It's hard to explain the last 5 percent of my image-making process, as it's a lot of experimenting to find what works best. This is what the final Layer palette looks like after I finished adjusting the image:

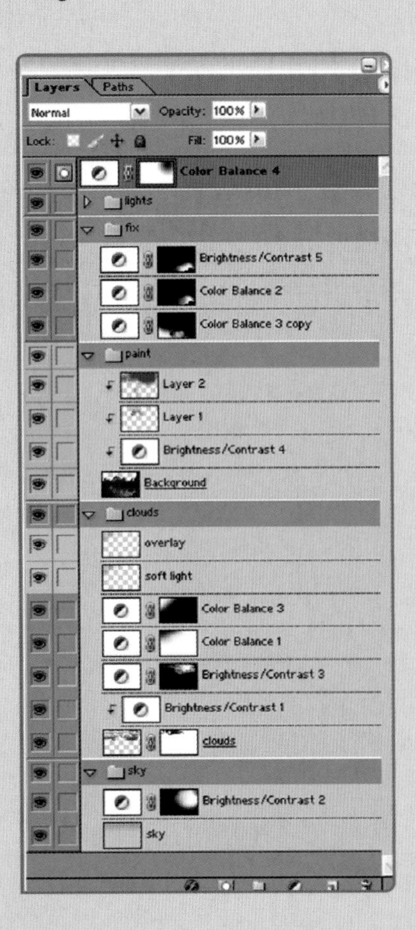

With that said, add a color balance layer right at the top of th layer stack and grade the entire image in a yellow/red tone. Us shadows, midtones, and highlight for this. The next thing to d is to brighten up the sky. For this, use a brightness/contrast laye on top of the cloud layer and push your clouds and sky bacl Brighten it all up and tone down the contrast if the clouc become distracting. You should now have a bright sky tha clearly differs from the dark red ground.

Next, let's create the light in the sky by adjusting the two laye individually for optimum control. Create a brightness/contra adjustment layer grouped with the sky layer. Invert this laye (CTRL+I) so that the layer affects nothing. Use a big soft brus and paint white through its layer mask. It might be slow to wor with such a big brush, but have patience and work in small slo steps. Lower the brush opacity from 100 percent to around 3 percent if the effect isn't subtle enough.

Work with the alpha channel and paint as you see the update using the X key to switch between black and white to paint nice mask. If too much light comes through, paint black an vice versa to tone it down. Paint the light sun rays on this mas

Repeat this for the clouds and group this layer with the clou layer so that it doesn't affect the sky.

dd a few color balance adjustment yers to clean up the areas that need olor adjustments, such as the water, hich could use a little more punch. You ight also want to darken or change ies in the sky on the left-hand side. Do is with either brightness/contrast ljustment layers or by painting it on a parate layer.

ne last thing to do is add a little red er the mountain edges where the sun ines through. Do this by creating a ew layer grouped with the ound/paint layer, (this enables you to aint on that layer only. A side effect of ouping is that you get the clean line ound your paint layer). Using a big soft ush, paint a soft transition with a ight red hue and set the layer blending ode to Color Dodge. Use the layer pacity to adjust brightness and hue and on't hesitate to duplicate this layer for ore intensity—or try different blending odes—to achieve the desired effect.

inal thoughts

nd so this is the end of my tutorial. I hope you had fun and njoyed reading it. Hopefully, you learned something that you dn't know already—something to take away with you.

ne techniques you've seen in this tutorial are certainly not the nly way to do things. For instance, people generally seem to se a lot more layers. I guess you can argue this forever, but hat it ultimately comes down to is that you need to find a way which you feel comfortable working. Whether this is through ainting everything accurately in the first place or by using ljustment layers and blending modes, and so on, doesn't atter a whole lot to me. Use whatever gets the work done!

I'm constantly pushing myself to try to find new techniques and methods of working. Sometimes it might be using new brushes, drawing images on paper and then scanning them, using digital photos, and so on. I recall several times when I have worked on big jobs but allowed myself to experiment through different mediums and approaches. The clients seem to like the result and, as long as it works, I keep at it. It's fun experimenting and I feel I have learned a lot by allowing myself to work this way.

Keep inspired and never stop learning.

09 PARAKEET

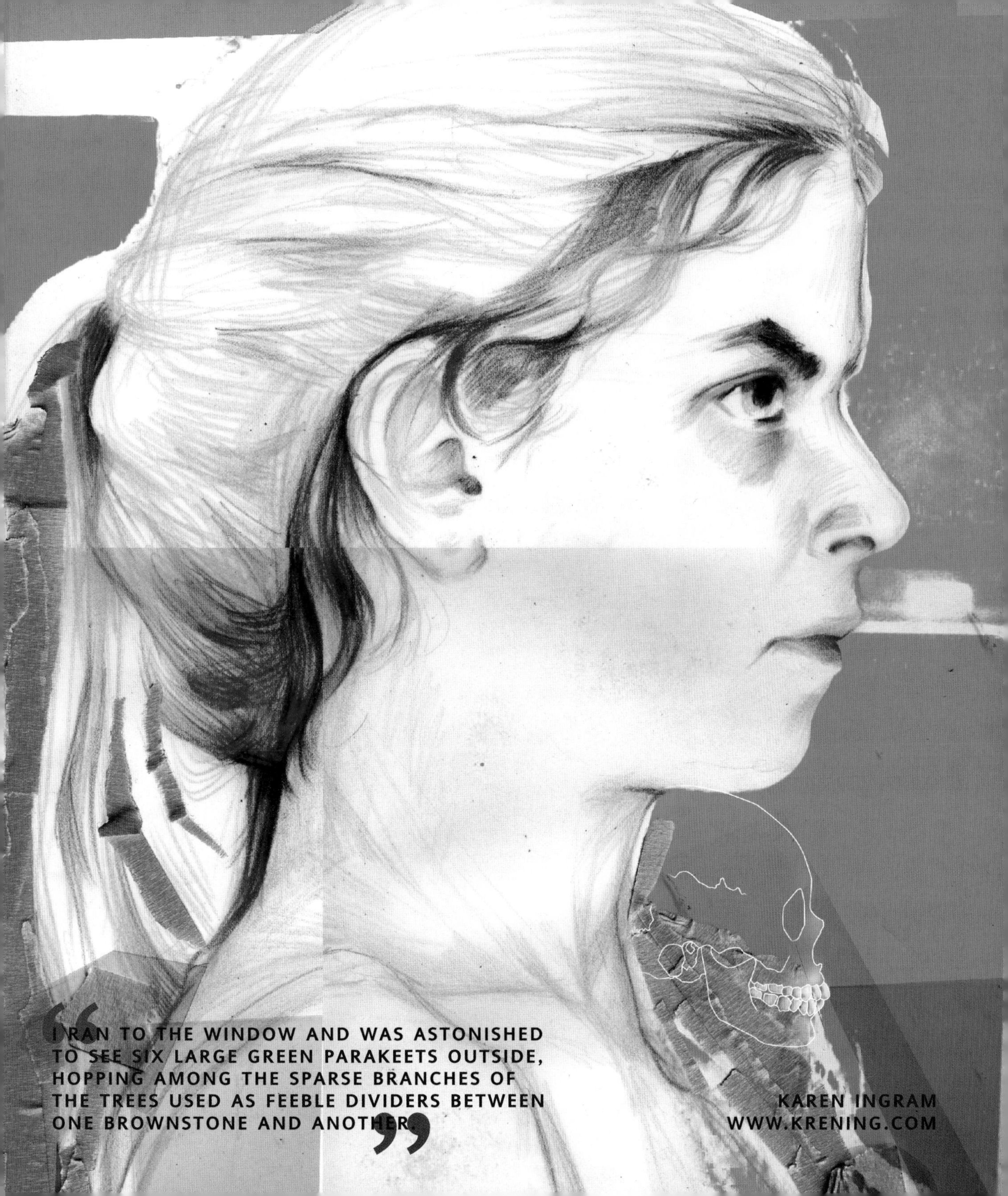
"I RAN TO THE WINDOW AND WAS ASTONISHED TO SEE SIX LARGE GREEN PARAKEETS OUTSIDE, HOPPING AMONG THE SPARSE BRANCHES OF THE TREES USED AS FEEBLE DIVIDERS BETWEEN ONE BROWNSTONE AND ANOTHER."
KAREN INGRAM
WWW.KRENING.COM

Tourism can be a good thing. This is something I notice every time someone comes to visit me in New York. I am taken out of my regular routine, my Walkman is removed, and my eyes, ears, and nose search out external stimuli, prodding my environment and taking in as much as possible.

My parents just left from a weekend visit, and while they were here, we talked about what a New Yorker I was. I am of the opinion that the typical New Yorker has a direction, a path, and a goal. The mission of the New Yorker is not to let anything get in the way of this directive. We are all tunneling through the sea of people, anxious to reach our end. This shows on the street and in stores where the target of your desire is something just over that person's (who you are aware of but don't quite see) head. Eye contact is a distraction. It's that object or destination that your eyes are pining for. The reason why this behavior has become such a New York cliché is because New York is a city where you are constantly bombarded with external stimuli and loads and loads of people. We have to be specific about what we focus on, or we'd all end up wandering around like a scene from *Dawn of the Dead*. In defense of New York, people are nice—you just have to get their attention! This "over-focusing" or lack of observation is not unique to New Yorkers. It can happen to anyone who gets stuck in the patterns of a routine.

The tourist is the person who is having fun getting to th
destination; they are distracted and inquisitive. It is in this sta
that inspiration is often found . . . for me, at least. Sometimes
is a delayed reaction. For example, the first time I saw the Mo
parakeets must have been over 3 years ago, squawking a
screaming outside my backyard window. The noise was so lo
I ran to the window and was astonished to see six large gre
parakeets outside, hopping among the sparse branches of t
trees used as feeble dividers between one brownstone a
another. It is only recently that this bird has found its way in
my work.

It's great to be a tourist, to observe and watch the world arou
you, and to look at it in a different light. It's nice to take t
longest route, to look at the shops, people, trees, and so on th
you come across along that path. You can visit different cities
neighborhoods and take a break from your routine. Clichéd
know, but it beats surfing the Web for inspiration. You'
certainly more likely to create more original stuff.

Inspiration is a tricky thing; you never know when it will pop u
The best thing you can do is allow yourself to be open to it. Th
doesn't have to be asset gathering. Inspiration can consist
simply taking an inventory of things that interest you—readi
magazines and books, taking pictures, and most important
getting away from the computer.

'onk Parakeets #1, 2004

Flower Sequence #1, 2002

I think it's pretty obvious that I get a great deal of inspiration from nature. A large part of why I choose natural subject matter i because I enjoy studying and scrutinizing the textures and forms. It's amazing how you can become familiar with the shape o something simply by drawing it a few times.

Stills from Candybar, 2004

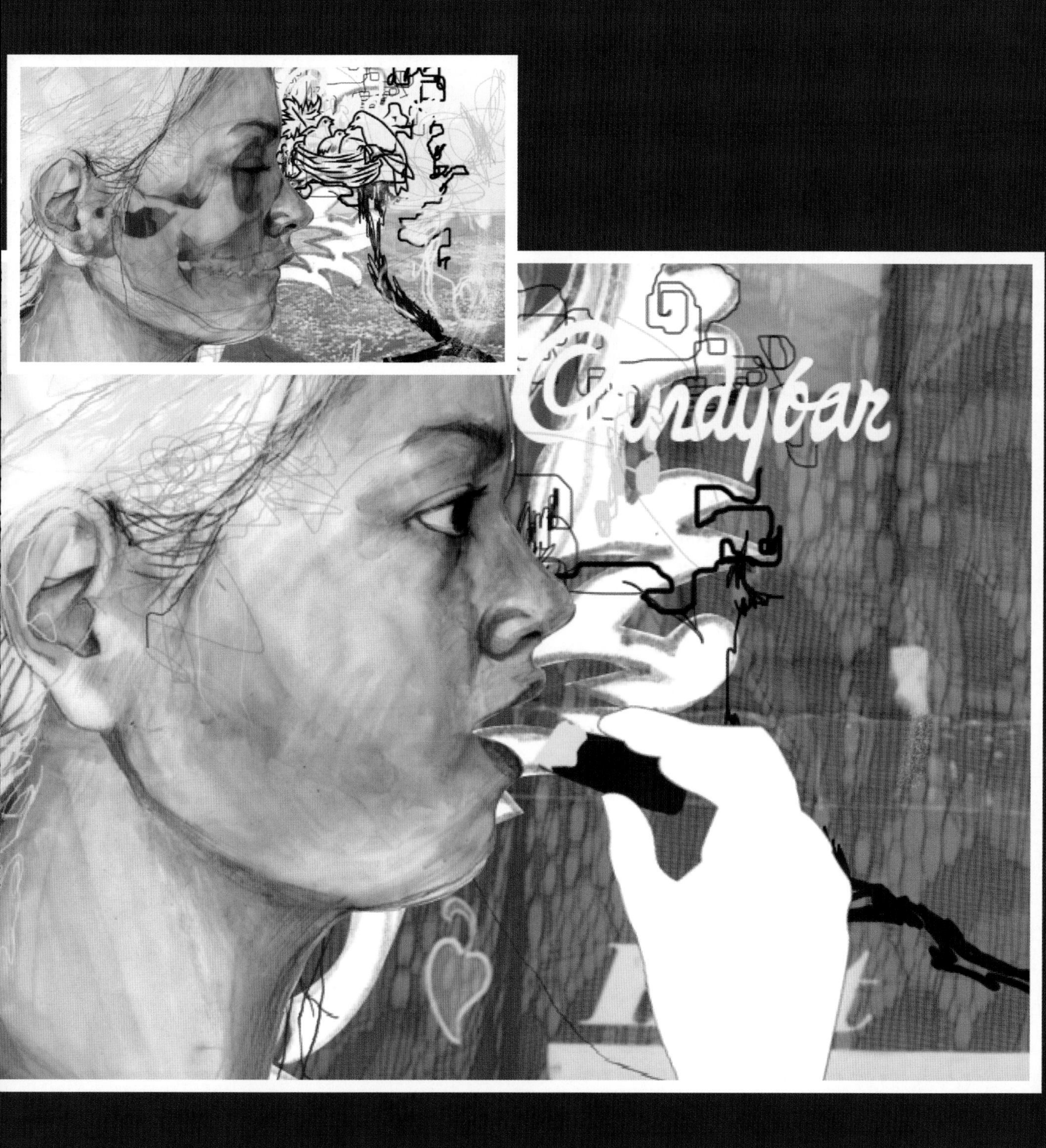
Candybar

My favorite reading material is the *New Yorker*. I also like the programming on National Public Radio. It's like watching TV except you get to use your imagination more. I try not to take my eyes for granted, though I am not one to wear sunglasses.

I enjoy drawing for the sake of drawing. I don't keep a sketchbook, but I think it's good to have one. Every time I try to keep a sketchbook, I never seem to actually sketch in it. I just end up taping receipts, ripped up credit card bills, or fruit stickers to the pages and taking illegible notes. I prefer to take out a large piece of paper, loads of markers and pencils, and sit over a drawing desk for a couple of hours with the radio on.

I have heaps of drawings that may never show themselves publicl

I started making visual art as soon as I could pick up a crayo as I suspect most people who are reading this sentence di Maybe you won a bookmark making contest in elementar school, made a card for a family member, or colored on you Granny's favorite antique chair? Maybe you drew a man-eatin alien and it was showcased on the wall of a family restaurant. A any rate, I make stuff now for the same reason that I made stu back then: because it's fun. The only difference is that now I a integrating more complex tools.

Scylla and Charybdis, 2003

Bouquet, 2003

My tendency toward art came quite early. My parents encouraged me to be well-rounded, participate in sports, and attend musical performances (I took piano for 2 weeks, it interfered with my after school art classes so I dropped it). They bought me a telescope and a microscope. Art just seemed to stick with me, and I was very lucky to receive lots of encouragement from my parents and younger sister. I would often perch myself in front of the TV late at night with a drawing board and some pencils and draw while the rest of my family slept. If anyone were to come into the living room at night en route to the kitchen for a snack, or just to see who was still up, I would feign sleep, or as my parents called it, "play possum." After the "intruder" had returned to bed, I'd pick up my drawing board again and continue. The next morning I would show my inquisitive family what I had done the night before. Nighttime was my private time, and this is how I became a night owl.

Spread from Fleur de lis,
created for This Is A Magazine, Issue 3, July 2002.
www.thisisamagazine.com

I've been told that my night owl tendencies are much like those of my Aunt Virginia Ingram (VI for short). She too is an artist and has recently been named "Artist of the Year" for 2004 at the Sawtooth Center for Visual Art in Winston-Salem, North Carolina. Aunt VI was a great influence on me while I was growing up, and still is. She has a wonderful studio with windows on all sides that overlooks a woody backyard with a small creek trickling below the downward sloping land. She works mostly in wood and her woodcuts of cats, alphabets, mandelas, flowers, and, more recently, planets, have always impressed me for their brave usage of shape, line, texture, and color. Aunt VI would always include a hand-lettered card with every present she gave us and we loved it. Her alphabet woodcuts and drawings are a large influence in how I do my work. When I discovered Photoshop, I saw a way that I may be able to integrate letters into my work. I try to follow my Aunt VI's example and do it by hand, or in some cases with the Pen tool, though I am not nearly as practiced and skilled as she is. I also enjoy letting a piece remain hand-drawn instead of digitized, and this may come from my appreciation of printmaking as seen in Aunt VI's work.

From A to Z: The Letter K, woodcut, 11"
Virginia S. Ingram, 1993

rom A to Z: The Letter S, woodcut, 11"
'irginia S. Ingram, 1993

From A to Z: The Letter I, woodcut, 11"
Virginia S. Ingram, 1993

I began using a computer for personal work after I started working as a pattern designer at a textile company in Greensboro, North Carolina. I had acquired the job in my junior year of college, in 1994, through professor recommendation (Bob Gerhart and Mark Gottsegen at the University of North Carolina at Greensboro), my drawing portfolio, and a color vision test. I knew little about computers, and nothing about Photoshop. In fact, at that time, I was a painter and very anti-computer. However, I felt as though the job offer was much better than working at a pizza place, so I took it. After years of learning and working on various CAD systems, I began poking around Photoshop and was delighted with the possibilities. I continued to paint and draw in my spare time. Slowly, though, I began to find more and more appeal in using Photoshop and making digital creations, and as a result, I bought my first computer. By the time I moved to New York in the autumn of 2000, Photoshop had become a necessary tool in everything I made, whether it was personal work or commercial design.

I'm a big fan of relevance when using tools and tricks in Photoshop. Someone asked me not too long ago if trends affected my work, and that was my reply. I think it's a great rule. A recent appropriate example of the success of relevance is *The Triplets of Bellville*. Due to the current and recent flood of pure 3D animations, this largely hand-drawn French film was a real treat. There are actually 3D elements in the movie, but it's always very appropriate, and this makes the film infinitely more successful.

Tulips, Splash screen created for www.creativebehavior.com, 2002

Spontaneity is important in my work. Often, I will begin a piece with a clear visual directive, but if I discover that a portion of my composition isn't going to work, I try not to waste a lot of time forcing it. A great idea will show up many times. A bad one usually doesn't stick around for long. I had an art professor in college—Nan Covert—who told me that. I was concerned about taking a piece in a direction that I wasn't certain I'd like, and she told me that if I ruined it I could always do it again. Thankfully, with Photoshop a bad composition can be remedied by simply deleting a layer.

I find that Photoshop is an excellent tool for composing because it allows me to change the composition of a picture over and over. It also enables me to add flat, perfect shapes, which I find to be a delightful contrast to the handmade drawings. That's the root of my work. Every fancy tool or filter in Photoshop is simply an accessory.

Tussle: Eye Contact, 2003

October, Lounge 72 PDF calendar for 2004, www.lounge72.com

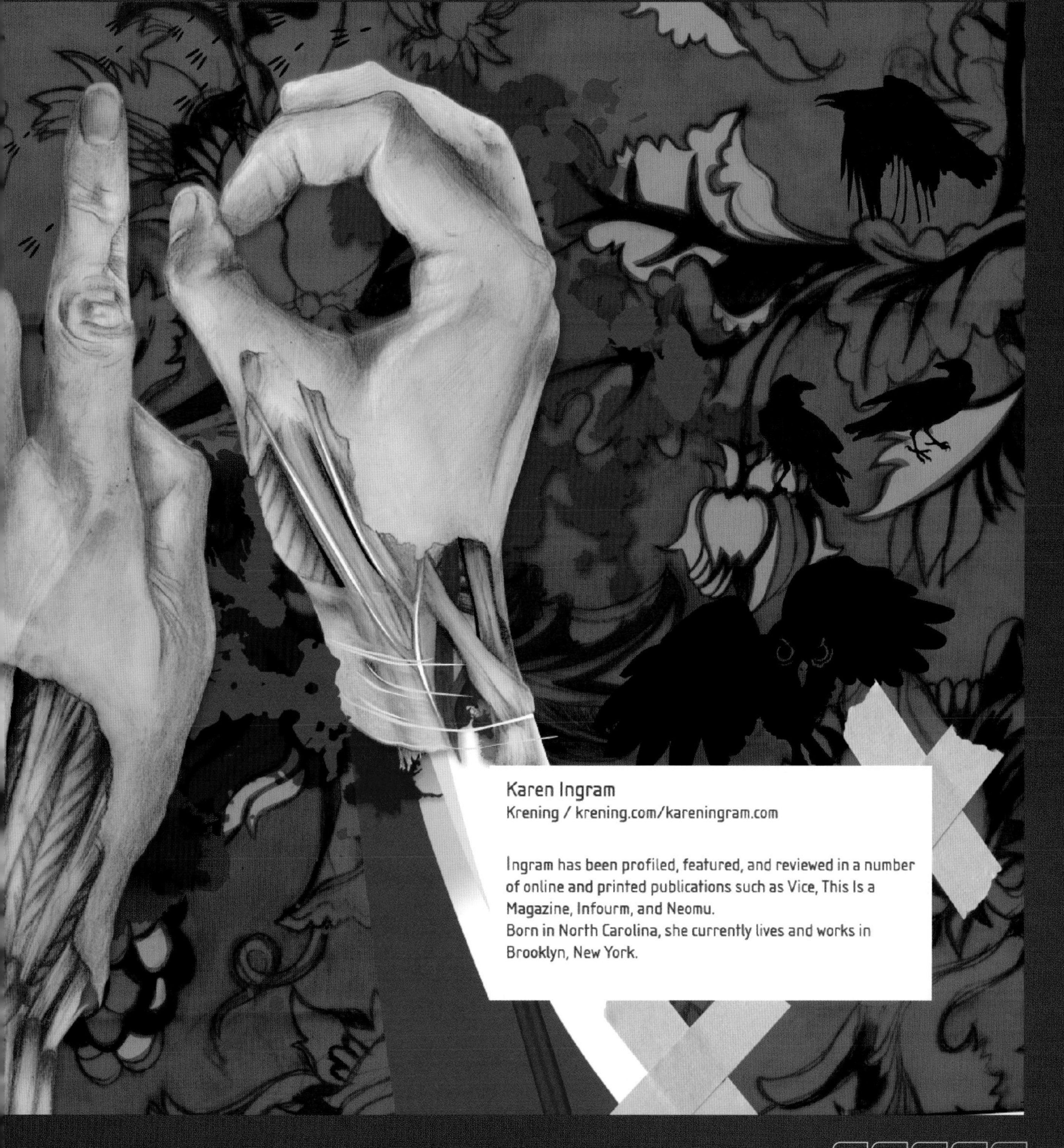

Karen Ingram
Krening / krening.com/kareningram.com

Ingram has been profiled, featured, and reviewed in a number of online and printed publications such as Vice, This Is a Magazine, Infourm, and Neomu.
Born in North Carolina, she currently lives and works in Brooklyn, New York.

The piece I created for this chapter was inspired by my immediate neighborhood, Park Slope, in Brooklyn, New York. I wanted to use natural beauty as an analogy for the merging of cultures in my neighborhood. One could easily and mistakenly overlook these cultural enhancements in favor of the commercial glitz and the consumerism of the city.

That's where my Monk parakeets come in. I wanted them to serve as the strange and unexpected bit of natural color and vitality that's present in New York. I am no ornithologist, but from my books and what I've observed, the Monk parakeet comes from South America and flies north during the spring, some come as far north as Park Slope, Brooklyn. The Monk parakeet serves as a nice analogy for self-imported culture and beauty.

Another example of the multiculturalism in nature is the annual Brooklyn Botanical Gardens Cherry Blossom Festival. I decided it would be very fitting to have a few South American Monk parakeets perching on the branches of a *Prunus serrulata*. The branches I used to draw from were purchased a few blocks away for $9 at a bodega. Even though Brooklyn lacks foliage, there are plenty of places to purchase beautiful flowers.

I originally started this piece thinking that I would play upon contrast by superimposing the tropical looking birds and the cherry tree over a dirty photographic Brooklyn backdrop. There would be a few splashes of color determined by some photos I had taken of construction in the Dekalb Avenue subway station while waiting for the train. An interesting thing happened while I was taking photos in Dekalb. A woman asked if I was photographing construction to chart its progress. I replied, "No it's even dorkier than that. I'm just photographing the colors." This is what I mean about being a tourist. You run the risk of being a dork.

At some point while I was working on the piece, I decided that I really wanted the birds to be the unobstructed focus of the drawing, so the dingy colorful subway photos went into the image library. I'm sure they'll surface again at some point.

So, what I decided to do was create a composition with th previously mentioned birds and cherry blossoms. After I ha decided the message and intent of my piece, I made a loos preliminary compositional drawing to see how many elements needed and what kind. This drawing functions more like a visu asset list than a clear plan of what imagery I want to have in m piece and how I want it to be composed. As you may be able t tell by the scratchy diagonals, I was still thinking I woul superimpose the birds and branches over an angular cit inspired backdrop.

I always draw elements separately to allow myself freedom i Photoshop for composing, so on the CD included with th book, you'll see a separate PSD for the birds (`birds.psd`) an another for the branches (`tree.psd`). One thing I like to kee in mind when I draw is that texture is more important tha precision. You can always move elements around in Photosho to make things look better, but the idiosyncrasies of a hand drawn line are harder to come by.

Being wary of Photoshop's tools and how you will use them very important in the first steps of making imagery that will b composed in Photoshop. Some examples of this are the lack o legs and claws on the birds and the blue color I made th flowers. When I drew the birds, I left the feet off becaus texture is not as important in them. We need the feet to latc onto the place where we will connect the bird to the branche so we don't want to set ourselves up with limitations. I made th flowers blue because I plan to use selection tools to isolate th cherry tree branches from the background and I don't want th blossoms to get lost. I can always lighten objects later i Photoshop, and it's easier to knock out the white paper if ther is no white in the drawing. We'll get to all this later, but it important to know that you can make technical decision before you even touch the computer.

I create all of my own imagery because I really enjoy drawin and I like the way the sketchy elements look when transpose with cleaner vectors, pixels, or photos. If you are not a perso who enjoys drawing, you can purchase illustrations or us photography. Photos will work great with these compositio tricks I am going to share with you.

Preparing imagery for the composition

The first step we want to take is to isolate the elements from their respective backgrounds so that we can place them on top of the cherry blossoms and move them around to create a pleasing composition. We'll start with the Monk parakeets. Open up `birds_start.psd` and select the Pen tool (P).

Use the Pen tool to draw a path around the outline of the bird. Photoshop will give the path the name Shape1, by default. Set the fill to zero in the Layers palette.

Zoom in very closely so that you can clearly see where the edges of the bird are. Because it's hand-drawn, the edges will naturally be pretty rough and sketchy. You can use this to your advantage when pathing the birds. I like to draw my path around the pencil marks in some places to give an illusion of stray feathers. You can hold down the spacebar and get the Hand tool to easily move the image around as you are adding points to the path.

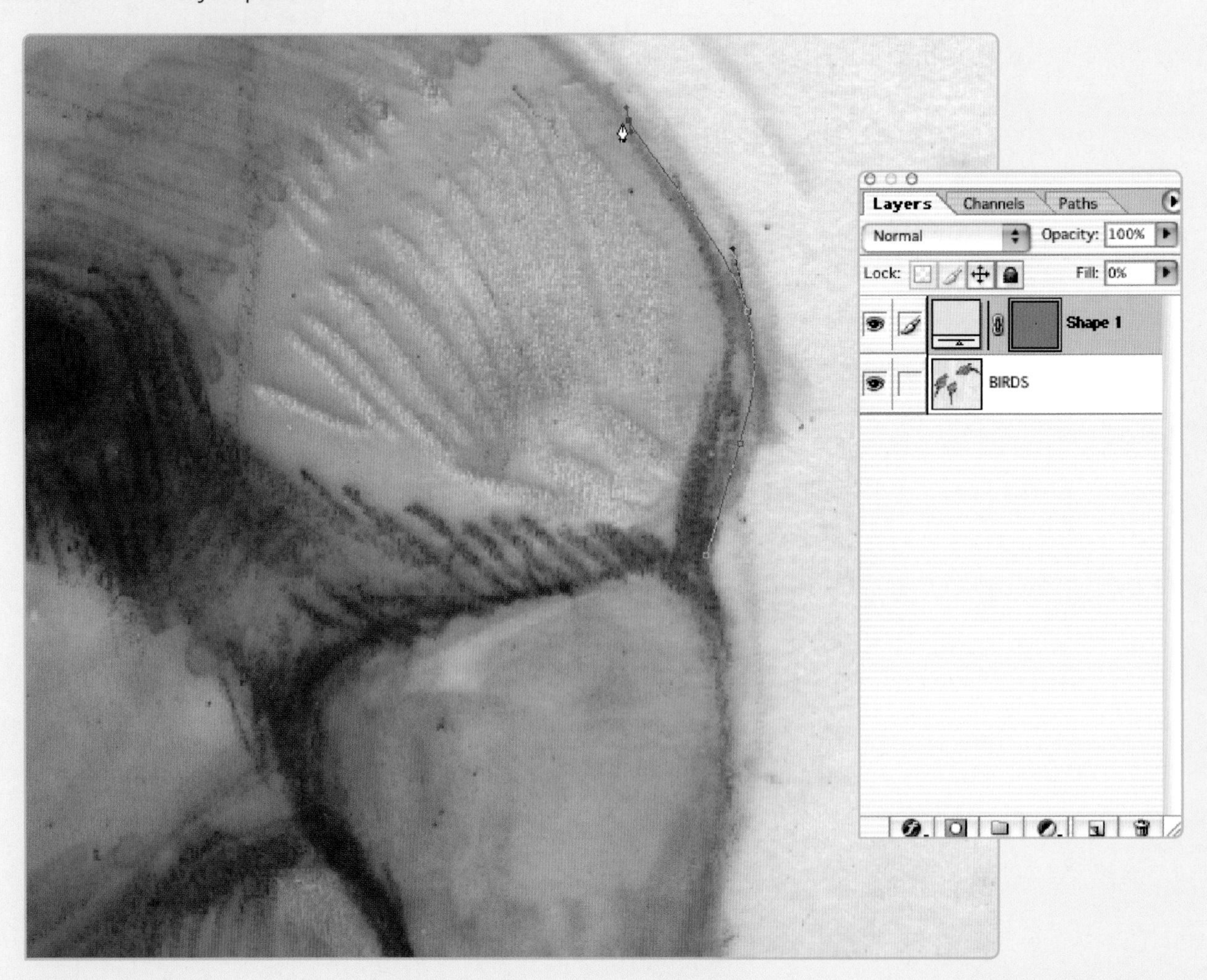

ere are a few tips for using the Pen tool:

- If you place a point in the path in a place that you don't like, hold down the CMD key to get the Direct Selection tool (which looks like a white arrow) to move a point or change the angle of both handlebars.

- You can use the Convert Point tool (an open V-shaped arrow) to move one handlebar of a point by pressing the OPTION key and mousing over a handlebar.

- You can also delete and add anchor points by mousing over the path, either on a specific anchor point (to delete) or just the path itself (to add). These tools look the same as the regular Pen tool with the minus (–) and plus (+) signs to the right of them, respectively.

fter you have finished this path, return to the nchor point from which you started. Notice a small rcle to the right of the pen, indicating that the ath will be closed after you place that point.

e Freeform Pen tool is great to use if you're not comfortable with the anchor points and lection tools of the regular Pen tool (on the yout menu of the regular Pen tool). The Freeform en tool allows you to draw a fluid line around an bject and it automatically places the points and andles, but you relinquish a certain amount of ontrol compared with manually placing your own oints. You can always go back to paths created by e Freeform Pen tool and manually adjust the ositioning of anchor points so that it fits the edges etter, but that can take a long time. The Pen tool an invaluable tool to learn. It may take a while to et comfortable with it, and you'll undoubtedly xperience many hours of frustration, but you'll be glad you suffered through when you are zipping ut paths and vectors like a racecar driver.

Another way of isolating the birds is via the Magic Wand tool (W). This is a good tool to use if you're not as concerned with clean edges and don't mind a few stray pixels. We'll use this tool later. You could also isolate the birds by selecting the white paper around the birds and removing it. We'll use this technique with the branches.

Continue making paths around the other two birds in the same fashion as you did for the first bird. You should have two additional layers of vector masks, or paths, for the other two birds called Shape 2 and Shape 3. You can take a look at the paths I made in the `birds.psd` on the CD.

We are going to leave this file for the time being and prepare the trees.

Open the `tree.psd` illustration.

First, duplicate the background layer, name the copied layer "trees isolated", and hide the tree layer.

All of these branches need to be isolated too because I'd like to put some elements behind them. However, we're not going to draw paths around them—we'd be here forever!

Choose Select ➤ Color Range. In the Color Range dialog box, make sure that Sampled Colors is selected in the Select: drop-down menu. Press the SHIFT key and click around the white background to take color samples. Make sure that the Fuzziness is set to zero, as this will give you a cleaner edge and make it easier to get rid of stray pixels. Pay attention to the flowers and the green stems as you are taking color samples, but don't make yourself crazy. This is only to minimize the whites; we don't have to get it perfect. The Selection radio button also needs to be activated so that you can see what colors you are selecting.

Once you are satisfied with your color selection, click OK and you'll see that a lot of the white area is selected.

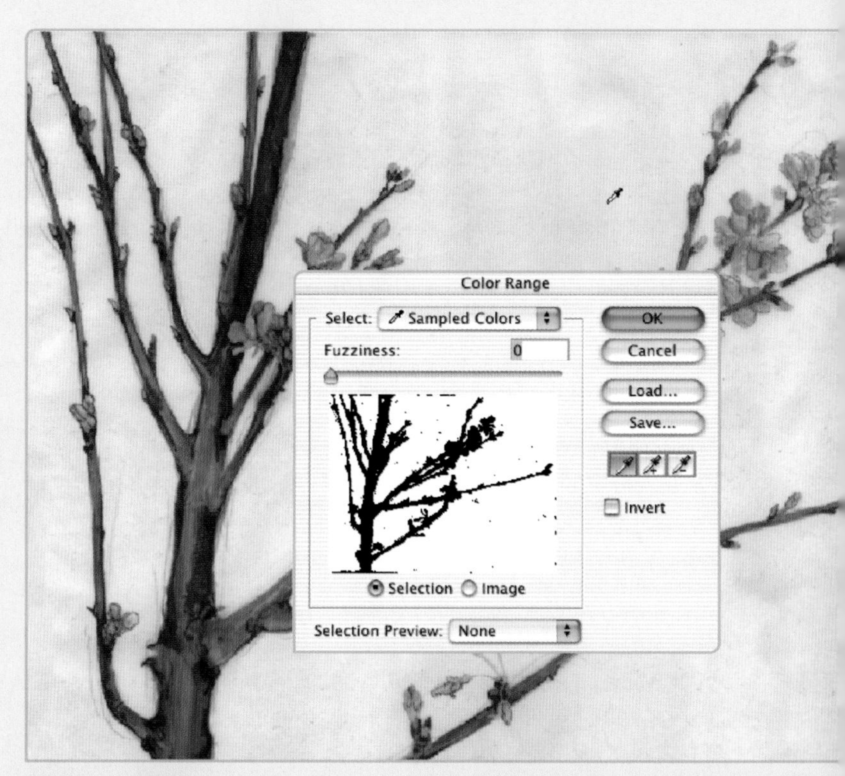

ow, go expand the selection by 3 pixels, (Select Modify ➤ Expand). Now you should see that lot of those stray pixels have been lost. Most ‹ely this is because some areas still need to be eaned up, such as petals that have been ·lected or branches that have sketch marks ound them. To fix this, we'll use the Polygonal isso tool (L), which has a more angular shape. nis tool works much like the Pen tool, except ɔu can only draw straight lines from point to ɔint. Press the OPTION key to deselect an area, ɔr example, a portion of a petal or a green em. Press the SHIFT key as you select to add an ·ea (like any stray sketch marks or marker lines) ıat will be deleted.

ake sure that you are aware that the lasso with ıe + icon is going to add to the area we are ɔing to take out of the tree drawing, and the ·eas selected with the – lasso will stay with the ·awing. Once you're happy with the selection, t DELETE.

ow you should have the tree drawing isolated om the background. Name this layer "trees olated". A little trick you can use to ensure that ıere are no extra stray pixels is to add a new yer below the tree and use the paint bucket to ıake it black. Any lightly colored stray marks ill stand out and you can delete them using the ɔlygonal Lasso tool. Throw the layer in the ash after you are satisfied with your edges.

ıis may seem like a lot of steps to isolate an ·ea from the background, but it's far quicker ıan drawing a path around all of those ·anches. Bear in mind that the reason I chose ∙ make the flowers in the drawing blue was ecause I knew it would make this selection ·ocess quite a bit easier.

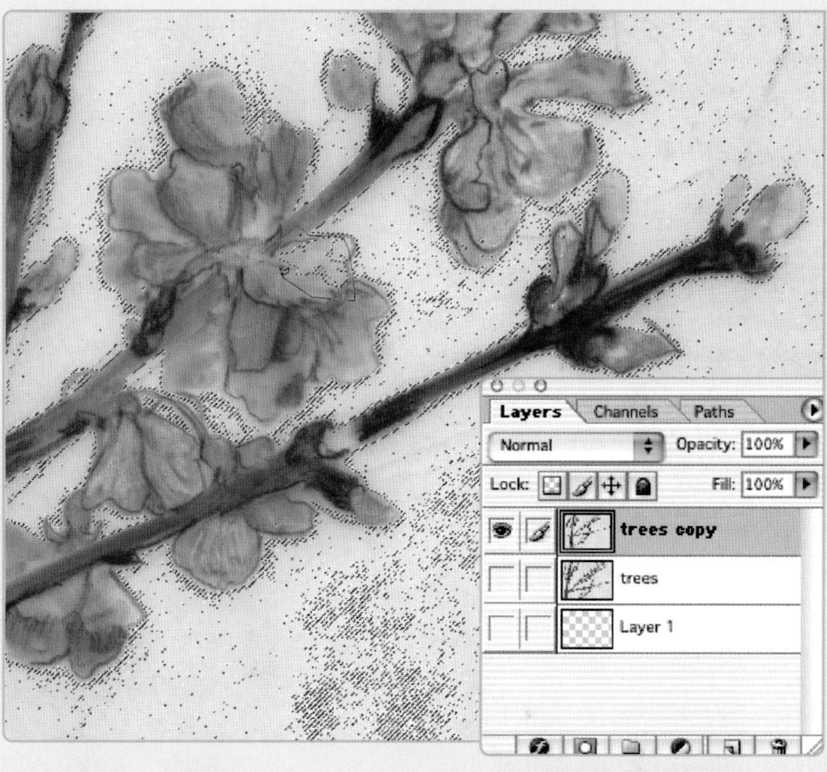

Go back to the birds.psd file. We are now going to import the birds into the tree.psd layout. Hide the Shape 1, Shape 2, and Shape 3 layers. CMD+click on the Shape 1 layer to select the bird. You'll see the "marching ants" around the bird. Drag the bird into the tree.psd file. Position and size the bird in a way that suits you. I've placed the first bird *behind* the branches and named the layer bird 1.

We'll follow this procedure with the other two birds, except we want them to be closer to us than the first bird, so we need to position them in layers above the tree.

Being a bit of a realist, I have placed the birds in ways that think they would actually rest on a cherry branch. Notice th I've placed the resting birds in the crook of the branch, whe their weight would actually be supported, while the third bird sort of teetering off of the smaller, more delicate branch. I ha also flipped the third bird to make it appear as though it about to fly out of the picture plane. You can flip the bird b going up to Edit ➤ Transform ➤ Flip Horizontal.

ow click on the eyeball next to the trees layer. It looks as though ıose birds have been sitting there all along, thanks to our expert election tool usage!

ow let's make the background a little bit darker. Duplicate the ees layer again and the default name will be trees copy 2. hange the trees copy 2 layer blend mode from Normal to Multiply and name it "trees multiply". This will make the ackground tree image a little darker and still retain the wrinkled aper quality we want to keep. You'll notice that having that Multiply layer gives the tree a slight illusion of a shadow, which I uite like.

o soften the edges of the tree branch a little, duplicate the trees olated layer and name it "trees isolated blur". CMD+click on that yer to select it, then expand the selection by 2 pixels. Now se Filter ➤ Blur ➤ Gaussian Blur with a radius of 2 pixels.

Detail of blurred edge on branch

The next step is adding feet to the birds. I used the Pen tool, but you could use a number of tools including the Brush tool, selection tools, or even the Pencil tool. The Pen tool gave me the cleanest edge and the most control, which is what I wanted. When you use the Pen tool, it automatically creates a new layer and gives it a default name, for example, Shape 1. I left the default names and put all of the feet shapes in a folder called feet.

Now is a good time to add accents and little retouches to the birds and leaves for the tree on their respective layers, specifically bird 1, bird 2, bird 3, and trees isolated. It helps to do this after you are happy with the composition because you can be more aware of where shadows and lights will fall. We'll start by adding a few dark areas around the birds' eyes and beaks. Select the Burn tool, with a brush size of about 17 with a fuzzy edge. The Exposure should be set at 25 percent and the Range drop-down menu should be set to Midtones. The Burn tool is aptly named in that it functions like it is actually burning the image a darker shade in the areas where you use it. You can also use the Burn tool in the birds' feathers or anywhere else where you'd like to add dark accents. While doing this step, I kept my Burn tool set at the settings just mentioned, but I used brushes ranging from 35 to 5 in diameter, depending on the area I was working on.

I wanted to add some highlights to the eyes of the birds, so created a new layer called eyes highlights. I selected a very sma brush and carefully dabbed a little bit of white in the eye c each bird. The beak highlights are painted in white (using larger brush) on a separate layer named beaks. I changed thi layer's blending mode from Normal to Lighten to make th highlights appear more yellowish over the beaks.

The flowers should be mostly white so I made a new layer calle white flowers and painted white where I deemed it appropriat You can be clumsy with the white as long as you don't hit an of the branches or green areas. You can always select the tree isolated layer and press CMD+SHIFT+I to get an inverse selectior and then hit DELETE to clean the edges up.

I used the Sponge tool (in the same menu as the Burn tool i the Tools palette) to perk up the saturation in some of th green areas and the Burn tool in some of the branch areas. T lighten feathers, I created a new transparent layer named ligh and used paintbrushes of varied sizes. I used white and mad the layer-blending mode Soft Light. I alternated between th paintbrush and Eraser to model the lights.

I did the same things for some portions that I wanted to mak only slightly lighter, except I gave this layer a 50-percent opacit I named this layer medium.

The parakeets could sit a little softer on the page, so we're going to blur the edges of the birds a bit in the same way that I blurred the edges of the cherry tree branches. To do so, you need to duplicate each bird layer and CMD+click on each bird to select it. Now expand the selection by 2 pixels (Select ➤ Modify ➤ Expand). Go to Select ➤ Feather and enter 2 for the Feather Radius. Click OK to make the edges of the selection a little softer. Now add a Gaussian Blur with a 2-pixel radius (Filter ➤ Blur ➤ Gaussian Blur). You'll see a very slightly blurre area around the birds. You may choose to use higher numbe for these steps to create a more blurred edge, or you may war to leave this step out and keep the hard edges on the birds.

I wanted to add a little ornamentation to the piece and mix u some vector shapes, so using the Pen tool, I added loopy an fluid lines and intermingled those lines with some paint splatter

hese lines give the picture a musical quality and a movement that nakes it different from a strictly observational composition. To dy up the Layers palette a bit, I put all of these elements into a yer set called ornament. Just to be sure that the ornaments will now up against the paper background, let's go back to the trees nultiply layer, pick Image ➤ Adjustments ➤ Brightness/Contrast, nd set the Brightness to –10.

For the final touches, I grabbed my Pen tool once again and drew some more sprigs of the cherry tree to make a connection between the positive and negative spaces. I placed these sprigs in a way that's complementary to the looping lines and splashes of paint so that the sprigs seem to bloom out of the other white area. I then placed these three elements in a layer set called sprigs.

Conclusion

I want to stress again that the techniques I have discussed in this chapter are not limited to Photoshop files that incorporate hand-drawn imagery. The concept here is simple—we are making an image that looks like it always existed "as it is now"—it just so happens that my elements are hand-drawn.

Isolating elements is also very important when you are preparing images for an animation. I have a number of pieces where I animate a human face and use one primary drawing as a base for different expressions. I drew the mouth, eyes, and nose differently for different facial expressions and used the selection features in Photoshop to superimpose the drawn expressions over the face, thus creating a believable flow and transition as the person's face changes (`opos.mov` on the CD). If Photoshop didn't exist, I'd be hand drawing each frame of the facial animation.

Have fun with Photoshop—enjoy the freedom it allows you!

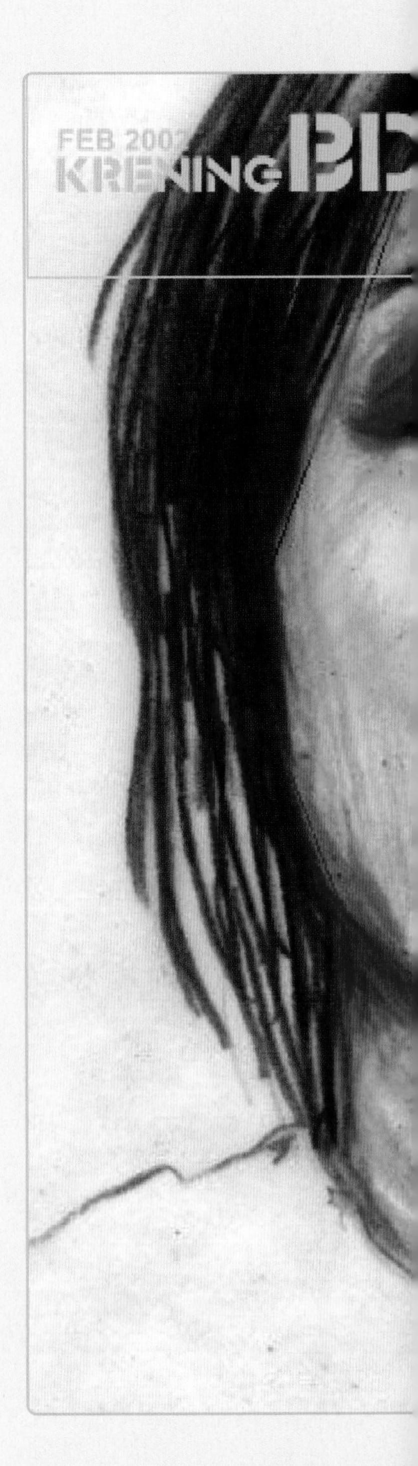

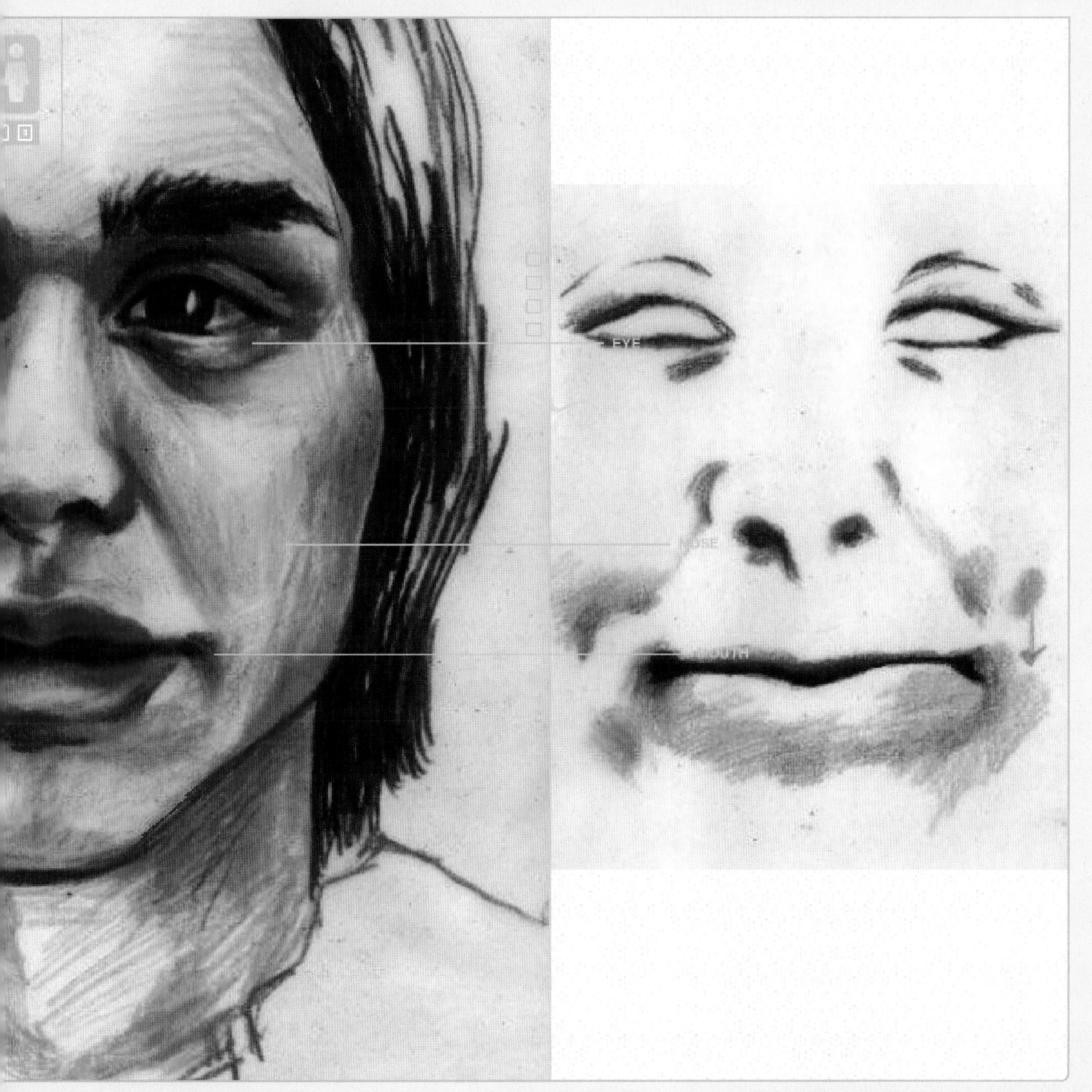

Brian Aznar still from BD4D presentation

10 **TARTART**

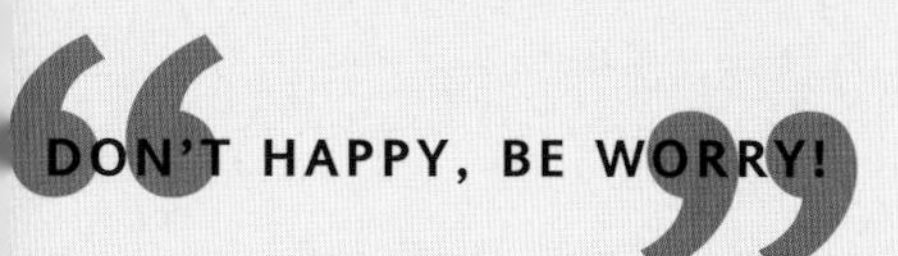

MARIN MUSA
WWW.TARTARTMAGAZINE.COM

First of all, let me introduce myself. I'm Marin Musa and was born in 1979 in Mostar, Bosnia and Hercegovina, where I still live and work as a graphic designer. When I first received an invitation to contribute to this second volume of *New Masters of Photoshop*, I was left speechless because I have never heard of the first volume. But I have to say that the idea sounded very good. But me, writing for the *New Masters of Photoshop*?! I was afraid that I might not be able to deliver what was asked of me.

When I say that I have never heard of this book, I should add that, up until just a few years ago, I had not heard of many well-known publications due to my inability to access information, all because I live in quite a strange part of the world. This world that I am part of is in the middle of 21st century Europe, but it somehow seems to be part of different planet. This odd place is part of the answer to why I decided to contribute to the book. Because I'm unaware of current fashions and other trendsets, I arrived at this point in my creativity on my own accord. And suddenly, it seemed that the work I was doing was considered "in."

I shall present some of my work in this chapter. However, I hav to point out that these are my noncommercial works, I publis in *Tartart* magazine (www.tartartmagazine.com), and they'r very different from what I do for my day job.

Tartart, my online magazine and noncommercial project, cam about as a means of expressing my views and myself to th outside world. The style I use in *Tartart* is completely influence by events that took place in this region over the last ten year Some of these events will be described in more detail later i the chapter.

This is the city of Mostar, my main source of inspiration. It wa destroyed in the war, and even now it is separated into tw parts (inside the minds of most of its citizens on both sides). A of its bridges were destroyed in war. In a symbolic way, this wa an attack on the people that loved Mostar, and most neve recovered.

1992, when war broke out in former Yugoslavia, I was 13. My hole life turned upside down. These four years of war dented eople's lives irreparably. Many died, whereas others fled, never return. Many objects were destroyed. This civil war changed eople, their way of living, and the city I live in.

These photographs were taken at Christmas in 2003. These buildings personify the collective state of mind of the people living in Mostar. Very few of the destroyed buildings have been rebuilt, even though it has been almost ten years since the end the war. Among these buildings are schools, business buildings, and hotels.

The city was systematically destroyed, both emotionally and spiritually during the war. People who used to live in it took part in the process of its destruction. As I said earlier, all of the bridges were destroyed, as were any remaining cultural and religious monuments. Even after the war was over, the destruction continued. Many historical monuments were renovated in a completely unsuitable manner, hence they now look even worse. The spirit of the city was destroyed. People who live in Mostar only required the very basics to live—nothing was replaced, and dirty objects were acceptable for everyday living. No one cared that Mostar was suffocating under tons of rubbish, that there was no street lighting, and that middle class society did not exist. Society consisted of two extremes. Many people concentrated on getting rich quickly instead of on rebuilding and aiding reconstruction. Now we all suffer the consequences of the war.

This way of life became the inspiration for my artwork.

Detail from my home

These mailboxes were originally colored by their owners and I have adapted this slightly using only Photoshop's contrast control. You just have to have an eye for interesting things and, of course, always make sure you carry a camera to capture the moment.

As I grew older and more mature, I looked for the best way to express my views. My priorities changed. It was not important that I was surrounded by destruction and theft, that there were no cinemas, no galleries, no theatres, or concerts. Now even the arrival of a cheap circus sounds like a good day out.

This original photo of the circus was taken at night using a long shutter. I then redesigned it and inverted it using Photoshop.

ost of my work does not have any meaning or any messages, or have I ever tried to deliberately communicate any messages the viewer. Any reaction to the image is based on the viewer's wn perception and their personal view and background, which ill be unique to them. I don't want to direct someone on how he should go about understanding a piece of art. If s/he mply likes the colors or composition, without me forcing a ear message on them, this is very satisfying for me.

y main aim is to cause some sort of blackout, a positive or egative shock, in the eyes of the viewer. Over time, I have eveloped a noncomplex way of working. My method of orking in Photoshop can be seen as a reflection of the way of e here: I take the shortest route to a desired aim. The final nage is all important; I want my audience to be able to look at the final image and get something out of it. I feel no need to use complex techniques in my artwork, because I think that such techniques do not help communicate in a better way. Once the situation in my head changes, those other techniques will surely be awakened from hibernation.

You can see this simple style in the photos above. You'll be introduced to some of these Photoshop techniques in the second half of the chapter.

The photo above was taken in the center of Mostar, and it shows that people are living in a partially destroyed building with an air conditioning system. The blue and red windows were already there, but I colored the rest of the windows using Photoshop's Paint Bucket tool.

Again, effective changes can be made with simple use of color. The following pair show the effects of changing hue and saturation parameters.

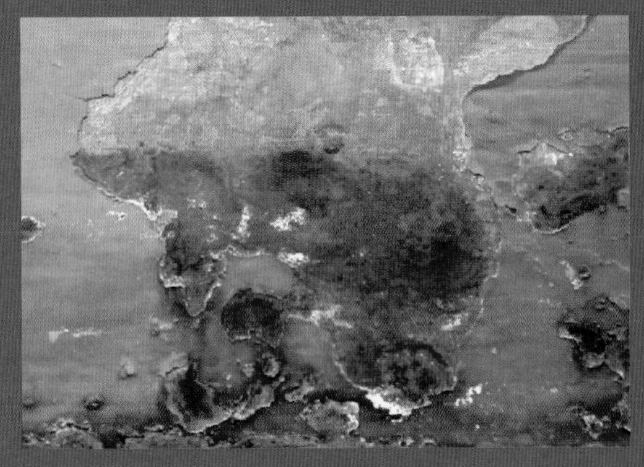

For me, the definition of Photoshop is a very simple form of expressing oneself. I never liked Photoshop because of its huge possibilities (layers, or its filters, and so on). Most of these tools, features, and additions are tiresome to me because I had to learn all of these advanced tools and features for my commercial work, which pays for my living and the life of *Tartart* magazine. I tend to avoid complex use of Photoshop tools in my noncommercial work because it's the final image that's really important here, not the process of creating it.

Taxi stand in front of my house

This is a building from the Communist period, built 30 years ago. After taking the photo, I transformed it into this artwork by changing the hue parameters.

Many of these photographs have been displayed in *Tartart*. This magazine came about as a result of my desire and need to learn how others live and work. By publishing *Tartart*, I've met many similar-minded people who have the same interests and joys in life. *Tartart* is an ongoing project and, I hope, a successful one. It's noncommercial, free, and available for download in PDF format (www.tartartmagazine.com). I print all of the publications too, but in limited numbers, because the magazine doesn't carry any text or ads (apart from the credits). I distribute these limited prints to friends and supporters. So far, *Tartart* has featured a number of contributors from all over the world. The fact that I have managed to bring people to one place through this magazine makes me very happy. I have never been sorry for investing my own money into this project and have never asked for support from commercial companies.

On more than one occasion I told my friend Martin Callanan (www.itakephotos.co.uk), one of the magazine's first contributors, that *Tartart* is as much his own property as it is mine, and this means that it is the property of all contributors who have helped shape it into what it is today. By working on this magazine, I have kept my belief that no matter where I live and what I am surrounded by, I can draw attention to the situation and to my work. Most importantly, I can draw attention to the work of people living in Mostar who supported me from the beginning and ever since the first issue of *Tartart*. Some of these people include Damir Sanje, who worked on one of the early (and still on-going) projects called Paus.Kruske that deals with some semicommercial projects (www.pauskruske.com), and Dalibor Nikolic (www.dalibor-nikolic.com) who supported my project from the beginning.

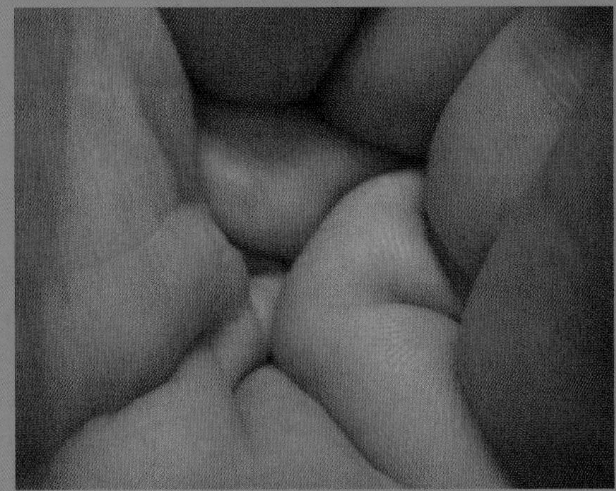

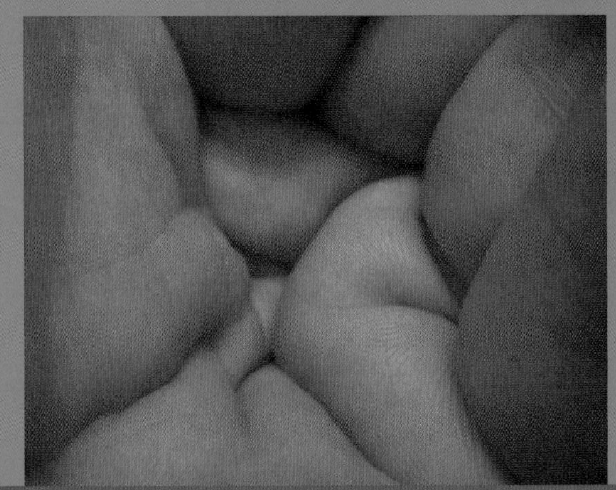

Image courtesy of Dalibor Nikolic (www.dalibor-nikolic.com)

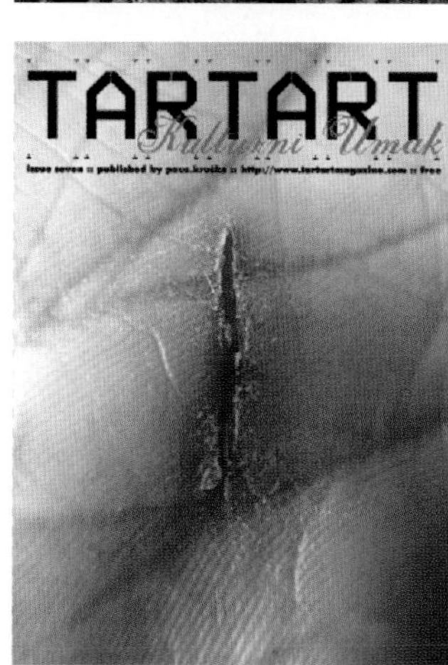

My plan is to publish ten issues of *Tartart* and then look for a new means of expression. The idea was to somehow unite all issues of *Tartart* in the form of a book or a web page. *Tartart* never had a theme or a definition. Contributors have recognized similarities to their own work in those printed in *Tartart*, and they send their work in to be displayed in the magazine. At the time of writing, eight issues of *Tartart* magazine have seen daylight!

Most of the works in *Tartart* do not have a message or a meaning. If some of the photographs can fascinate someone by what they are looking at—and they do not necessarily understand it—I would consider this a success. If an individual can find a message and meaning in any artistic work, then I believe that is the best reward for any artist.

I have found that society needs magazines like Tartart that are devoid of advertising and messages. When, sometime in future, I realize that things have changed, another form of expression is bound to surface. My personal opinion is that *Tartart* has achieved its best under these current conditions and that I should not aspire to better it further. It's highly unlikely that I can possibly create anything with a bigger impact on the outside world while still living here.

Postage stamps designed for Croatian Post Office Ltd., Mosta

In this chapter I would also like to show some of my commercial works that sustain *Tartart*'s life and existence. I created all of these works using Photoshop, but they are mainly works for print that were not published on the web. Some of the projects are similar to work I've done for *Tartart,* and I would like to thank people who have financially recognized and rewarded my designs.

Other major inspirations in my life are films and music. These enable me to concentrate, to rest, and to reflect on current topics and issues. Songs have, some with only one particular line, inspired part of my work, whereas films have influenced others. *Singles* (Cameron Crowe, 1992), left an important mark on me and my work. This film shows young people living a normal life, faced with normal problems, at the time when the unrest in my country was becoming stronger than ever. It gave me hope that one day I would be faced with the type of problems they have, instead of those I was facing.

Another important aspect of the film is its soundtrack, which includes music by Alice in Chains, my favorite band at the time, Soundgarden, and Pearl Jam. At the time, the film helped me find my own identity, as there was hardly anyone around me that could have been envisaged as a role model.

Another important influence was a film directed by Wim Wenders called *The Million Dollar Hotel* (2000). This film helped shape my ideas into reality; it helped me pull them from my head, put them on paper and in the computer, and start working. It gave me energy to create something that can, and will, be seen by people outside the borders of the country I live in. I hold Bono's soundtrack to this film in high regard, and also the soundtrack of Tarantino's *Pulp Fiction* (1994). Many other films have given me a push in the right direction and fed my creative strength, such as Vincent Gallo's *Buffalo 66* (1998). This is a film I wish I had made.

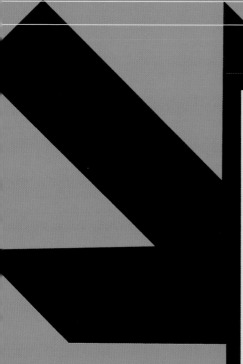

Vhen writing for *Spatium Magazine* vww.spatium-newsletter.de), I was asked here I find inspiration for my work. I had ɔ admit that my biggest drive comes om the inability to have everything ıat I want at the same time, or to ather all I want in one place (for xample, music or film) when I please. ubjects that excite me most come from ıy surroundings, both material and onmaterial in nature. I find people's lives, ıy life, and occurrences that happen here ısightful in an unconventional way.

ve attempted to show what drives me to reate the work that I do, and in the econd half of the chapter, I shall show ow some of them were created using hotoshop.

Most of my artwork is based on using only basic elements of Photoshop's image controls. In my opinion, most of the work shown in this chapter would have never been made if it weren't for this extraordinary software. And, of course, I have to thank my Olympus Camedia c4000 zoom digital camera, which satisfies my needs because it supports all kinds of manual control over the picture and has a satisfying 4 megapixels of picture resolution. This is enough for my publishing needs, because the format of *Tartart* magazine is 15cm x 20cm and is printed on digital print equipment. As far as file sizes are concerned, I tend to use an A4 page format at 300dpi in CMYK and, with that, I'm sure I can get good results in print. When those files are stretched to a larger format, such as posters, the resolution decreases, but it's still acceptable because posters are viewed from a greater distance.

I must say that I've tried using software other than Photoshop for working on digital images, but none of them give me what I need—simple control over images, and yet some very complex options for my commercial work needs.

However, before we get started, if you think you're about to learn some advanced Photoshop techniques, you're wrong. The main message of this chapter is that if you bought this book to learn some complicated operations, you should skip to one of the other chapters. I will show you what you can make using just the basic Photoshop controls that you already know. When I say "basic," I mean that we'll be using one-step actions such as controlling the basic image parameters: hue, saturation, desaturation, contrast, level adjustments, and so on.

I want to wake up your creativity that's been imprisoned by the complexity you see in other people's work. You don't have to spend hours or days in front of the screen to create an image you can be proud of. So, if you're afraid that you can't achieve some satisfying results, now is the time to get rid of these fears.

Two things I try not to use in my art are photographs made by other people, and Photoshop's artistic filters, which give eye-catching results but become parts of one boring image after about a minute of looking at it. I hope I can show you how t accept some "back to basics" controls, save your images, an return to them each day.

My idea is that great things happen in a moment (or at least i few minutes). Those works on which I spend hours and hours o time in Photoshop don't satisfy me. Now, if I spend 30 hours o one piece of art, that means I think about it for 29 hours an 50 minutes, make a coffee, drink half the cup, turn on m computer, check my e-mail, and then start up Photoshop.

OK, I will start to show you how I developed some of my art int finished images. I hope you'll enjoy this preview of using ver basic tools in order to achieve (at least) interesting results.

Electric fire

This will be a kind of "what to do with that photo I accidentall took" tutorial. This is a pretty ugly image and it shows nothing I was supposed to take some commercial photos in an offic and, while I was waiting, I played around with my camera's ligh settings. During this time, I took a dozen other photos, but thi is the one I thought I could make something out of. Why? don't know, and I can't teach you how you should recogniz exactly which one among the many photos has possibilitie Sometimes you shouldn't look at things the way everyone els does. These images surround us saying, "hey I'm here, use me! Or at least I can hear them doing so.

his image probably has no inspirational ıfluence on anyone, but what I see is a rid of tiny metal bars that provide secure eating and prevents other objects in the oom from touching the fire. Another ning I see here are the colors. I always 'anted to have them in my camera but ave never taken my camera with me to barbecue.

fter I took this photo and opened it in hotoshop (`fire_start.tif` on the D), the first thing I did was crop it down o just the electric bars.

This is the result after cropping, but it lacks contrast, amongst other things. So what I will do here is add more contrast and color saturation, and the final result is something you would never expect to get from the starting image. When doing this, edit the image directly with Image ➤ Adjustments ➤ Brightness/Contrast and then play with the settings. Remember to turn on the Preview option so that you will see the results immediately. Take my advice and try not to use automatic contrast adjustment because you'll never get what you expect from it. You need to have complete control over these settings.

Interesting grid isn't it

This image is now ready to be used for a commercial poster. Try deleting some of the fields created by the grid, then set up a solid black background, and place some information on these black areas. Of course, you can use your creativity and imagination to keep playing around with this grid format.

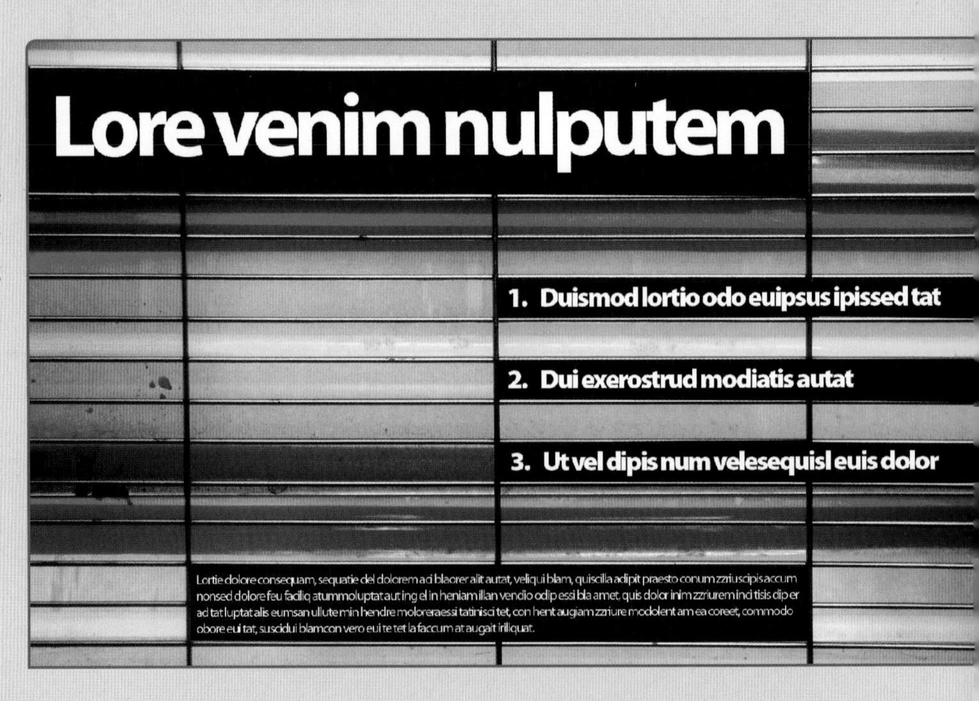

ou could leave this as your final result, but I think that ugly arting image has more to offer. Why not use it? What I ccidentally did on this picture, and liked a lot, was apply the aximum motion blur effect with an Angle of zero and a istance of 999 pixels.

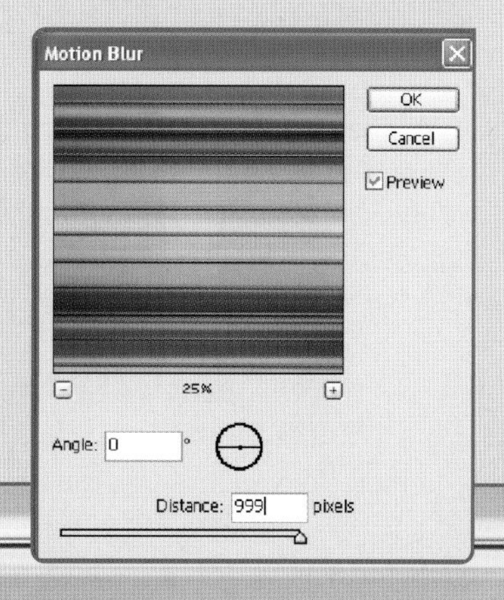

K, I think this is pretty enough as it is and no more can be leaned from the starting picture. Let's move on to another twork that's also based on an accidentally taken photo.

ectric fire, but astonishing colors...

Radio display vs. long shutter: display wins

As you can see from this section's title and the following image, I'll try to introduce you to the world of long shutter photography and what you can do with it using Photoshop. This image shows the display on my A/V receiver. At first glance, it's an ordinary image with very little to see.

But, have you ever tried taking a photo like this in a room with the light turned off? I did; in fact, I did it 20 times for this photo, using the manual controls of my Camedia c4000. I set a long shutter time, shook my hand a little for a second or two while taking the picture, and this is the resulting image (`display_start.tif`).

The photo with the lights turned on in the roor

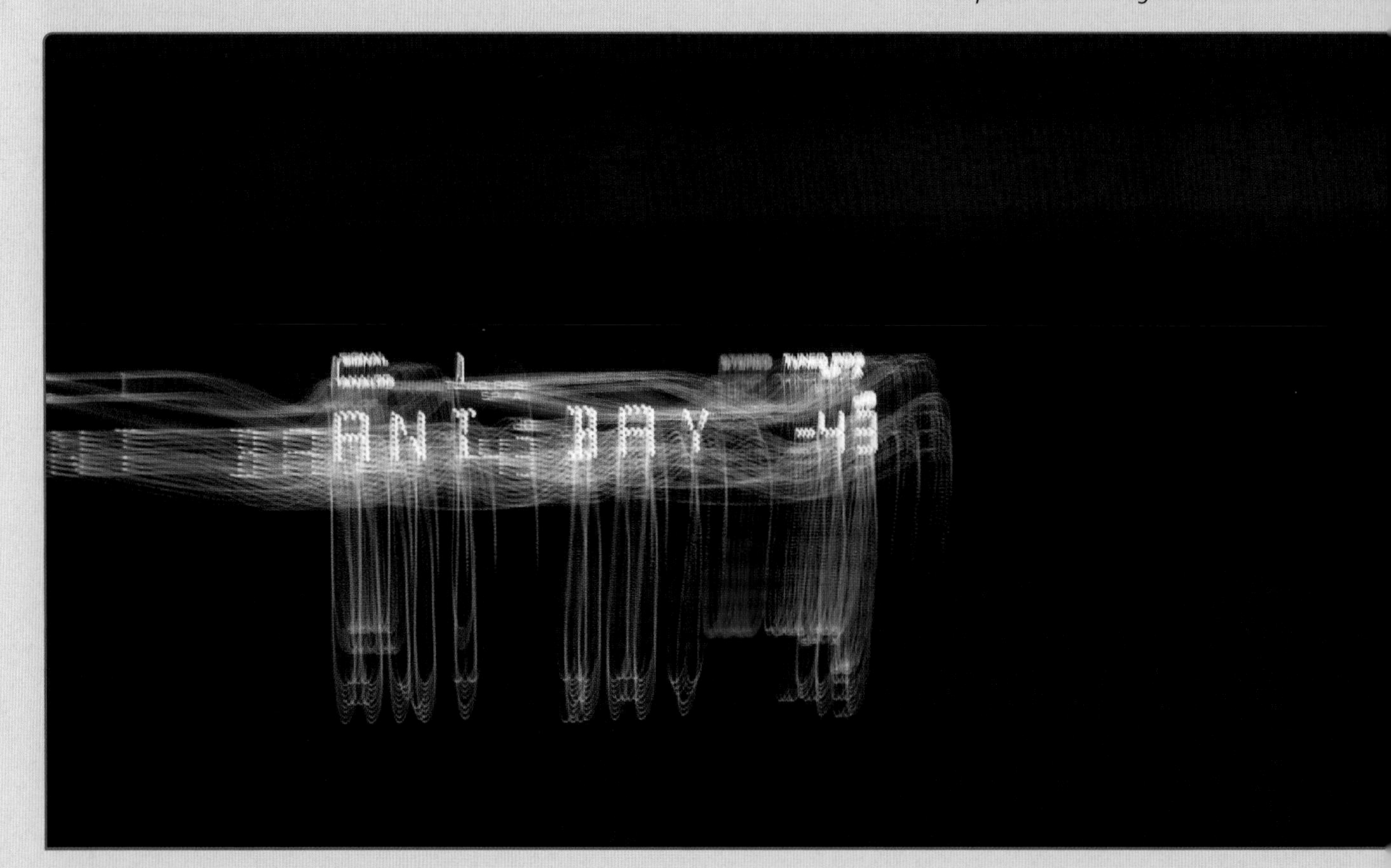

K, this image represents what I was talking out. A little bit of darkness, some hand aking, a long shutter, and here's the result. t you won't stop here, will you? Now try anging the levels to remove semidark parts of e image and convert them to solid black. Also cent the bright parts of the image, such as the aces of light. Once you've done that, try iting the levels for the whole image. Now we ve a much better starting point for our periment.

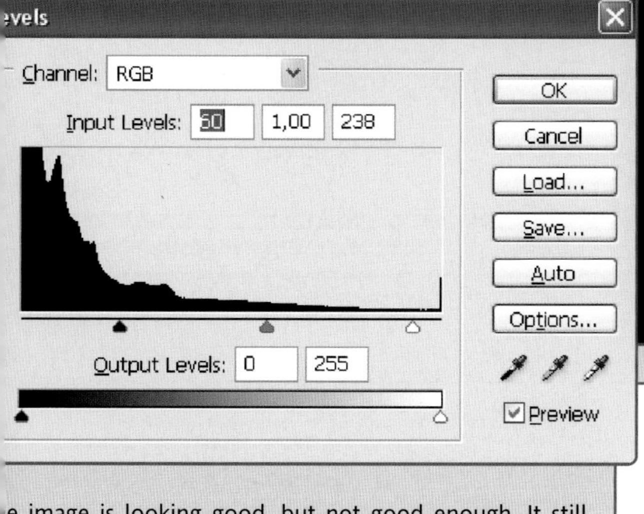

e image is looking good, but not good enough. It still minds me of the original display and I don't want that. I ant to make something that's going to make people ask e what it actually is. The first step now, and the easiest e, is to press CTRL+I to produce an inverted version of e image.

This looks cool but the colors are kind of impersonal. Their combinations mean nothing to me and I would like to change this but withou changing any other part or parameter of the image. Now, we'll use my favorite option from the Image ➤ Adjustments menu, the Hu and Saturation controls. These controls are my favorites because in my work I expect only the unexpected, and you can see this in lo of my work, some of which are displayed in this chapter. Most of them are published in *Tartart*. In my opinion, I expect that the peop from Adobe never thought their controls would be used in this way. Their intention was to help people correct and adjust specific colo components or simultaneously adjust all the colors in an image. In this case, I have nothing to correct, so I don't have anything to los

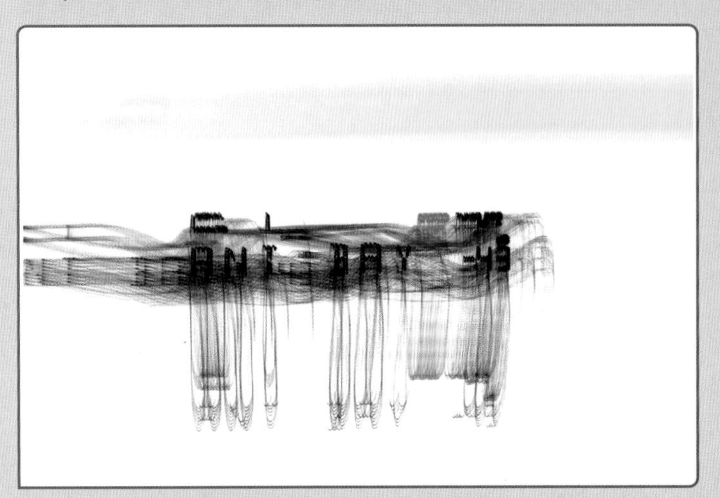

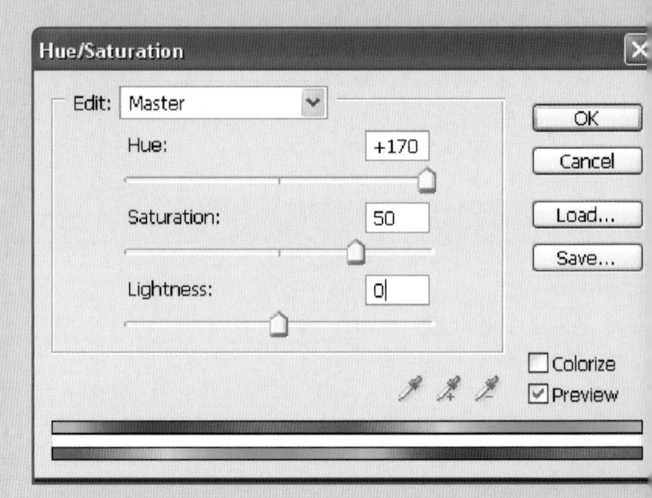

What you see below is the final result. This combination of colors is more acceptable to me now. I left the bright red on the top the image because it reminds me of a cloud.

ere are some more images that illustrate what you can do by taking a picture of a radio display. I used one of them on a *Tartart* agazine cover, and the other is shown here just as it was taken.

You should help your mother dust on Sundays

This sounds funny but it's the truth, at least for those who still live with their mothers. I live alone, so I do all the cleaning myself. In every aspect of my life, I try to see something that catches my eye and makes me think what it would look like on paper or on a computer screen. So, what has this got to do with Photoshop?

Right then, let me explain. One day I was using a dust rag to clean my TV. I had made the rag a little bit wet so that it would collect more dust.

Back to the story. After I finished cleaning the TV, I stretched the dust rag out flat to see what the dirt pattern looked like. It looked interesting, so I said, "why not take a picture?" After all, my camera is always somewhere near me.

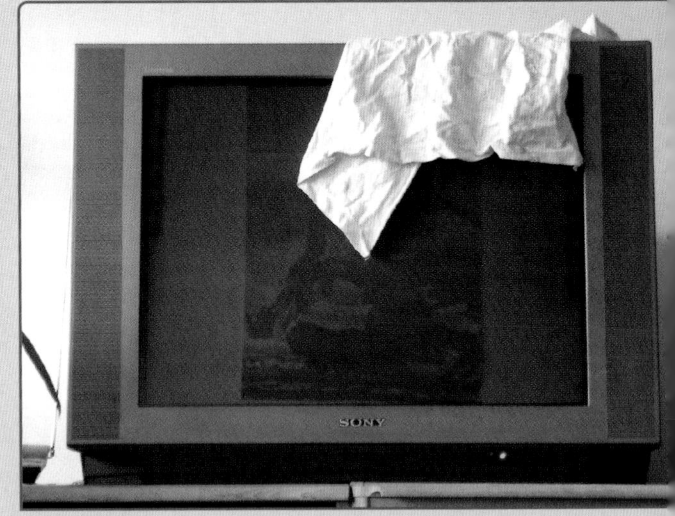

"All you need for this experiment is a dusty TV and a white dust rag

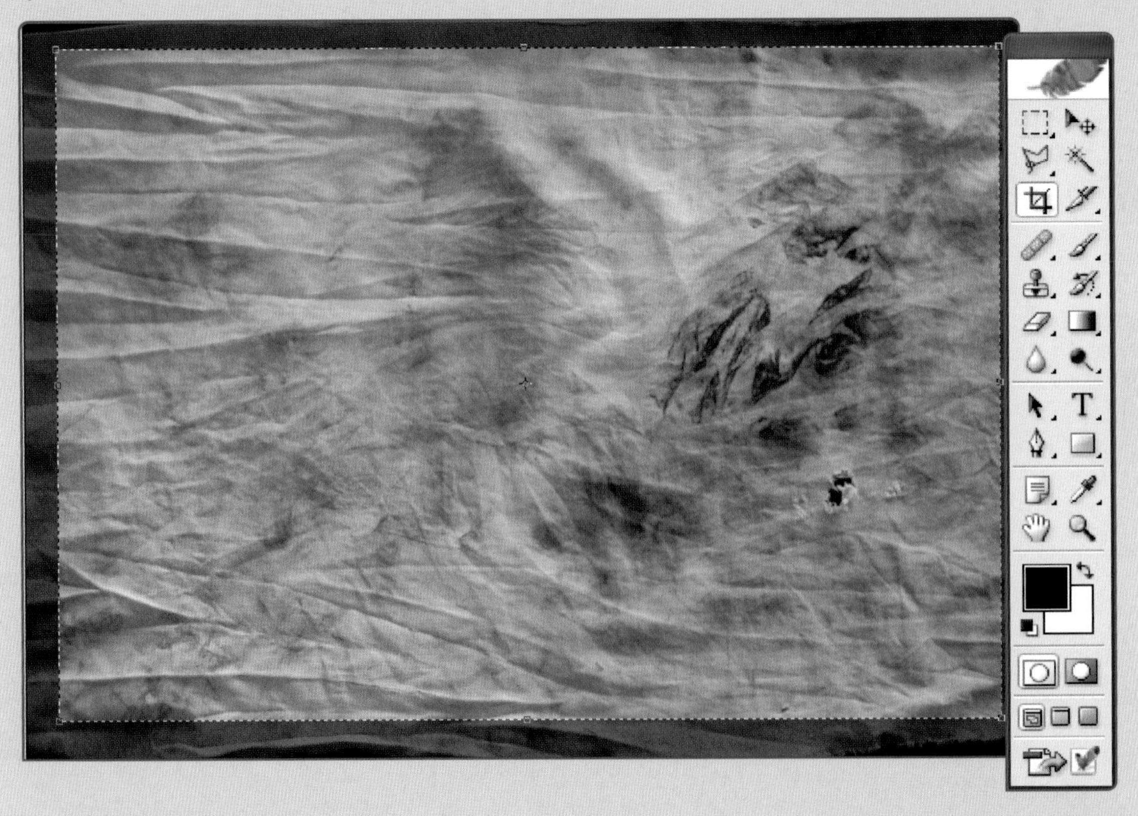

ɔu must admit that it looks interesting, r at least you have to admit that I did my est to try to convince you that ordinary ıings can sometimes become very teresting. Let's get back to Photoshop • see what we have. This is a cropped ıage of a dust rag, and we'll correct its ɔntrast to give it some more style (I efer high contrast images).

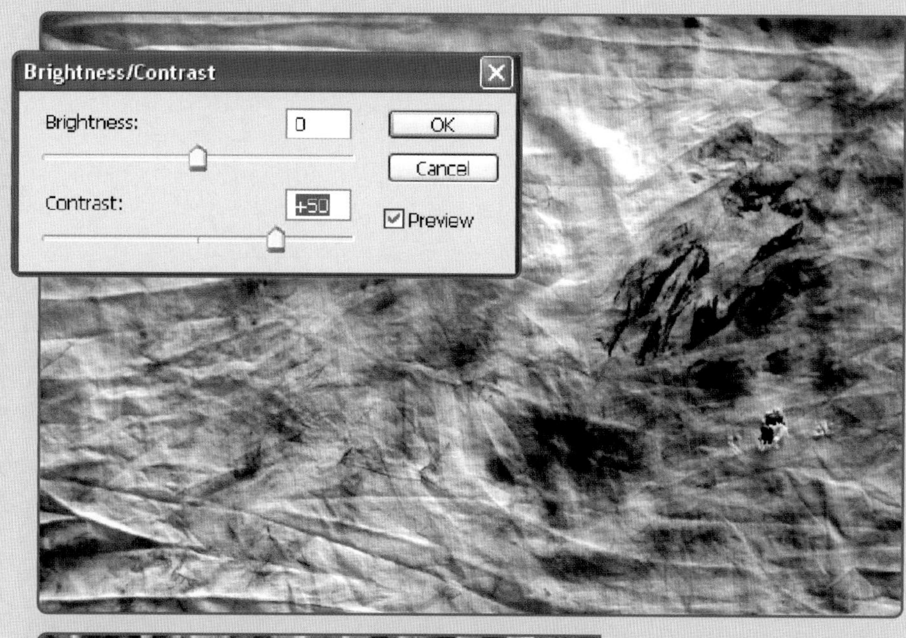

fter correcting the contrast, I rotated e image by 90 degrees and converted it • grayscale because it's actually a ayscale dust rag. The dust rag is white, ıt when you clean something, it ecomes dirty and, in my case, it was a nd of grayscale result. When you take a ıoto of the dust rag with a camera, you t an RGB version of the image, which rries unimportant information about her colors in the picture, which are tually not visible and could cause some ouble later. So what I did was convert to ayscale in order to reset the picture. ecause I still wanted some yellow in ere, I used the Convert to Duotone tion where I choose black and yellow the two dominant tones. This is a very ong combination that gives a clear idea what imagery *Tartart* carries inside and ıat you can expect from viewing that agazine. The other reason I used this mbination is because I like it and I use in many of my commercial works— mething of a personal style.

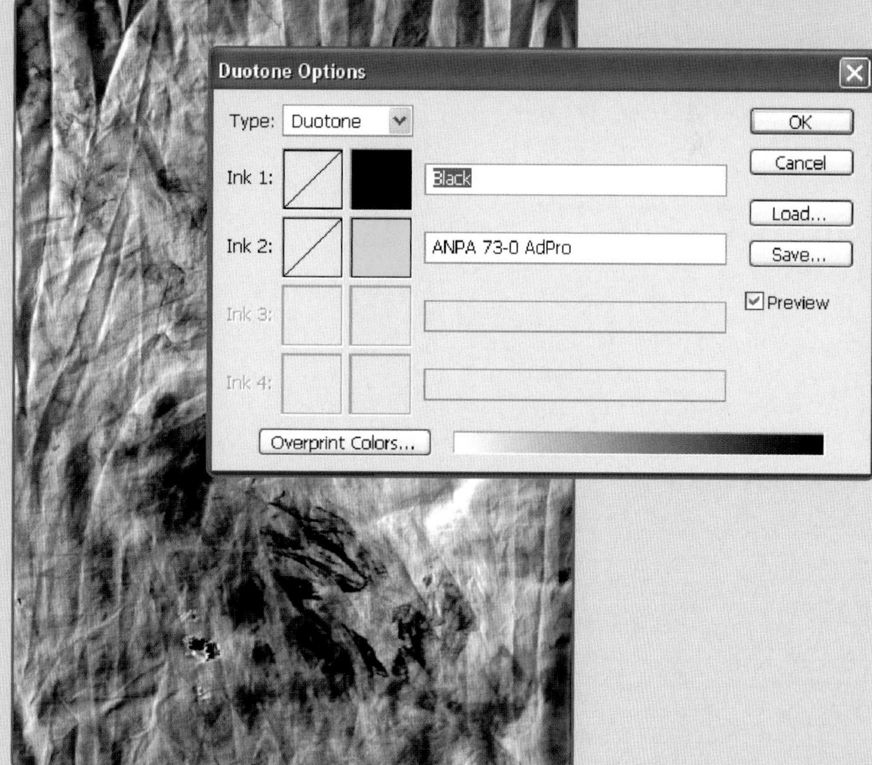

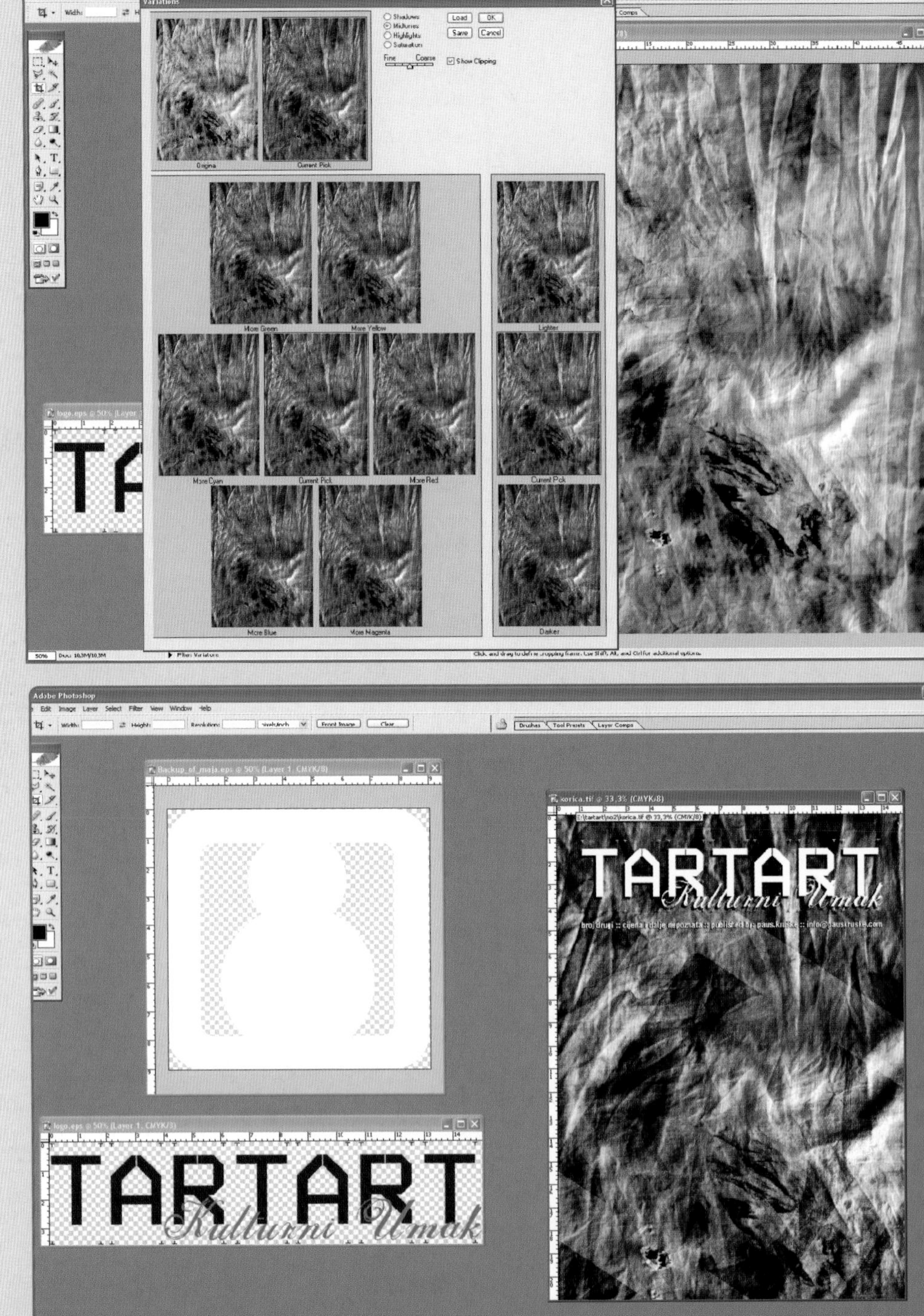

Now I'll go back into CMYK mode, because I will use the final image as a digital print. An interesting option is Image ➤ Adjustments ➤ Variations. This lets you adjust the color balance, contrast, and saturation of an image, and shows you thumbnails of the alternatives at the same time. I find it very useful, especially when precise color adjustments are not required.

Let's see what this image looks like when mocking up a *Tartart* cover.

I rotated the Paus.Kruske logo you see here and added it to the cover using the transparency option in the Layers palette. I then added the Tartart head and applied a drop shadow.

OK, as you can see, the *Tartart* cover is now ready for publishing. How many people would guess what the image really is?

TARTART
Kulturni Umak
broj drugi :: cijena i dalje nepoznata :: published by: paus.kruške :: info@pauskruske.com

Rastafarian color scheme in your room

This is the last image I'm going to deconstruct/reconstruct in this chapter. It deals again with simple commands that are common to all bitmap graphic software. This photo shows my living, working, and sleeping room; the room is the place where Tartart magazine is made, and where my connections to the world of art and design are made, as well. So, let's start and see what this section title actually means.

First of all, I go to Image ➤ Adjustments ➤ Posterize using five levels. This command lets me specify the number of tonal levels and I can have as many levels as I want. In this way, I can get flat areas that are suitable for applying color to later when I go back into CMYK color mode.

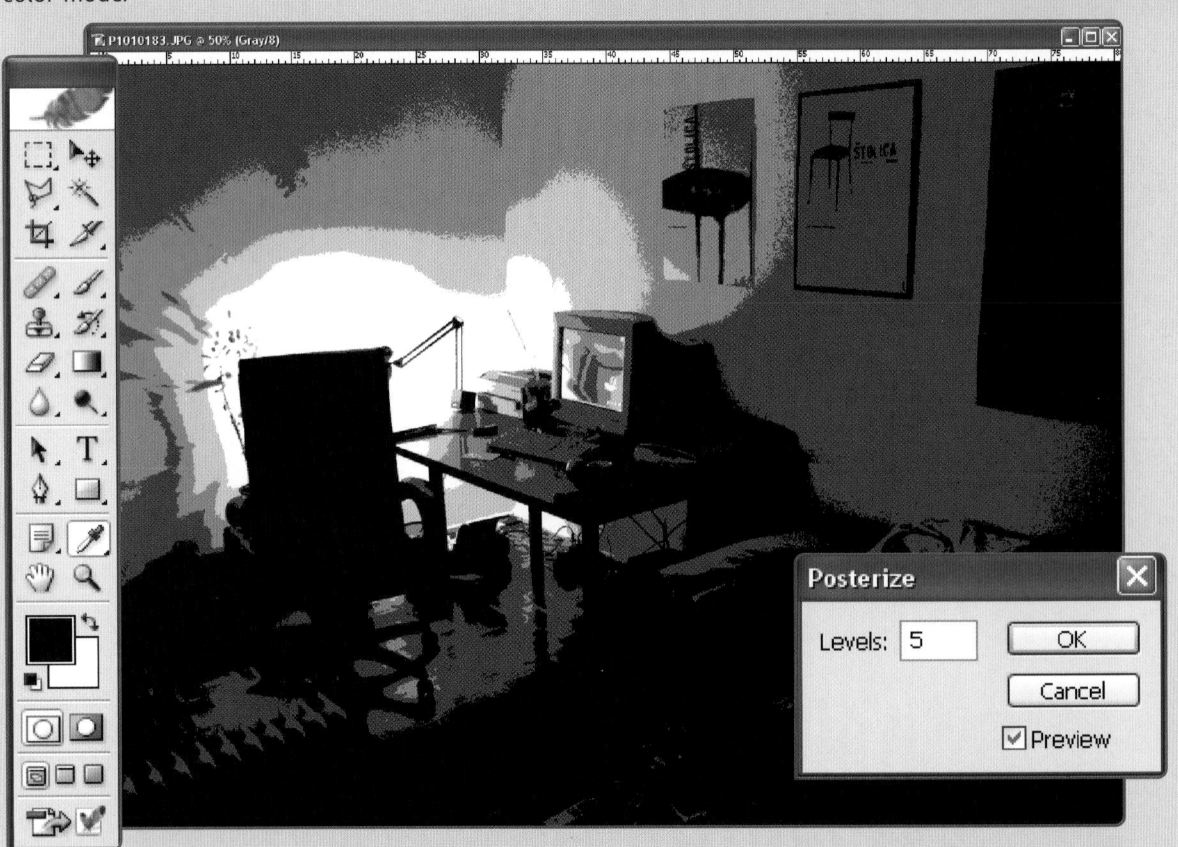

lecided that five levels is enough for what I wanted to do. Any ore would make things complicated and I'd lose connection etween parts of the image. Less then five levels would make e image too boring with little scope for experimenting. When hink of color combinations, the first combination that comes mind is a kind of Rastafarian color scheme. I was sure of one ing though; the colors must be very intense to accent the portance of this space for my production. No other mbination seemed correct to me.

ter you have chosen the colors you want to use, all you have do is apply them to certain areas, connecting them in a eaningful combination. Let's see what the start of the coloring ocess looks like:

Turn the page to see the final product after I added a small image title in the upper-left corner. You should, and could, try this trick with any photo you have in your collection. I think you'll be surprised by the results.

Okay. I hope you've managed to rest your head while reading this chapter. I also hope that you did not learn any new features because everyone should be familiar with most of the work I show here. I hope I helped you open your eyes more and made you look deeper into those things that carry no particular meaning or message. Sometimes they can be very useful in your everyday work. I wanted to show that the amount of Photoshop knowledge is irrelevant if you don't go around and look for inspiring stuff in your everyday life. Open your mind and good luck!

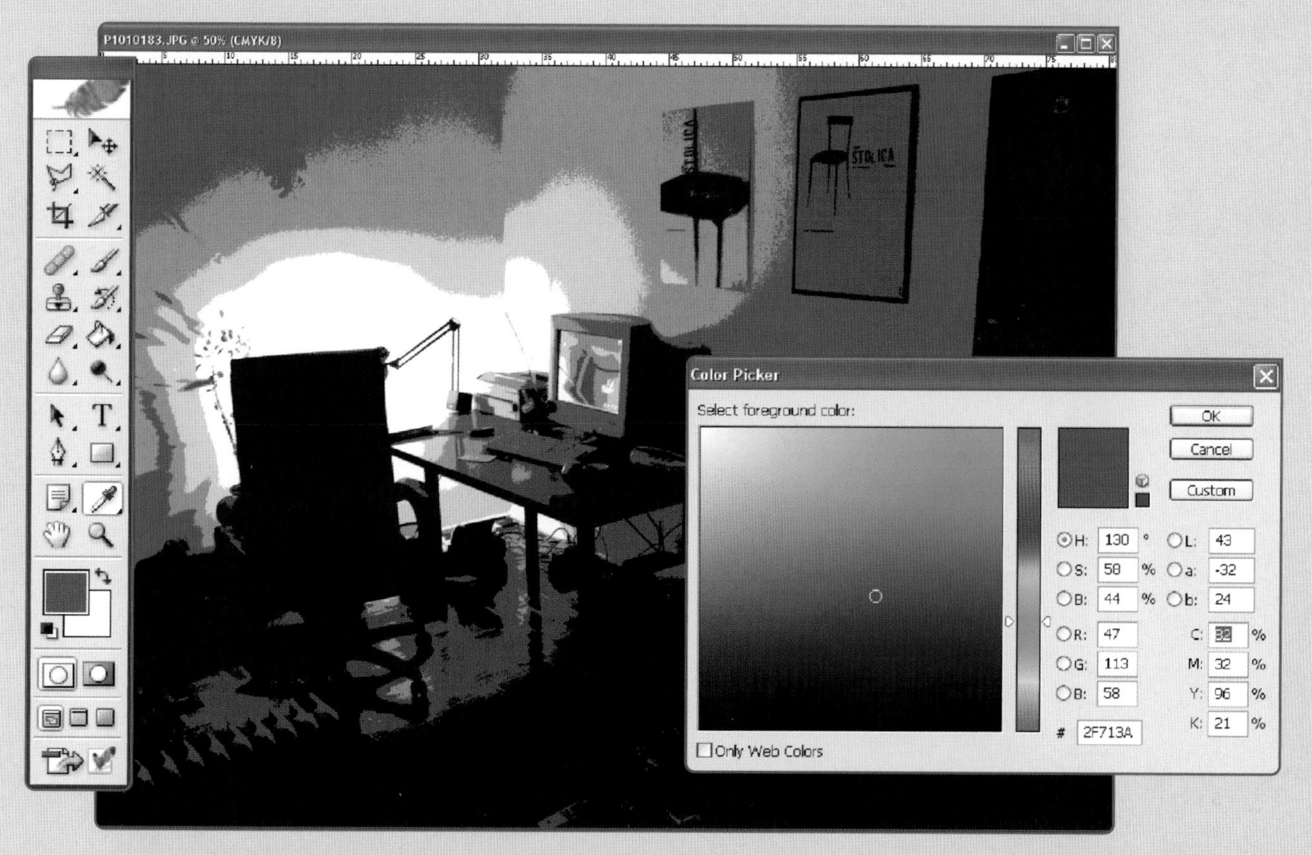

TARTART BIRTHPLACE

STOLICA
STOLICA

11 COLLAGE

"TAKE ADVANTAGE OF ERRORS AS PART OF THE EXPERIMENTATION PROCESS. LEAVE BEHIND THE FEAR OF MAKING MISTAKES, OF MAKING BAD CHOICES."

JORGE RESTREPO
WWW.WONKSITE.COM

When I was asked how I began studying design after nearly completing my IT studies, I could only say that it was an accident. Back then I didn't know the design discipline well at all. I liked art, but because I thought there was a clear difference between art and design, I wasn't completely sure which path to follow, and I continued searching for something that could fulfill my expectations.

I was already 27 years old and feeling sort of lost. I was only certain that graphics and image manipulation were among my greatest interests. I got enormous pleasure from looking at posters and ads. Although I knew very little about the field—what was really meant by graphic design, that is—and had very little drawing ability, I decided to take it on.

Not being any good at drawing was a little traumatic at first. Not only were the other students all drawing geniuses, but they were all pursuing very different paths than mine, such as comic art and illustration. What I wanted was to achieve something important as a graphic designer; perhaps I would publish a book, take on huge advertising campaigns, or simply create my own website. I had lots of doubts up to this point; for example, how much of an artist did I need to be if I was going to be any good at design? Not long after, I found out that drawing wasn't necessary at all—I could use photography as a medium for illustration.

The process of reaching this point wasn't easy, however. My first encounters with illustration were not very comfortable. At the university, part of the curriculum dealt with illustration, which didn't sit well with my few skills. I researched different painters to find a style to which I could adjust to meet my graphical requirements, and it was then that I encountered the work of Toulouse-Lautrec. I enjoyed his pastel techniques with their very flowing strokes, his choice of color palette, and the strength that he transmitted through his work. So, I started to experiment on a small scale and made a little progress, but nothing truly meaningful.

Ambassadeurs: Aristide Bruant, 1892 (litho) by Henri de Toulouse-Lautrec (1864-1901), San Diego Museum of Art, USA / Bridgeman Art Library

t this point, I began to think that maybe graphic design wasn't r me. But a couple of semesters later, I was taught a technique at I didn't think much of at the time, but which would later ecome my personal style and my letter of introduction to the orld: **collage**. I must say that the pop artists of the 1960s, such Andy Warhol and Jasper Johns, interested me greatly. I felt a een desire to discover how they carried out their compositions, ut when I tried to work it out for myself, the results didn't npress me. I became discouraged because, instead of feeling imulated or inspired by these artists, I felt dejected because I ad so much to learn.

owever, this dejection didn't last. A short time later I discovered e multiple applications of photography and how they could nction as the basis for an illustrative process; I then understood at I could attain the same results as an illustrator by composing y work with photographs. So, I started exploring this notographic area. Initially, I felt that photography was the urest and most honest form of the image itself; I wouldn't tervene by editing the image. But then I was inspired by e work of the Colombian, Leo Matiz (www.leomatiz.com), r his compositions within the framework of photographic ortraits. My greatest inspiration, though, was Richard Avedon www.richardavedon.com).

And so I began experimenting, more as a photographer than as a designer. Though the female nude interested me, I was more interested in creating an abstraction based upon the female form. I created my Catarsis (Catharsis) project based upon a photographic exploration of the woman, and Algo Mas Que un Pepino (Something More Than a Cucumber) shows me searching for the female form in vegetables. These black and white projects gave me my first foundations for photographic composition.

When I encountered color photography, my viewpoint changed from being so artistic to being more graphical, more design oriented. I became interested in urban forms, architectural structures, and urban typography. I felt that, in some way, photography allowed me to be more sensitive to my surroundings and to the language of the city. But how did photography help me to discover the benefits of Photoshop as a useful tool for my profession?

My first influence was David Carson's *Fotografiks* (Gingko Press, 1999). After reading his book, I realized how it was possible to illustrate with pictures in an innovative way. Elixir Studio (www.elixirstudio.com) also inspired me back then.

So, ever since those early years, my own photographs have functioned as the starting point for my images. The process is quite basic: I look for an angle that can portray the concept I'm looking for and, after that, I perform small adjustments to color, contrast, and so on. Finally, I add the type to the image. Quite simple, isn't it? However, the complex part isn't in controlling Photoshop, but in finding the perfect shot. It must be one that guarantees the impact I require of each of my designs and, later on in the process, it must integrate well with type. At the end of the day, this is what I mean when I say "design."

In establishing this basic approach to working with Photoshop, I realized what a great piece of software it is. My first experiments probably weren't great, and I didn't find my photos transformed into negatives or completely distorted an enticing enough capability. On the contrary, I was very subtle when retouching—I simply eliminated the obstacles to my design from the photos. I've always been careful when applying filters to my photos. Slight changes to the levels still appeal to me, but I don't like departing too far from the original.

You could almost say that, at first, I was more a photographe than a designer. This thought worried me a little because photographer wasn't what I was trying to become. When I firs tried to manipulate my photos, I felt as if I was stabbing a dea friend. Okay, that's an exaggeration, but I didn't fee comfortable changing something that I had already put a lot c work into. I aimed to take the perfect image the first time.

I gradually learned how to recognize design through photc graphy: urban design in building structures, typographic desig in posters, kitsch design in Bogotá's slums, and so on. Mayb this happens to all photographers—that when they loo through the camera lens, the world is just in a frame that the can control to their liking. When I looked through the lens, found a new opportunity to portray what I saw, and to captur this, I tried every possible angle: I lay down, I stuck my head ou of the car, I went to the top of high buildings . . . I thorough searched for the angle you're not used to seeing. After that, a that remained was scanning it in, adding type, and voila! Th design was ready.

Deadline Pictures Contest, 3rd prize. 2003.
www.deadlinepictures.com

owever, time went by and this process wasn't enough—I eeded more photos. I tried modulating multiple copies of one nage, overlapping them in such a way that I could create depth nd thus I achieved highly contrasted images such as night lights r very pale skies. This technique didn't require too much hotoshop knowledge. This is how I participated in the Deadline ictures Contest, where I came third with the preceding image.

he objective of the contest was to come up with a design using ne of their photo stock images. The result was a 15-layer file which every layer had a slight blend and transparency djustment (multiply, luminosity, lighten, etc.). On top of all nese, I added a layer that was meant to unify them all in one luish tone. It was when I was producing this image that I ealized how important photography was in my creation process nd I didn't feel depressed at all this time. Many designers I dmire and respect use the same design process.

In those days, I was also working on my degree project, *Urbano*, in which I was exploring the process of overlaying multiple images. A new stage began after this. Somehow, with every photo I shot, I could see beforehand in my mind how I would lay out my design; it was like having a little version of Photoshop inside my head. Therefore, after shooting, I already had my design finished mentally, with filters and blends already applied. Not long after that, I found out that everything was also already organized and structured in my head; it was only when I made a "mistake" that things would change completely. Thanks to my mistakes I learned that accidents can be interesting and I felt attracted to applying the wrong layer with a clumsy cutout, even a jagged image. As if by magic, I could see a collage; a technique that I had found so out of reach with illustration was now available thanks to Photoshop.

rbano, degree project, 2001.
ww.eject2.org

Urbano, degree project, 2001.

At this point in my life I started working at the Incubeit agency as a graphic designer, and my time was taken up completely between the university, my thesis, and my work at the agency. The time had come to apply all that I'd learned and take the greatest possible advantage of it. The change was really pronounced, as I discovered that everything experimental must be reduced to function within the corporate parameters. I had to be careful to use the correct corporate colors, make sure the composition of the logo was correct, use the correct kind of font, and become familiar with many other restrictions that didn't encourage experimentation within the design, but nonetheless, I found that the creative process must not be staunched. I began by designing Incubeit's web site (www.incubeit.com) and soon became the art director of *Cambio* magazine, one of the most important printed publications in Colombia. A short time later I carried out part of the design for General Motors, Colombia, and then took part in designing for Telecom, Colombia.

At the agency, we then decided to create a parallel corporate portfolio that would focus on graphical design. Thus IncubeitMedia (www.incubeitmedia.com) appeared, a site I designed with Julio Gómez. This was basically a place where we could exhibit the work in graphics we'd done during our first year at Incubeit, along with a small sample of our own experimentations. The site is mostly made up of photographs used as backgrounds along with an unusual, but simple, navigational system.

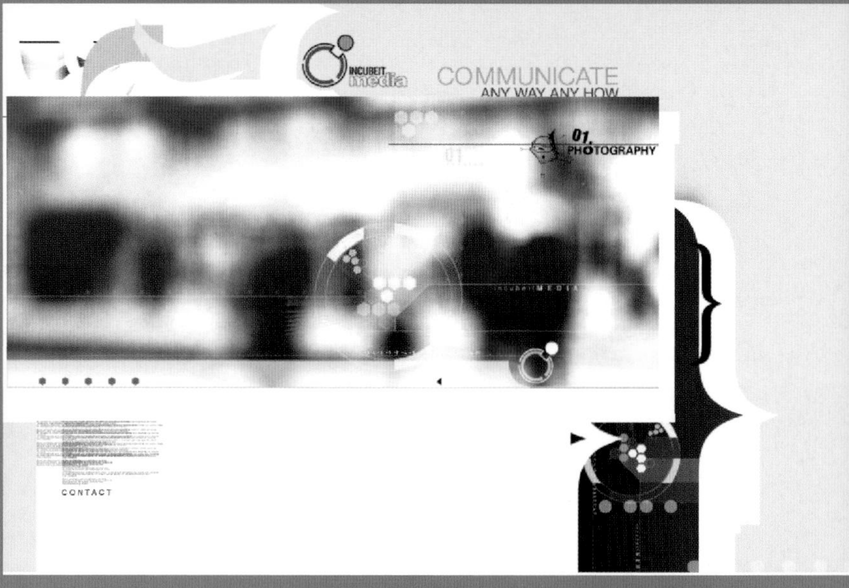

IncubeitMedia agency website, Bogotá/Colombia, 2001
www.incubeitmedia.com

The New
AMERICA

N.65

THE PERFECT FAMILY

WONKSITE .COM

TRIKE

eatured in Tartart magazine, Issue 8, 2003.
www.tartartmagazine.com

On the experimental side of things, I was interested in developing what I couldn't in the corporate world. I needed to explore new methods of finding this style for aesthetic reasons. Though I would label my style as purist, simple, and structured, I was striving towards the styles inspired by Elixir Studio, Joost Korngold, Onyro, and 2Advanced, among others. Despite not having any 3D skills, I managed to create interesting atmospheres. But the world goes round and eventually I dared to face my biggest fear: drawing. I made a number of scribbles, cut them out and glued them together in a collage, which I sent to a group show called the Silicio Project. It was here that my work was exhibited side by side with Microbians and Doma, among others.

For this collage, I was chiefly influenced by Rauschenberg's work (Black Market, 1961, and Axle, 1964). I collected all sorts of stickers, security tape, old posters, cans, and so on. This was a collage more than a design piece.

The reception of my work in this venue obviously exceeded my expectations and so the following week I decide to participate in *thedesigner* magazine (www.thedesigner.co.uk) competition "My Favorite Toy." This PDF magazine allows designers from around the world to show their abilities. Unlike some of the other PDF magazines, *thedesigner* keeps an open mind and aims to show a wide range of talent and style, as all peoples' tastes differ. It's up to the audience to determine what pieces they like or dislike. I named my submission "My Family" and tried to replicate my Photoshop work on paper. I surrounded myself with all kinds of cutouts, overlapping them until I reached a point where I was satisfied, despite the limits of my illustration experience. Step by step I built a style without realizing it.

I mentioned earlier that unintentional mistakes can have an interesting effect upon my designs. But why is this? The answer isn't quite as simple as you might imagine, because an accident is just that—a mistake, something outside your plan that brings about unexpected results. Perhaps my secret lies in doing everything I was always told not to do: I mix filters, change colors, and make bad selections. Around this time, I started creating clumsy vectors, miscalculated and free, which resulted in producing the disorder that I was interested in building. In a single design, I might combine hand-cut images, vectors, handwriting and digital type, and some brushes. I found the secret formula I was seeking, and began experimenting more and more with this method.

Image created for Proyecto Silicio collective exhibition, Medellin/Colombia, 2003.
www.proyectosilicio.com

y Family created for thedesigner magazine, Issue 3, UK, 2003.
ww.thedesigner.co.uk

I participated further in several other magazines and portals such as:

- *manzanazeta* magazine (www.manzanazeta.com)
- *Tartart* (www.tartartmagazine.com)
- *thedesigner* (www.thedesigner.co.uk)
- Texelse Boys (www.texelseboys.nl)
- *Form & Form Magazine* (www.formandform.com)

Some of the pieces I made for these are only collages without computer intervention, and others contain a balance of non- and computer-based art.

After working non-stop for five years and after spending one year as a lecturer for a postgraduate multimedia course, I decided to put the computer aside and move on to making real life cut-and-paste collages. I was inspired by THS (www.ths.nu), Eduardo Recife (www.misprintedtype.com), 1950s graphics, retro fashion, color, type, and so on. But instead of copying, wanted to give my work a personal touch.

Around this time I decided to upgrade my little online portfoli (www.wonksite.com) and, by working on this new version, found what I was looking for. To start with, I created background, scratching and messing up a photo to get th grunge effect. But I had trouble deciding what I should do wit all the other subject-specific content, like covers for my link and contact pages. Well, I tried to make a collage directly on th computer, but the result looked similar to many other website so I wasn't satisfied. By accident, I incorporated a vector imag that I had created for another project into the design an without wanting to, I mixed two styles that weren't th common or, at least, not very popular. I then decided to sta creating clumsy vector shapes. In the same space, I place manually cut images as well as digital counterparts, vecto shapes, both handmade and digital type, and some brushes. had found my secret formula and this is when my mad race t explore this method began.

The Girl created for Form & Form Magazine, USA, 2003. www.formandform.com

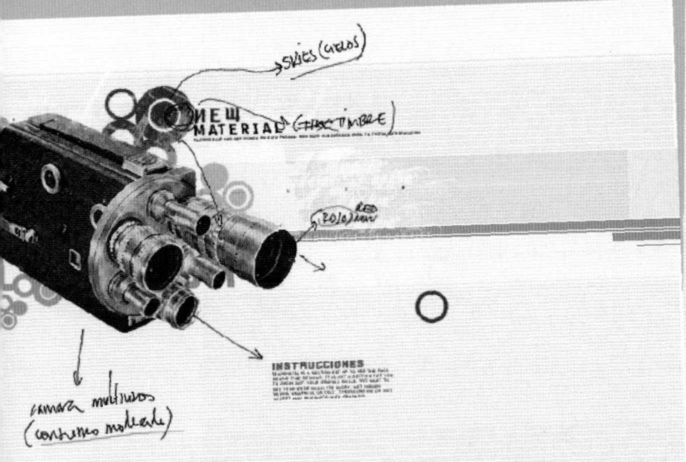

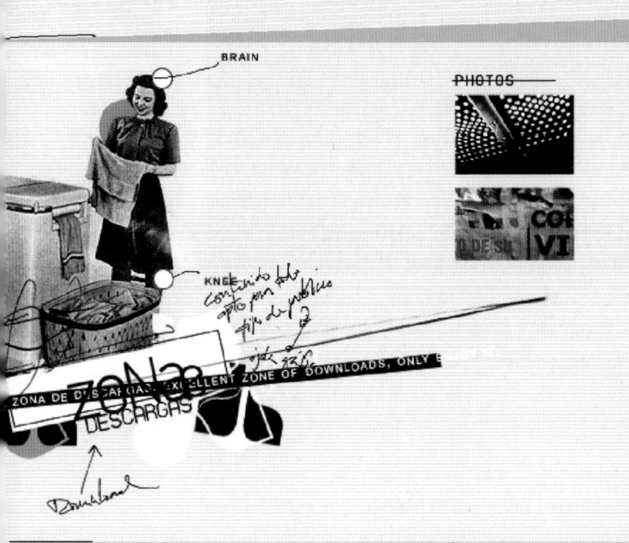

Restrepo,www.wonksite.com

I contributed a series of pieces called *Kings and Queens* to the online magazine *manzanazeta*—my personal interpretation of the story of Adam and Eve. This was a long process and probably one of my more complete projects. I made a collage on a solid base, and then I added witchcraft imagery that I bought in downtown Bogotá, phone book pages, masking tape, and other things too. After scanning the collage, I added vector shapes and was finished. I used Photoshop's Magic Wand tool to select, and whatever came up in the selection, perhaps because I didn't care if it wasn't perfect, actually worked best to create a whimsical texture in the design.

I think chaos is a large part of what inspires me. The chaos of the city in which I live stimulates my mind. The things I see include signs on the side of buses, promotional leaflets, posters, signs on walls, and popular Latin graphics that are full of mockery and color. Type also plays an important role here: a cow promoting a politician, a pig in a store front, a curious 13 that appears in the window of an abandoned house. It's all very spontaneous and this is what feeds my work, as do the aesthetics of advertising in the 1950s and 1960s, and pop art by Warhol, Rauschenberg, Rand, and Lubalin, the pastel palettes, and images of happy families. It all attracts me and I've found a very comfortable way of working using these sources.

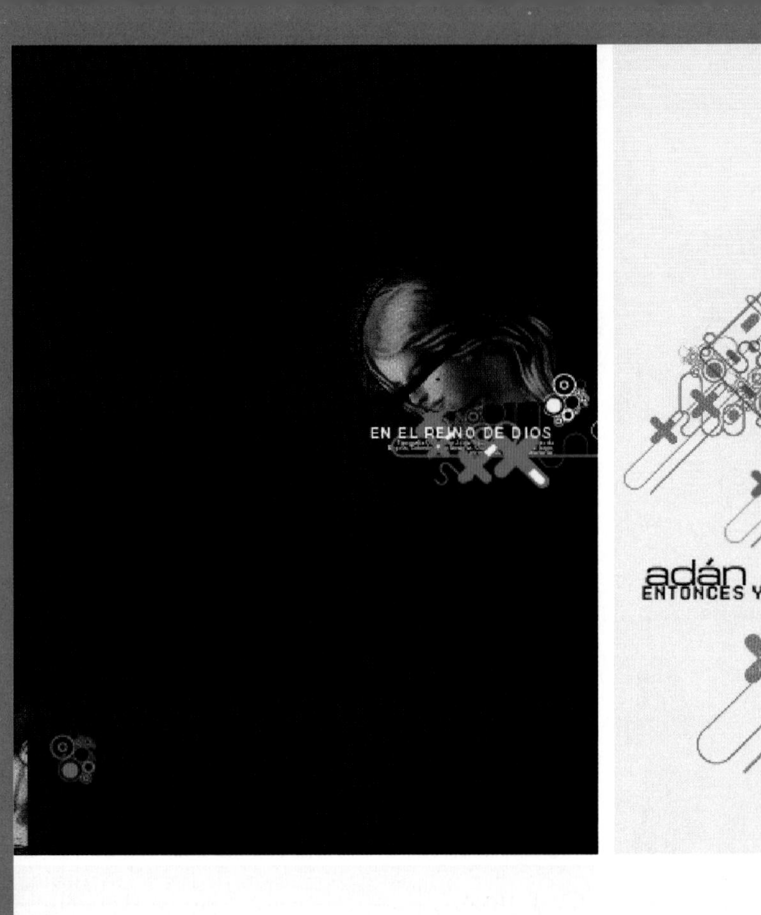

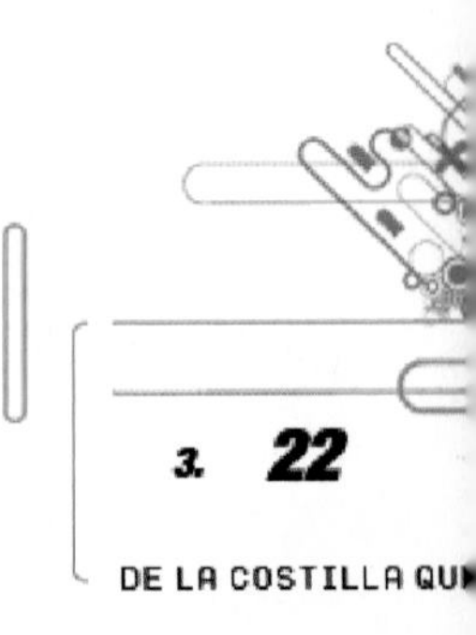

Kings and Queens for manzanazeta magazine, Medellín/Colombia, 2003. www.manzanazeta.com

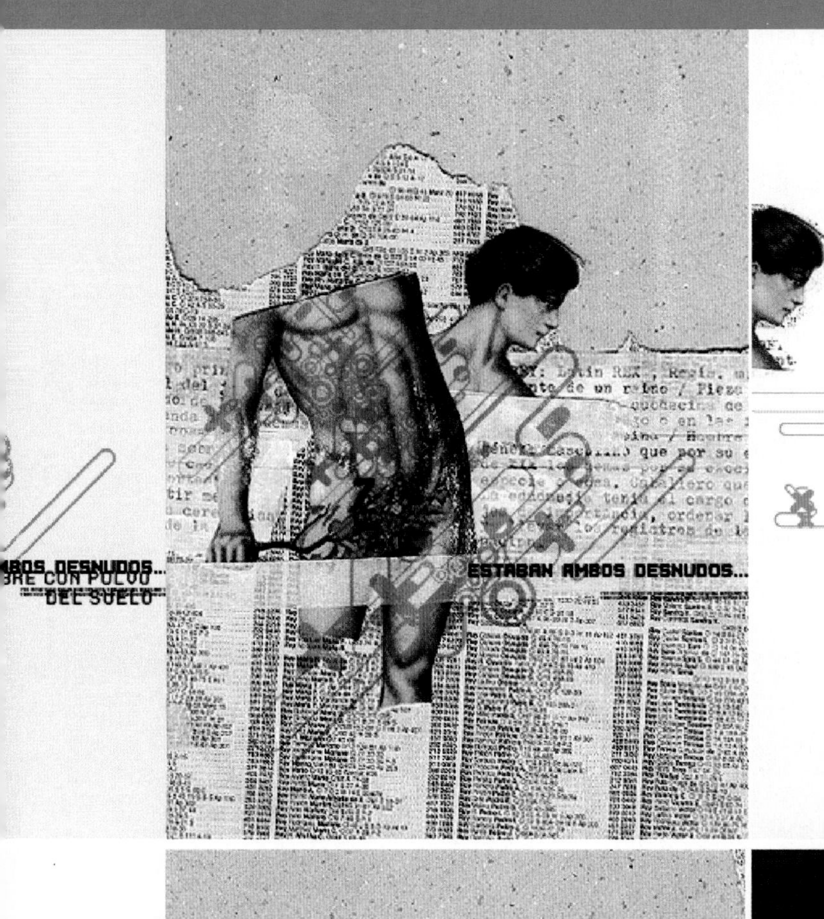
MBOS DESNUDOS...
BRE CON POLVO
DEL SUELO
ESTABAN AMBOS DESNUDOS...

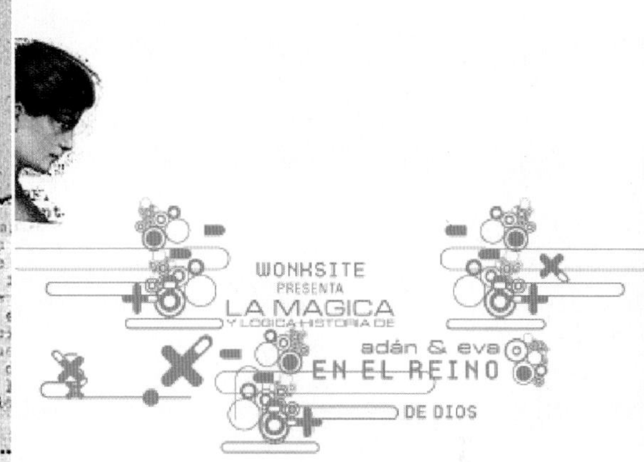
WONKSITE
PRESENTA
LA MAGICA
Y LOGICA HISTORIA DE
adán & eva
EN EL REINO
DE DIOS

eva
OS DESNUDOS...
ADO DEL HOMBRE
ESTABAN AMBOS DESNUDOS...
DE LA COSTILLA QUE YAVEH DIOS HABIA TOMADO DEL HOMBRE

EN EL REINO DE DIOS

My style consists of cutting, tearing, pasting, and overlapping, but I mainly take advantage of errors I make as part of the experimentation process. Sometimes, when you're inside a program you make two mistakes. The first is to look for the most obscure effect possible and apply it to the image. Then, after a while, you get stuck using the same four or five effects. Soon, you can only see the Blur, Drop Shadow, and the Sharpen effects. You forget how to experiment and leave behind the fear of making mistakes, of making bad choices.

In preparation for earning my ACE (Adobe Certified Expert) 2003, I learned the software in depth and therefore my im creation process became more efficient and structured. time it took me to develop images shortened and I knew exa which tool to use and how to take more advantage of each and, at the same time, I gained the knowledge I needed to s being so organized in my projects.

For instance, I found that adventuring into a program usin known filter on the wrong layer is quite interesting. What be the outcome?

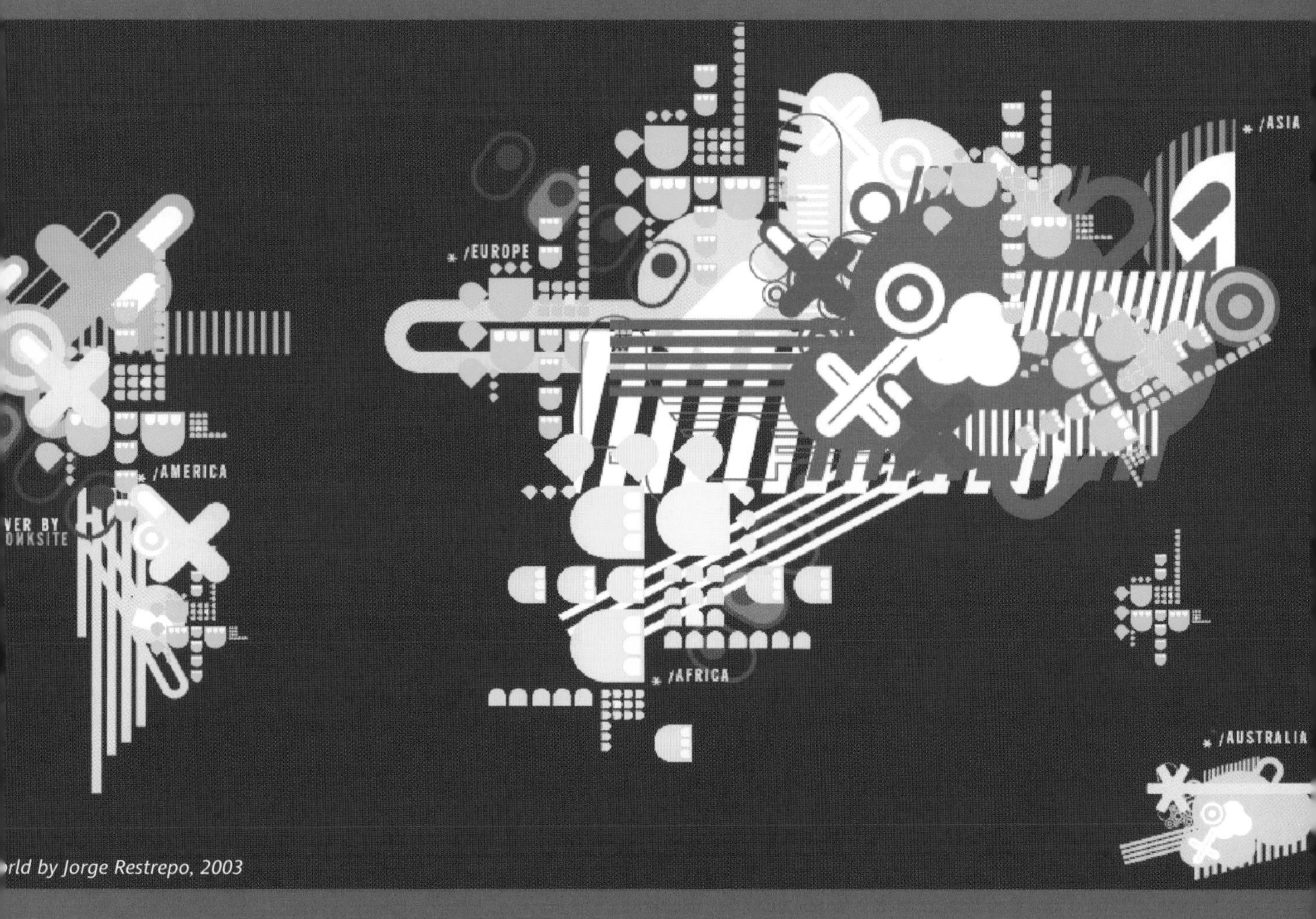

rld by Jorge Restrepo, 2003

ıen I choose to do something like this, I have no idea, and obably 70 percent of the time it will be a failure, but the maining 30 percent is what I try to take advantage of. My erest in Photoshop is not to use it to create all my designs, t only as a meeting point for all my different experiments. In style until now, the bitmaps and vectors melt into one, but ways import the vectors from Illustrator because it allows me stock up on these shapes. Also, with the Pathfinder I can ild these shapeless shapes I'm interested in, whereas otoshop doesn't handle them in quite so friendly a way. I also nually create my collages with hand drawn type, and scan them in later to incorporate them into a design using Photoshop. Sometimes I take photos focused on a particular concept.

Every time I create a new design, I feel like it's a puzzle where the pieces are separate and need to be gathered in one spot: Photoshop. I could define my use of the software as a very simplistic act, without exaggeration or endless multiple steps. The digital pieces are combined with those created by hand, and I make small adjustments and combinations subtly to try and bring something chaotic out of something simple.

In this tutorial, we'll create the image I made for the *thedesigner* PDF magazine. This tutorial is aimed at those of you who don't have a great understanding of vector-based illustration, and its goal is to make you conscious of the results you can obtain by using the available tools in a moderate yet precise way. In other words, less is more.

But why use Photoshop to develop these images? Why not spend a little more time and create the image entirely with vectors and get a significant savings in file size? The answer is simple: time. The time I save is far more than if I use a different technique, and although it's true that because of file size, Photoshop may not be the ideal solution, if your work is destined for the Web, this factor will eventually be irrelevant. The image will be optimized at the end of the process.

My designs use images that are partially created using vectors and are always accompanied by scanned photographs or images. This means that the final files, whether they are JPGs or TIFFs, will end up rasterizing those vectors to pixel-based images and their final weight in bytes will be the same whether they've been created with vectors or with some other effect in Photoshop. I'll now show you how this happens. At the end of this tutorial, I'll show some printed applications that I produced for an exhibition at the MAMBO (Bogotá Museum of Modern Art) where the file resolution was 300dpi and the final size of the native file (PSD) ended up almost the same as a file generated by using just vectors. This is because Photoshop rasterizes the vectors when it imports them from other applications like Illustrator or Freehand. I also use Photoshop as the application for creating my designs because it allows me to integrate multiple elements from different platforms (typography, scanned illustrations, photographs, and vectors) into the same end result.

This tutorial is divided into three simple parts and, in additi to teaching a series of steps to achieve a certain goal, I hope demonstrate the attractive results that can be achieved throu the integration of these elements.

My starting point is a photograph, which I usually use as the ba for a design. I use it to try to establish the focus or the center the composition, and so it becomes the main support of t image. Then I use two new elements, vectors and typography, accompany the photograph. These two elements stabilize t composition and produce the balance that I'm looking for. T photograph, vectors, and typography are then developed with the composition through repetition, color management, a intentional error. I use a graphic style without the innumerab filters that can be applied to any kind of image in any setting.

What elements do we need to achieve such an image? First of we need a photograph that contains sufficient contrast betwe the background and the foreground object. It must be possib to easily adapt the color scheme within the photograph to single color range without altering its sense. Above all, we ne to remove all our fears regarding error and badly constructed imprecise things; we need to feel that part of the graphic proce lies in experimentation, based upon simple use of effects and t moderate repetition of elements.

Bad image (low contrast)

Good image (high contrast)

Now let's start working with the central element of the composition. Remember that the subject of the work was My Favorite Toy, so we're going to use an old Mickey Mouse pencil sharpener as the representative element. To get started, I take a couple of quick photographs without worrying too much about their quality. The idea is to create a quick, well-made, silhouette.

To see the results, open `mickey.tif` from the CD. The image is 300dpi, so we must keep in mind that the size of the brushes and the selection tool options may vary considerably when working at a lower resolution. Double-click the locked Background layer and rename it "mickey." Then, add a new layer called "blue background," and fill this layer with a blue color. Drag it below the mickey layer.

Here I'll take a moment to show you my graphic process and how you can visualize an optimum result in Photoshop from the photo itself. When I was taking the initial photos, I was conscious that my goal was to take a photo that was as clean as possible, that is, one without any additional elements that would interfere with the final silhouette. As a result, I placed the pencil sharpener on a white background and took a photo against the shadow; I was looking for direct lighting without any contrast. The conditions may not have been perfect, but it doesn't really matter because Photoshop will ensure the quality of my image. So, any image that fulfills these requirements will do for our purposes.

The next step is to silhouette our image. To do this, we can apply selection tools such as the Magnetic Lasso or the Pen tool, but we should do this as exactly as possible without leaving any pixilated borders, so we'll use Extract (ALT+CTRL+X) on our mickey layer. We use Extract to carry out some difficult selections that require a more sophisticated way of isolating a foreground object from its background. This is really the best tool for intricate elements or elements without well-defined borders that must be removed from their background with a minimum of effort.

In the Extract window, select a Brush Size of 20 and check Smart Highlighting. This option helps you keep the highlight on the edge, and applies a highlight that is just wide enough to cover the edge, regardless of the current brush size. Additionally, set Smooth to 25 percent to increase the smoothness of the outline.

Now we will define the area we want to maintain isolated. Press B to select the Edge Highlighter tool and draw over the silhouette of the Mickey toy. The mouse acquires the same attraction, or snap effect, as it does when we use the Magnetic Lasso tool. This is because we chose the Smart Highlighting option. We must take into account that our selection must cover areas of high contrast, that is, areas with well-defined colors that are tonally differentiated, such as those we would use the Magnetic Lasso tool to select. For this reason, we need a photograph with a background that contrasts well with the foreground. We must also remember to trace the borders of our selection carefully, but if we make a mistake, we can erase by pressing E (Erase tool), and marking the areas we want to redo.

It's likely that we will come across areas where the contrast isn't high enough. In these cases we should overlook these areas we'll go over them more thoroughly later. We should also keep in mind that the selected area must be closed, as shown in the following screenshot, so that we can later fill the area that we need to leave intact using the Fill tool (G). Press G and go ahead and fill this area, then click OK. We must keep in mind that when we fill in this area, the selection is marked in green. If the fill goes outside of the selection, it's probably because the selection isn't properly closed.

However, our object has not been completely silhouetted. The lower area contains imperfections that need correcting. Now use the Lasso tool (L) with a 5-pixel feather to carry out a rapid selection of the small areas that have been left undone. Press the DELETE button to clear these areas.

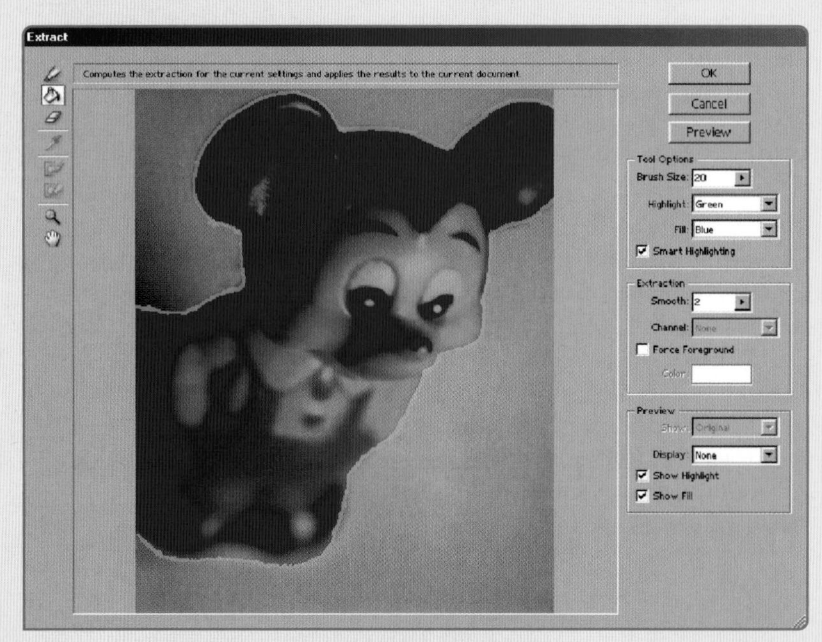

ːmember, it doesn't matter if the selection is not exact, because e feathering will help correct the problems. Sometimes as I ɔrk, I find areas that are hard to fix, but this isn't a problem ːcause I can always cover these areas over with the vector apes later. It's probably quicker to use the Magnetic Lasso tool, ıt in my experience, I prefer to invest a little more time and gain little on quality. This is possible when I use the Extract tool's ush Size and Smart Highlighting options. They give me control ʼer the degree of smoothness with which I want to isolate my ɔject by assigning different degrees of diffusion around the ıage (remember that Photoshop does all this automatically) and thout generating a constant range around my selection, as I uld do with a feather when I'm using the Magnetic Lasso tool.

Finally, we need to balance the colors slightly using the Levels dialog box (CTRL+L) and try to increase the image's tonal contrast because so far it has none. Slide the black arrow to 12, the gray slider to 1.23, and the white slider to 220. The idea is to create a soft transition between the image and the background. Remember, the blue background is here only to set the definition of the borders in the image, and this background will eventually be removed.

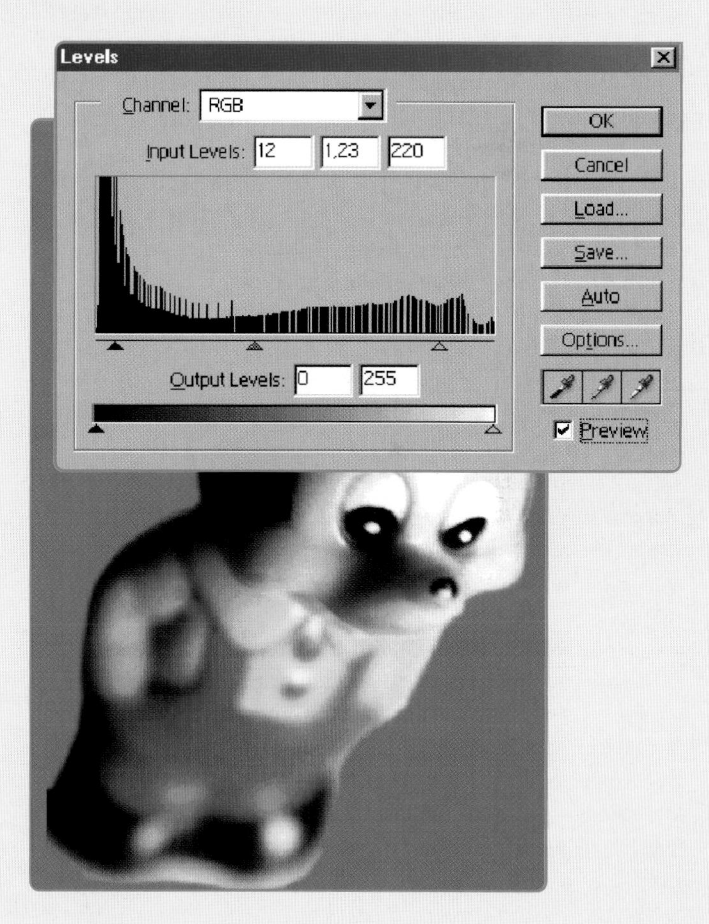

Save the file as mickey.psd, with both layers intact; once you do, our first image is ready.

The second image for our design comes from the Military Hospital of Colombia; I took this picture midway through 2003. The goal of this picture is to achieve a vectored effect without having to create a single node. The steps are very simple.

First, open `building.tif` from the CD. Now quickly select over the roof of the building with the Polygonal Lasso Tool to remove the sky from the image. It really doesn't matter how exactly this is done, but I recommend taking a few extra minutes to silhouette it properly.

Once you've done this, I suggest saving this selection (Select ➤ Save Selection) and naming it "sky." This is a constant operation for me when I am working, and I recommend doing it whenever you carry out a selection that needs a little extra effort. Why do this? It's important to always keep a selection on hand within the PSD so that you can retain the possibility of recovering it easily in case you wish to reuse it. In this way, we can add and remove areas from our selection without having to start from scratch each time. As the process for saving is very simple, my philosophy in these cases is as follows: we lose nothing, but we might save ourselves a lot of time later.

Erase the selected sky area with the Delete key. Some of the borders will probably be jagged or pixilated, and some of the sky could still remain in some areas, as we carried out our selection manually. For the moment, this doesn't matter too much. We'll correct it like this: with the arrow keys, move the selection down by a single pixel (remember that we're using the Lasso tool) and apply a 3-pixel feather (Select ➤ Feather). Press the Delete key and Ctrl+D to deselect it.

Now that we have our first part, we're going to simulate our vector effect on the image. This is, in fact, very simple, because what we need to do is convert the image into a single color hue. To do this, use a threshold (Image ➤ Adjustment ➤ Threshold). This command converts grayscale or color images to high-contrast, black-and-white images. In the Threshold dialog box, change the Threshold Level to 161 until the image is sufficiently defined. The building's silhouette must be clearly visible, including its windows and structure.

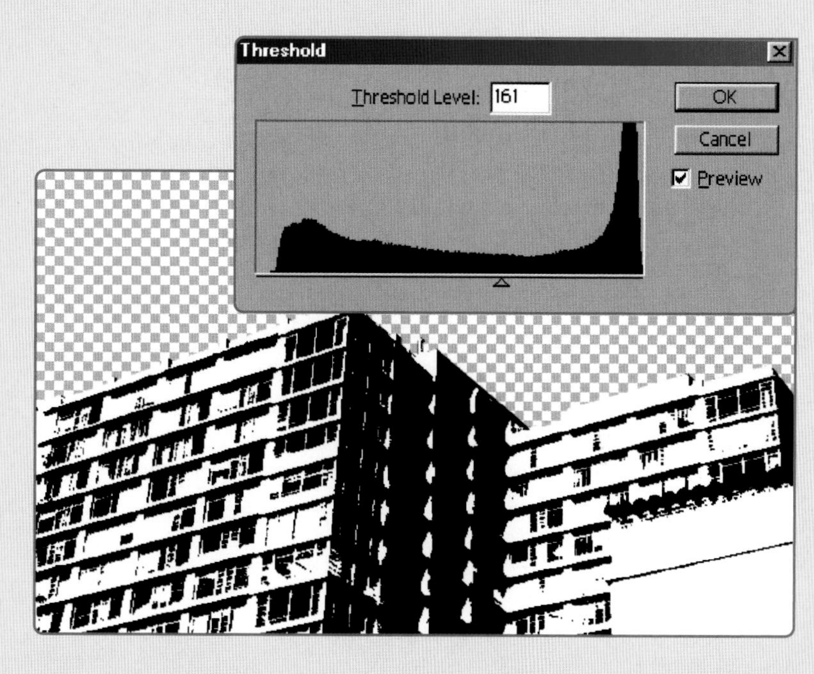

Save this file as `building_final.tif`. Now we've finished adjusting this image and it's ready for our design.

Now let's begin work on our final image. Create a new 5cm~TMS20cm document at 300dpi in RGB mode and name it "my_favorite_toy". Here we'll integrate the images we've worked on so far and construct some others using vectors and typography.

First up, drag and drop the mickey layer from the `mickey.psd` into this working PSD file. Next, we'll import the vectors I've created earlier for this tutorial.

At this point, though, I'd like to take a moment to explain my point of view regarding my graphic style of mixing photographs with vectors. Nowadays, there is a tendency to create designs with a marked appearance of vectors, many of them constructed through repetition and following a retro aesthetic. When I discovered this marked graphical expression, I began a process of graphical experimentation using vectors.

But how did I end up creating vectors, if illustration isn't really my strong point? I think it all started with my interest in experimenting with new forms within my designs. Because I didn't see a great future in creating well-defined forms and highly defined silhouettes of objects and people, I decided to start with a predefined vector (generally a dingbat) and deconstruct it in Illustrator. I would take random nodes and move, repeat, join, and separate them. By doing this I lost my fear of what might happen, and came to the point at which I started working as a graphic designer, the point at which I started to fashion something pleasing to the eye out of all the chaos I had created previously. The result depends on what goal I'm working toward. To be honest, with this project, everything was created somewhat randomly, with very fluid strokes and without a predefined sketch or concept of the final composition. Occasionally, I will create a node that is exaggeratedly far from the center of the composition or a chance combination of random strokes.

In this way, I have created two different kinds of vector shapes for this project (`vector_one.ai` and `vector_two.ai` on the CD).

Back to the tutorial. Let's import our first vector shape, `vector_one.ai`, using File ➤ Place. Before rasterizing the image, let's adjust the size and rotation of the imported object. Resize it to 52 percent by typing directly into the Width and Height fields in the Tool options bar.

Here a new question arises: Is it ideal to have our vector scaled to the exact size before importing it? No, it isn't really necessary, because Photoshop allows us to scale and rotate the vector when we import it. So, we can work comfortably in Illustrator without having to worry too much about the exact proportions of the shape when transferring between the two programs. This is a great advantage.

Currently, the color might not be ideal. Remember that the colors created in Illustrator must be RGB because our document in Photoshop was created in this color mode. Therefore, we can guarantee vivid colors that are closer to those we're seeking. To change the colors, I recommend always using the Hue/Saturation tool (CTRL+U). Double-click the vector once you're happy with its size and position, then edit the colors to get them how you like (I'm going to stick with the magenta, though). Before clicking OK, let's save the color adjustment you just made by clicking the Save button in the Hue/Saturation dialog box.

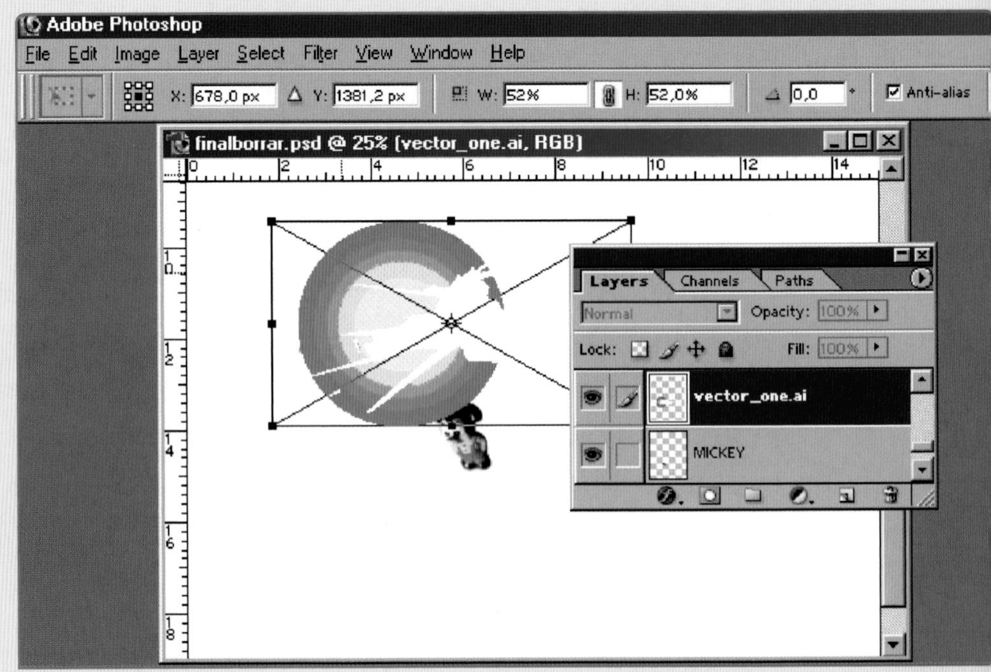

Now it's just a matter of incorporating both the building and Mickey images, and adjusting them until you're happy with the composition. Drag and drop the building layer into the `my_favorite_toy.psd` file. Remember that, although this is a tutorial, the choices of design, composition, and color are your own, and don't necessarily depend upon the parameters that I suggest. Feel free to change the colors and layout of the three elements in this image.

Now duplicate this building layer, name it "building 2," then resize it with the Free Transform tool (CTRL+T). Move it elsewhere in the image if you prefer.

Now let's add another vector shape (File ➤ Place); this time it's the `vector_two.ai` file on the CD. Before we rasterize it, scale it to 80 percent, remembering to keep the aspect ratio constrained.

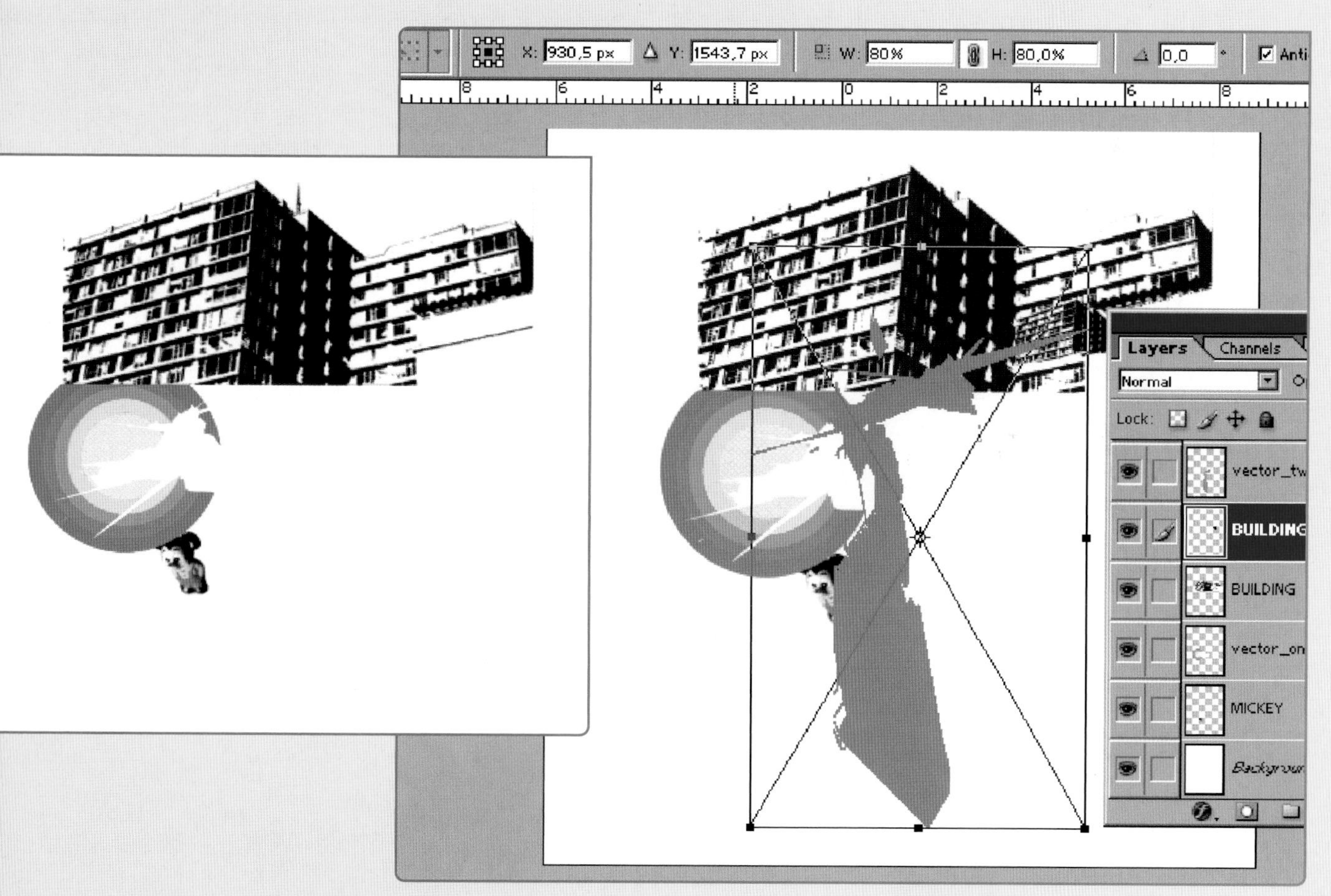

Now I'll explain the text effect I use in My Favorite Toy. I could, in fact, create the text directly in Illustrator and then import it into Photoshop, but I prefer doing it with greater freedom in Photoshop because I have more control over the effect regarding the composition as a whole.

First of all, we need to create a new layer set to keep our layers in order. I suggest working with as much organization as possible, so the more layer sets we can create and name, the more control we have over our file, and the quicker it is to get to the desired result. Nonetheless, I suggest using about five layers per layer set to make good use of this feature. Create a new layer set called "my favorite toy." Now we'll create the text, for which we use the Helvetica Rounded font. If you don't have this font, any font with a Rounded version will create a similar effect.

If you don't have any rounded fonts, a similar effect can be achieved using an Arial Black font. Type in "TOY" in a white font color.

While holding CTRL, click the type layer to select the text exactly. Go to Select ➤ Modify ➤ Smooth and create a 4-pixel border and hide this layer. Now add a new layer called "stroke" and click the TOY layer while holding down the CTRL key. Notice that Photoshop selects the area around the TOY text. Now put a stroke over our new layer (Edit ➤ Stroke), selecting the magenta color that we've been using elsewhere in the image, giving it a value of 15 pixels, and choosing the Outside option. If you wanted to, you could repeat this process with additional layers, increasing stroke levels and reducing the color hue gradually.

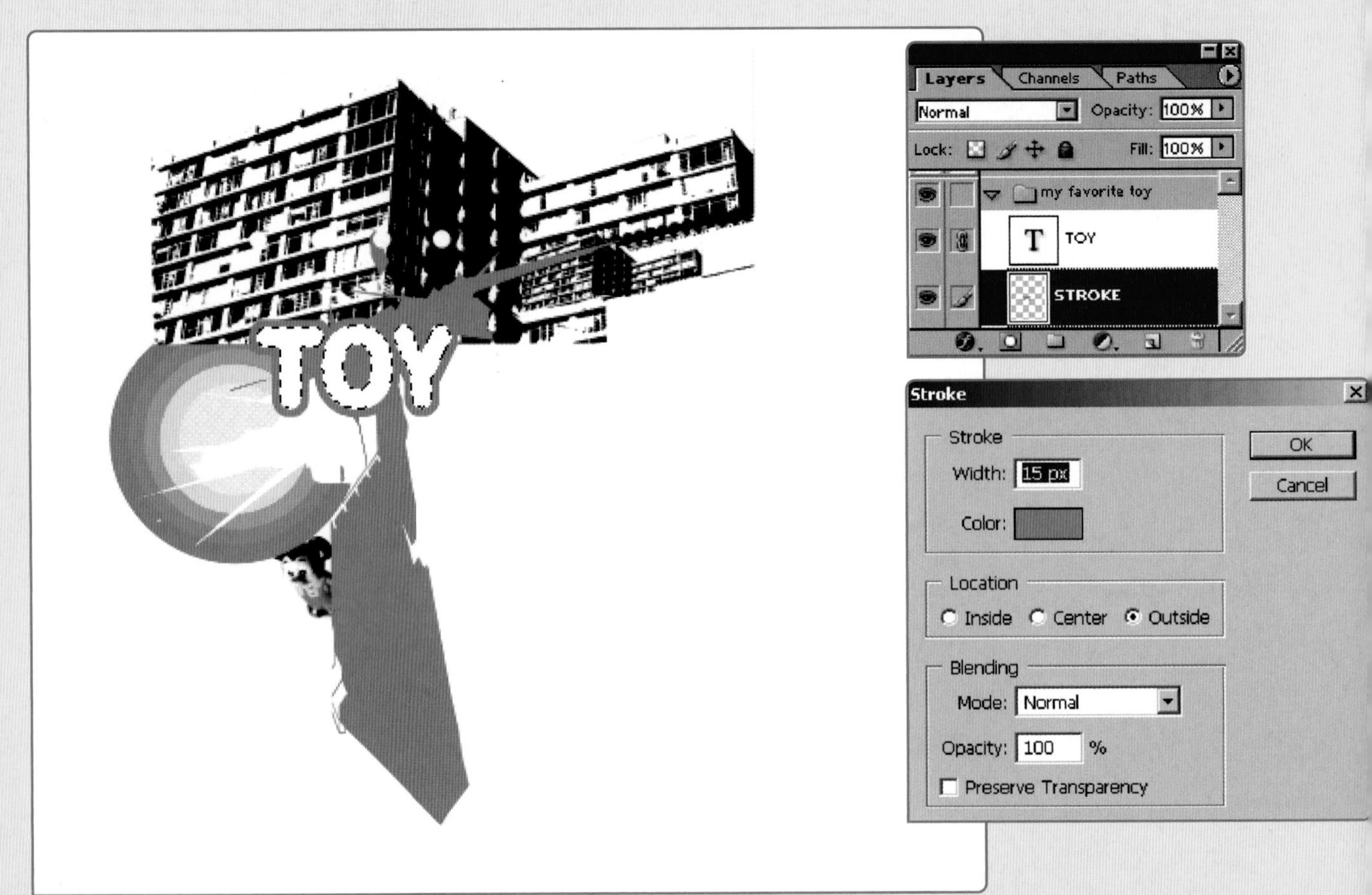

ep going and add in the rest of the My Favorite Toy text. Feel e to play with the stroke settings, placement, and number of xt elements.

Now add a new layer with the Mickey toy by dragging the mickey layer from the `mickey.psd`. Also add another `vector_one.ai` to the `my_favorite_toy.psd`. After positioning these elements, bring the my favorite toy layer set that contains all the text to the front of the composition (Layer ➤ Arrange ➤ Bring to Front).

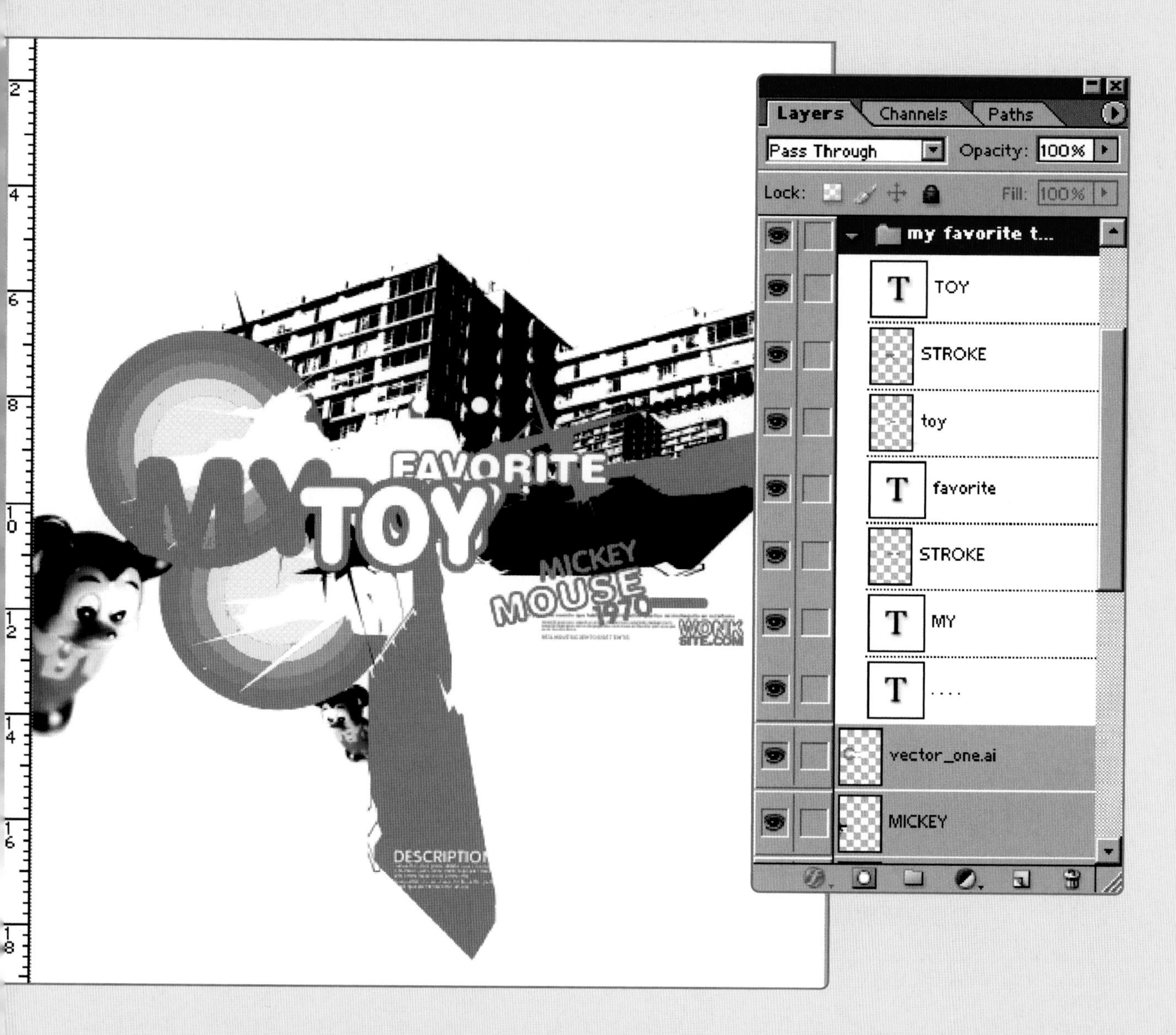

To finish everything off, we'll fill the sky area with a pattern. Open `grid.gif` from the CD. Select the entire canvas (CTRL+A), go to Edit ➤ Define Pattern… and call it "grid." In the working `my_favorite_toy.psd`, create a new layer and freely select the sky area (this doesn't have to be exact, the idea is to be as loose as possible). Right-click, select Fill, choose Pattern from the drop-down menu, and search for the grid pattern. The pattern we're using is one option, but you also get interesting results when using a degradé or some other repetitive pattern.

And so we come to the end of this tutorial. I hope that i served as a good workshop in graphic design as a whole, a not just training in the program as such, the application vectors, and how they can be included within Photoshop. I' tried to show how we can save time by simulating a vect effect based upon high-contrast images without having create a single node. My goal in this tutorial was to explain t use of simple tools without much ornamentation and witho many repetitive steps that result in a saturation of filters. I al hope to have resolved any doubts regarding my work. As I w writing this tutorial, I was thinking about the many email receive every day regarding my work with questions like: Whe do my vectors come from? How can I get such and such image? Why do I use color in this way?

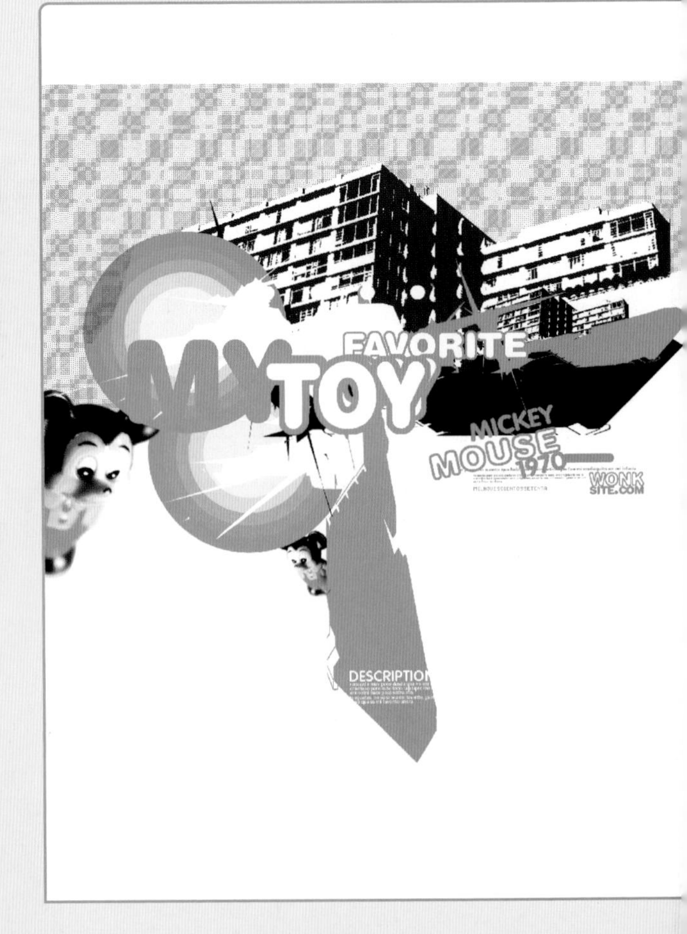

n not a genius at filtering, nor do I hope to become one. I elong to the less-is-more school, and I prefer working with ery few effects to get good results that are attractive to every- ne. I believe that there is greater value in obtaining a lot from ery little. Another thing that is characteristic of my work is the umber of layers I work with, and the order I try to impose pon my native files: I always name my layers, create new layer ts, rename the vector masks, and so on. I feel that this always uarantees success. Along side Germán Olaya, I created some osters for the RAD collective exhibition in the MAMBO 3ogotá Museum of Modern Art) where I applied the same rocesses that I've shown in this tutorial—creating interesting nd attractive pieces without constructing elaborate vectors.

Above all, I suggest finding elements that might help you to work toward a good design, unlike what I see sometimes in my students and coworkers, who work according to the program, making their designs a somewhat strange mixture of senseless filters and effects. In my designs, I try to invest in the three aspects outlined in this tutorial: a photograph (taken by myself) or an image scanned from a collage, a couple of freely created vectors, and some text that will create an impact and lend strength to the concept. I then join all these elements together in Photoshop. I hope that this has been useful and insightful and that it has given you the desire to explore a little bit beyond the program, moving away from the filters to seek new possibilities in the fields of design and illustration.

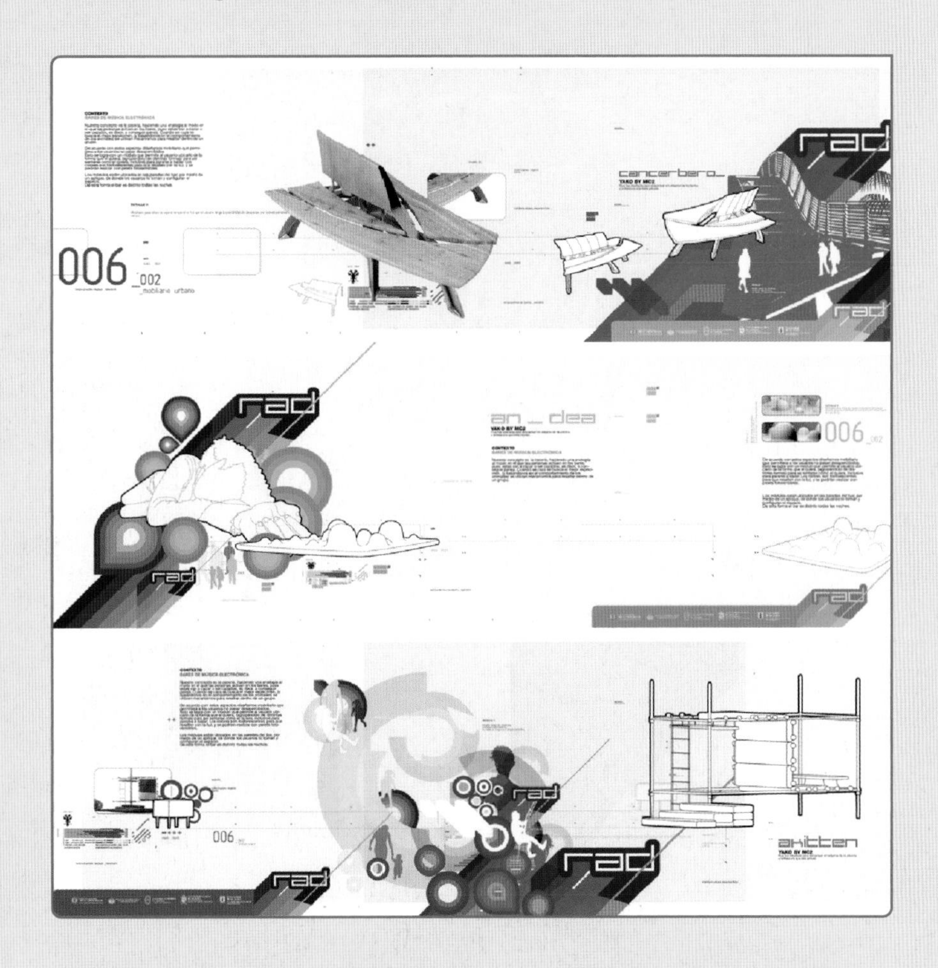

MY
FAVORITE
TOY
MICKEY
MOUSE
1970
cuento que habl... fue mi muñequito en mi infacia
recuerdo muy poco cuando yo era... pero este lindo tajalapiz me lo encontré hace poco entre mis jugu...tes, no se si sea mi favorito, pero si se que es mi favorito ahora.
WONK

I was born and raised in Taiwan, later immigrated to the United States, and have resided there ever since. As I was growing up, illustration was my passion and drawing pictures for children's books was my desired career. In my college years, I took some drawing and airbrush classes and fell in love with these media. At the same time, I was introduced to graphic design in a computing class. However, although the instructor showed us how to lay out an ad, he didn't explain how to do it step by step in either Photoshop or QuarkXPress. As a result, I didn't realize the illustrative capabilities of the computer or design software like Photoshop.

However, in 1995, I met a funky looking Asian dude named Eric Quach, the graphic designer behind www.KingKongShrimp.com. Using some distortion tools in Photoshop, Eric demonstrated a really eye-opening interpretation of a classic image—he made the Mona Lisa look high. This really drew my attention and generated a new curiosity in me to learn more about the software, despite my lack of affection for the computer.

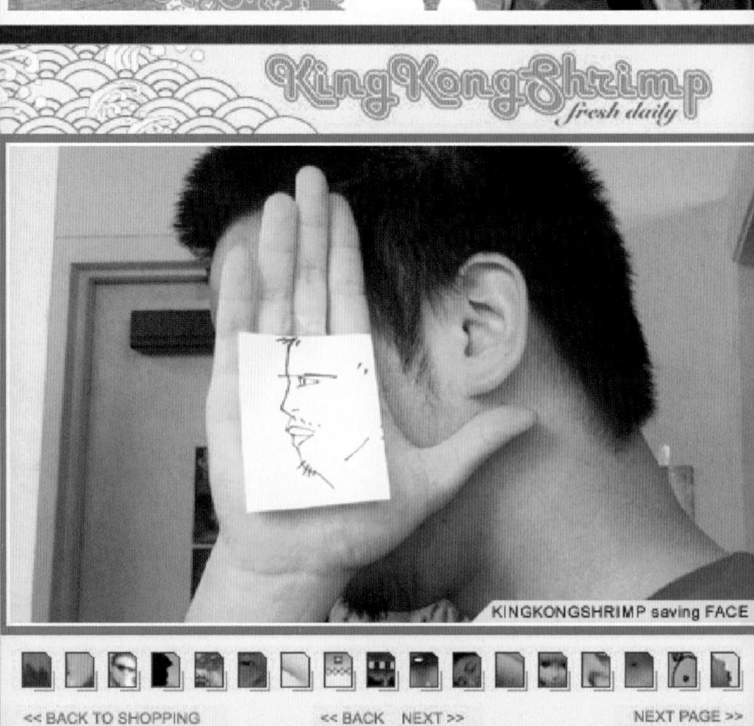

Eric Quach, www.KingKongShrimp.com

m Hsieh © 2004

Around this same time, I met Mario Sanchez, a wonderful graphic designer who is currently working at www.Idealab.com. Looking at Mario's layout style really inspired me.. They were so clean and beautiful. On Mario's recommendation, I subscribed to *Communication Arts* magazine (www.commarts.com). This magazine has such a wealth of information about graphic design for print especially. It was this magazine that inspired me to pursue a career in graphic design.

In 1997, I began furthering my education in the UCLA Extension Program, hoping to explore the field of design more deeply. At that school, I relearned how to use Photoshop, Illustrator, and QuarkXPress; this process was a lot more interesting and fun than the same classes had been in college. The instructors had already been full-time designers and had gained a lot of valuable experience out there in the field. This made whatever they taught much more informative and useful, because the theory was backed up by real professional insight. At the end of the program, I enrolled in a portfolio presentation course and subsequently saw an ad for a job opening at Moxie Girl. I got an interview and was offered a graphic design position. An art director there, Agnes, asked me if I wanted to join their web department. She encouraged me to pursue a career in the dotcom industry. At that time, I wasn't really prepared for the World Wide Web, but I jumped in anyway.

A good friend of mine, Mike Wandell, was a music editor a Moxie Girl. His knowledge and taste in music is nothing short c astounding. It was Mike who introduced me to the Anti-Po Consortium (www.warprecords.com/antipop), DJ Krush, and host of other talented artists. This music would later come t affect my designs in many ways.

After my stint at Moxie Girl, I got hired at a subdivision c ZeniMax Media Inc. called Vir2L Studios Inc. (www.Vir2l.com This was about the time when I discovered the works c Mike Young (www.weworkforthem.com), James Widegre (www.idiocase.com), and Gmunk (www.gmunk.com), and I wa completely in awe of these designers. They took graphic desig to an entirely different level. I personally believe that they a had a huge impact on the web design industry and deserv much respect. During that time, I continued to learn an explore more techniques by experimenting with layer blendin modes in Photoshop. To me, it was headier than mixin cocktails. When applied, these effects helped me blend photc in so many new and interesting ways. On top of that, I began t learn the trick of adjusting the opacity to match the right flavo With these skills under my belt, I understood why Photosho was an indispensable tool for any designer.

gmunk vs DIK, www.gmunk.com, 200

design is kinky
KINKY IS AS KINKY DOES

I started working at 65 Media in 2001, which also marks the time I met many more talented designers. Brian Lin of http://secretsquare.com and http://statesunited.com is one of these. He revealed even more possibilities of what Photoshop has to offer, including how to customize the Brush tool. Instead of using the typical soft/hard round brushes, he showed me that you can actually choose from many more options in the Brush Shapes flyout menu in the tool options.

These different brushes allow you to paint or erase in a unique way. It's like painting on a real canvas where you can use different brushes to create natural strokes. As my learning experience in Photoshop continued, I developed more techniques. I would spend time away from work and create my own personal art at home.

In 2003, I joined Bleu22 Studios (www.bleu22.com), working mainly on movie websites, such as *Beautiful Creatures*, *Tomb Raider: The Cradle of Life*, and *The Score*. During this period, mainly learned the importance of controlling levels and hues properly to emphasize the design. Although I developed while working at Bleu22, somehow and somewhere along the way felt that as an artist, my creative needs were being stifled and neglected, and I decided that I needed to find an outlet for this growing discontent. To quell this feeling, I decided to create second website, a personal one, at www.FistsOfCurry.com. This site became my much-needed therapy from the stresses of the corporate work in which I had become so embroiled.

use I am fascinated by the varied beauty of oriental and dental cultures, I wanted to interpret them into a new aesthetic, creating stimulating audiovisuals reflecting elements that affect deeply.

Within this site, the Gallery section is where I translate my thoughts and emotions into images—it's the canvas where I paint my meditations. While building the site, the only tool I was comfortable using to create these visuals was Photoshop.

Because I live in Los Angeles, I have the great privilege of observing street art in the many places I go. So many unknown artists create the awesome works that surround me. This art is so pure and personal that it inspires me to use my Photoshop skills to explore it. When I first came across this type of expression, it made such an impression on me that I really wanted to combine it with my interests in Far East culture and hip hop music and display the results on my personal site. I see many similarities between Asian culture and street art and hip-hop music; for example, some strokes of graffiti remind me of Chinese calligraphy. I want to examine these further to unify these similarities.

Man One, copyright 2004, www.ManOne.com

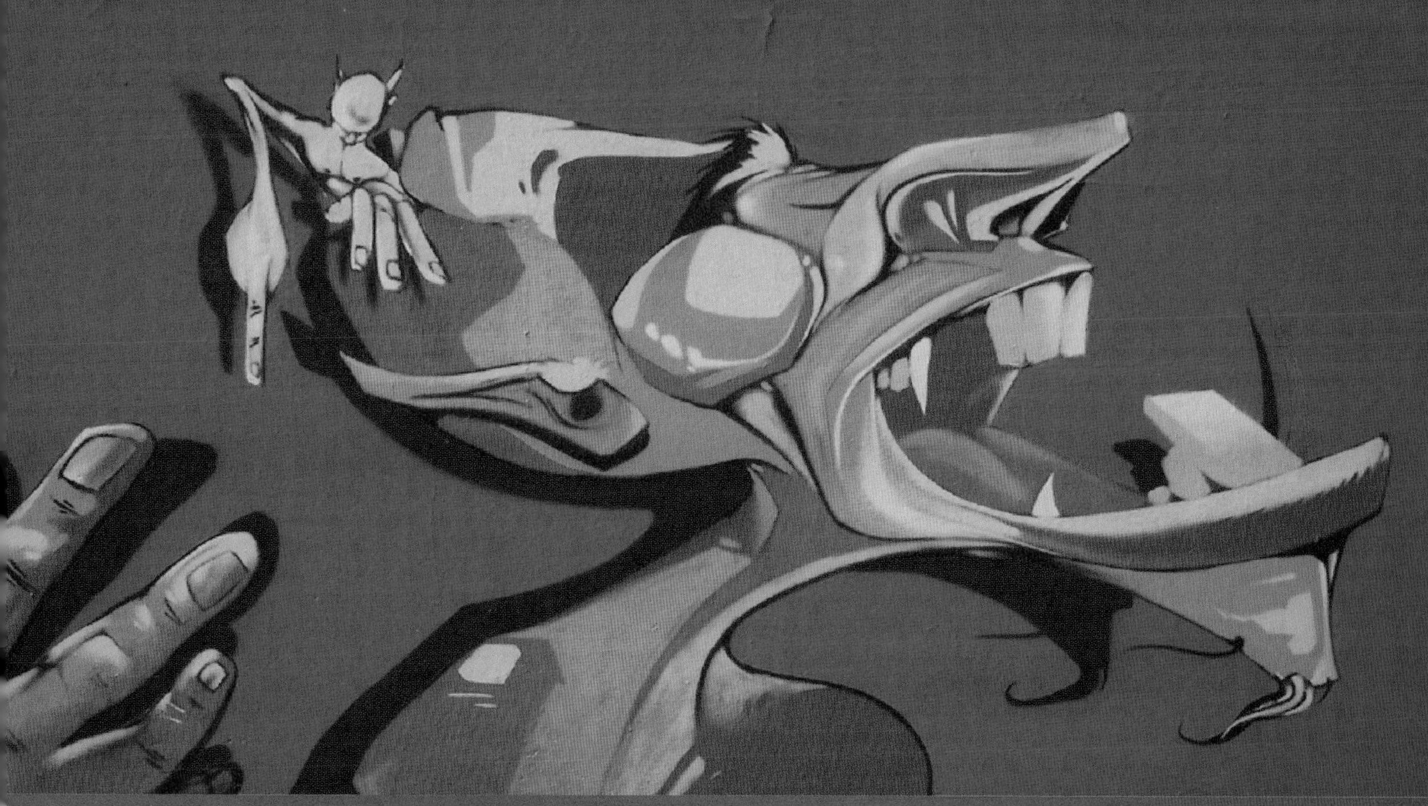

Man One, copyright 2004, www.ManOne.com

In addition to music and graffiti, I am blown away by break dancing. It is just as physically amazing and fascinating to me as Shaolin monks demonstrating their martial arts skills.

ven the ancient Chinese language of the scholars is like p—both are so heavily involved in the poetics of xpression. Fists Of Curry brings all these influences gether.

so, I have built up music around the site. My personal vorites are DJ Krush and DJ Cam, two of the most spected DJs in the underground hip-hop world. Their usic has had a great impact on my Fists Of Curry project. mazing listening experiences somehow trigger my nagination. Those beats from DJ Krush and DJ Cam are so illed and groovy. I really recommend you check out their oums.

Hip Hop Dynasty, Jim Hsieh, 2004

After much procrastination, I finally bought my first digital camera. As a graphic designer, I've found that this is one of the handiest must-have tools, especially if you want to learn and create images with Photoshop. On the way to work, or whenever I fancy, I stop my car and shoot photos of anything that catches my eye. It's great! Shooting photos helps me research, builds my working library, and creates a wealth of images for me to experiment with in Photoshop.

Boy, Jim Hsieh, 2004

In the following tutorial, I want to elaborate on the process I used to create one of my artworks from Fists Of Curry. It is entitled *Chinatown* and is one of my favorites within the entire Gallery section. My approach was to employ certain effects and apply them on a regular color image. The method is simple, yet effective. The idea behind the piece is to combine a traditional example of Chinese architecture with an urban color theme.

What inspired the idea for this piece was an event I attended in LA's Chinatown recently. At this event, DJ J.Rocc from the Beat Junkies was spinning up a chill and groovy vibe while an artist by his side was free-style painting on a sheet of 6-foot tall, white-frosted fiberglass. A big, bright spotlight was shining behind the glass, and this light illuminated the oil paint the artist was using, making the colors very shiny and beautiful. While I was enjoying this scene, I happened to look away at a wall and saw the coolest thing. The light behind the sheet of fiberglass was projecting the colors and shapes of the painting onto the lime-green walls. The entire venue was transformed into an ethereal and vividly colorful atmosphere.

Though I was not physically within the painting, I felt I ha somehow become a part of it. I wanted to capture the essenc of that feeling with Photoshop, and thus *Chinatown* was mad

Before we begin, let's first analyze the starting pho (`original_photo.psd` on the CD). It's always good to stu your material before you begin working on it. I chose th picture because it contains a good number of elements to wo with. Though the quality of the image isn't so great, with t magic of Photoshop, a lot can be done to transform Moreover, it is perfect for what I want to create for *Chinatow* The columns on the left and right of the photo are a good s of elements to work on. They act as a natural frame for t entire composition, and the roof that connects the columns al has some nice detail. In addition, the stone lion's head is a ve important element of the piece. Contrasting the color a brightness of the image will allow me to create more dep within the image. In the center of the photo, there's a sculptu to work on too. The last two elements I'll deal with are the inn roof and background walls.

his piece was originally made for the Web, so let's begin by reating the file in RGB color mode—we'll make it 6.747"x7.05" ith a resolution of 300 dpi.

start by creating two layer sets. I name one Images, which will ore any original image files, and the other China Town layers, hich will contain the extra layers I add while editing the image. eep in mind that it's good to be organized early on so you on't be confused during the later stages of the process.

o begin with, we'll add the main colors to the image that will t the mood, and then we'll work on the columns that ill frame the piece. Next we'll move into the center and add etail to the column behind the lion's head—this column presents the frosted fiberglass that the artist was painting on at chilled out night in Chinatown. Finally, we'll add more ghttime atmosphere in the rest of the piece by adding smoke nd stars.

et's start by giving the background some color. Remember, e're choosing an urban color scheme.

Make the foreground color a purplish pink (R:195, G:115, B:151) and the background color bright pink (R: 254, G: 205, B: 216). Now, select the Gradient tool (G), and in the tool options, set a solid gradient type from foreground to background.

On a new layer named "Background 1", drag from top to bottom, holding SHIFT to constrain the gradient to the vertical.

Create another gradient on a new layer named "Background 2". Use the same gradient type as on the Background 1 layer, but change the foreground color to R: 176, G: 58, B: 108 and the background color to R: 173, G: 134, B: 193. Again, hold SHIFT and drag from the top to the bottom of the image. Now lower the opacity of the Background 2 layer to 70 percent. Now, we have some funky purple pink colors with an appropriate brightness combined together. With this color theme as the foundation, we'll start building above it.

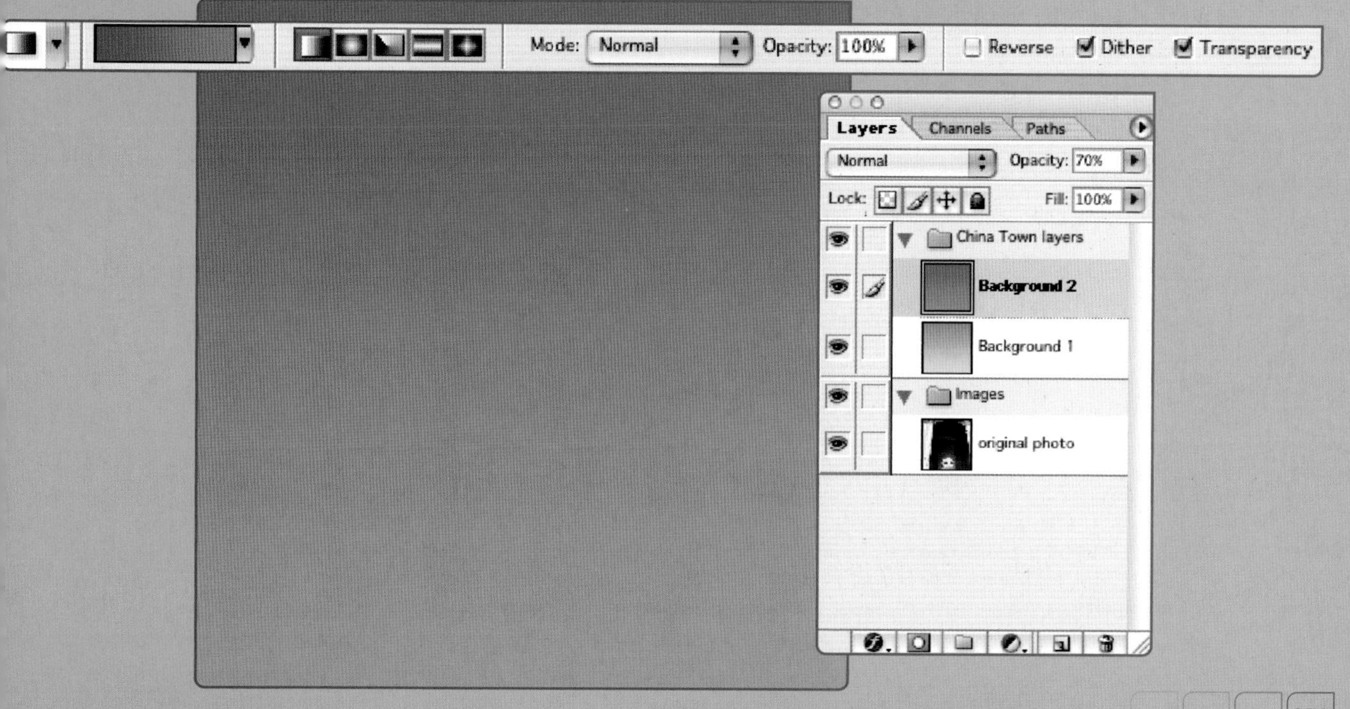

Now let's convert the color photo into a black and white one. Open `original_photo.psd` from the CD and copy it into your Images layer set in your working document on a new layer named "original photo". Duplicate this layer and completely desaturate it (SHIFT+CMD+U) to make it grayscale. Then duplicate this layer, call the copy "Black / White", and place it above the Background 2 layer at the top of the China Town layers layer set. Now increase the contrast of this Black / White layer, via the Brightness/Contrast dialog box (Image ➤ Adjustments ➤ Brightness/Contrast) to give it more of a vector look.

You may see some stray white areas left over at the top of th columns, so use the Brush tool with a black foreground color t clean it up. At this point, change the layer blending mode fro Normal to Overlay and reduce the opacity to 60 percent.

In the coming step, we're going to separate the columns and th center sculpture by creating a path. Initially, we are going t focus on the columns and the head, but eventually each elemer of the image will have its own path, as you can see in the Path palette when you look at `chinatown_tutorial.psd`.

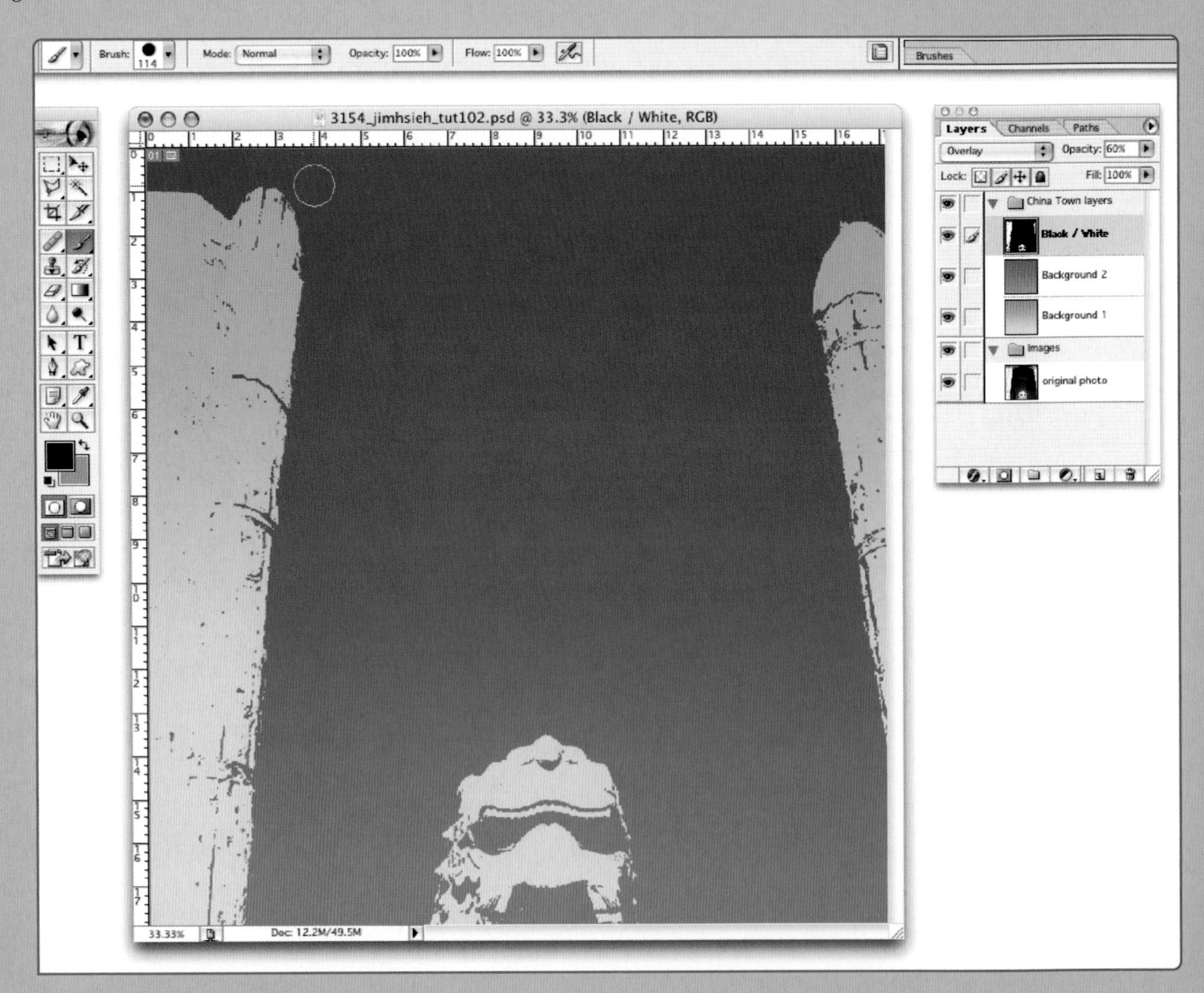

›y taking a bit of time to create an accurate path here, we will ave time later when we wish to alter the different parts of the mage, because we'll be able to select each element quickly and leanly.

›efore, when designers used to cut out a part of an image, they vould have to use scissors or a craft knife. Today's computer rograms have tools to perform this task to perfection. In hotoshop, a simple way to do this is by using the Pen tool (P). usually like to start from the corner of the image. In this articular case, let's begin from the bottom of the left column. Aake sure to use the Zoom tool (Z) to get a close-up view of ne image. (Another shortcut is to press CMD+SPACEBAR at the ame time and click to zoom in).

Now, go ahead and click your way up on the edge of the left column. Using the Path tool can be tricky at first. To get a good command of it, you will definitely need to practice. Once you reach the top frame, turn your attention to the right column. When you approach the end of the top frame, go ahead and click down to the bottom of the right column. To complete this path, click back to the original point where you started the path by going down to the very right corner and "around" the lion's head back to the left column. Next, save your path using the options menu in the Paths palette. Name it "Path 1".

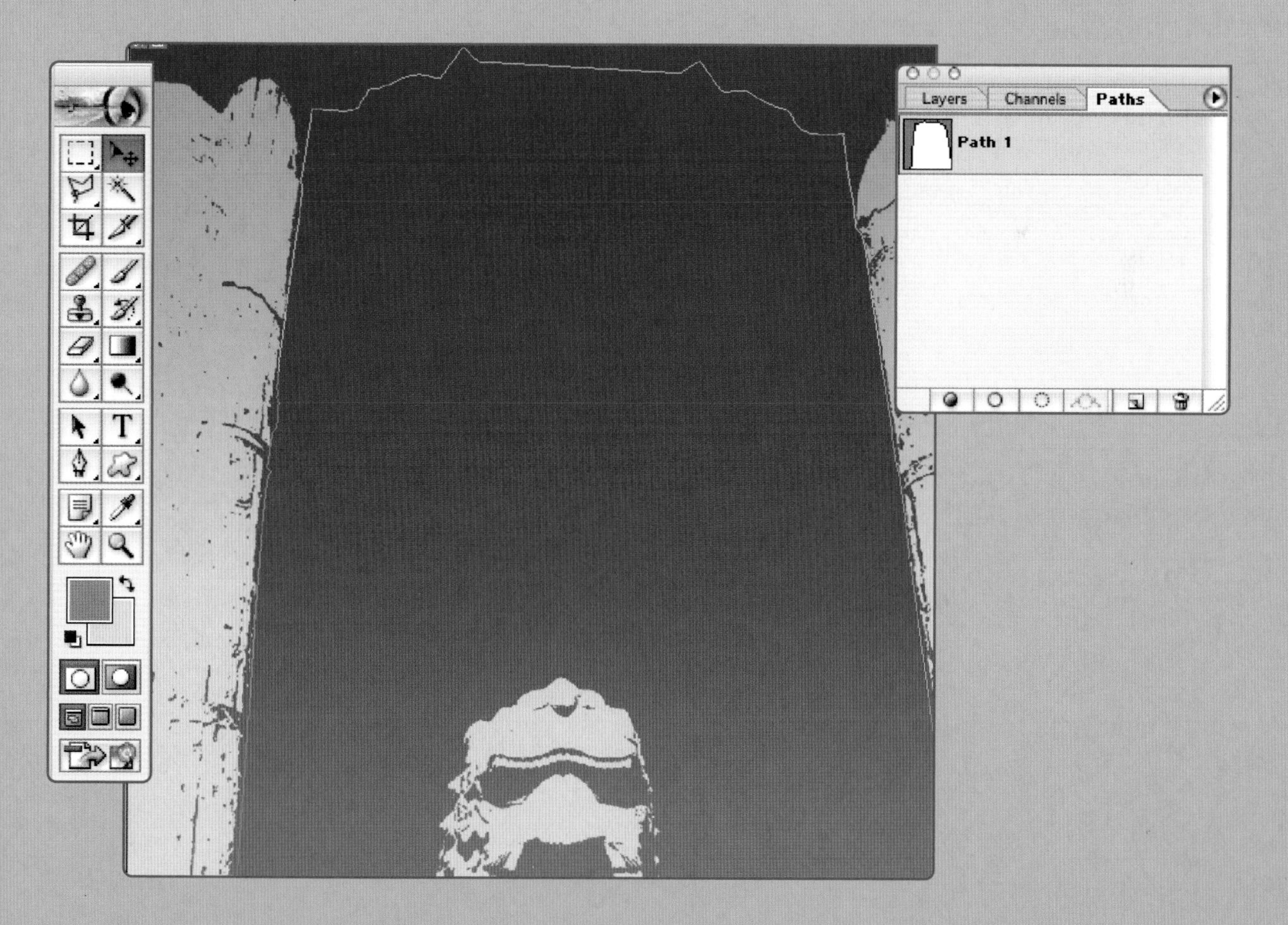

Once you've saved the name, make sure to stay on that particular path layer. Go ahead and click on the bottom middle icon in the Paths palette (Load Path as Selection). Now, everything else but the columns is selected.

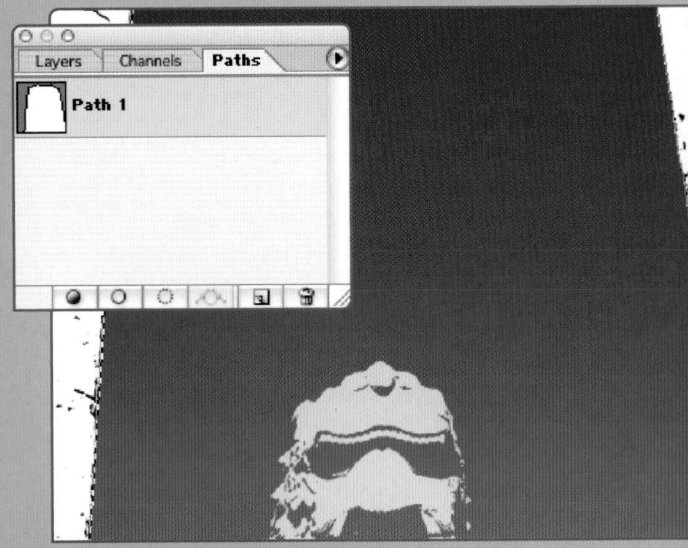

Go back to the Layers palette and copy the Black / White layer, then press the DELETE key. Another option is to use CMD+X to cut off the selected part. Make sure you deselect (CMD+D) everything afterward. The last step on this layer is to contrast these columns by using Levels (CMD+L). Input levels of 172, 1.00, 210 give the extra definition to the columns that I was looking for, and changing the blending mode to Multiply helps the columns blend in with the rest of the elements (I also increased the layer opacity back up to 100 percent). Because this new layer helps frame the whole image, we'll call it "Top Frame".

o far, we have enough pinks and purples. Let's add some blue o balance and darken the overall bright pink color. Create nother layer called "Solid Blue". In this step, we'll go back to the ath 1 layer we saved earlier. Go ahead and click on the Load ath as a selection icon, then select the inverse (SHIFT+CMD+I). se the color picker to choose the blue color (R: 151, G: 169 B: 81). To fill the selection with the new color, go to Edit ➤ Fill (or HIFT+back space). Once you've done this, deselect everything CMD+D). We'll blend in this new blue with the background by hanging the layer blending mode to Multiply. Because of the nixture of blue and pink with the Multiply blending mode, the oles look a sort-of dark purple now.

Next, we'll lighten them up and make the image more lively. After that, we'll add a new layer called Gradient. There are a few ways to do this. I like to go back to the Solid Blue layer and use that same cutout shape to duplicate another one. To do this, back on the Solid Blue layer, select everything with CMD+A. Once it's selected, press CMD+UP and then hold CMD and press DOWN. This way, the column shape is selected again. While it's still selected, go back to the Gradient layer we named earlier, and select the Gradient tool (G) with a 100 percent white foreground color and 100 percent black background color. Make sure to go to the Gradient Editor (by clicking in the image of the gradient in the tool options). Choose Foreground to Background, Solid in the Gradient Type drop-down menu, and 100 percent Smoothness.

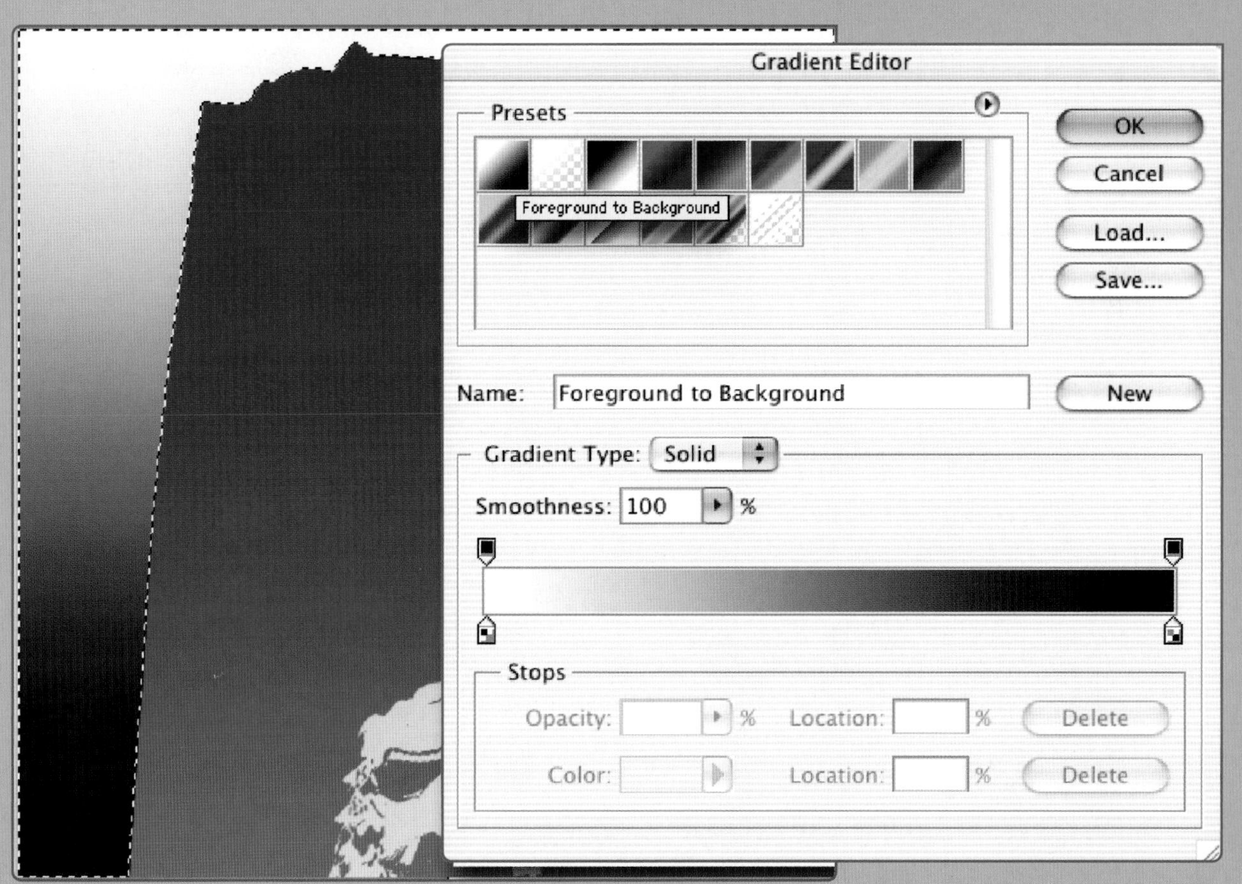

Click OK and go ahead to use the Gradient tool (G). Hold the SHIFT key and drag from the top to the bottom of the selection. Once it's done, deselect. Now, we are ready to make this layer into a 100-percent overlay. Adding different treatments to the columns will help create more depth to the image.

Because we are now done with the columns, let's head on over to the centerpiece sculpture. Go back to the original photo layer and, to help make things clearer, hide the other layers. Go back to Path 1 and load it as a selection. Then go to Layer ➤ New ➤ Layer Via Copy (CMD+J). Name the new layer "Stone".

efore we begin working on this sculpture, we'll have to change nis centerpiece into black and white by pressing CMD+SHIFT+U. s you can see, there are shapes behind the lion's head—we still ave the inner roof and the rear walls to work with. Let's keep verything but the center sculpture for now. To do this, we'll eed to use the Path tool again. Zoom in to around 66 percent o begin with. Start from the left bottom corner of the culpture, go around the top and back down the lion's head, round the center rectangle, and back to the original starting oint. When the path is complete, name it "Path 2".

With Path 2 selected, click Load as a selection icon at the bottom of the Paths palette, jump back to the layer Stone, press DELETE, and deselect. Now, move this layer above the Black / White layer and make all the layers visible again.

You might be able to see that the inner roof could still do with some minor touching up. To do a clean job, use the Polygonal Lasso tool (L) to select just the inner roof area. Once you get back to your original starting point with the cursor, press CMD+UP and DOWN to select the top roof. Go to Edit ➤ Fill and fill with a black color to achieve a clean look (CMD/CTRL+DELETE).

Using the same method, we'll also touch up the walls behind the sculpture. This time, use a dark gray (R:18, G:18, B:18) to fill the center wall. There are also two smaller areas of the walls at the right side. We'll use a mid gray (R:95, G:95, B:95) for the second wall and light gray (R:195, G:195, B:195) for the third wall. When this is done, change the Stone layer blending mode to Overlay at 60-percent opacity.

(At this point, you may wish to compare your progress to th final source file `chinatown_tutorial.psd` on the CD.)

At this point, we pretty much have everything but the cente sculpture and the final touches to add some atmosphere. Th next step is to work on the top part of the sculpture; we'll ad more detail and some lighting effects.

elect Path 2 in the Paths palette and load the path as a election. While it's selected, go to the original photo layer and uplicate another image (just to make sure the original remains ntact). Once this is done, drag this new layer back on top of tone layer and name it "Stone Head". We are now going to ork on the stone head without the bottom rectangle frame.

Again, use the Polygonal Lasso tool (L) to get rid of the bottom. This time, you may just simply delete it. Next, switch the stone head to black and white (CMD+SHIFT+U) and adjust this layer to Overlay at 60-percent opacity. With this effect added, it blends nicely with the rest of the elements.

When I first created my *Chinatown* piece, I felt like there was something missing. I realized that it lacked a moody visual. So, I created an effect to remedy this. It's easy, has a nice look to it, and you can try applying this technique to your other work as well. To do this, you need to duplicate the Stone Head layer and call it "Glow 1".

Before we start, make sure the layer blending mode is back t Normal and 100 percent. Select all (CMD+A) and press CMD+U and DOWN to grab the stone head shape. While it's selected, us the Gradient tool (G) with a black foreground color and whit background color to begin with. Hold SHIFT, and drag from th top to the center of the image, deselecting when you're finishec

is time we'll set the blending mode to Screen. Next, we'll ed to soften the shape using Filter ➤ Blur ➤ Gaussian Blur th a blur radius of 11 pixels. To exaggerate this effect, let's plicate Glow 1 and call it "Glow 2". You don't need to do ything else to this layer—just duplicate it.

Now, we should have a good amount of white-colored glow around the stone head. Things are coming together nicely, but there are some more touches that we'll quickly go through.

Behind the lion's head is an empty frame around the central piece, which we are going to fill with a new layer called "Frame" above the Stone Head layer.

First, go back to the Paths palette and choose Path 2. Load the path as a selection. Second, jump back to the new Frame layer, fill it with black, and then deselect it. Next, go to the Stone Head layer and CMD+click on its layer name. Then, go back to the Frame layer, press DELETE, and deselect. Finally, select the frame.

To emphasize the lighting, use the Gradient tool (G) and set mid-gray foreground color. In the Gradient editor, set th gradient Name to Foreground to Transparent, Solid type, an then choose a 100-percent Smoothness. This time, drag fro the bottom to the top with the Gradient tool and then deselec To finish this off, set the blending mode to Overlay with a opacity of 80 percent. So far, you'll see that it still has a goo amount of purple around the whole work.

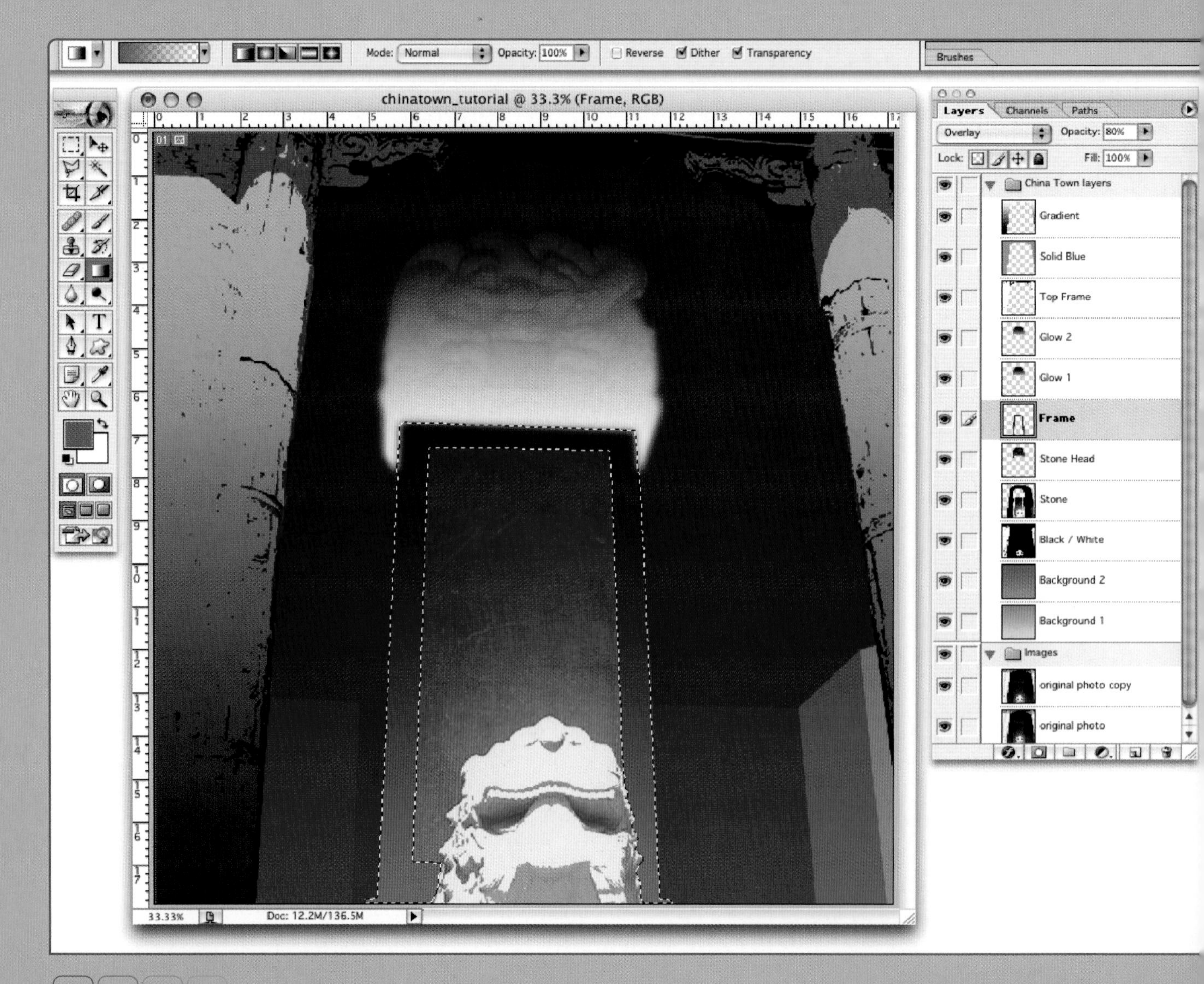

› tone down the color, we'll add another color to the center ›ctangular box. Create a new layer above the Frame layer and ›ll it "Mud Green". We're going to use a specific green with an ›verlay effect to create a dark reddish color in the central ›iece, behind the lion's head.

› be as exact as possible, first zoom in to about 66 percent, ›d then select the center piece using the Polygonal Lasso tool ›). First click the lower-left corner of the rectangle as the ›arting point and then work your way all the way around to the ›p right of the lion's head. Fill it with the mud green color ›:123, G:116, B:53).

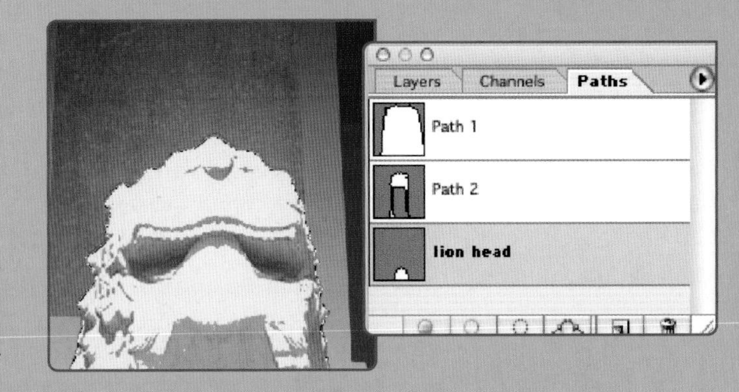

›rn off the layer visibility for now and use ›e Pen tool (P) to select the lion's head. ›ake sure to save the path in the Paths ›alette and call it something appropriate, like ›ion head". Now load this path as a selection.

›o back to the Mud Green layer, make the ›yer visible, press DELETE, and deselect all. ›astly, change the Mud Green layer blending ›ode to Overlay at 100-percent opacity.

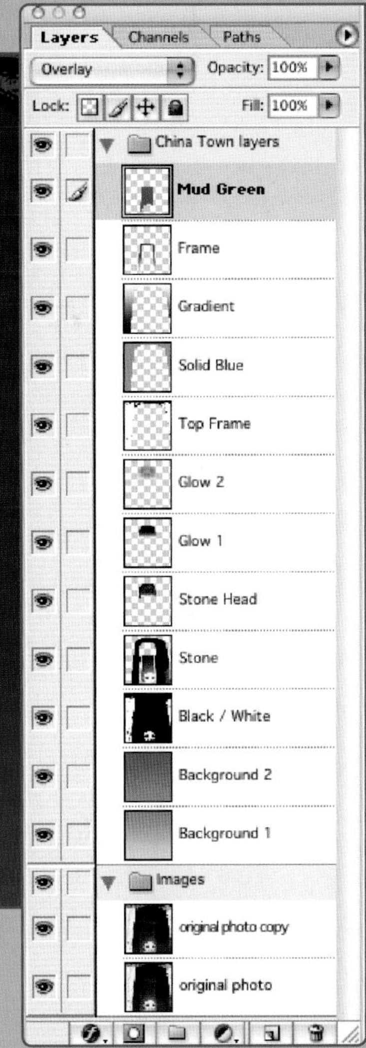

Although the color has been toned down quite a bit in the previous steps, it still looks a bit flat. To fix this, we need to add a new shade above the mud green. Duplicate the Mud Green layer and call it "Gradient". Use the Gradient tool (G), with black foreground and white background colors, and a Foreground to Background solid gradient. Drag from the top of the rectangle shape to the bottom. Lastly, change the Gradient layer blending mode to Overlay with 60-percent opacity.

The following steps are actually my main focus throughout th entire art piece. I wanted to create a painting in that rectangul shape that is just a simple, fun, visual experiment with th Photoshop tools. In a way, it's related to the inspiration I ha when I was immersed in the fiberglass painting experience that Chinatown event.

ow we are going to add some xternal, natural imagery to the image. uplicate the Gradient layer and call it Park". Select it and fill it with a mid- ray color (R:186, G:186, B:186).

created the trees by using the Path ool. I have drawn them and saved em as Tree 1 and Tree 2 in the Paths alette of `chinatown_tutorial.psd`. ou could also get the shapes from `ree1.psd` and `tree2.psd` on the CD.

or Tree 1, add a new layer and fill it ith black. For Tree 2, add a new layer nd fill it with mid gray (R:125, G:125, :125). When this is done, link the gray ackground and two trees by merging em together (CMD+E). Lastly, change e Park layer blending mode to verlay at 100-percent opacity.

To make the painting even more interesting, I decided to make a pattern called "strips"; this functions a bit like patterned wallpaper to add some interesting texture to the central piece.

Open `strips.psd` on the CD and place it in your working Chinatown file on a new layer called "Strips".

CMD+click on the Park layer to select the rectangular shap Select the Strips layer and press SHIFT+CMD+I to invert th selection. Press DELETE and then deselect afterward. Finally, s the blending mode for the Strips layer to Multiply at 60-perce opacity.

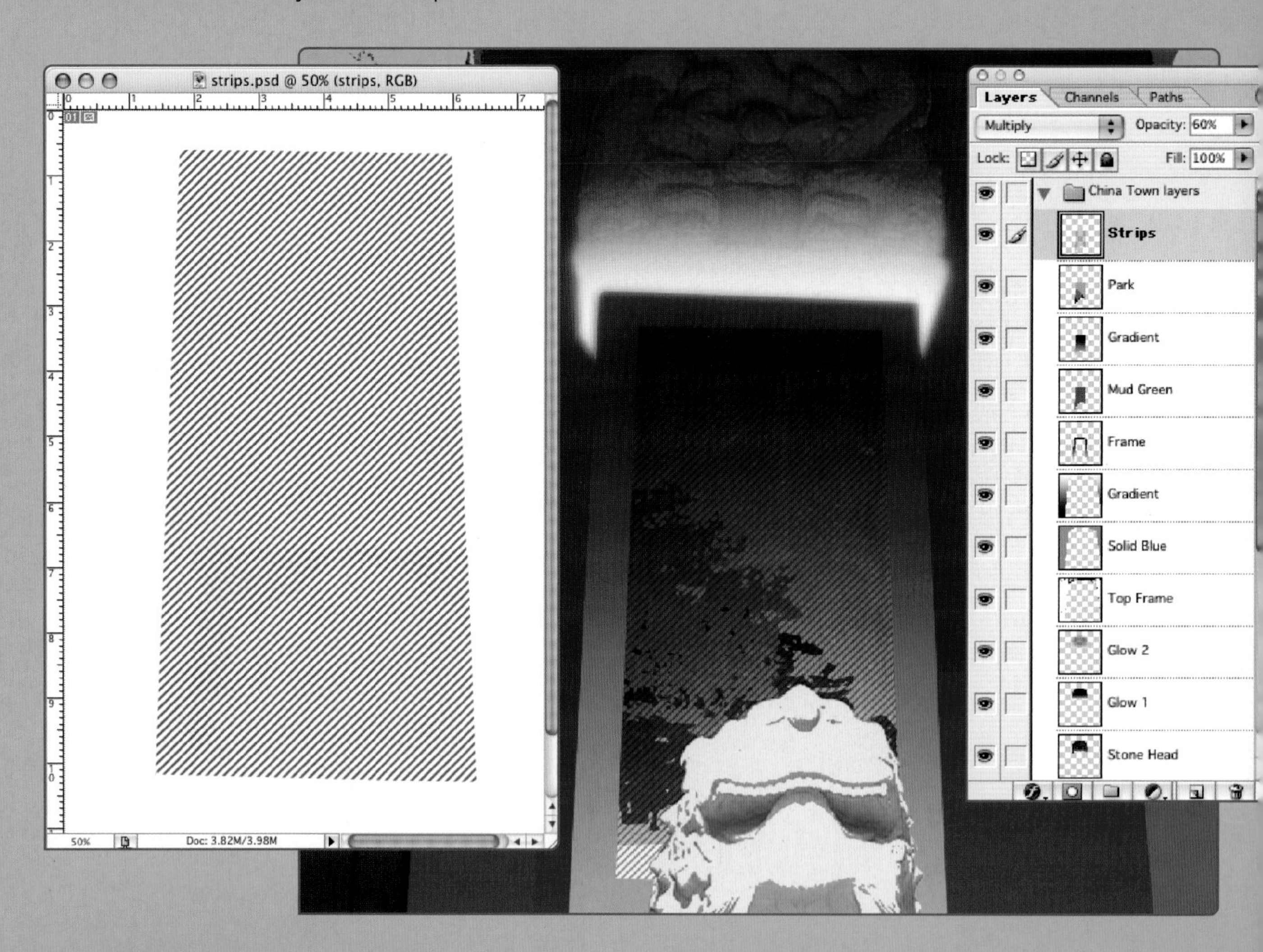

Now, to finish this center section, add a little more flavor to it by placing `purple_trees.psd` (this file is only available at www.friendsofed.com/downloads) on a new layer called "Purple Tree" directly above the Strips layer. Make the Purple Tree layer's blending mode Multiply at 100-percent opacity.

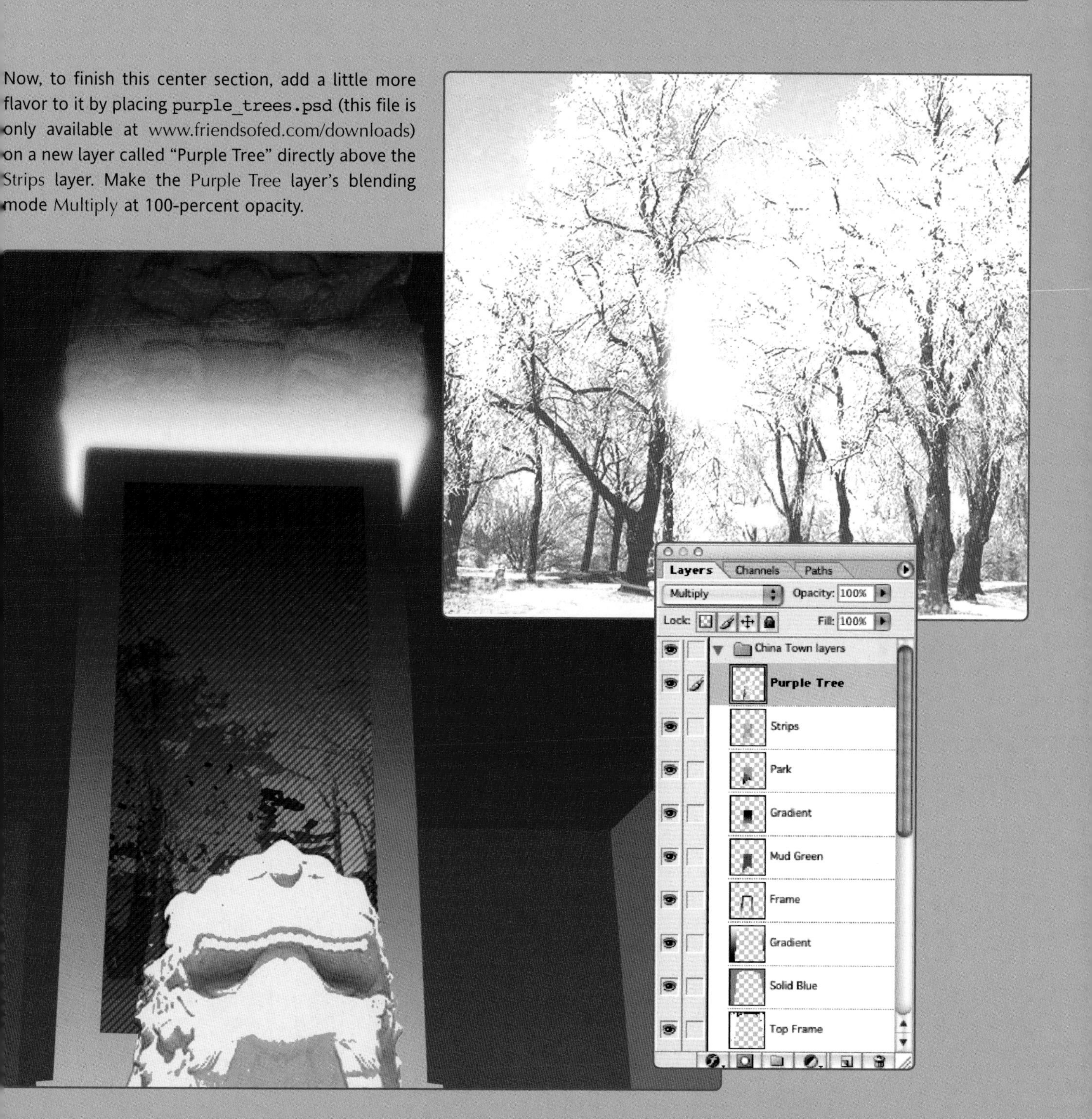

Now let's move on to adding some more atmosphere. I've provided another image that you can use (`smoke.psd` available at www.friendsofed.com/downloads) or you can grab it from the Smoke layer in the Images layer set in `chinatown_tutorial.psd`, where it has already been cleaned up. These two images were found from a free stock photo exchange site (www.sxc.hu).

Place the smoke image on a new layer called "Smoke" above the Background 2 layer to ensure sure that it's not too dominant in the picture. The blending mode is Screen at 100-percent opacity.

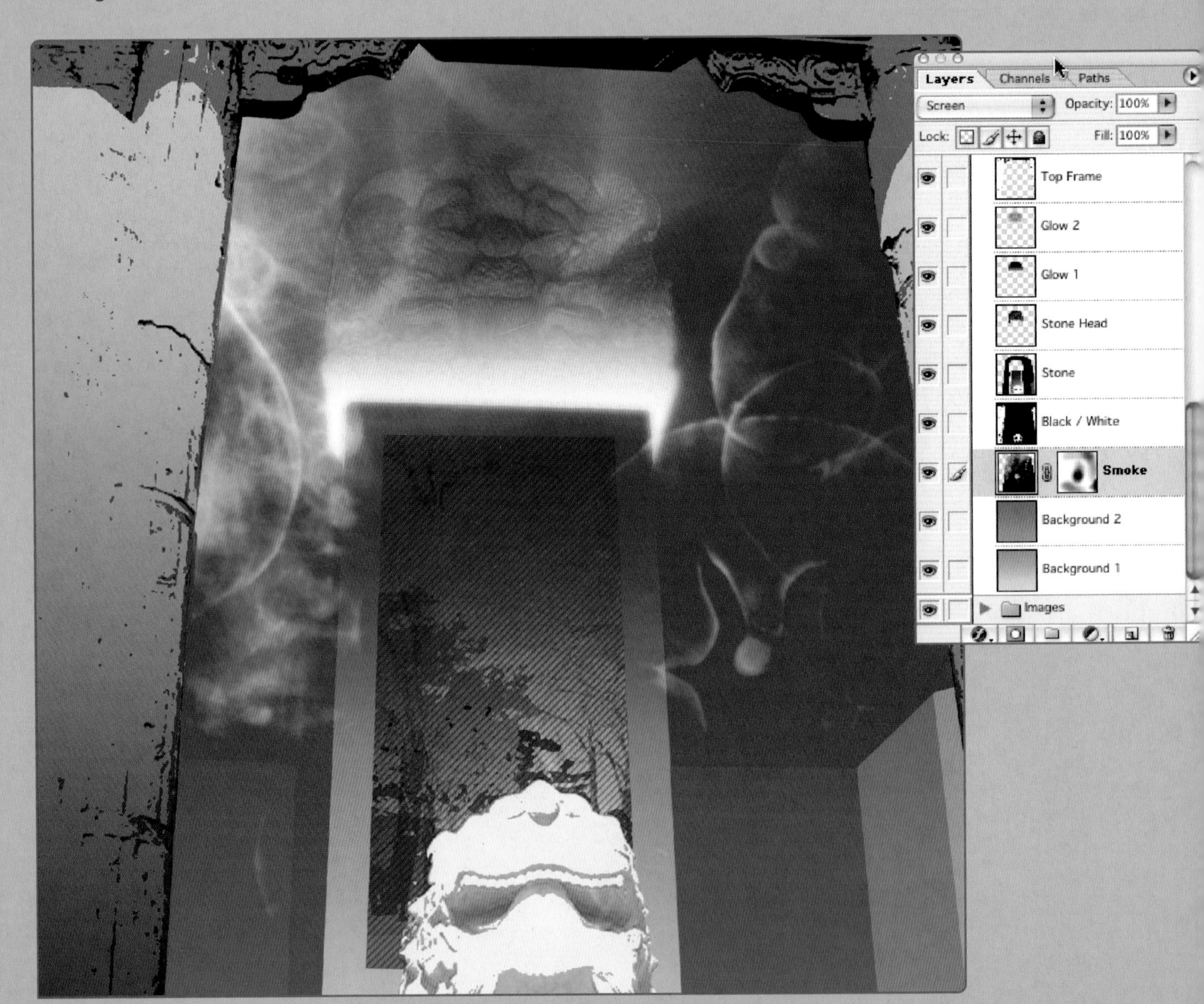

Next, add a new layer above the Purple Tree layer and name it "Moon". Choose the Brush tool (B), select a Hard Round pixel brush, and adjust the master diameter to 102. Make sure the color is white and then simply click once at the upper-left corner of the image. Next, use the Eraser tool (E) with the same diameter and take out part of the circle by clicking once; this should create a crescent-moon shape.

Let's add a glow effect to the moon now. Duplicate the Moon layer and called it "Moon Blur". Add a Gaussian Blur with a radius of 24.3 and set the blending mode to Screen on this Moon Blur layer.

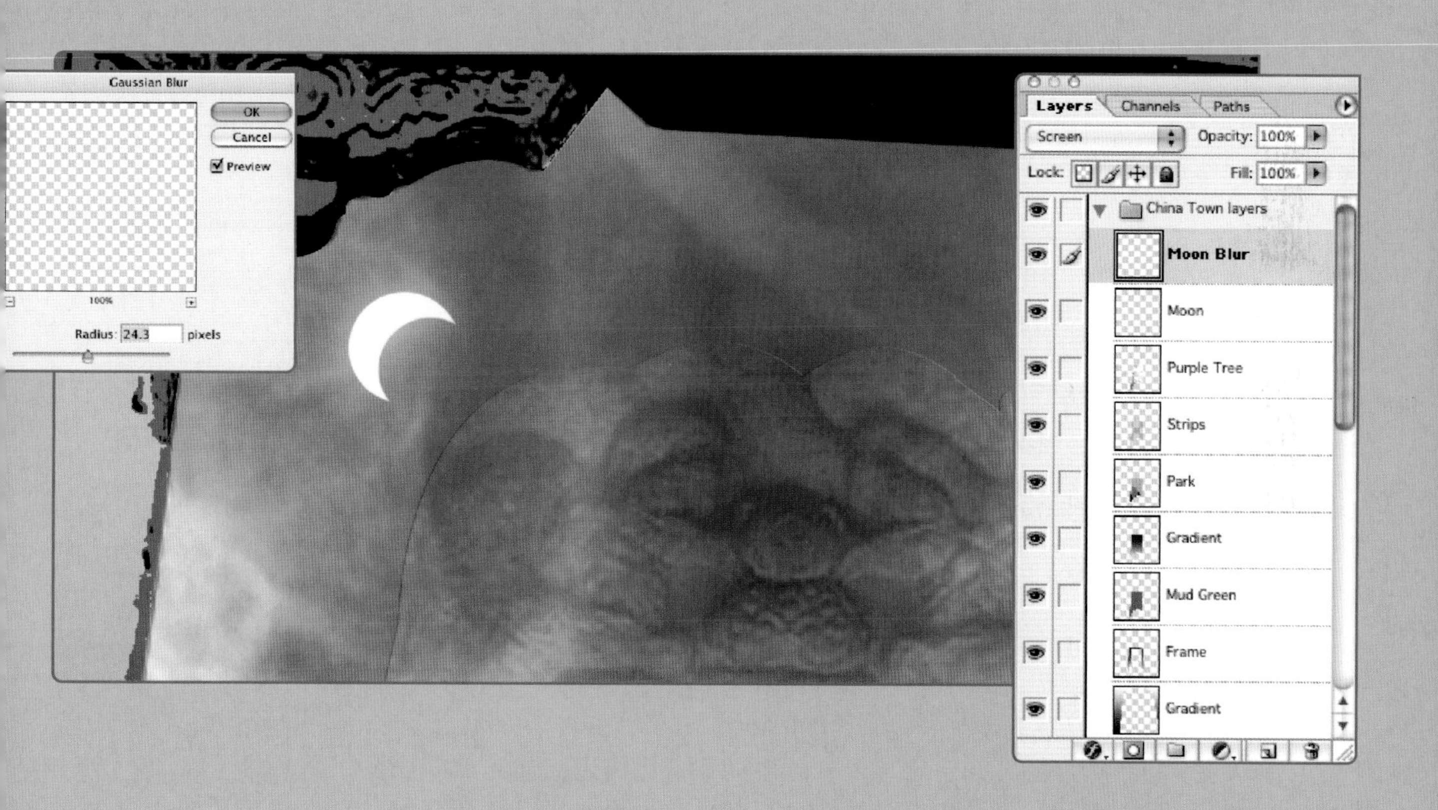

To accompany the moon, a handful of stars should fit the bill quite nicely. Create another layer at the top of your Layers palette and call it "Diamond Stars". Select the Rectangular Marquee tool (M), press SHIFT to draw a small square, and then fill it with white. Next, use the Eraser tool (E) to remove the corner by simply clicking it once.

Using this method, go on to create another three squares wit their corners cut off and position them together to make a sta shape. Also, make sure that each individual square has a differen color of gray to emphasize the shading. Once you've finishe creating the stars, set the layer blending mode to Screen.

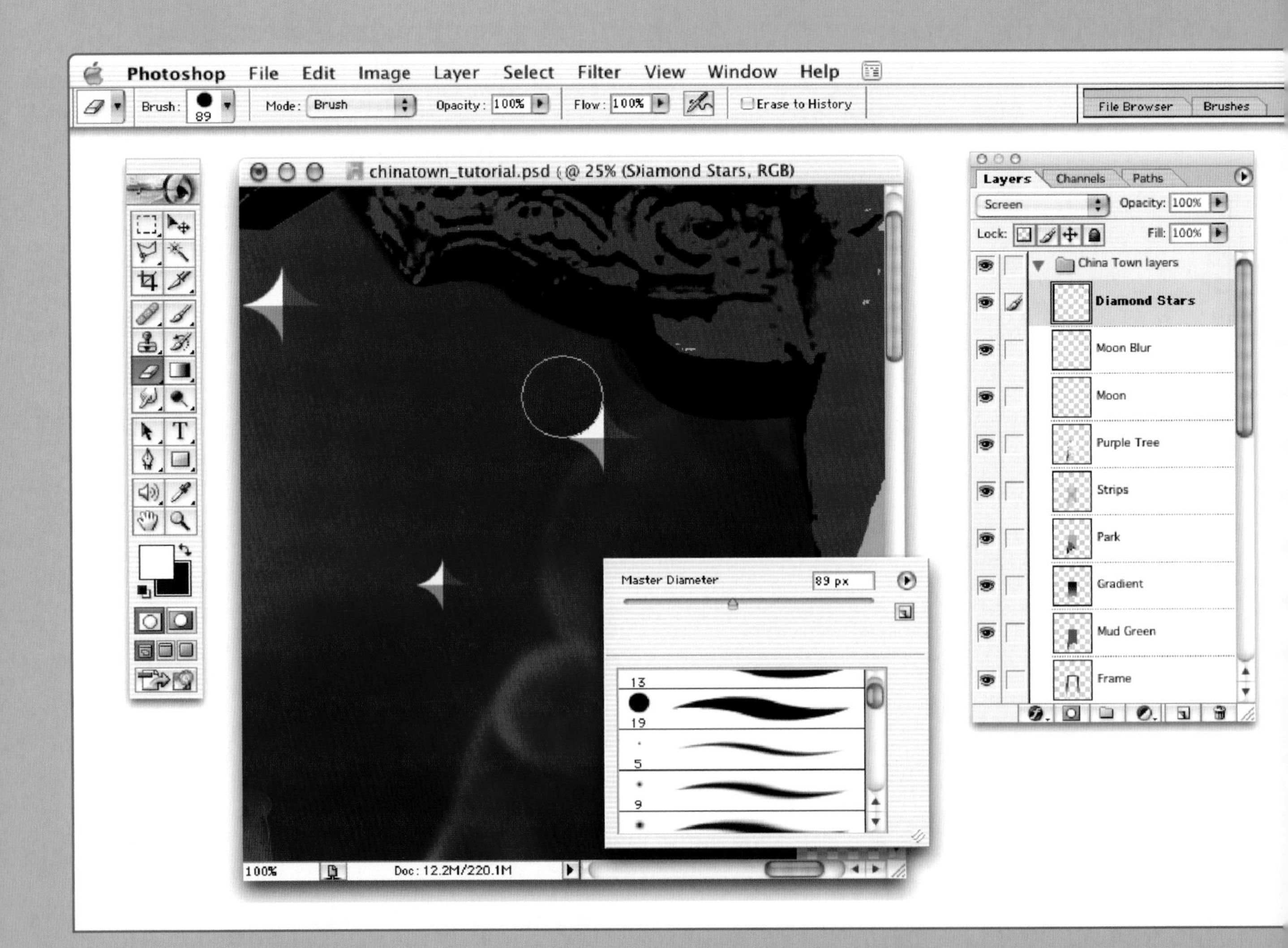

'or the very last step, we'll add some white-colored Chinese ext to the painting. It's almost like a kind of signature. I created his clip art with the Path tool, but it is also provided on the CD n `chinese_words.psd`. Copy the path into your working Chinatown file and click on the Load path as a selection icon in he Paths palette. Fill the selection with white. I positioned the ext over the pattern in the center area of the image.

This concludes my tutorial on the process I went through to create the *Chinatown* piece for my site. I hope this Photoshop demonstration has been helpful. The style and techniques demonstrated are simple and practical, yet so versatile that they can be applied with ease in today's graphics world. Enjoy and explore the many possibilities open to you that are made possible with new and ever-improving software. I wish you all a fun and happy time with Photoshop!

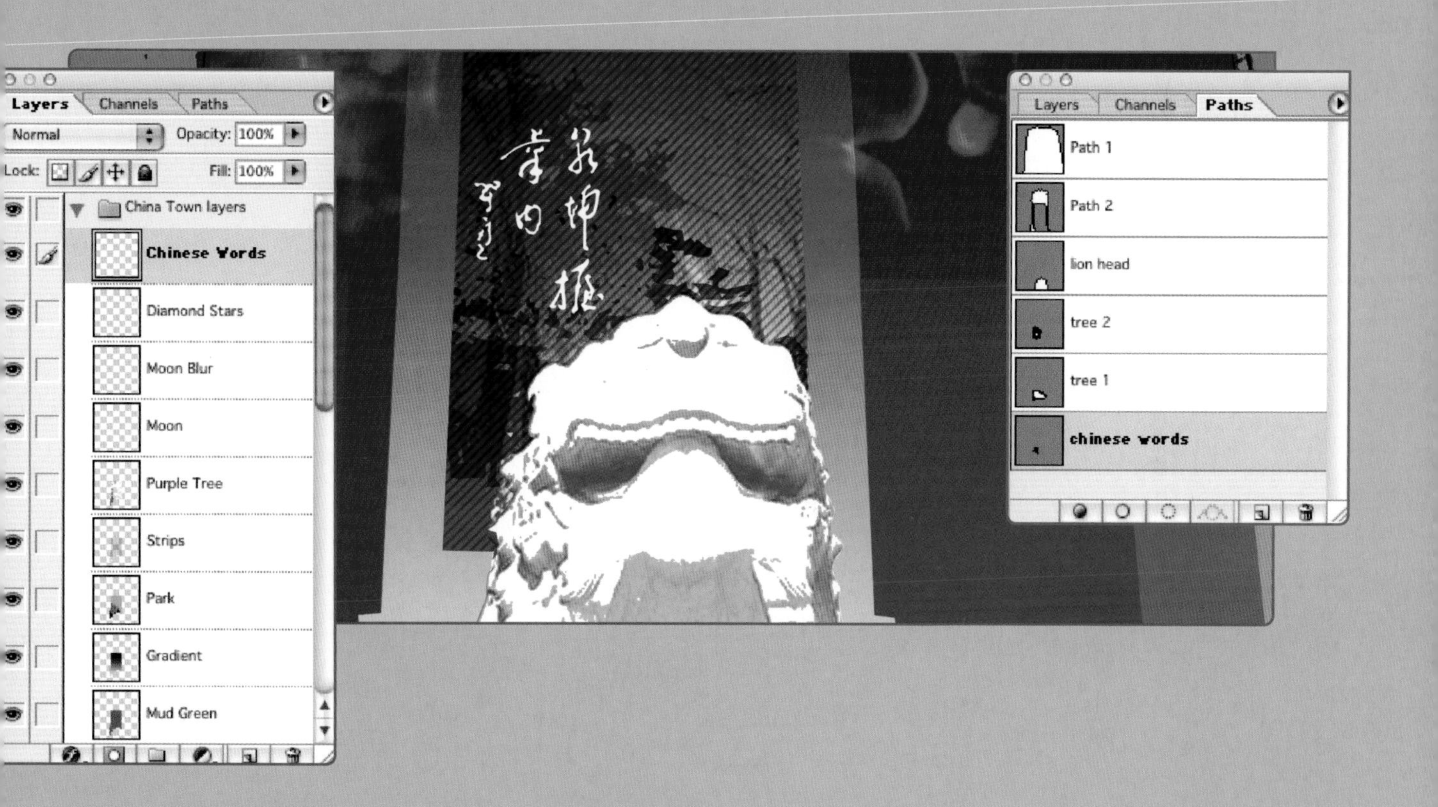

13 NATUREMORPHOSIS

“THE ESSENCE IS USING YOUR BRAIN AND PATIENCE.”

OLIVER OTTNER
WWW.EFFECTLAB.COM

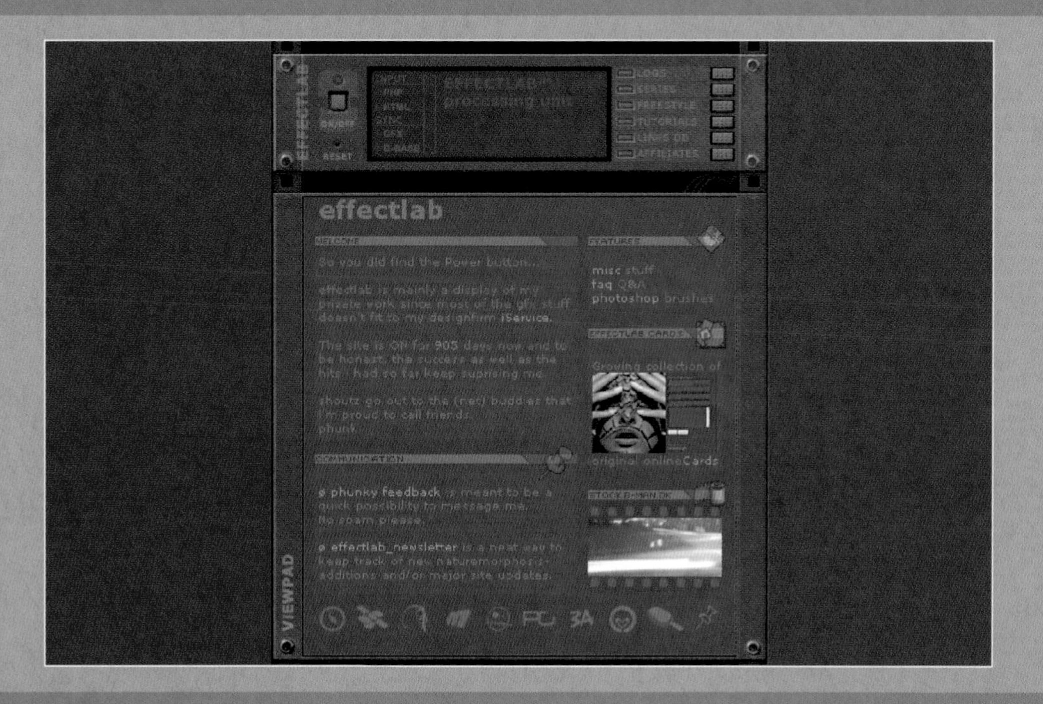

When I started working in the graphics field and experienced my first all night surf sessions, the graphics community was small. Very small, actually. Just a few artists were displaying their portfolios, hardly anybody was using Google, and the "state of the art" search engine, AltaVista, would find maybe 2,000 sites containing the term "Photoshop tutorials." Now Google lists around 582,000 sites, some of which may lead you to deviantART, various "art groups," and Photoshop-dedicated forums full of people. I began working with Photoshop 3 shortly before version 4 was released and brought the all new Navigator, adjustment layers, and actions. When I started, my Photoshop work was quite chaotic and the results were ugly. Going through all the filters and applying half of them gets boring with time, but I guess that's a stage most have (or still have) to go through. Because Photoshop fascinated me, I spent a lot of time working with it and my skills grew quite quickly. Soon I discovered that photomanipulation was my main area of interest. Combining elements together into a single image that wouldn't actually fit in real life was an amazing thing for me.

One step followed another as I learned to use as many deskt publishing tools and web techniques as I could find. I decid to continue studying psychology at the University of Vienna b in addition to these studies, I opened an advertisement ager with one of my best friends. Though I worked like mad clients during the day, I slowly got back into the graph community again in my spare time, offering help to the starting out in Photoshop just like the help I received whe started. I thought that the only logical next step would be register my own domain and host some tutorials, as well artwork. This is how my main site, www.effectlab.com, w born.

The resulting site has been online for over two years now, a the attention it has received has gone far beyond wha expected. My new site, www.naturemorphosis.com, conce trates on my artwork and allows visitors to buy high quality well as high-resolution prints.

naturemorphosis _ dualism _ various _ info _ ordering info

WELCOME

naturemorphosis.com is dedicated to the art of Oliver Ottner, digital artist living and working in Vienna, Austria.

As founder and art-director of the advertising agency iService he works for clients such as Estée Lauder and the famous Zoo Vienna.

The main purpose of this homepage is to give a detailed sneak peek into his works as well as provide the opportunity to order high-quality prints, shipped worldwide.

You will find all background info as well as technical and order support within both **_info_** sections above.

NEWS

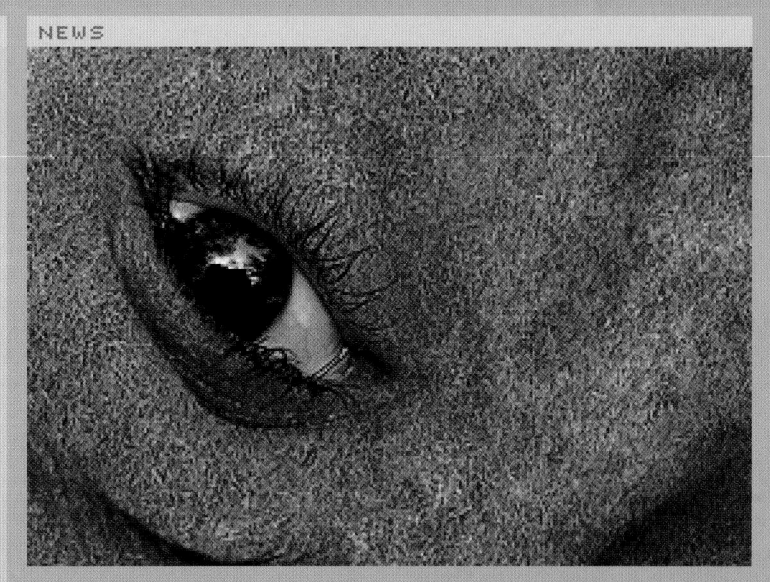

UNSORTED

Now that you know a little bit about my background, let's see what inspired me when I started five years ago. Two centuries, two masters, two completely different approaches, and two completely different techniques. The first of these, Hieronymus Bosch, might be the artist who first brought the combination of flora/fauna and humans to canvas. Bosch is widely acknowledged as one of history's most popular and most intriguing artists; he is a true master of symbolism and is especially famous for his fantastic demon-filled works. He was a painter rich in ideas with a seemingly irrational fanaticism that enveloped his work. It's this enigmatic characteristic of his paintings that separates him from the mainstream art of fifteenth century.

Bosch keeps inspiring me with his attention to detail. Look closely and you'll find a hundred little things that make his work so believable. He draws creatures and figures that never existed but, due to his addiction to perfect highlights, shadows, and realistic shapes, they look almost real. Bosch's demons, often symbolized by humans strangely combined with animal bodyparts, feed the captivating effect. He must have had a pretty interesting inner life to give birth to such weird creatures.

The central panel of this triptych illustrates the kneeling figure of St. Anthony being tormented by devils. These include a man with a thistle for a head and a fish that is half gondola. What is so extraordinary is that these imaginary creatures are painted with absolute conviction, as though they truly existed. Each bizarre creation is drawn with the same realism as the natural animal and human elements. Bosch's nightmarish images seem to possess an inexplicable surrealistic power. I could stare at this for hours and still learn something. The main impact his work has on me has to do with the quality of these creatures. He brought them out into a perfect state by finding good combinations and balancing them perfectly. I have never thought that Bosch rushed his work to achieve a quick effect. His ideas make sense, fit the overall scene and, due to 100 percent accuracy, manage to trick the eye into believing that the scene is real. This level of patience is something I learned from Bosch.

The Temptation of St Anthony (c.1500; Museo National de Arte Antiga, Lisbon)

When I was staying in London for the first time at the age of 16 (6 years before I bought my first PC), my attention was captured by a pretty strange book cover—the cover for *Horripilations: The Art of J. K. Potter* (Overlook Press, 1997). I've never been that interested in dark art, but this book really got to me because of Potter's technical and imaginative skills. His work intrigues me because he creates all his pieces using only photographic and darkroom techniques—no computers, no Photoshop—just knives and glue combined with (as far as I know) subtle airbrush retouching. By combining art and photography, Potter creates stunning effects; an intensely dark and psychological vision that is as horrifying as it is beautiful. He shows superb imagination and perfect technique, which is why he really inspired me when I started with photomanipulation.

Illustration created by J. K. Potter for H. P. Lovecraft's "The Music of Eric Zaan"

Just imagine the tools he is using! Where we're used to switching to the Clone tool, he must spend a long time airbrushing, cutting, and glueing. Imagine, no Undo! But then again, look at the realism in his works. The lighting is correct, even within the weirdest combinations or locations. It's breathtaking. What I learned from Potter is mainly to look at things very closely, learn from them, and then try hard to create a vision that looks realistic. Of all my influences, his artwork has had the biggest effect on my work style.

Do yourself a favor and get your hands on one of Potter's books; he is the true master of photomanipulation. This field contains a lot of very good artists, but nobody comes close when it comes to quality. The difference between a good and bad photomanipulation is **realism**. Swap a person's head for another and you can work on it as long as you like, but if the light falling on the face or the shadow around the nose is not 100 percent correct, you will never trick the viewer.

uite often, I get asked for assistance with photomanipulation someone simply wants insider information on the "trick" hind my naturemorphosis series of images. Although I can nd a helping hand, it's impossible to really explain this trick, cause there isn't one. naturemorphosis is a combination of eas, hard work, and creativity in finding ways to bring the ion to canvas. Because English is not my mother tongue, it's ficult to find the right words, but what I'm trying to explain that there isn't a particular skill or single technique that I can sily communicate that will allow you to re-create these ages (though hopefully you'll get very close to re-creating em and will gain insight into the process from the tutorial ction of this chapter).

As far as I can see, two different requirements back up my Photoshop work: my **brain** and **patience**. Now, before you start laughing, let me explain. Thinking—it doesn't matter whether I am creating a new Dualism piece (my second art series) or working as an art director of an advertisement agency—is essential to my design. This doesn't mean that you can open a blank canvas and start to draw using a mad frenzy of filter and layer effects until, by a fluke, you find something acceptable. You might have a small chance of creating something really good, but most people will see that it was just wild trial and error, because the result will have a cheesy, unskilled feeling. By thinking in depth and preparing solidly before you even open Photoshop, you can remain in control and accurately transfer your vision exactly as you see it, not by accident.

lism III – sex

dualism V – culture

Let's take a closer look at the theme behind this chapter: **naturemorphosis**. This is a series of images displayed o www.effectlab.com that I began once I had the ability to really create the pictures and ideas I had had in mind for a long time. Th idea for imagery containing wild combinations of humans and nature elements began when I looked closely at Bosch's painting These images were like my dreams from when I was small. Of course, memories fade over time, but I do remember that some these dreams were filled with imagery from the fairy tales my parents read to me. All those witches and angels had strange sk made of wood and fur. You can see where I am going with this—Bosch's work brought back these visions and dreams. Because wanted to recover these and remember their ambience, I decided to attempt to create them in an artistic way, as realistically possible. However, I felt that Bosch's transformation and combinations went too far. I had something more subtle in mind—n joining human legs and animal heads, but working in my dreams of skin changes.

At first, I did a few sketches in Photoshop... a cat's skin on a human face, leaves wrapping around noses, and so on, but it still looked somehow dull to me (as it really was). When I discovered that Photoshop's blend modes, if used in an unusual way and combined with shading layers (more on this in the tutorial), could help get things looking more realistic, I kept trying and practicing until I had the knowledge and skills to create something that matched my idea of quality—something that I could display to the community.

I was already working on the next two additions to the series when I realized that it was about time to find a name for these images, as a whole series seemed to be growing out of it.

With the benefit of my experience as an art director in an advertisement agency, I quickly found a strong brand that would fit this growing series. It's all about morphing from one stage to another, what we call metamorphosis (such as from a tadpole to frog). By using something phonetically similar that made sense content-wise (as I'm morphing humans with parts and textures from nature), the name **naturemorphosis** was born and was quickly recognized by the community. People seemed to have understood and used it when they talked about the "stuff on effectlab."

naturemorphosis #.

Let's have a look at naturemorphosis #XIII to explain further what I'm heading for.

You can see that I planned to create an elephant-themed naturemorphosis. Sounds easy but, then again, look at the real elephant photo. How would you merge this logically with a human face?

What I did was sit back and have a good look at the "logic" of an elephant's face. How do the eyes look? Is the nose really part of the face or does it look like it's attached to the forehead? Where is the mouth located? Where are the nose, eyes, and ears? What are the main proportions? Giving the girl an elephant's nose would have broken the idea of my series—it is always a mixture, never a full transformation.

Okay, the decision for no nose transformation was ma what about the tusks? If a girl slowly morphs into an e where would the tusks be located? Looking closely elephant shot, you'll see that the tusks should be part cheekbones (let's assume an elephant has got someth these, I have no idea), so I had to create them in this to make them look realistic.

> *What ruins (and in my presketches, ruins more t once) a perfect naturemorphosis is a small part of image where I think for a moment, "Uhmm, th something wrong in this vision; it looks good, somehow it makes no sense." If this happens, I've mi my goal.*

After it was clear how the image could fit together real I opened my model shot and started to work. As I said it is essential that you use your brain and patience here

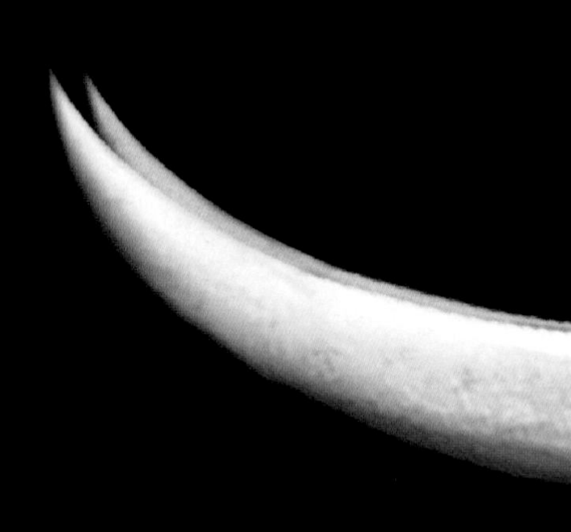

naturemorph

Look at naturemorphosis #VI. In this one I only had one challenge—how to paint those cracks so that they looked realistic. If I had worked in a 72dpi standard screen resolution, it would have been much easier—I could have browsed the Web, gotten a cracked-earth photo, pasted in a new layer, and played around a little. But as you know, I'm working with much higher resolutions, so I wouldn't be able to find a free photo on the Web that would provide the necessary quality. Also, Austria doesn't have a desert where I could take a shot like this just before it rains.

What I did was look at the logic of such earth cracks—the lights, the shadows, how the cracks create structures. I then re-created this in Photoshop, using the Airbrush tool and the noise filter, which appears to be resolution independent. I created it all on new layers above the face.

naturemorphosis #VI

aturemorphosis #VII is one of my favorites. The whole feeling n this shot as well as the ambience is great. If you saw it anging on a wall, 120cm wide, printed on Kodak professional hotopaper, and framed with a black wooden frame, you'd nderstand.

he giraffe fur was tough to draw. I used a lot of reference hotos to see which giraffe pattern (there are at least three ifferent patterns) would look best. When I started painting, I ealized that all the results would look very plain. Within the utorial, you'll see the technique I had to "develop" to vercome this and get the shapes back into the image.

While I was bringing my visions into Photoshop, I needed to develop my techniques permanently. Some of the key features of my creations involve blend modes. I thought I knew all about them and how they reacted until I started the naturemorphosis images. Nearly every new piece still brings me back to an almost beginner status when it comes to blend modes. The challenge is always completely different; I haven't learned any special gimmick. Depending on color, sharpness, the light situation, shades, the base picture, and more, only one solution for the problem exists and you have to find it.

naturemorphosis #VII

Next come masking problems. I've tried every possibility Photoshop has to offer to make a selection and I always come back to using paths and/or the masking mode. You might laugh when I tell you that when it comes to clean deleting, I'm still using the Eraser tool a lot. I do prefer it for the final touch-ups.

The last main issues I need to deal with are resolution and quality. It seems that my work depends on the source images that I can get my hands on, but that's not quite true. I spend time searching for pictures I can use (large, 300dpi files) and if I don't find them, I draw the desired effect. For example, in naturemorphosis #III, the whole reptilian skin is painted with the Airbrush tool and then brought to realistic life with a combination of distortion filters.

The average time I spend on a naturemorphosis image is around 35 hours of concentrated work time. Because I take a few days' break, it's at least three weeks until they're finished. This timeframe also includes photoshooting, scanning, and searching for source images. I design each image to be printed, so I work at 300dpi and around 80cm width, minimum. In the end, each file is around 900MB, with a PSD workfile size around 1.5GB. You need patience for this, and a fast machine (I work on a PC).

As mentioned earlier, people ask me for tips and hints on a daily basis. In most cases (if they don't have a specific question), I have one simple answer: **don't stop too early**.

There are a lot of really good artists out there in our community, both old and young, experienced and new. I see many mainly younger people who show talent and admirable skills, but when I look at their work, I can tell that they have been rushed. Their images look quick and dirty, and thus they ruin a good idea and bring the overall level of the artwork down by several degrees. Most are satisfied with the result way too early, and they overlook the fact that (especially in photomanipulation) realism is *the* crucial factor if you want to stand out from the crowd. You need a little patience so that you can make the artwork grow—unless you're a genius, that is. Don't get me wrong, but there aren't that many geniuses out there.

I try hard not rush things, release them too early, or, in my professional graphics life, give my clients an early glimps before major elements are completed and accurate. I know tha I'm as impatient as most people are, but I realized that I can ruir a piece if I display it publicly (such as a graphics forum) toc early. We all develop better with constructive criticism, but let' get criticism on final pieces, not on sketches!

Remember, take your time, rethink your concept, learn you beloved Photoshop, and practice, practice, practice. If you thin that your skills are good enough to begin creating your visior begin working on it hard. If you think you're done and ready leave your image untouched on your hard disk for a few days anc then look at it again. If you're still satisfied with it, upload it to forum (such as deviantART), and ask for some criticism. If thi criticism happens to be negative, rethink the image and b honest with yourself. Could it be improved? Did you rush it? I finc myself ironing out the last wrinkles after some criticism mor often than you might think. I give some friends a sneak peek anc try to get as many honest reactions as possible. If what they sa is true, I start up Photoshop, open the file, and start ironing.

Even after a lot of naturemorphosis pieces and some significan experience in the area, I still have to be careful not to rush it I've had times when I haven't released a piece for a month afte I was "finished" with it, as I was unsure if it was reall completed. It might be hard to wait, but in my opinion there i no way around that.

I learned a lot while working on those pictures; I had to start t think along the right paths and find solutions that you can't finc in any tutorial or Photoshop book. I'm not sure if it is eve possible to explain those base techniques, because they are no really techniques—remember, as I mentioned earlier, it is a about your thinking skills at the beginning. Once these firs important steps have been taken, it isn't a miracle to complet it. You just need a solid understanding of Photoshop, som time, and plenty of patience.

Now on to the first detailed naturemorphosis tutorial in prir (image #XVI), which has been created specifically for this boo

First of all, naturemorphosis #XVI took around 30 hours to create, so even after cutting out preparation of thinking and testing, I have had to shorten things a bit here. I haven't cut on quality but, for example, I won't fully explain how you mask the model in order to delete the background. You'll have to figure that out using tutorials from other books, the Web, or Photoshop's manual. You should follow the tutorial as closely as possible to produce an image similar to my example. For instance, ensure that all layers are in the correct position with the given blending modes (and use the same layer names as I have).

Basically, what you're going to do is re-create naturemorphosis #XVI from scratch. You'll have to figure out a few things on your own, but I've explained all the basic steps, which are the important ones. The rest is up to you and depends a lot on your taste and your idea of realism.

You'll find all the source files on the CD at 300dpi and in RGB mode. My intention is not to enable you to completely copy my piece but to give you an insight into how I created it, give you ideas on how to start solving problems in Photoshop, and, last but not least, give you an impression of how I think graphics-wise.

Enough talk; open `liz.tif` in Photoshop and rename the Background layer "girl". Choose your favorite masking tool. The first thing you need to do is separate the girl from the background.

I would like to encourage you to use the Pen tool because it allows you to make the most precise selections possible in Photoshop. When you're done, create a selection from it, invert it, and hit DELETE. Getting used to the Pen tool is not too easy, but keep practicing; you won't need anything else once you've mastered it.

ou should make sure that your mask is accurate, because you'll eed it quite often to crop textures, shadows, and other masks. ou can handle the area around the hair as you like (I am saving his work for later because it falls under the final touches ategory, in my opinion).

)pen `leopard.tif` and paste it into your document above the irl layer. Name this new layer "texture" and reduce its layer pacity to 40 percent so that the body shines through. Drag the exture around, resize, and rotate it until you like how the spots re positioned on the body. This part is difficult, but you need o spend a bit of time on it.

)nce you're happy with the positioning of the texture and you hink it looks as realistic as possible, load the selection by olding CTRL and clicking the girl layer. Make sure the texture ayer is active, invert the selection (SHIFT+CTRL+I), and delete it.

ide the texture layer for a moment, grab the Eraser tool, and elete the area over the head and hair. Basically, you should ow have the texture and its shape in the right place.

ow comes the interesting part—finding out which blending node will fit. Cycle through all the blending modes of the exture layer until you think you've found the one that makes nost sense. To help a little here, try starting with the Multiply lending mode. It lets the body shine through, brings the orrect spots into play, but doesn't look too washed out like nost of the other modes.

There is one big problem—now the texture fits but the color isn't correct. It looks much too transparent, the spots are not black enough, and the fact that this is fur isn't very clear.

Part of the naturemorphosis technique is in using copies of the same layer with different blending modes and, according to the effect, different opacity settings. You'll need a fair bit of experience here, as the combinations are almost endless (don't forget that the stacked order within the Layers palette does affect the image a lot, too).

In this case, copy the texture layer, rename it "color", place it below the texture layer but above the girl layer, and start testing. What you need, which you may have discovered already is the Color blending mode to retain the yellow fur as well as making the dark spots more visible.

You're on the right path now. You should be able to see that it will work but also that you need to make some changes in terms of realism.

With the color layer still active, bring up the Hue/Saturation dialog box (CTRL+U), check Colorize, and change the color layer to a decent yellow. Play around with the three settings until you like the color.

Do the same for the texture layer and find a good combination for the spot contrast versus fur color. You should apply levels or curves (as you like) to fine-tune the tones, referring to the screenshots as a guide.

The whole skinning part seems to be complete if you worked accurately.

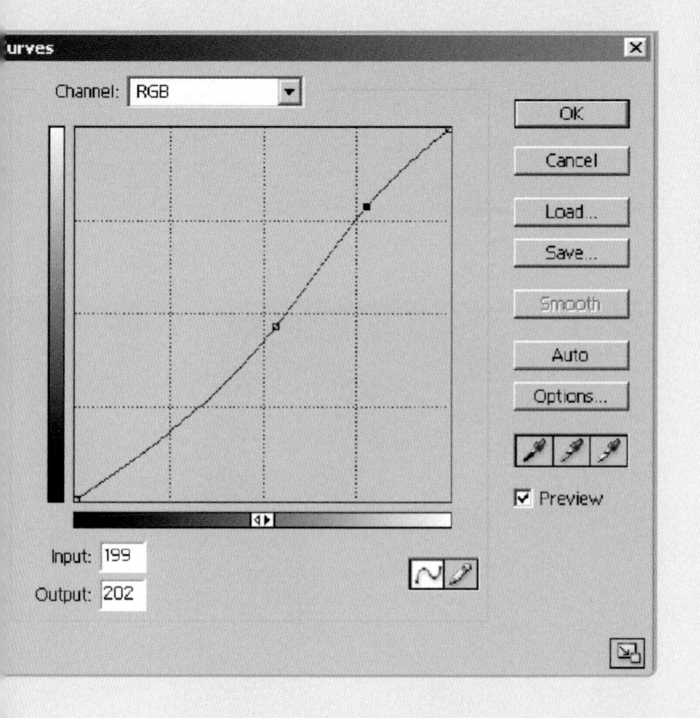

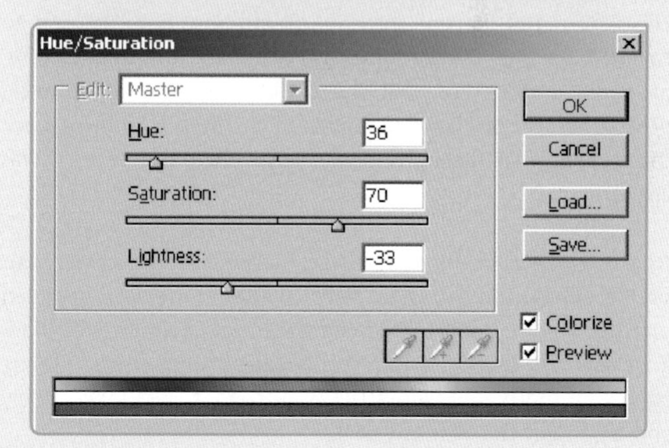

Everything you'll add now is to enhance realism. These highlights and shadows help the body look more shaped and lift the whole texture out of the plain feeling it currently has.

Open `concrete.tif` and place it below the girl layer. Name it "back" and color it as you like. I changed it to make the concrete look a little more weathered by playing with the Noise filter (but that is a matter of taste).

Create a new layer below the girl layer but above the back layer, and name it "shadow". Change the foreground color to black (if it isn't already), choose a round brush (with a diameter of around 90) with soft edges, and paint a shadow around the body on the background. As you can see here, I'm assuming that the light comes from the top left of the image, so the body will throw a shadow that's slightly larger on the right side.

Apply a Gaussian Blur filter with a setting high enough to make the shadow look realistic. Also try reducing the layer opacity of the shadow, if you like.

You now need a new layer right below color called "shades". This isn't a 100-percent accurate description, but I'm used to calling it like this. Using a soft brush and black foreground color, paint along the edges that shape the body—the arms, neck, breasts, and so on. The whole idea of this step is to bring back the dimensional feeling that was lost when the texture was applied.

As you can see in the final image (`naturemorphosis16.psd` on the CD), I used two layers with "shades". One has a reduced opacity of 49 percent, while the other was painted with dark gray and was blurred a lot. This is where your artistic feeling comes in; there is no way strict way to do it. Just look closely and try to get the best out of it.

ook at the picture here to see how I did the final shading; I also used the color Burn tool a little on the girl layer. I hardly ever do his, because painting on the base layer is irreversible, but sometimes there is no way to create the desired realism by simply adding nore and more shadow layers. The Burn tool lets you use different settings when you are applying it to the girl layer shadows/highlights/midtones). If you want to re-create this effect just with additional layers, you need a lot of them, all with lifferent blending modes and brush settings.

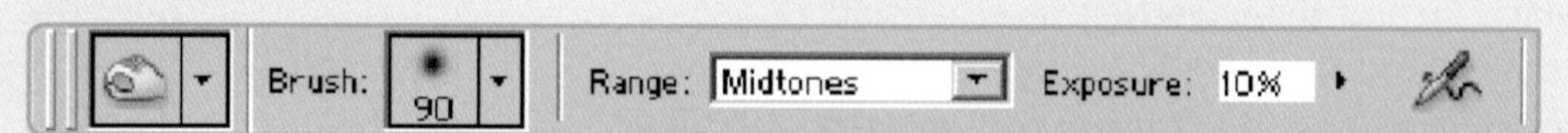

ook at just the girl layer in the aturemorphosis16_final.psd to ee what I mean. You should be able to ee the difference. The body is imensional again, the arms are ounded, and overall it has lost that lain feeling.

: seems like all is done and we can tart talking about the final touches. irst, the girl's head needs a shadow as : lies on her right arm. It looks plain nd wrong without a shadow, so create nother shadow layer and apply the ame technique I described previously. e careful with this shadow as it will ook inaccurate if it isn't similar to the xisting shadow.

nother necessary layer is FaceShapeHelp. ook at the final PSD and switch this yer on/off to see what it does. asically, it distinguishes the outline of ne face from the shadow, which brings out a little more. Keep in mind that nis image is made for print, so think of viewing distance of at least 1 meter. way from the screen with the nose!

The final touch is to color the face on a separate layer and, if you like, color the background too to give the whole scene a bit more dramatic lighting. In this case, I created an adjustment layer (faceColor in the final PSD), using levels that sit above the girl layer, with a layer mask that has some black to gray masking on it (depending on which parts of the underlying layers should be affected or not). As you know, the more black you used, the more the pixels below disappear. Also, don't forget that you get very soft edges if you use Gaussian Blur on a layer mask!

here you go. You've reached the end of a naturemorphosis ıtorial. I hope that you have gotten a good glimpse behind the :enes of how I create these images. It's not a lot of magic; ather a lot of patience and thinking.

m pretty sure that the future will bring more and more new ieces; I'm only limited by my ideas, nothing more. In fact, in ne process of writing this chapter, I came up with four new oncepts for naturemorphosis works! I've already sketched all f them and started three of them, which are now sitting on my ard disk as 600dpi files.

he naturemorphosis series and the work I do on it has brought lot of new things to my life—a reputation and recognition as n artist, clients for my firm, some great buddies within the raphics community, and a big bag of new skills and ways to ring my inner life and ideas to life on paper.

eeing your own creations printed at high quality, with large imensions, and hanging in a room or office is a feeling you nouldn't miss. Wouldn't it be great if your very own series or ork had the same impact on you?

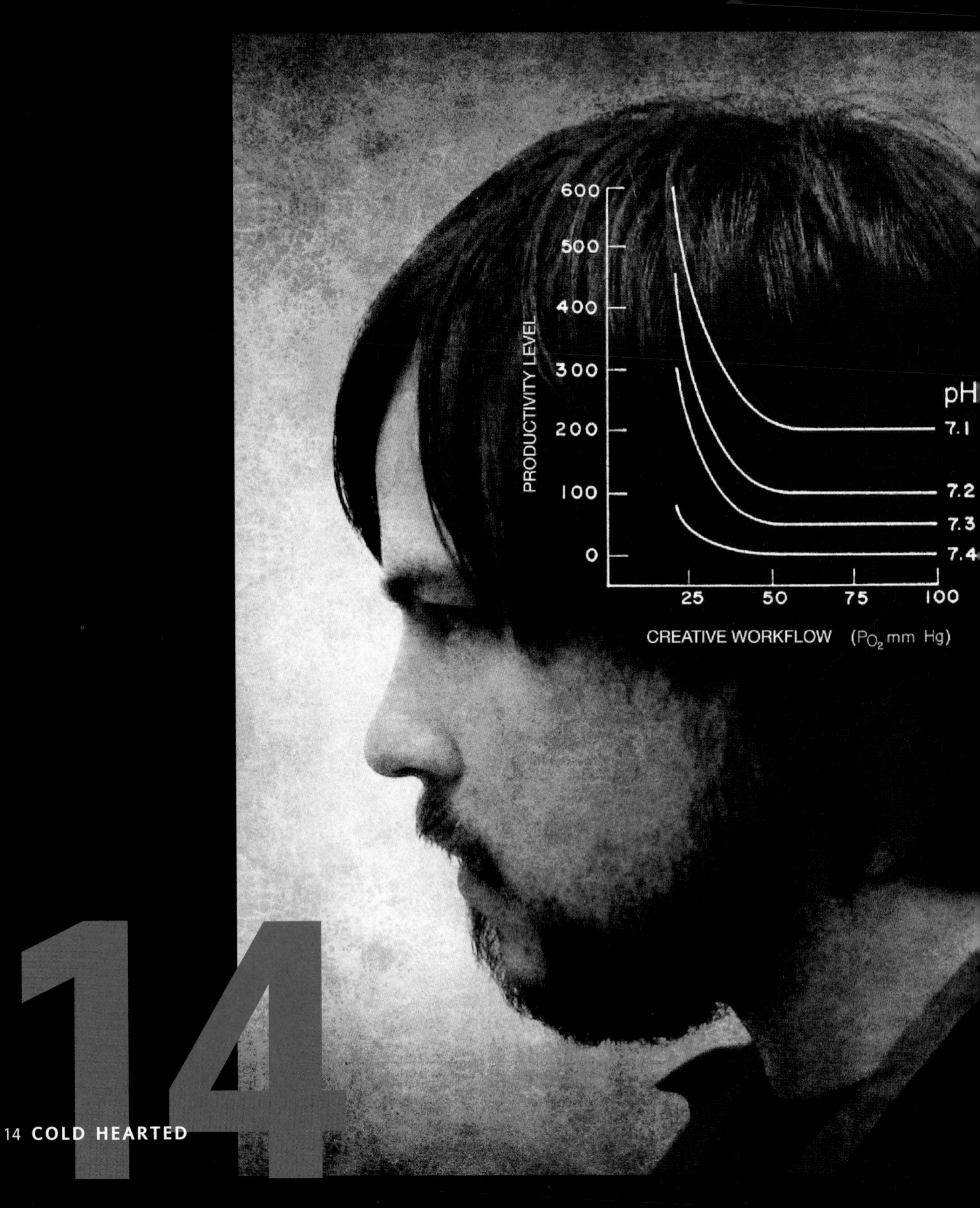

14 COLD HEARTED

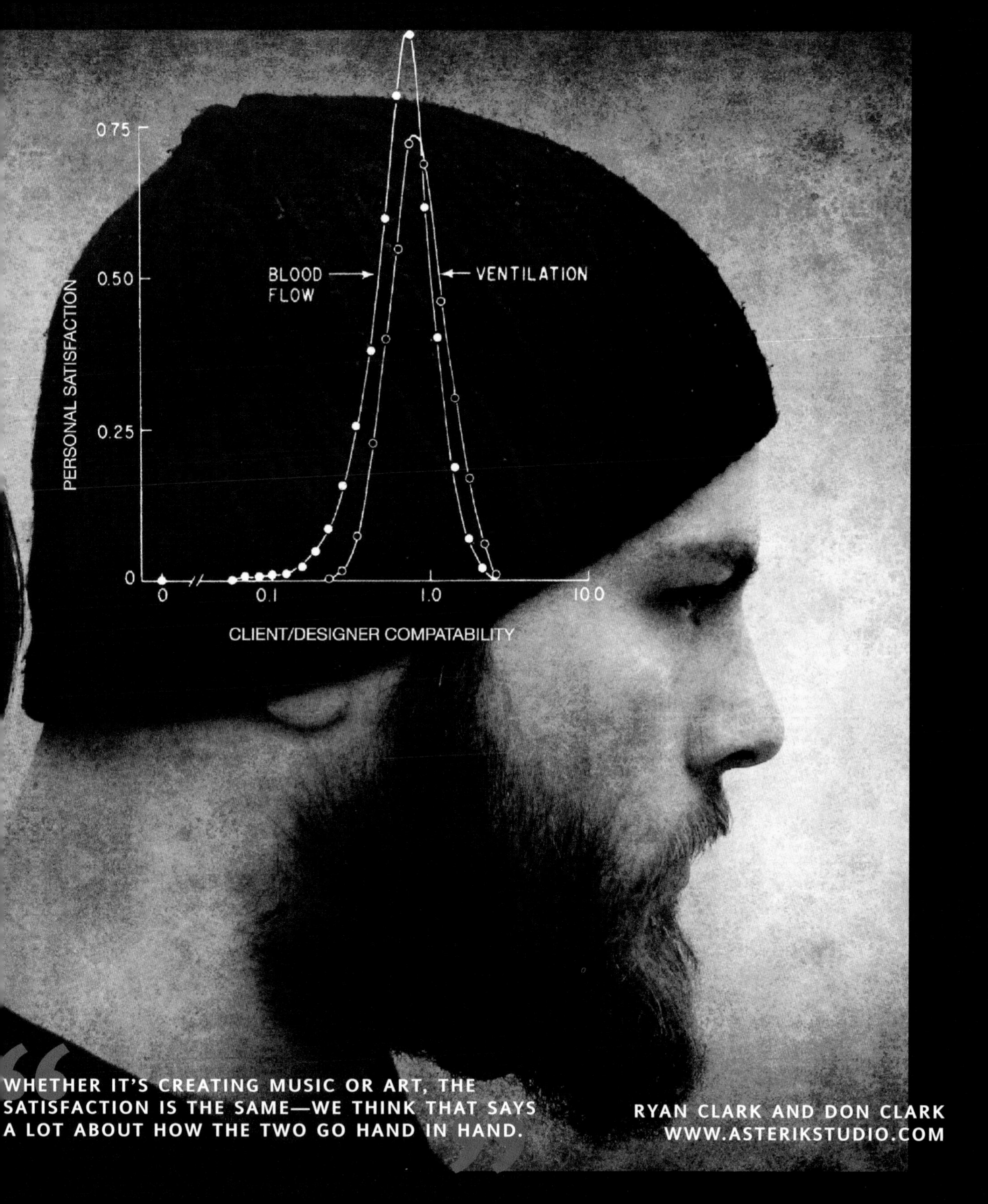
0.75
0.50
0.25
0
PERSONAL SATISFACTION
BLOOD
FLOW
VENTILATION
0
0.1
1.0
10.0
CLIENT/DESIGNER COMPATABILITY
WHETHER IT'S CREATING MUSIC OR ART, THE
SATISFACTION IS THE SAME—WE THINK THAT SAYS
A LOT ABOUT HOW THE TWO GO HAND IN HAND.
RYAN CLARK AND DON CLARK
WWW.ASTERIKSTUDIO.COM

My love of art began when I was just a small child. I remember drawing whenever I got a chance and always telling people that I was going to be an artist when I grew up. Either that, or a major league baseball player, I would say. Well, it turns out that I wasn't so hot at shortstop. As long as I can remember, I always knew I wouldn't have a normal job. My goals and aspirations were too high to work the normal 9-to-5 job that I would hate. I knew God had a plan for me, I just didn't quite know what it would be. I was focused on becoming involved in art, so I had always planned on doing that as my career.

My grandfather was a graphic designer. He was a designer at NASA years before he set out on his own and started his freelance business, Imaginators. He would do political cartoons, illustrate for catalogs, periodicals, and newspapers, and even make paintings. I remember looking at my grandfather's work and realizing that this is what I wanted to do. I wanted to use my imagination, like he had. And I wanted to do it for the rest of my life. He was, and always will be, a huge source of inspiration for my brother and I.

My father bought an Apple Macintosh in 1984. I remember the tiny screen, the small compact size, and the amazing ability to draw and create images digitally—something I had never seen before. This was completely different than the Apple II I had worked on in elementary school. Instead of a green cursor and a black screen, you had this machine that was quite user-friendly, with all of the tools you would need, right in front of your eyes. It was amazing. MacPaint was my new favorite friend. I was in front of that machine for hours on end. I was able to draw and create images using a computer instead of a pen and paper. Something about that really intrigued me.

POISON THE WELL + EVERY TIME I DIE + THE BRONX

My brother would tell you the same story. You see, we share the same love of art. My parents encouraged us to pursue our goals in art and were always willing to help when they could and, to this day, we are very thankful. We were very involved in school activities when it came to art —we would always enter state fair art contests and any other competitions that the school would hold. In high school, I was highly involved in the art department and had wonderful teachers. I look back on those days as a real time of growth in my creativity.

After finishing high school, I was still int design, but I was also getting heavil involved in the music scene, along wit my brother. Design started to take a bi of a backseat, thanks to our newfoun love of playing/listening to music. W were learning how to play guitar, startin bands, and going to shows. Ryan and started a band called Training for Utopia.

After three months of playing, we go signed to a large independent record labe from Seattle, called Solid State Records, division of a larger label called Tooth Nail Records. Music was taking over ou lives. We were involved in this larg underground genre called "hardcore, which mixed punk and metal. The early t mid nineties were a real defining time fo this type of music, and we were in th thick of it. Our band was touring, releasin records, and having a blast.

I met so many people in the music industr because of the band. They were finding ou that I was also a designer, and that reall opened the door for me. I started design ing 7-inch record sleeve covers, CDs, an merchandise for small bands. My love o design was starting to come back to me a full throttle. This is when I started findin out about designers who were working i the music industry. Designers who wer doing things to change the look of musi and breaking rules, like Vaughan Olive Stefan Sagmeister, Art Chantry, Dir Rudolph, David Carson, and others.

Image created for Seattle Design Association by Art Chantry, 1987. www.artchantry.com

I was in love with their use of type, color, balance, and depth. Everything about it was intriguing to me. I loved the way that Vaughan Oliver used elegant and classic typefaces with dark and dirty imagery. The way that David Carson completely broke every rule known to man when it came to type. I was in awe of the massive amount of thought and creativity that went into Stefan Sagmeister's CD packages and book covers. To this day, Art Chantry still doesn't use a computer, but his classic xeroxed, cut-and-paste style of design inspired me as well. I was a fan of his posters, his logos, and the whole dirty look that he created. He was definitely the visual voice for the whole Seattle grunge movement.

My love for music and design were starting to go hand in hand. At the time, I was just as excited at seeing a poster by Art Chantry as I was when I was listening to my favorite band. They were becoming one—one love I guess you could say. I was using all of these inspirations to fuel experiments with my own work. I was trying to understand how these artists attained their style, and the techniques they were using. It wasn't easy. I always tell people that I have learned the most about design over the last four years. As soon as I got involved with other designers and started learning from other people, that's when the magic started happening. That's when the creativity was really starting to take shape. I was learning how to do things the right way, to attain a certain look.

I remember using Photoshop for the first time. In the beginning, I was just happy scanning in a picture and seeing it appear digitally on the screen. As time went on, I found it to be an amazing tool. Photoshop was a program with as many functions as I had ideas in my head. I could literally create anything I wanted using it. After studying pieces from the designers I looked up to, I began to get a glimpse of what they were doing by getting better at Photoshop.

My first design job was designing the real estate flyers that ar posted outside homes that are for sale. I know, really fun. Bu that was a job where I used Photoshop heavily. I would go tak a picture of a home with a digital camera, bring it back to th office, and patiently get rid of any parked cars in the drivewa kids toys outside, and so on. The goal was to make the hom look as appealing as possible, even if it wasn't in reality. This wa I learned a lot about retouching in Photoshop. It wasn't the mos fun job, but it helped me learn a lot of important techniques.

fter that job, I toured quite a bit with the band and put design n the back burner again. A few years later, I got offered a osition as a graphic designer at an up-and-coming new dotcom nterprise in Seattle, where I had always wanted to live and work s a graphic designer. It was my little dream, I guess you could ay. Well, I accepted the job, and we made the journey to Seattle. t the time, my friend Demetre Arges was a web designer, who ras doing freelance work for bands. I got him an interview and oon enough, he got hired along with me. So, my wife, my rother, Demetre and his wife, all moved to the Northwest.

This is what I would consider my first *real* design job. I was making good money and working really long hours. I learned so much about workflow, deadlines, and corporate design. It was the best training I could ever have had. Because I didn't go to art school, this ended up really preparing me for what I am doing today.

Soon enough, the dotcom company went under, and Demetre and I got jobs at another dotcom. Six months later, we lost those jobs as well. That's when we decided to take the plunge and start our own company, Asterik Studio.

We had both been doing freelance work on the side for different bands and labels, working all hours of the night, after our regular jobs. We felt like this was the time to try and make it work. If we could score some type of contract work with a label, that would help us get on our feet wet in the business.

We ended up doing just that. We had developed a grea relationship with Tooth & Nail Records over the years (fror playing in bands and being signed to the label), and we wer able to get quite a bit of work from them in the beginning. Th helped us get where we are at today.

: has been almost three years now. Asterik Studio is myself, emetre Arges, my brother Ryan, and Greg Lutze. We do CD ackaging, web design, rock posters, tour merchandise, and verything in between for the music industry. We've worked ith hundreds of bands, from Slayer to DC Talk. We work with very genre of music, and we have a passion for all types—we re music junkies and consider ourselves to be the happiest designers on the planet. We work in Seattle and don't plan on ever leaving. Also, Ryan and I still play music; we record and tour with our new band, Demon Hunter. We release our second record next month, so you can see that music is still a big player in our lives.

I attribute our success to many factors: working hard, always keeping our eye on the goal, knowing the right people, chances that have been given to us, our work atmosphere, the people we choose to work with, learning how to use software in a correct and efficient way, and developing our talents every day. I am still learning every day—I learn something new about the field I work in all the time.

I am always hungry for something else to better my skill. I thin that's important, never settling, that is.

To this day, I see Photoshop as a tool, a tool just like a pen, piece of paper, or a paint palette. But I don't see it as the end-a to design. If you use Photoshop in addition to other tools, it ca really bring your work to life.

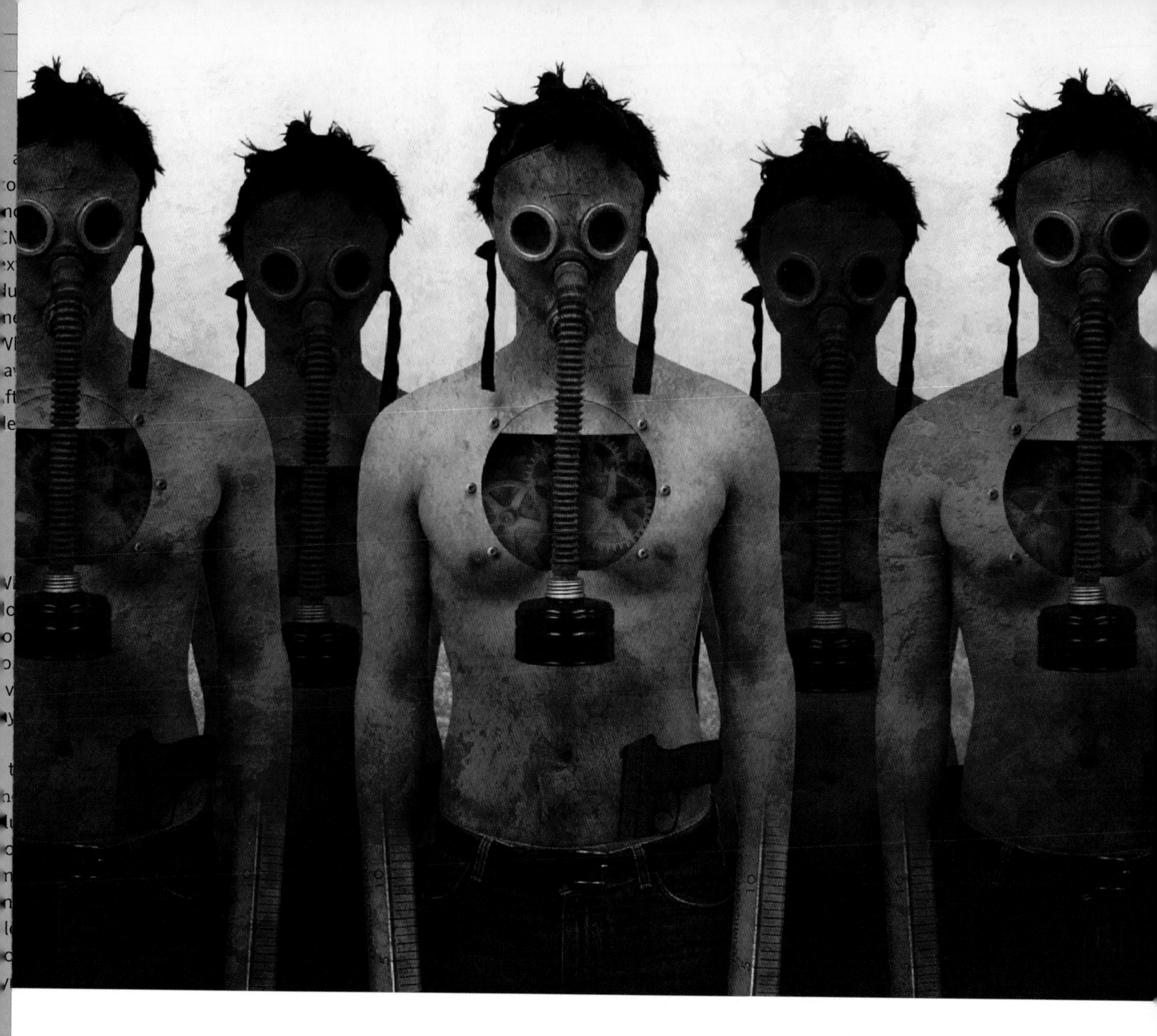

t's been a huge resource of our business. We have developed ways of doing things in Photoshop that we use to create our overall look. By just learning some simple techniques and ways of doing things in Photoshop, your work will start to look different and you will become more proficient in the program. My brother and I have found some really great, easy ways to add depth to your design, including using layers, masks, and effects.

These steps are really easy, and if you are able to use these tools, you will find that your images will really start to gain depth. We will be the first to tell you that there are so many things that we don't know about Photoshop, but we thought we'd share the little that we do know.

Hiding my background layer, I create a new layer called "background highlights," and using a 200px-wide soft paintbrush, I paint some vertical blue (values: 72%C, 20%M, 29%Y, 0%K) highlights to break up the monotony of the solid blue background.

I hide the blue background layer so that I can see what I'r doing a little better. I change the blend mode of this layer t Soft Light to help it subtly blend into the background. I also ad a Gaussian Blur to this layer to soften the edges a bit. I want th color to blend in nicely and just be a slight accent.

import an image of a distressed wall (`texture01.tif`) as a texture and change this layer blend mode to Soft Light. Overlaying this ayer would provide a more drastic contrast, but in these initial stages, I'm looking for soft and subtle.

Now that I have my central image in place, I want to start building around it. Because the title of the record is *A Snowcapped Romance*, I'm getting ideas involving ornate line art and details. The word "romance" brings to mind thoughts of beautiful, flowing, Renaissance-style art. Here at the office, we have a very large library of books and magazines that we like to use for things like this. Clipart books, texture books. You can find them at many bookstores, and they serve a very important purpose in our day-to-day designing.

For this design in particular, I want something circular to revolv[e] around the heart. I look through a book of old ornate border[s] and find exactly what I'm looking for. I scan in the ornat[e] circular border (`ornate_border.tif`) as an accent to m[y] background and I hide all of my layers so that I can focus o[n] this piece by itself. These background layers should all b[e] underneath the heart layer. In situations like this, sometimes [I] hide the heart layer for the time being if it makes it easier to se[e] what I'm working on.

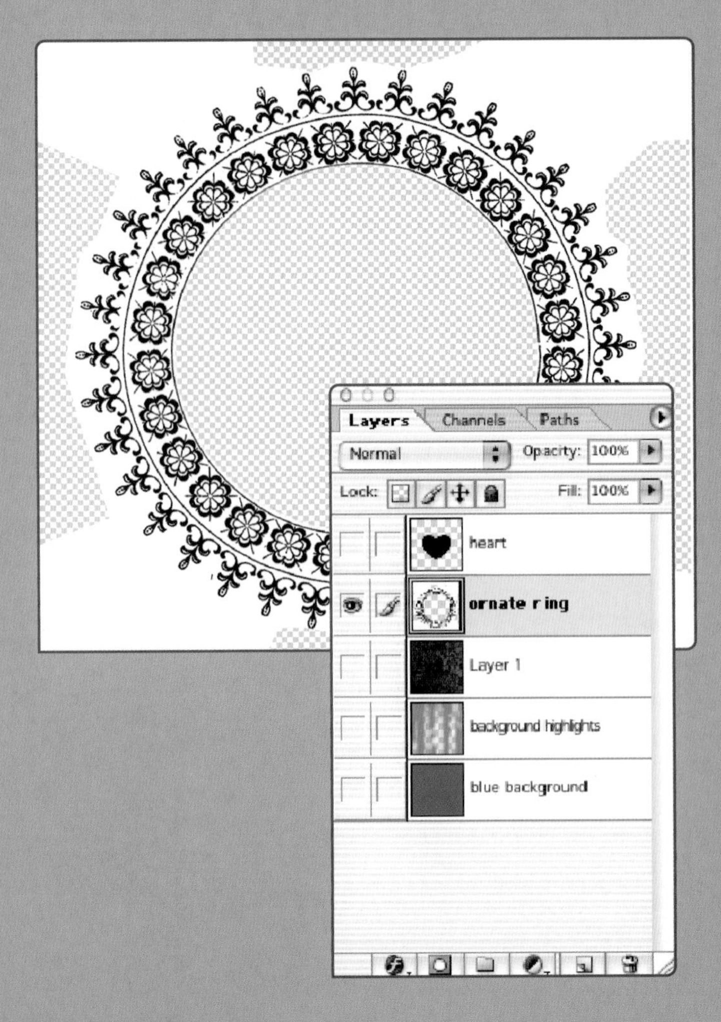

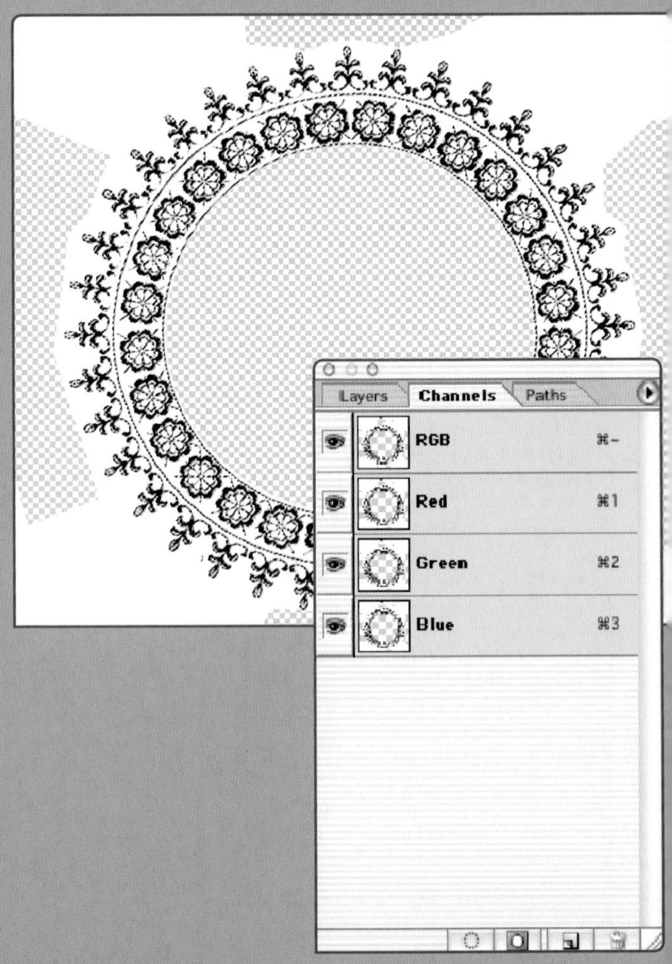

witching over to my channels, I CMD-click the RGB channel and hen select the inverse (SHIFT+CMD+I) to select just the black ortion of the image. Switching back to my layers, I then hide his layer and create a new one and fill the selection with 55- ercent gray. I chose gray because it is neutral and won't affect he color of my background, just the shade.

Duplicating this layer, I stretch my new layer to make a larger ring around my original ring. To give the impression that the rings fade darker towards the center, I lower the opacity on my small ring to 80 percent.

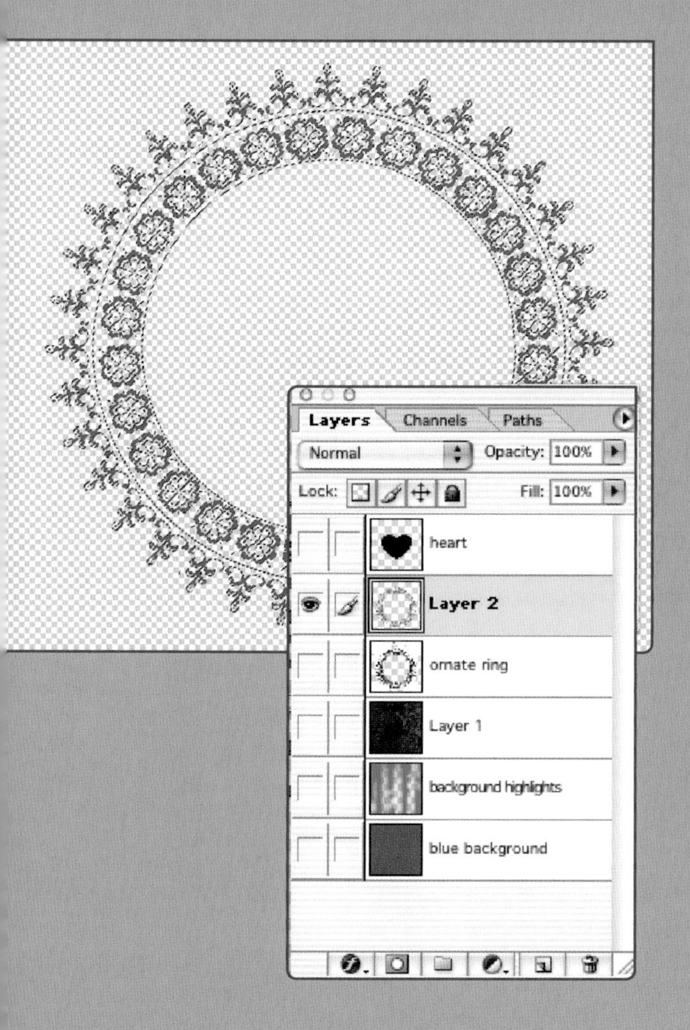

Now I make all my layers visible again, discard the original ring layer, and set both of my gray rings to Screen blending mode.

Using the Polygonal Lasso tool (L), I magnify my image to 100 percent and draw a choppy, inconsistent edge within the heart. I want this heart to appear icy and hard with a cracked outer shape.

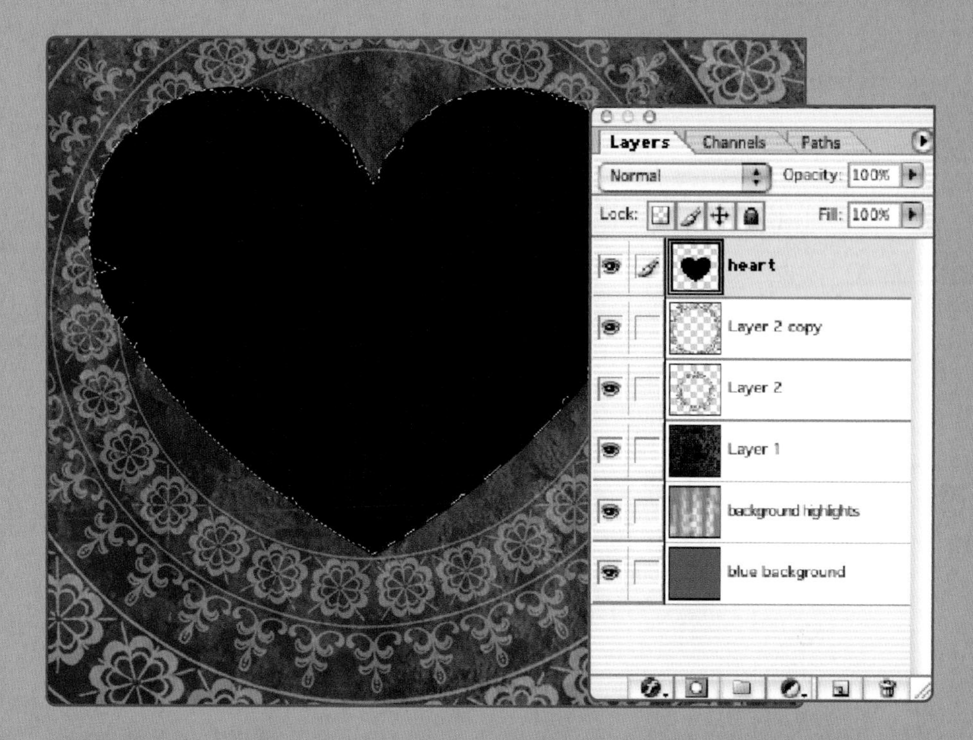

I select the inverse and delete the soft edges of the heart leaving the new, chiseled heart shape. Now I hide the original heart layer.

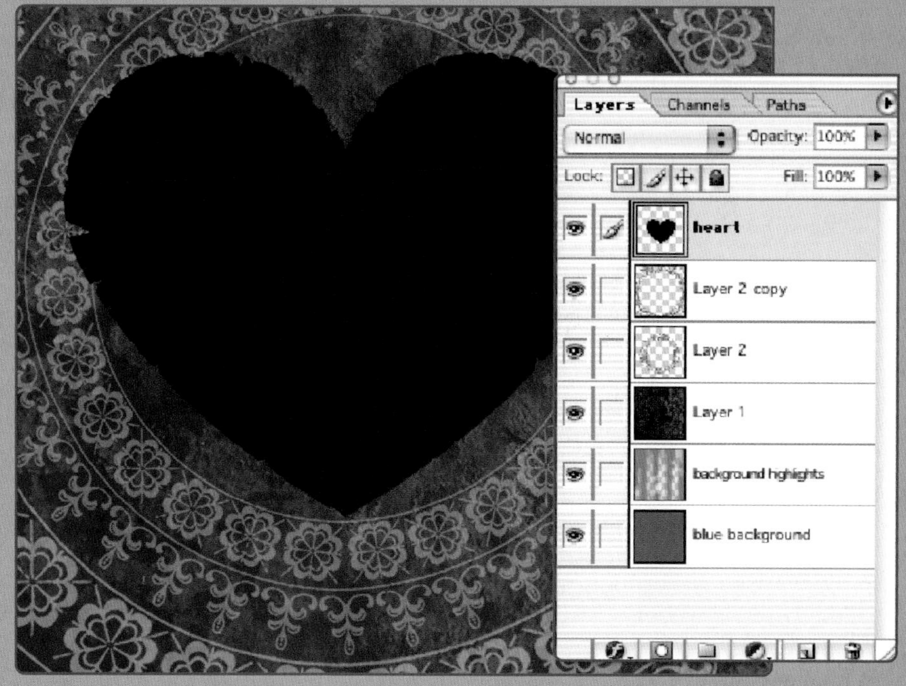

I import an image of an ice texture (`ice_texture.tif`), desaturate the image (CMD+SHIFT+U), and adjust the levels, raising my lowlights and highlights, to give the texture a much higher contrast.

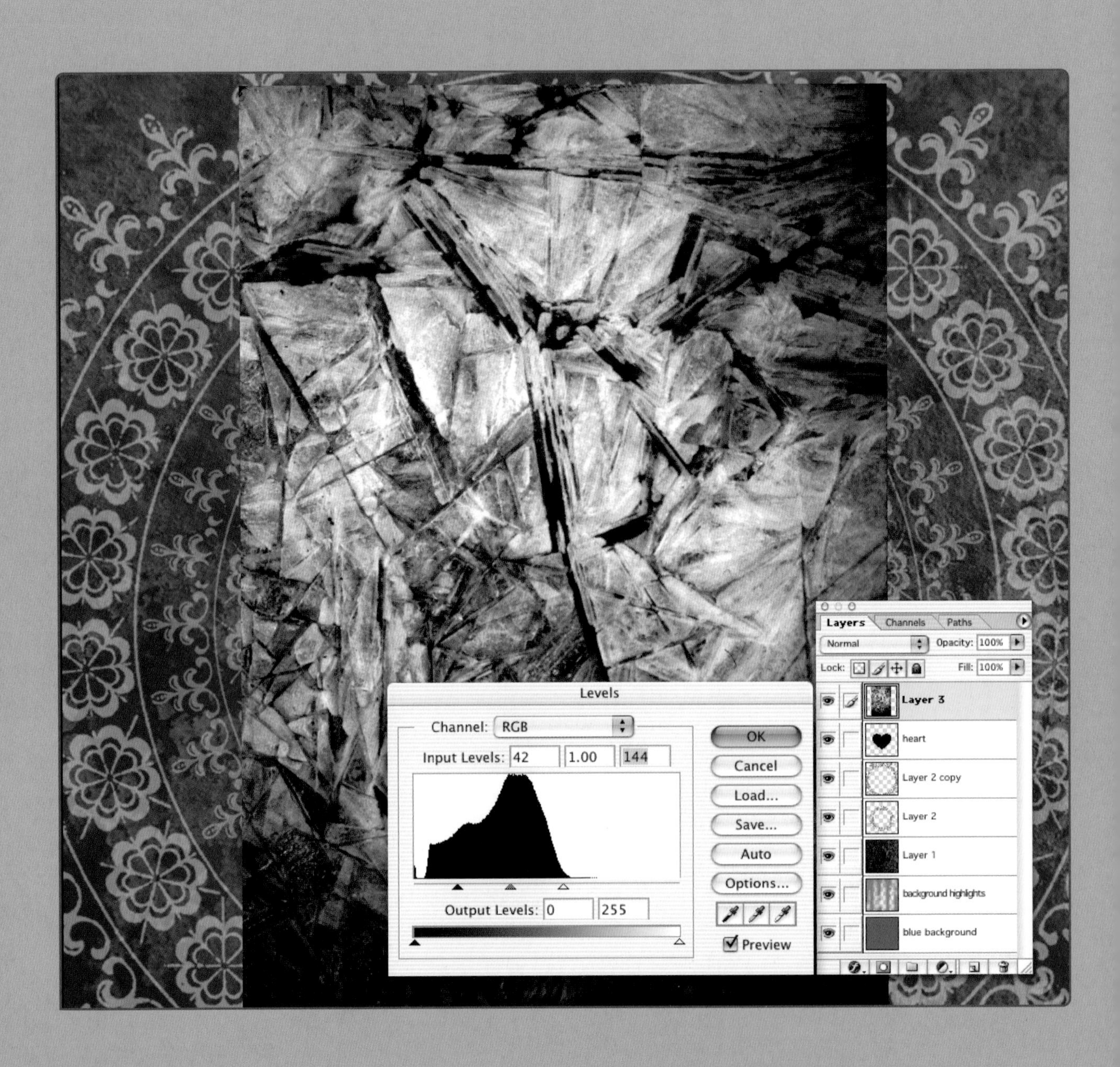

y CMD-clicking the heart layer, I select just the heart shape. I ıen go back to my ice texture layer, select the inverse, and elete the unwanted portion of the texture.

I'm now left with my ice image in the shape of the heart.

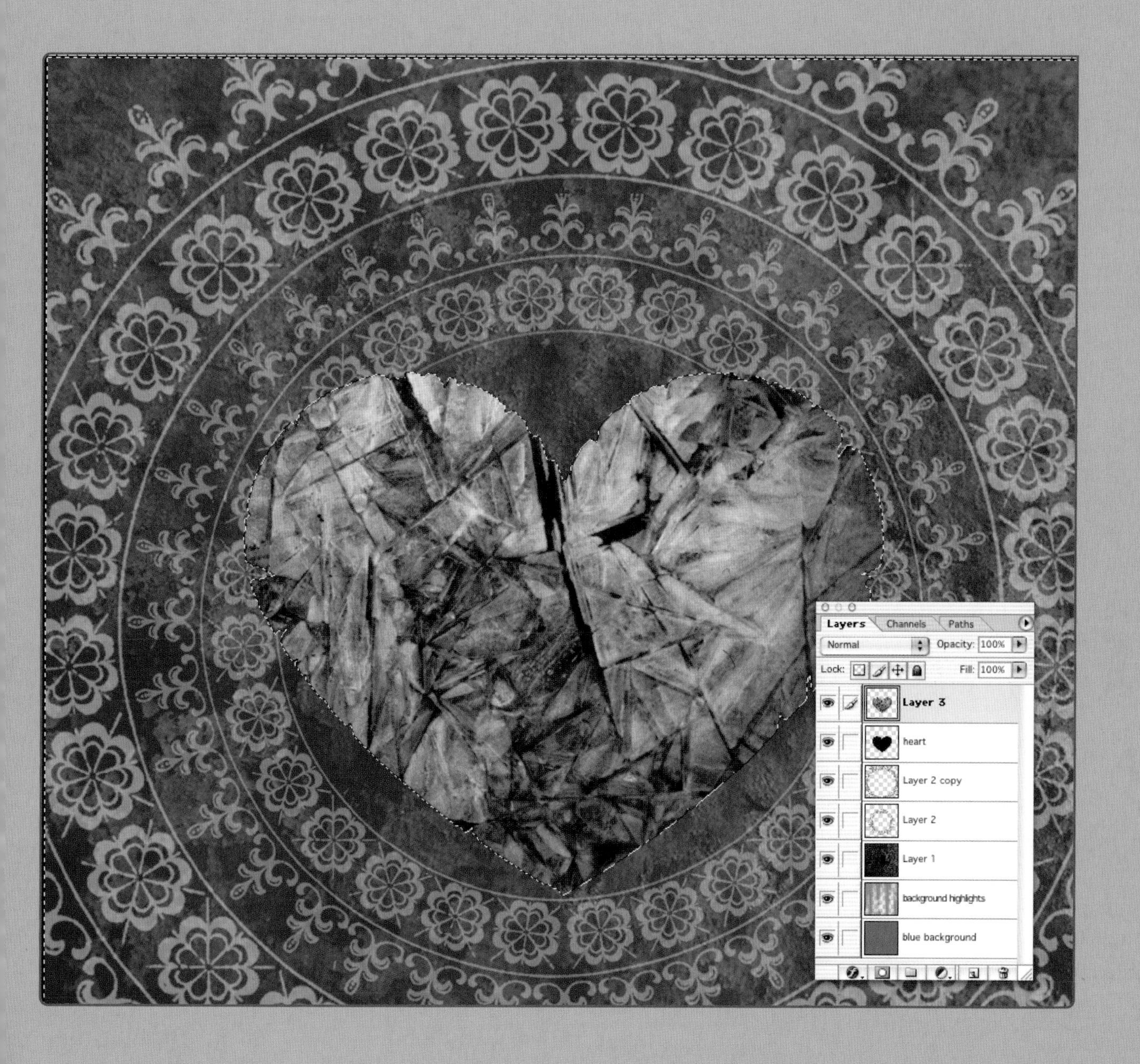

Just above my ornate ring layer, I create a new layer called "heart shadow." Using a 300px-wide soft paintbrush with the opacity set down to 30 percent, I draw a shadow coming from underneath the heart to help it pop off the background a bit.

I multiply this layer, add a slight Gaussian Blur to help it blend and turn the opacity down to a desired level, in this case, 8 percent.

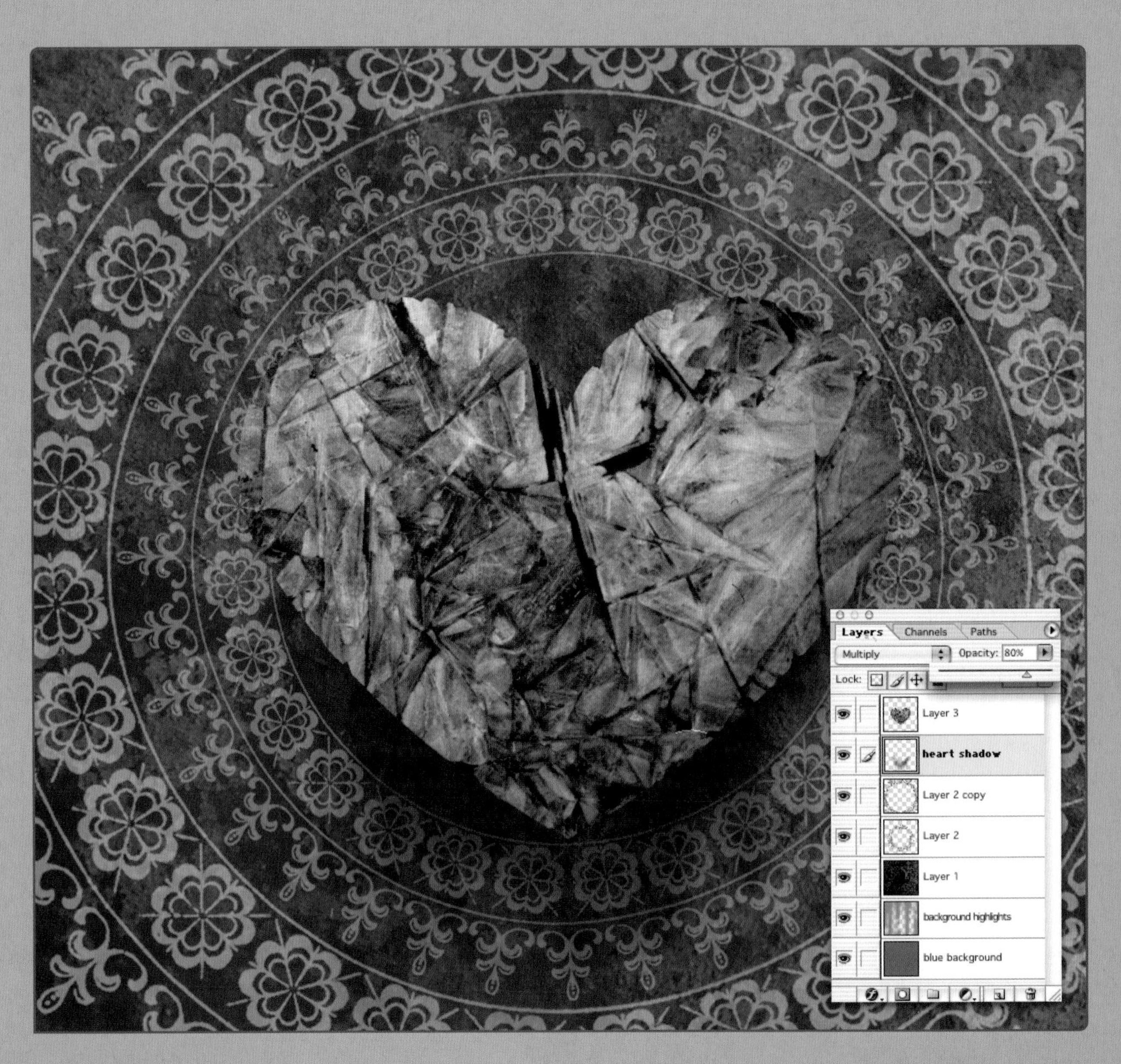

)n a new layer called "heart outer glow," I want to add a glow oming from the top of the heart, one that imitates the flame hat would appear in a traditional sacred heart and juxtaposing the shadow below the heart. I do this also with the Brush tool (200px-wide soft brush) and the Gaussian Blur filter.

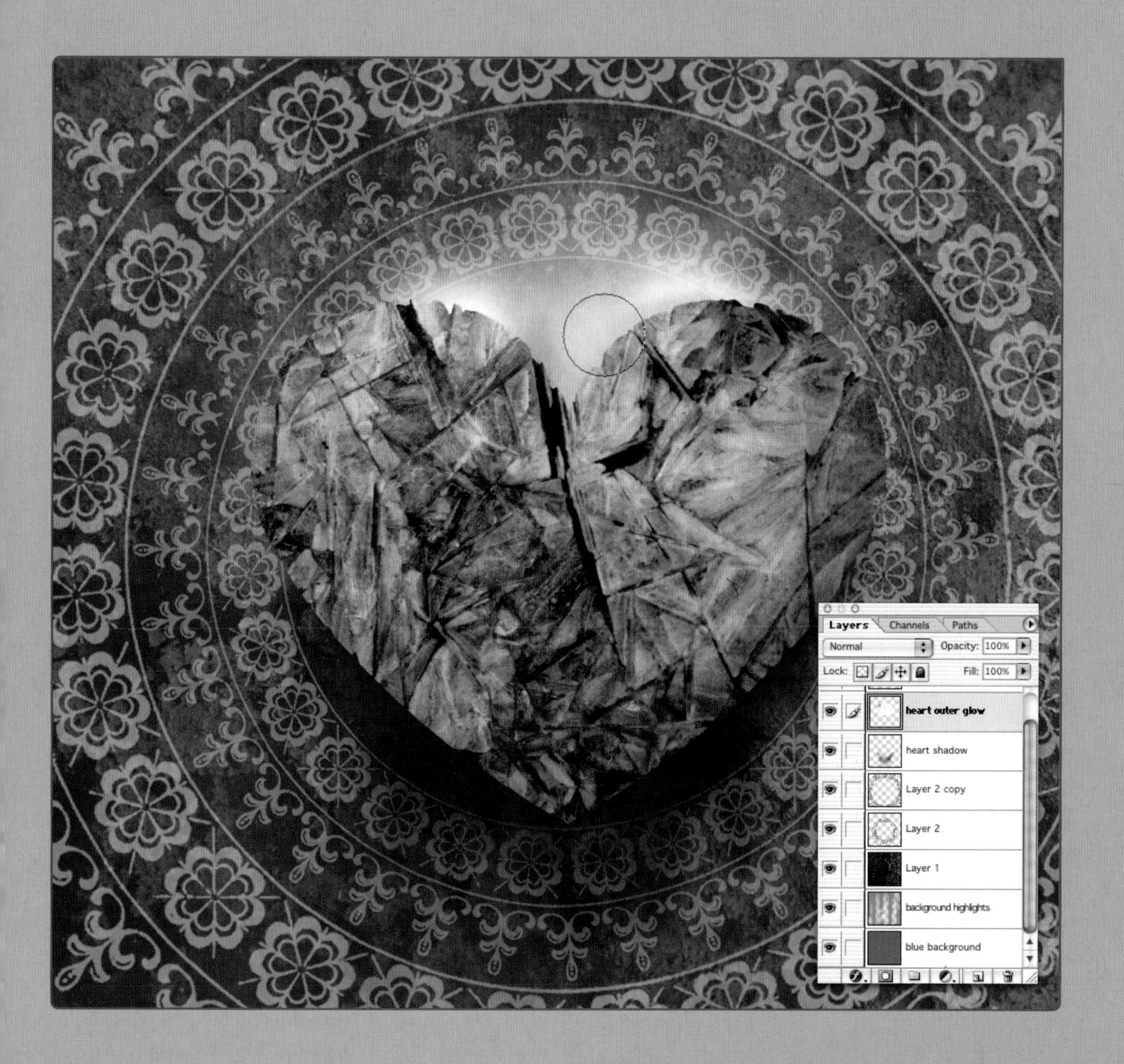

I'm now going to incorporate some smoke rising from the top of the heart and bleeding off the page. I create a new layer called "smoke 1." Using a soft paintbrush at varied sizes, I create wispy lines above the heart.

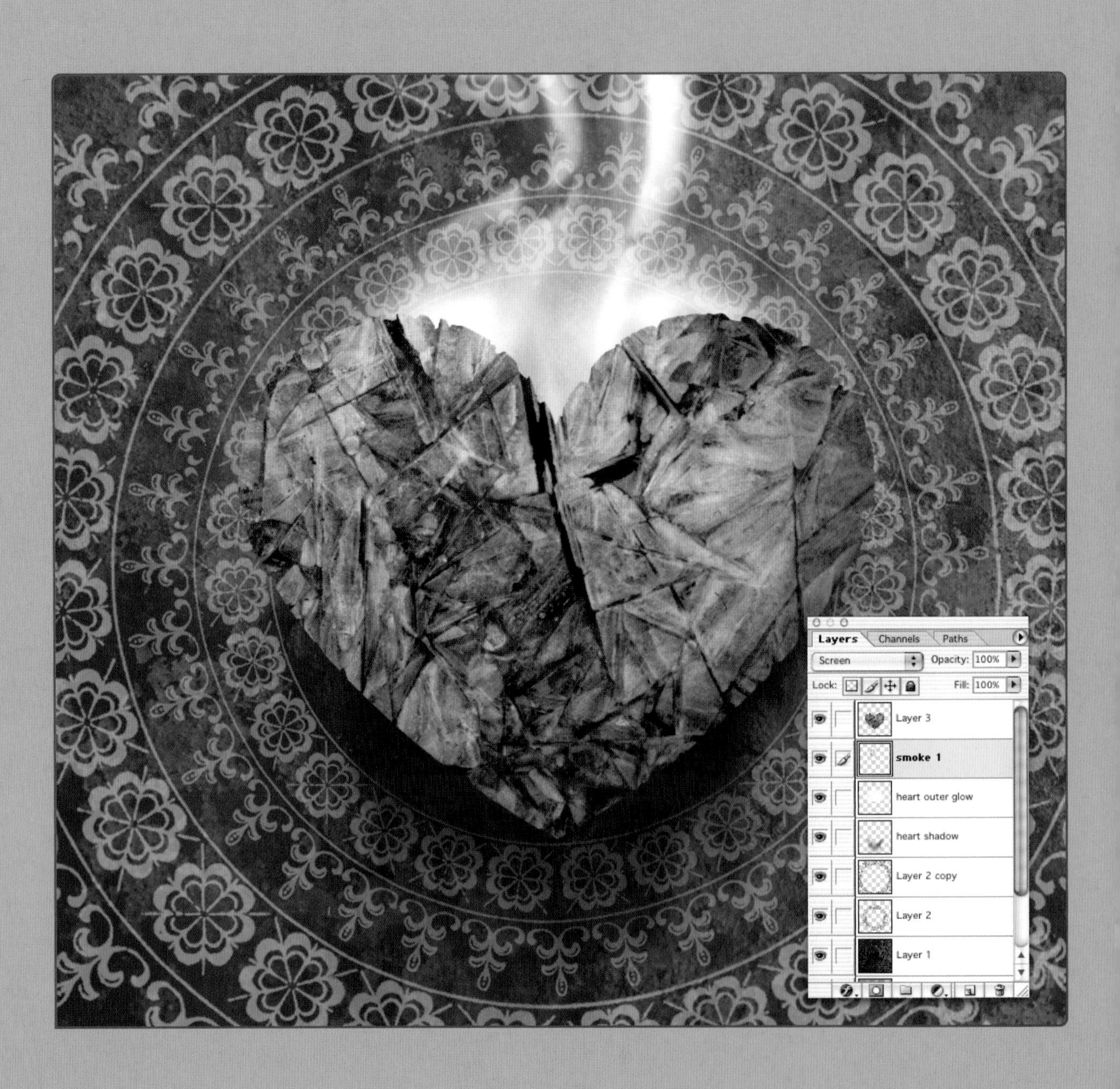

Creating a new layer, "smoke 2," I add more lines to give the smoke depth. I change the blending mode to Screen for these two layers and blur them to help them blend and to take off any hard un-smoke-like edges.

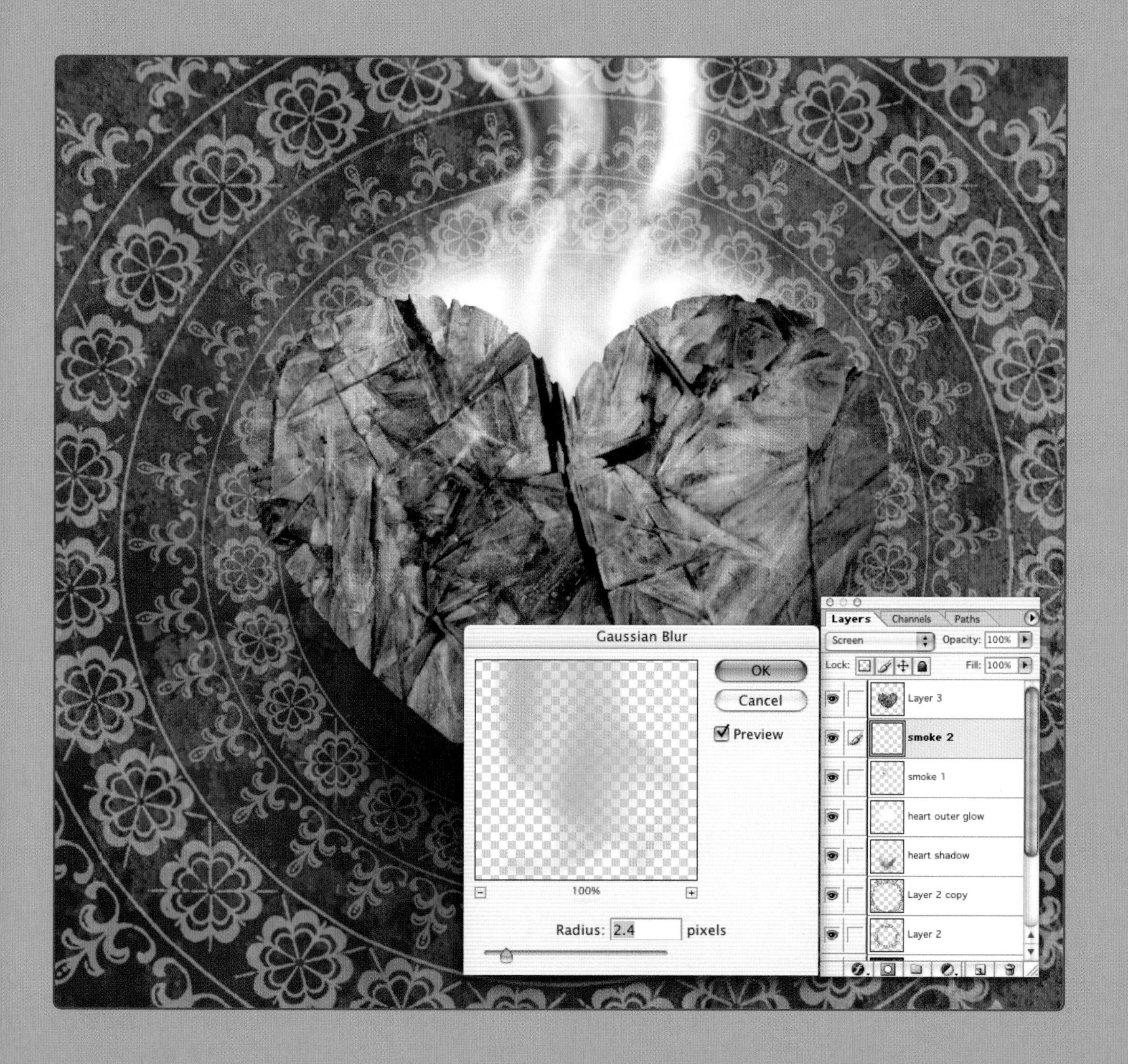

Now I import an Illustrator-based file (`icicles.eps`) that I created of icicles descending from the bottom of the heart and fit it perfectly. I adjust the levels of the icicle image, bringing the highlights all the way up and making the image entirely white.

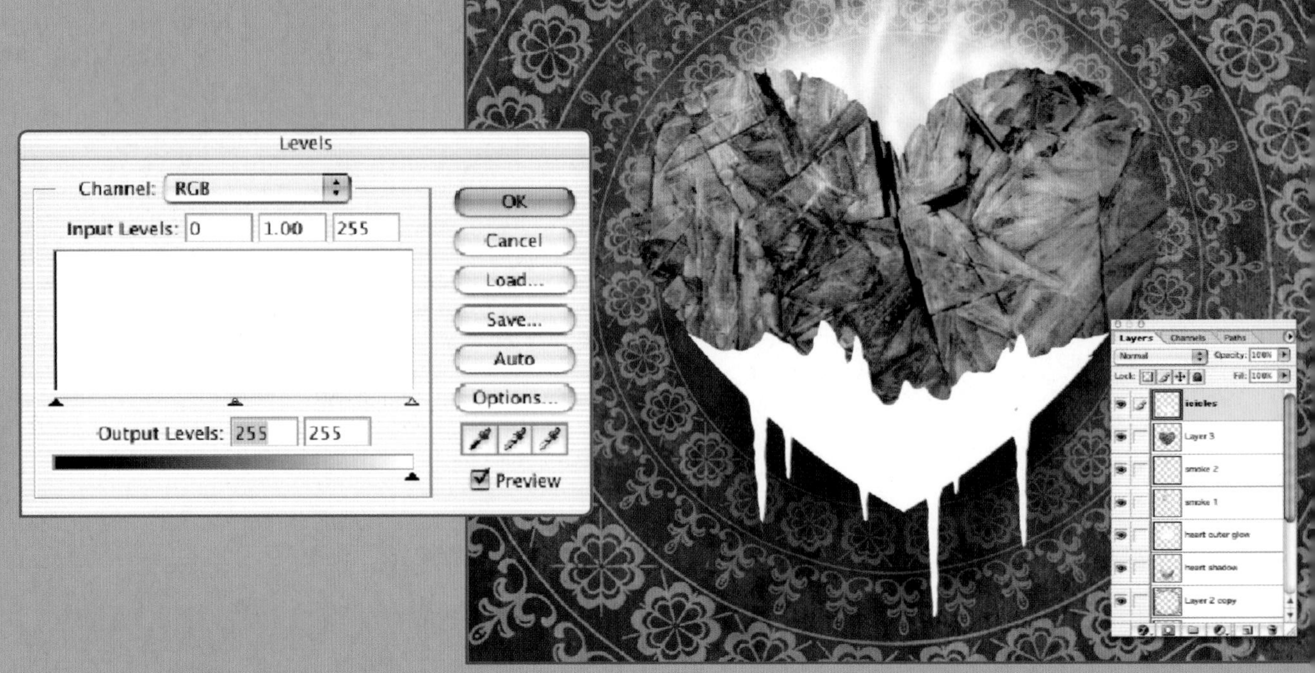

et the opacity of this layer to 75 percent and erase pieces of the top using a 200 or 300px-wide soft brush eraser set to 50 percent pacity. This is all in an effort to make this layer blend in.

Now I'm going to shade the heart to give it a sense of depth and realism. On a few new layers that I've titled "heart right shading" and "heart top shading," I switch from the eraser to the paintbrush and shade the heart with a large, soft paintbrush using black. I select the heart layer by itself and create a new layer, where I softly shade the sides of the heart where it makes sense.

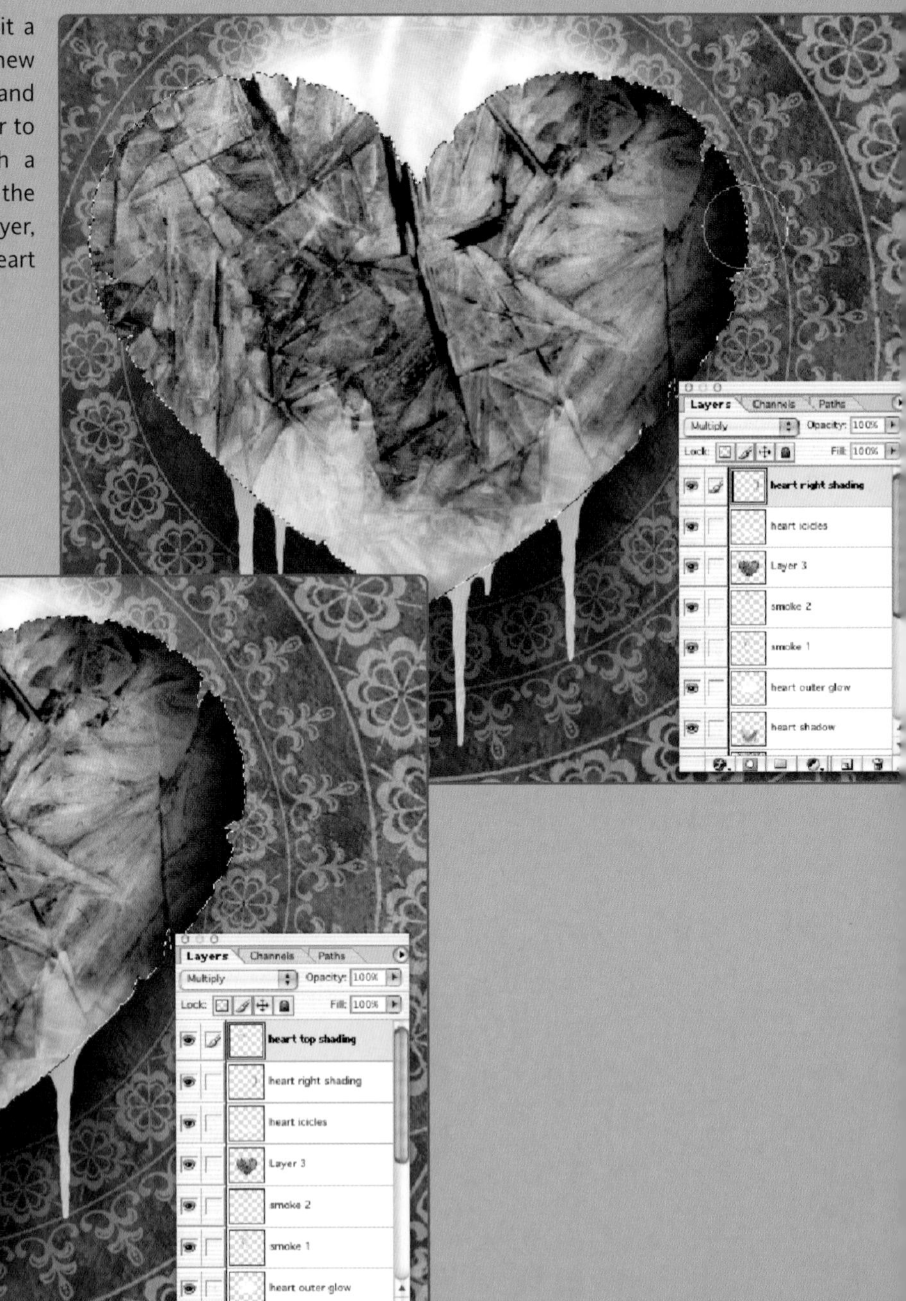

ı this case, I'm trying to give the heart a emirounded shape, so I'm shading just the right side nd small parts of the top accordingly. I also change ıese layers' blending mode to Multiply. On two new ıyers titled "heart left highlight" and "heart top ighlight," I highlight the opposite side of the heart ith white to give it some sense of dimension. I hange these two highlight layers' blending mode to)verlay because I still want to see the cracks and revasses of the heart. I also give a slight highlight to ne side of the icicles as well.

On a new layer, I use my Elliptical Marquee tool (M) to create a circle shape and fill the selection with a bright red (values: 0%C, 95%M, 100%Y, 0%K). After deselecting, I Gaussian Blur the red dot to soften the edges and make the red fade out gradually. I then change the layer blending mode to Soft Light and duplicate it to intensify the glow.

Normal
Dissolve
Darken
Multiply
Color Burn
Linear Burn
Lighten
Screen
Color Dodge
Linear Dodge
Overlay
Soft Light
Hard Light
Vivid Light
Linear Light
Pin Light
Difference
Exclusion
Hue
Saturation
Color
Luminosity
Paths
Opacity: 100%
Fill: 100%
glow 1
highlights
top highlight
left highlight
heart top shading
heart right shading
heart icicles
Layers
Channels
Paths
Soft Light
Opacity: 100%
Lock:
Fill: 100%
red glow 2
red glow 1
icicle highlights
heart top highlight
heart left highlight
heart top shading
heart right shading

On a new layer titled "center glow," I repeat the steps I took to make the red glow to make a small white glow in the very center. This helps give a subtle, bright burst right in the center. This layer blend mode is Overlay.

ow I want to draw more attention to the eart image in the foreground and tone own the background imagery. Creating a adial gradient, from black around the edges transparent in the center, will help make ne heart really pop on the cover. After reating a new layer called "radial shading 1," electing my Gradient tool, and setting it to a adial, reverse gradient, I go to the Tool ptions and set the gradient to Foreground to ansparent. I've chosen black for my color.

hen I create a new layer, click y cursor in the center of the nage, hold down, and drag ne gradient just outside of the ocument before I let go. This ill create shading, graduating om nothing in the center of e image to black around the dges.

I create a new layer and fill it with blue (values: 80%C, 28%M, 32%Y, 01%K). I want to tie all of these elements that I've created in with the blue background to start to give the overall image the cold feel that it needs. I choose Soft Light for this layer and again erase portions of the blue over the smoke so the white from the smoke can show through. I erase these portions completely, so my 300px-wide eraser brush is set to 100-percent opacity.

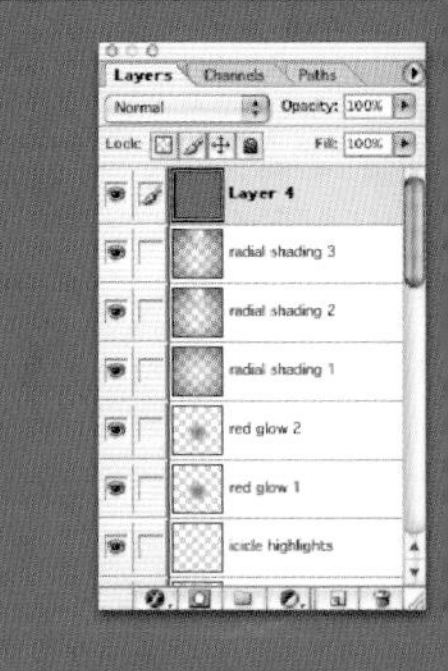

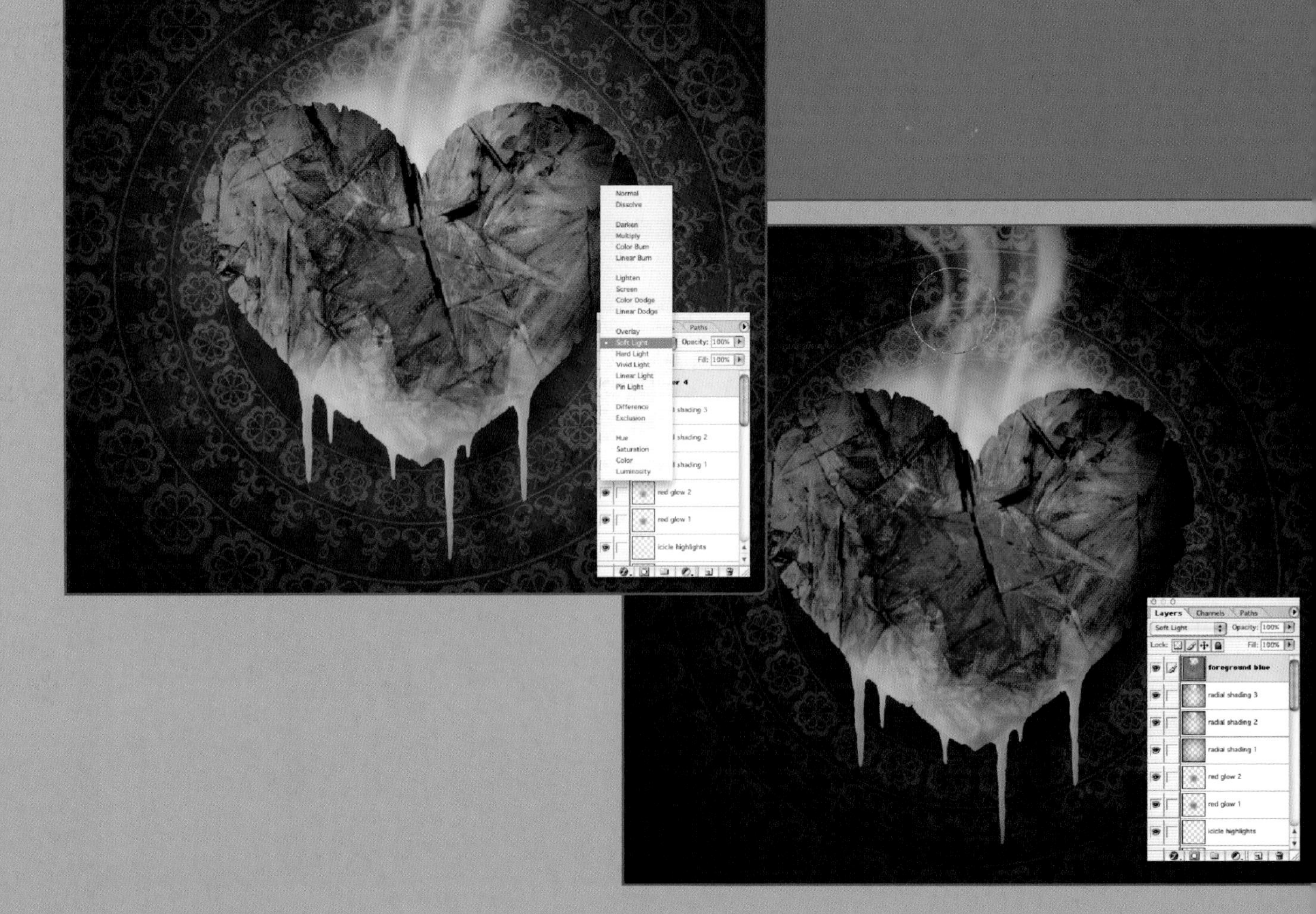

›n top of my blue layer, I create a few new ›yers to give the heart some extra highlights. name these layers “heart left highlight 2” ›nd “heart top highlight 2.” Some of the ›ghlights that I created on the heart before ›ave been softened by the blue layer, and I ›ant to bring some white highlights to the ›reground. I make these layers’ blend mode ›creen to let the heart’s texture show ›rough.

I now import another texture layer (`texture02.tif`) that I'm going to drop over the top of all these layers. By using Soft Light on this layer, I will give the image an overall distressed look and help tie all the elements together.

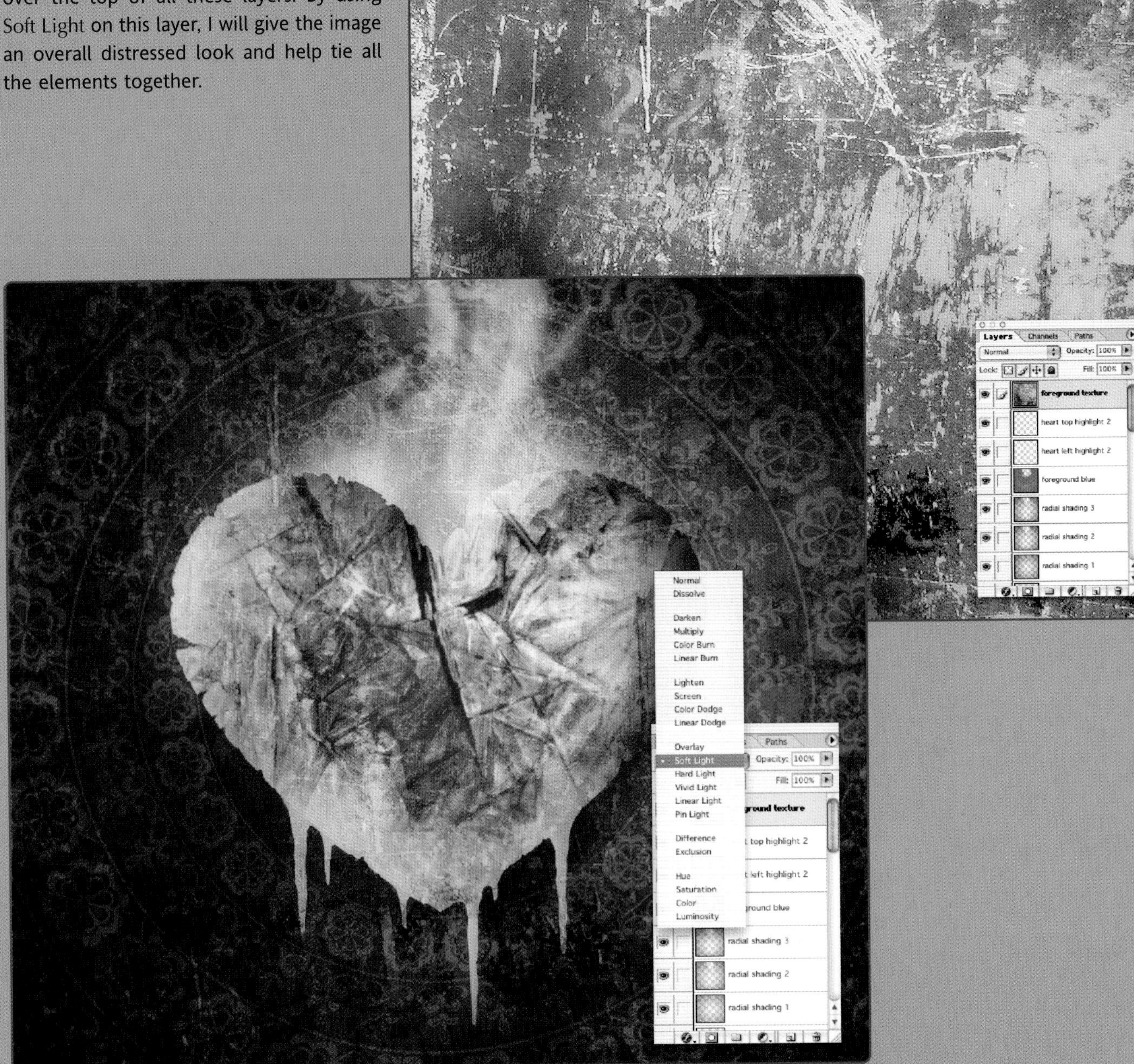

nally, I drop the band logo and album title on the image and 's done. This last step is only to show the client the final image ith the type included, but when it comes time to lay out the nal package, I will do all the type and logo work in the layout oplication, QuarkXPress. This will help keep the type easily ditable and will transfer cleaner and clearer in the final printed roduct.

had fun creating this cover. I enjoyed the challenge of taking n image that I don't have as a print or a scan and creating it tally from scratch.

A lot of the time, for album covers, I'll have imagery to work with and all it will take is some minimal Photoshop coloring and texture and a type treatment and I'm done. I do like creating something on my own though, without any imagery other than the textures and line art to help.

The record label and band were happy with the cover and they agreed that it was exactly what they were looking for. I'm happy with it as well. I think the hard, surrealistic edge gives it a cold, dark feeling, which I think is important, but the ornate line art in the background and the textures help to convey the sometimes beautiful and melodic contents of the album.

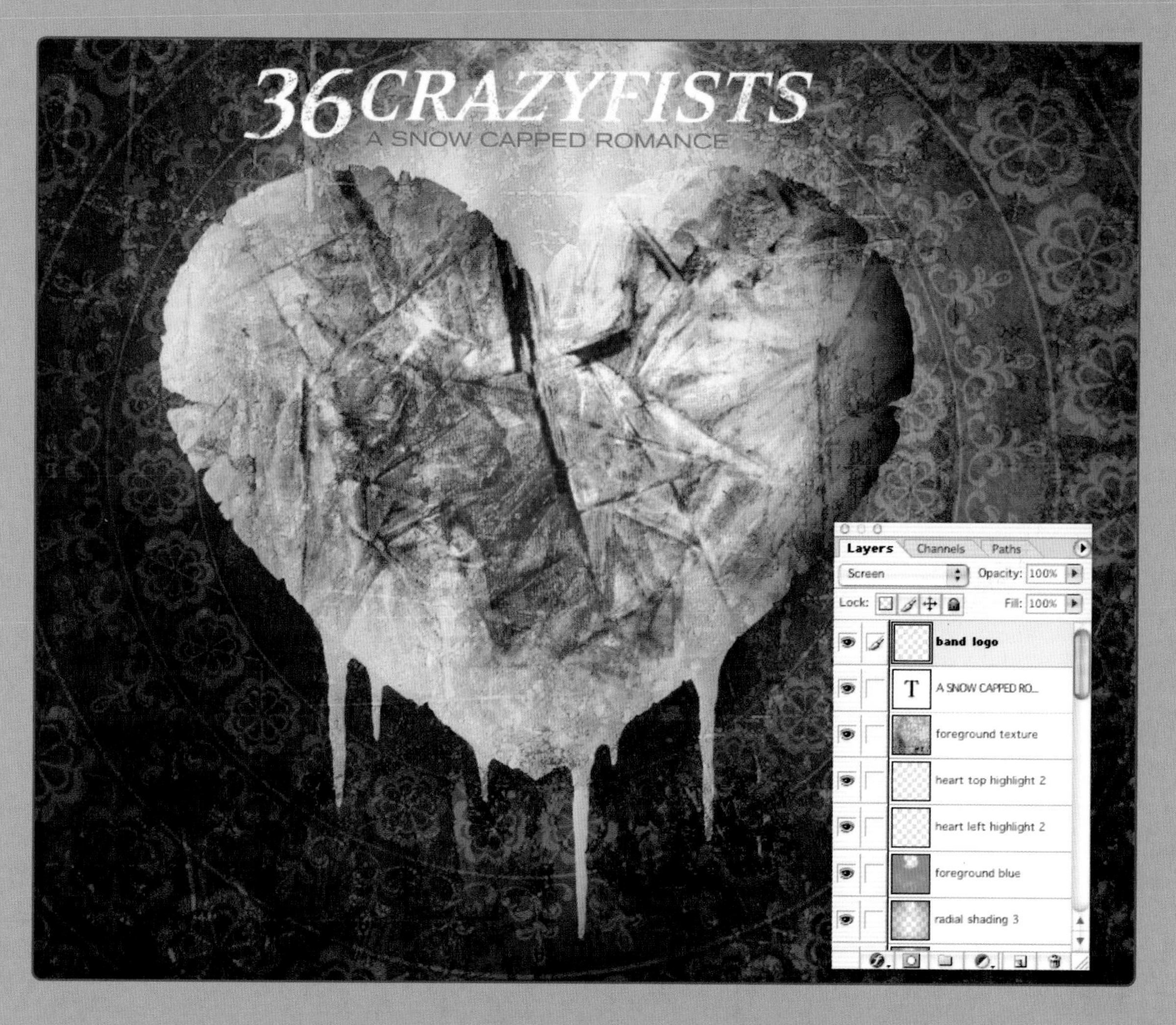

36CRAZYFISTS
A SNOW CAPPED ROMANCE

INDEX

INDEX

INDEX

Numbers

A

B

1-59059-303-0 $29.99 [US]

1-59059-305-7 $34.99 [US]

1-59059-308-1 $34.99 [US]

1-59059-336-7 $34.99 [US]

1-59059-210-7 $34.99 [US]

1-59059-306-5 $34.99 [US]

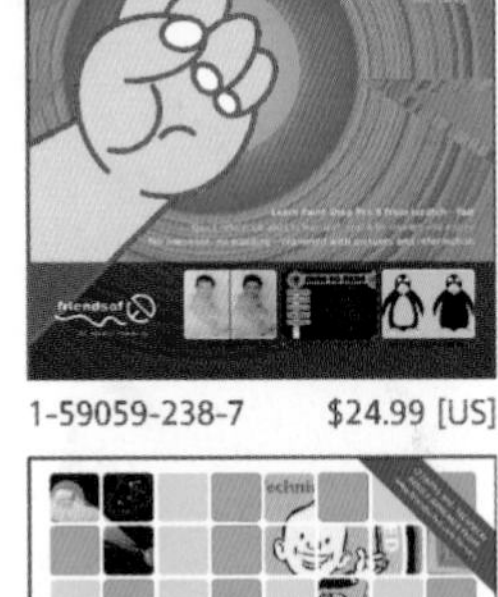

1-59059-238-7 $24.99 [US]

1-59059-149-6 $24.99 [US]

1-59059-224-7 $39.99 [US]

1-59059-221-2 $39.99 [US]

1-59059-236-0 $39.99 [US]

1-59059-372-3 $39.99 [US]

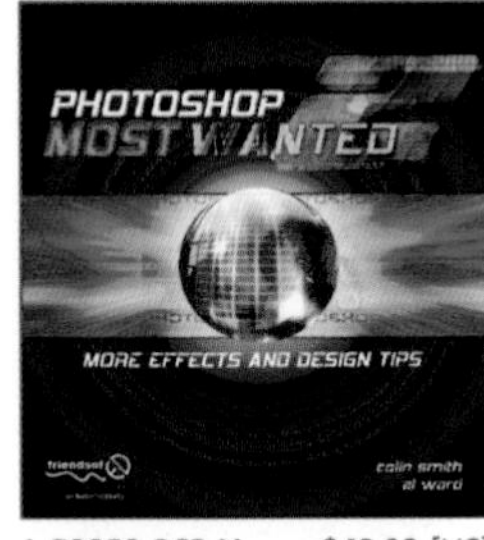

1-59059-262-X $49.99 [US]

1-59059-304-9 $49.99 [US]

1-59059-309-X $49.99 [US]

1-59059-399-5 $44.99 [US]

1-59059-110-0 $49.99 [US]

1-59059-231-X $39.99 [US]

1-59059-408-8 $34.99 [US]

1-59059-355-3 $39.99 [US]

1-59059-381-2 $29.99 [US]

1-59059-409-6 $39.99 [US]

friendsof
DESIGNER TO DESIGNER™
an Apress® company